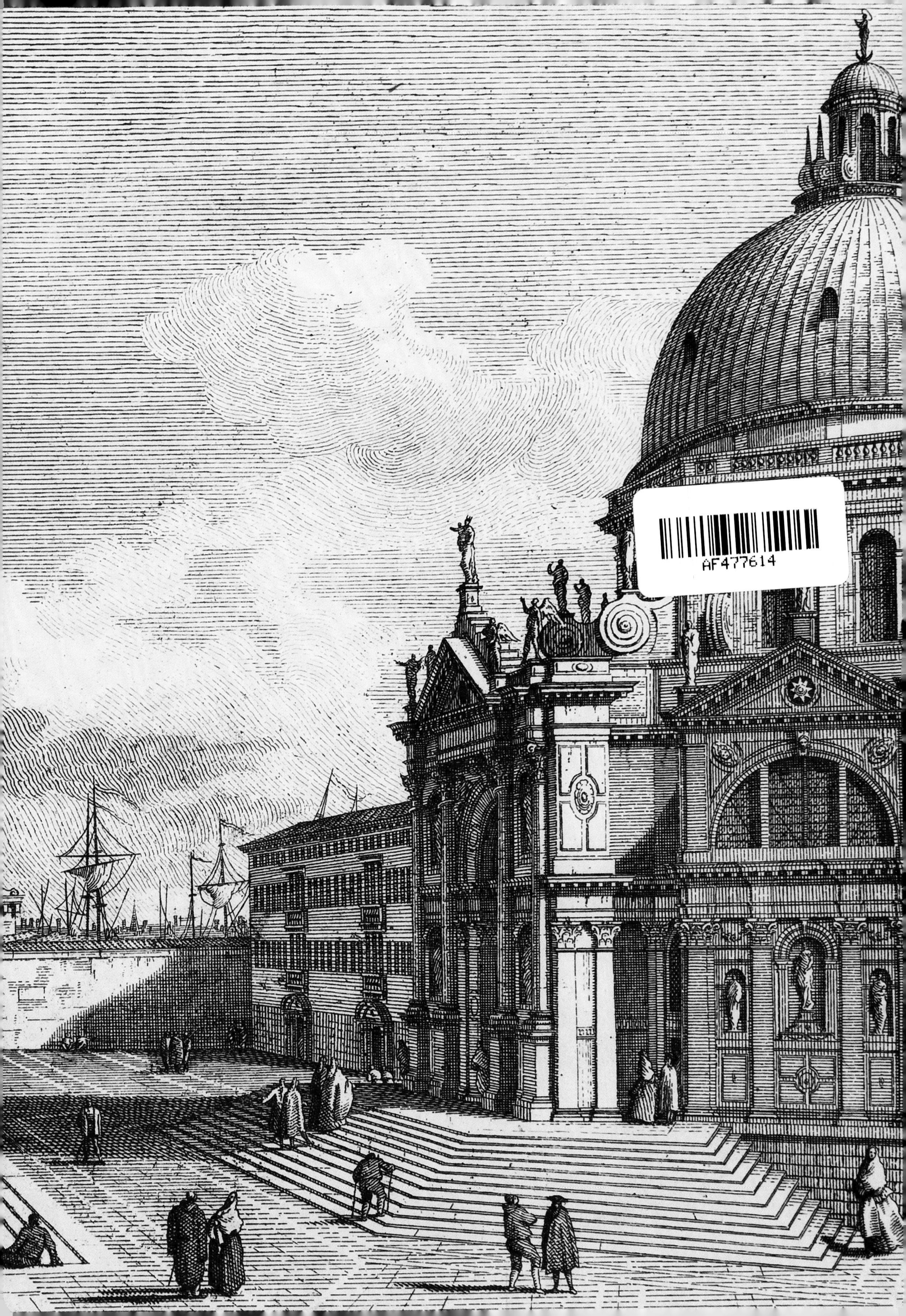
AF477614

Venice in the Age of CANALETTO

Venice in the Age of Canaletto

Exhibition at the:
The John and Mable Ringling Museum of Art
October 8, 2009 – January 10, 2010

Memphis Brooks Museum of Art
February 14 – May 9, 2010

Published by Memphis Brooks Museum of Art
Design layout: Heather Kurtz Klein
Editors: Alexandra Libby, Marina Pacini, and Stanton Thomas
Copy editor: Carlisle Hacker

Printed and bound by Paulsen Printing Company, Memphis, Tennessee, USA

Distributed Worldwide by Prestel Publishing.
Prestel books are available worldwide. Visit Prestel's website at www.prestel.com or contact one of the following offices for further information:

Prestel Verlag
Königinstrasse 9
D-80539 Munich
Germany
Tel: 49 89 242 908 300
Fax: 49 89 38 17 0935

Prestel Publishing Ltd.
4 Bloomsbury Place
London WC1A 2QA
United Kingdom
Tel : 44 20 7323 5004
Fax: 44 20 7636 8004

Prestel Publishing
900 Broadway, Suite 603
New York, NY 10003
Tel: 212 995 2720
Fax: 212 995 2733
E-mail: sales@prestel-usa.com

Library of Congress Control Number: 2009929824
ISBN 9783791380001

This publication was supported, in part, by grants from The Samuel H. Kress Foundation through the Old Masters in Context program, The Assisi Foundation of Memphis, Inc, and The Gladys Krieble Delmas Foundation. Any views, findings, conclusions, or recommendations expressed in this publication do not necessarily represent those of The Samuel H. Kress Foundation, The Assisi Foundation, and The Gladys Krieble Delmas Foundation.

The John and Mable Ringling Museum of Art
5401 Bay Shore Road
Sarasota, Florida 34243
941.359.5700
www.ringling.org

Memphis Brooks Museum of Art
1934 Poplar Avenue
Memphis, Tennessee 38104
901.544.6200
www.brooksmuseum.org

Cover:
Canaletto (Giovanni Antonio Canal), 1697-1768
The Grand Canal from the Campo San Vio (det.), ca. 1740
Oil on canvas. 44 7/8 x 63 1/2 (114 x 161.3 cm)
Memphis Brooks Museum of Art;
Gift of the Samuel H. Kress Foundation 61.216

Endpapers:
Antonio Visentini, 1688–1782
Prospectus Magni Canalis Venetiarum adduti Certamine Nautico et Nundinis Venetis (cats. 13f and 13k)
(Venice: Giovanni Battista Pasquali Press, 1751)
Etchings, each 10 13/16 x 16 7/8 in. (27.5 x 42.8 cm)
Matthew Nimetz Collection, New York

Contents

Directors' Acknowledgements

Venice in the Age of Canaletto provides a new examination of the context and influence of one of Western art's most beloved figures. Nearly three centuries after Canaletto's emergence as a highly sought after painter of Venetian views, his work retains a power and mystery that mesmerizes on each occasion. The Memphis Brooks Museum of Art and The John and Mable Ringling Museum of Art welcome you to see Canaletto anew through the exhibition and this accompanying catalogue.

We often attempt to place artists of Canaletto's fame into a continuum of art history, seeking to identify the artist's precursors and successors. While Canaletto's work references artistic traditions and has been studied widely by later artists, what is too easy to overlook is the singular nature of his aesthetic vision. His skill and, we must say, imagination contribute greatly to how we see eighteenth-century Venice itself.

Venice in the Age of Canaletto brings together the glory and mystery of the eighteenth-century city in which Canaletto produced his finest work. It also unites two American art museums fortunate to hold Canaletto masterpieces in their collections. The collaboration between the Brooks and the Ringling has been a joyous partnership for both museums and reaffirms the importance of dialog and interchange among American art museums. We are pleased that our curatorial exchange contributes to the study and appreciation of Canaletto and welcome you to *Venice in the Age of Canaletto*.

Our most sincere appreciation first and foremost to Stanton Thomas, Associate Curator at the Brooks, and Alexandra Libby, Assistant Curator at the Ringling. Both have led the museums' respective efforts and deserve our immense gratitude for their research talents, creative skills, and curatorial vision. Marina Pacini, Chief Curator at the Brooks, also deserves accolades for managing the project with diplomacy, grace, and countless hours of dedication.

Thank you to Max Marmor, President, and Lisa Ackerman, Executive Vice President, of the Kress Foundation for believing deeply in this project and granting the financial resources to publish the catalog. We are also grateful to Wil and Sally Hergenrader for their generous gift to this project and their lifelong support for the Brooks Museum. Further, the catalog would not have been possible without the support of The Assisi Foundation of Memphis, Inc., and the Scheidt Family Foundation. Alice Whelihan at the National Endowment for the Arts and the entire Federal Council on the Arts and Humanities were the key to federal indemnification of the project, an important statement on the quality of the exhibition and the high standards of museum practice at both institutions. Matthew Nimitz generously loaned essential etchings to the project, giving it a wider and more representative view of Canaletto. Alan Chong, Curator of the Collections at the Gardner Museum provided important objects in the exhibition and was an outstanding colleague.

At the Brooks, our great gratitude goes to Kaywin Feldman, under whose directorship the project was launched. Thank you also to Kip Peterson, Collections Manager, and Marilyn Masler, Associate Registrar, for their steady and professional hands managing the immense logistical effort entailed by the project, and to Heather Kurtz Klein for her elegant and sumptuous graphic design befitting the age.

At the Ringling, thank you to Françoise Hack, Chief Registrar, and Ashley Burke, Assistant Registrar, for their expertise and skills, and to Aleesha Nissen, Collections Management Fellow, and Stephen Borys for his early guidance as Curator of Collections.

Finally, thank you to all who contributed, edited, and coddled the catalogue throughout the project: William Barcham, Professor at Fashion Institute of Technology; Fausto Calderai; Victor Coonin, Professor at Rhodes College; Catherine Hess, Curator of European Art at the Huntington Library; Eugene J. Johnson, Professor of Art at Williams College; and Leslie N. Johnson. Curt DiCamillo served as an invaluable resource for provenance and collections history. Thank you to Phil Freshman, who helped shape and refine the catalogue essays and entries.

It is our hope that the spirit of collaboration that infused the entire project carries forward throughout the catalogue for *Venice in the Age of Canaletto* and we invite you to return often to the Brooks Museum and the Ringling Museum.

Sincerely,

Cameron Kitchin
Director
Memphis Brooks Museum of Art

John Wetenhall
Executive Director
The John and Mable Ringling Museum of Art

Curators' Acknowledgements

To embark on an exhibition and publication as ambitious as *Venice in the Age of Canaletto* is necessarily to rely on the cooperation and expertise of a great many people. We owe an enormous debt of gratitude to those who encouraged and supported the project from start to fruition. We offer our most profound thanks to the lenders of the exhibition. As all museum professionals know, the loan of even a single object is a complicated and time-consuming affair; replacements must be found, conservation reports completed, crates built, and of course, for the length of the loan, that object is missing from its home collection. In this light, we are thrilled that so many institutions have graciously agreed to part with their magnificent paintings, prints, and decorative arts for the duration of the exhibition in Sarasota and Memphis. The enthusiasm and support of directors, curators, conservators, registrars, and art handlers from across the United States have been essential to the success of the exhibition. We would also like to extend our sincerest appreciation to Matthew Nimetz for his generous participation in the project by consenting to share his private treasures for the benefit of the public.

To our directors, John Wetenhall and Cameron Kitchin, who have given the exhibition their absolute support and commitment—and continual encouragement to its curators—we are extremely grateful. It has been their guidance and enthusiasm that have brought the project to its culmination. A debt of gratitude is also owed to the Brooks Museum's former Director Kaywin Feldman, under whose guidance *Venice in the Age of Canaletto* was first conceived. We are also deeply indebted to Marina Pacini, Chief Curator at the Brooks, who oversaw this project, and to Stephen Borys, former Curator of Collections at the Ringling, who enthusiastically embraced the creative collaboration between our two institutions.

Venice in the Age of Canaletto also owes much to the participation of William Barcham and Eugene J. and Leslie N. Johnson, our distinguished authors. It is a far superior publication thanks to their insightful and articulate essays. To them we also owe our sincere gratitude for their patience and unfailing good humor throughout the long editing process. These scholars, as well as Alan Chong, have also provided invaluable guidance and assistance for so many aspects of the project. In addition, we must thank Ralph Lieberman for his luminous and evocative videos of the Grand Canal. We would also like to thank those scholars who have contributed entries to the catalogue: Fausto Calderai, Victor Coonin, and Catherine Hess. Even under the tightest of timetables they never failed to produce excellent, polished, scholarly work, and always with good humor and patience. We also thank Phil Freshman, who oversaw the preparation of the manuscript with unparalleled care and attention. And to Heather Klein, we express our deepest gratitude for designing this elegant and beautiful exhibition catalogue.

Venice in the Age of Canaletto has been a rewarding collaborative effort that has drawn on the expertise of a great many of our museum colleagues at The John and Mable Ringling Museum of Art and the Memphis Brooks Museum of Art. To name a few is to risk omitting the many who helped in inestimable ways. But we owe a particular gratitude to (in alphabetical order): Bob Arnold, Aaron Board, Virginia Brilliant, Ashley Burke, Richard Gamble, Louis Giberson, Liz Gray, Francoise Hack, Carlisle Hacker, Gussie Haeffner, Matthew Harmon, Barbara Hyde, Diane Jalfon, Linda McKee, Aleesha Nissen, Kip Peterson, Dave Piurek, Donn Roll, Amy Sankes, Michelle Scalera, Jean Speaker, Heidi Taylor, Peg Thornton, Claudia Towell, Paul Tracy, and Artis Wick. We must also make special mention of the individuals outside our institutions whose dedication and generosity were crucial to the project, in particular Christine Edmonson of the Cleveland Museum of Art, Peggy Morrison of Hendrix College, and Klaartje Proesmans of the Katholieke Universiteit of Leuven, Belgium.

The exhibition would not have been possible without the generous financial support of The Samuel H. Kress Foundation through the Old Masters in Context program, The Assisi Foundation of Memphis, Inc., The Gladys Krieble Delmas Foundation, and indemnity from the Federal Council on the Arts and Humanities.

Our greatest debt is, of course, to our families. Their unwavering encouragement and endless patience throughout the years leading up to the completion of this project have been both humbling and inspiring. To Scott and Genevieve, thank you.

Alexandra Libby
Assistant Curator
The John and Mable Ringling Museum of Art

Stanton Thomas
Associate Curator
Memphis Brooks Museum of Art

Curators' Preface

Canaletto's landscapes are arguably, even today, the most familiar artistic products of eighteenth-century Venice. For those with the requisite means, no visit to the city would be considered complete without the purchase of at least one of the artist's views, which captured the city's topography and urban activity with apparent verisimilitude. *The Grand Canal from the Campo San Vio* (cat. 20), which inspired this exhibition, is just such a picture. George Proctor, a retired merchant and entrepreneur who visited the city, bought the painting and its pendant *View of the Molo* (cat. 21), as well as other vistas of Venice, to adorn the walls of Langley Park, his country estate near Norwich. Proctor's choices were versions of very popular compositions by Canaletto, and reflect the range of subject matter beloved by English tourists. These include such panoramas as the Rialto Bridge (cat. 19), or vistas of and around the Piazza S. Marco (cats. 22 and 23). For those of lesser means, etchings after original compositions by Canaletto, which were both more easily transportable and widely available, provided an affordable alternative (cats. 13a–o).

View painting, not a favored genre during the preceding several centuries, gained considerable popularity in the 1700s. Its ascendency corresponded directly to increased foreign travel and in particular to the aristocratic Englishmen who, having embarked on the Grand Tour—an itinerary which necessarily included Venice—sought mementos of their travels. Indeed, view paintings functioned not just as visual records of places visited on travels, but as aide-mémoire, that is, souvenirs of their time there. However, for all Canaletto's popularity and his ability to capture the fabric of Venice at its most appealing and evocative, his work is curiously devoid of the rich coloring, sensuality, and exuberance of most Venetian art of the period.

His canvases, in fact, are quite distinct from other cityscape paintings produced by the artist's compatriots, such as Francesco Guardi (cat. 28) or Luca Carlevaris (cats. 7 and 8), whose atmospheric colors and flickering brushwork reveal a more dramatic and expressive approach. Even Canaletto's nephew Bernardo Bellotto, though he trained with his uncle and initially emulated the elder master, soon evolved toward a much darker and more dramatic style (cat. 31). Instead, Canaletto focuses his attention upon a more controlled, seemingly realistic, and detached evocation of Venice. Granted, by definition *vedute* or view pictures must record vistas of famous cities or landscapes with at least outward visual fidelity to subject matter, thus seemingly precluding the qualities of invention and fantasy—the stuff of which capriccio paintings are made. And while Canaletto is well-known for his ability to distort his subject matter creatively, using the canvas like an architectural photographer with a wide-angle lens, his *vedute* always *appear* to be accurate depictions of the city. When compared to the works of the other *vedutisti*, Canaletto's canvases are revealed as beautiful but rather anomalous creations.

There is an even starker contrast between Canaletto's paintings and other works from eighteenth-century Venice. Compared to the decorative arts—Rococo objects distinctive for their sense of fantasy and almost confectionary decoration and coloring—his canvases are models of restraint (cats. 9, 32–42). Likewise, Canaletto's pictures are no less surprising when juxtaposed with images of aristocratic life from this time, lacking as they do the emphasis on luxury, pleasure, and indulgence recorded by Pietro Longhi (cats. 24–27) and Domenico Maggiotto (cat. 30).

Perhaps most telling is the disparity between Canaletto's work and the great trinity of eighteenth-century Venetian artists who dominated the city: Sebastiano Ricci (cats. 1–6), Giovanni Battista Piazzetta (cat. 12), and Giambattista Tiepolo (cats. 14–16). Measured against the chromatic mastery of Ricci, the coarse naturalism of Piazzetta, or the heroic theatricality of Tiepolo, Canaletto's works appear almost proto-Neoclassical in their restraint and rationality. Although his ability to stage a scene and his sense of color and light are no less extraordinary than his accomplished compatriots, his artistic vision is a decided contrast to their expansive ceiling frescoes, dramatic altarpieces, easel paintings, and dynamic decorative cycles that evoked religion, myth, and history. Here again Canaletto's paintings are revealed as beautiful yet rather anomalous creations. This is also true of his works when compared to other great proponents of the Rococo in Venice, such as Antonio Pellegrini (cat. 10). *Venice in the Age of Canaletto* provides the opportunity to explore the strange tension that exists between Canaletto's austere, seemingly realistic cityscapes and the magnificent, pastelline fantasies, religious pictures, and historical dramas of the Venetian eighteenth century.

Standing at the heart of this project is Canaletto's splendid canvas *The Grand Canal from the Campo San Vio*, a gift from The Samuel H. Kress Foundation to the Memphis Brooks Museum of Art. When compared to the more ebullient Rococo works with which it usually is displayed, the painting embodies a sense of restraint and realism, reflecting a seemingly literal sensibility within the more exuberant strains of most eighteenth-century Venetian art. It is this juxtaposition, the contrast between Canaletto's apparently more rational, measured vision of Venice and the dramatic, expressive works of his contemporaries, that inspired the exhibition. Indeed the aim was never to take a monographic approach to Canaletto—scholarly understanding of whom has advanced significantly in the past decade thanks to the contributions of Charles Beddington, Martin Clayton, Bożena Anna Kowalczyk, and Filippo Pedrocco—but rather to consider him within the Venetian context. Seeing Canaletto's paintings thus, whether against the grand mythologies and transcendent religious scenes, exquisitely lacquered furniture, or delicately crafted glass, reveals both the painter's place within the city of his birth and the way he is an exception to it.

To help elucidate the complicated forces that shaped Canaletto and the city of Venice during his age, this catalogue offers a range of essays. Alexandra Libby's biography of the artist gives a review of the social and artistic circumstances that influenced Canaletto throughout his life. It also reminds the reader of his theatrical origins, and how painting stage sets and scenery contributed to his predilection for architecture and landscapes. The biography also traces his evolving market popularity, thus laying the groundwork for Stanton Thomas's essay on the taste for Canaletto in England. Thomas's study focuses upon how the British interest in Palladian principles of restraint, pleasing rhythms, and harmony mirrors Canaletto's rise in popularity. Reading the artist's work in this way helps explain his canvases within the otherwise ebulliently Rococo environment of his compatriots.

Complementing Thomas's essay is a study by Eugene J. and Leslie N. Johnson of Antonio Visentini's famous series of prints after Canaletto's paintings. Their work offers a refreshing exploration of the nature of these etchings, and how they functioned as so-called "armchair reminiscences." In particular, this essay reveals that the prints were prized for their ability to replicate the experience of moving sequentially through Venice's unique urban highway, the Grand Canal. The Johnsons' study is particularly valuable as it notes precedence for this approach

in seventeenth-century Dutch prints, as well as in images of Rome associated with Papal projects in the city and related pilgrimages. The final essay, by William Barcham, focuses upon Roman Catholicism in Venice. His study explores the rich and vital religious life of the city, in relation to both the clergy and the general population. It offers a compelling backdrop to the public, international image of Venice as a place of sensuosity and luxury, where its citizens lived a licentious way of life. Based upon the extraordinary number of ecclesiastical building and renovation campaigns, and, perhaps more critically, upon the deeply pious imagery that permeated the private and public sectors, Barcham's essay reveals that Venetians were manifestly committed to the Catholic faith. His study shows that Christian life, with all its rituals, dogma, and saints, was alive and well—despite the visitors who flocked to the fabled city to sample its worldly pleasures.

Venice in the Age of Canaletto focuses upon an era when the city, perhaps more than any other in Europe, cultivated a civic image of pleasure, fantasy, and escapism. To some extent Canaletto's work perfectly captures this adjusted view of reality, one that emphasizes Venice's perceived charms: its glowing light, reflective canals, exotic setting, and imposing buildings. Even during the artist's lifetime his celebrated representations became the preferred way of recalling, and perhaps even seeing the city, and quickly emerged as key elements in fashioning the identity of the Venetian Republic. At the same time, the artist's vistas of Venice maintain a certain distance, keeping the viewer ever a tourist, a visitor looking into another world. Perhaps Canaletto's most brilliant achievement is this ability to beguile the viewer as if from afar. His canvases are so persuasive that, in our minds, we wander upon glistening canals and through cramped streets, mingle with the crowds in squares and churches, step into gilded gambling houses and palazzi. In Canaletto's paintings we see—more marvelous through recollection or inner vision—the richness of his world and the vanished splendor of that age.

Alexandra Libby
Assistant Curator
The John and Mable Ringling Museum of Art

Stanton Thomas
Associate Curator
Memphis Brooks Museum of Art

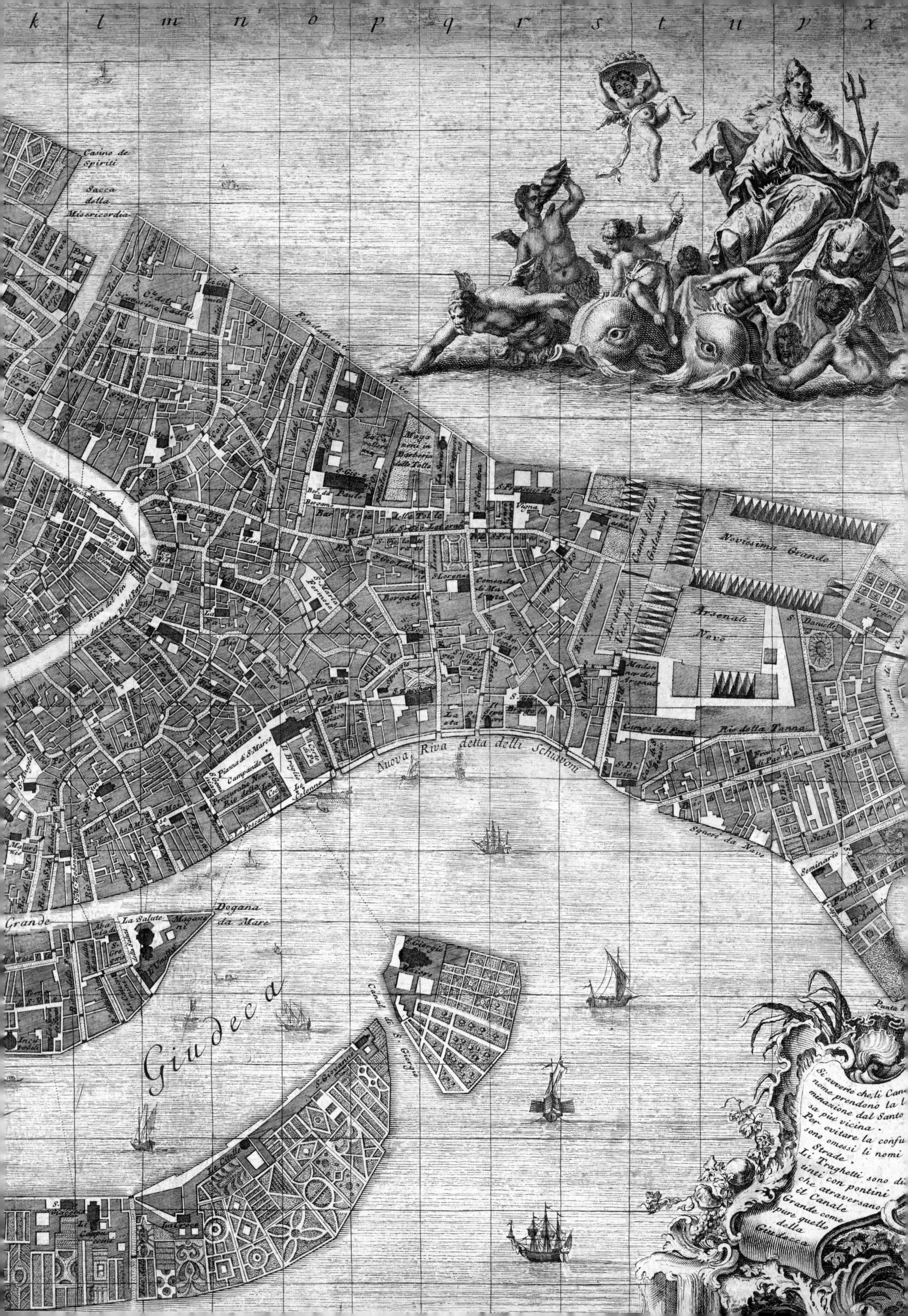
k l m n o p q r s t u x
Casino de Spiriti
Sacca della Misericordia
Novissima Grande
Canal delle Galeazze
Arsenale Vecchio
Arsenale Novo
S. Francesco della Vigna
S. Lorenzo
Comenda di Malta
Borgato
S. Giustina
Campo dei Forni
Rio della Tanna
Squeri da Nave
Seminario
Piazza di S. Marco
Campanile
Procuratie Nove
Le Colonne
Nuova Riva detta delli Schiavoni
Dogana da Mare
La Salute
Magazzini
Grande
Giudeca
S. Giorgio
Canal di S. Giorgio
Punta
Si avverte che li Canali
prendono la denominazione dal Santo
più vicina. Per evitare la confusione
sono omessi li nomi delle Strade.
Li Traghetti sono distinti con pontini
che atraversano il Canale come
pure quello della Giudeca.

In the notes to the essays and catalogue entries, all books, articles, and exhibitions are cited in abbreviated form. Such citations are also found in the Reference section of each catalogue entry. Full citations for all referenced works are given in the Bibliography.

Objects exhibited only in Sarasota are indicated by †.
Objects not included in this exhibition are indicated by ‡.

Unless otherwise stated, measurements are given in inches and centimeters, with height preceding width. For the decorative arts, measurements are given in inches and centimeters, with height preceding width, followed by depth.

Catalogue entries are signed with author's initials, which are listed in the following key.

FC   Fausto Calderai

AVC   A. Victor Coonin

CH   Catherine Hess

AL   Alexandra Libby

ST   Stanton Thomas

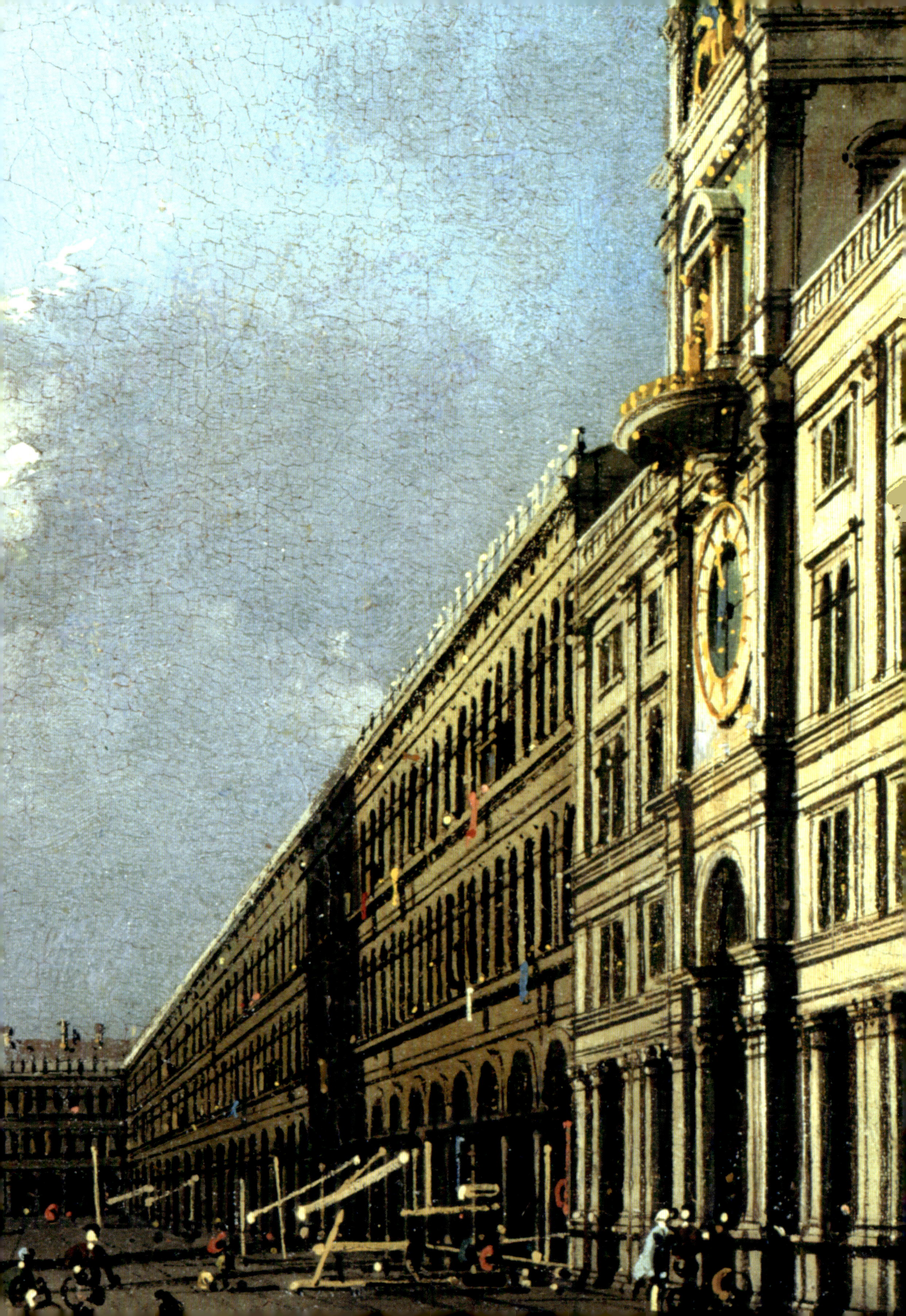

Canaletto:
A Brief Biography

ALEXANDRA LIBBY

Giovanni Antonio Canal was born on October 17, 1697, into a high-ranking Venetian family near the Campo S. Lio—in the heart of Venice, not far from the Rialto Bridge.[1] Because the honorable status of *cittadino originario* had been accorded to his paternal great-grandfather, Canaletto could rightly describe himself as "Origine Civis Venetus" on the frontispiece of a volume of etchings after a group of his view paintings by Antonio Visentini, who was himself described only as "Venetus" (cat. 13a).[2] The artist's father, Bernardo Cesare Canal (1674–1744), was a highly regarded theatrical-scene painter, and it was from him that Canaletto—"the Little Canal"—learned his trade. Not surprisingly, this early training in scenography significantly influenced Canaletto's later work.

Among the few surviving records documenting Canaletto's life and career are the paragraphs that Pellegrino Antonio Orlandi, Antonio Maria Zanetti, and Pierre Jean Mariette devoted to him in their respective *Abecedari,* or encyclopedias, of Italian artists.[3] All agreed that Canaletto traveled to Rome in 1719 to assist his father on scenery designs for two operas by Alessandro Scarlatti, *Titus Sempronius Graccus* and *Turno Aricino.*[4] Apparently he did not stay there long, since he registered as a member of the Venetian painters' guild early in 1720.[5] Nevertheless, he must have been active in Rome given the existence of a series of twenty-three drawings of that city by him, generally dated to 1719.[6]

The nature of these works, which were executed in pen and brown ink with gray and brown wash, suggests they were preparatory drawings. Several of his paintings of Roman subjects rely heavily upon these early compositions. That each is numbered and inscribed in the lower border "Antonio Canal Dellineo IN ROMA" conforms to the conventional format used by printmakers working in series; presumably, then, Canaletto initially intended these drawings to be reproduced as prints and only later used them as the bases for paintings. They exhibit a controlled use of the pen, painterly handling of wash, and careful attention to incidental detail that prefigure his mature draftsmanship. Because, on the whole, the drawings

vary in quality and execution, some scholars have questioned their authorship.[7] Yet the presence of awkward passages and uneven execution may simply reflect Canaletto's artistic immaturity.

Although the paucity of surviving documentation makes it impossible to reconstruct the sequence of events following Canaletto's trip to Rome definitively, a group of pictures may plausibly be dated to this period based on style. One of the first paintings, if not the first work he produced upon returning from Rome, is the large capriccio *The Piazza del Campidoglio* (fig. 1).[8] Clearly based on a drawing from his Roman sojourn, the painting also reveals the hand of an artist involved with the theater (fig. 2). The sharp separation of foreground and background, which Canaletto achieved by plunging the former into extreme shadow, was a classic scenographic technique used to produce the illusion of distance and space. Furthermore, when combined with strongly blocked areas of light and dark as well as carefully rendered atmosphere, this effect creates a heightened sense of drama. Attesting to Canaletto's familiarity with contemporary Venetian theatrical-painting practice is the abundant architectural ornamentation: pilasters, columns, and pedestal sculpture as well as acroteria—all motifs popular in eighteenth-century Venetian theater.[9]

In style and subject matter, this early work closely resembles that of the Dutchman Gaspar van Wittel (called Vanvitelli, 1653–1736), who was also active in Rome at that time. Although there is no hard evidence that Canaletto had any personal contact with Vanvitelli—or any other artist, for that matter—during his stay there, he certainly would have been familiar with the older painter's lively and luminous work. Rather than focusing on the poetic, often melancholic themes associated with ruins, as did many northern European artists working in Rome, Vanvitelli concentrated on the city's modern topography and urban activity (fig. 3). Canaletto similarly took the spirit of Roman life as a subject, which he set against the backdrop of ancient and modern sites. He delighted especially in portraying such homely details as the woman hanging her

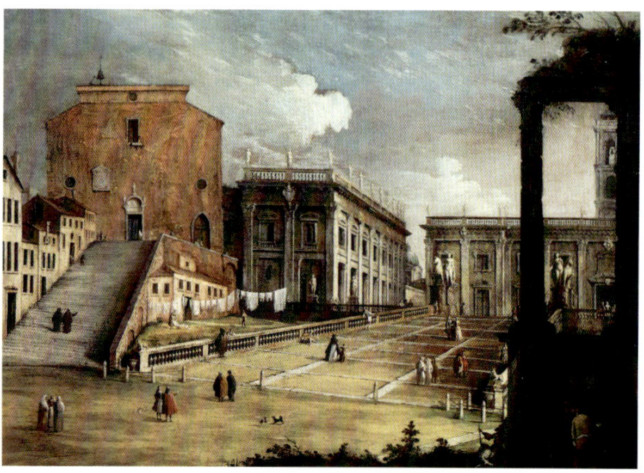

Fig. 1. Canaletto (Giovanni Antonio Canal)
The Piazza del Campidoglio, ca. 1720
Oil on canvas, 58 1/4 x 78 3/4 in. (148 x 200 cm)
Szépmüvészeti Múzeum, Budapest 53.483

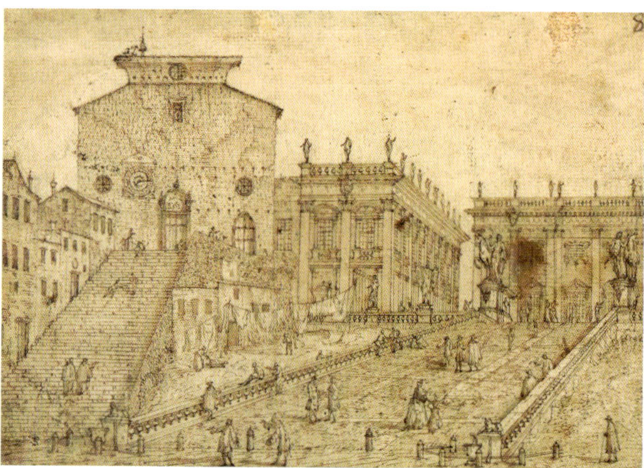

Fig. 2. Canaletto (Giovanni Antonio Canal)
View from the Capitoline, ca. 1719
Pen and brown ink with gray wash over traces of graphite, 6 1/8 x 8 3/4 in. (15.7 x 22.4 cm)
Hessisches Landesmuseum, Darmstadt, AE 2186

laundry alongside the church steps in *The Piazza del Campidoglio.*

Another early influence on Canaletto must have been Marco Ricci (1676–1730). The nephew of the highly successful history painter Sebastiano Ricci, Marco was an accomplished landscape painter best known for his imaginary views and picturesque capriccios (cat. 11), a genre with which Canaletto first experimented in the Roman drawings. The distinctly fanciful feel of his Roman work is evident in, for example, the depiction of foliage sprouting from the architectural edifices in *The Piazza del Campidoglio.* His technique at this time recalls several other aspects of Ricci's style, including the use of a dark reddish-brown ground and the dramatic contrasts of light and shadow in the circa 1720 painting.[10]

Luca Carlevaris (1665–1731), the "father" of the *veduta* (view painting), was the most significant of Canaletto's predecessors. Although certainly not the first artist to paint in the topographical mode, he was the first to specialize in that genre and to base his reputation on it. However, it was not until 1703 that Carlevaris definitively declared his status as a *vedutista* (view painter). In that year, he published *Le fabriche, e vedute di Venetia disegnate,* a 103-plate topographical survey of Venice's churches, palaces, and other buildings as well as its canals, *campi,* and bridges.[11] Although the etchings are not especially lively and do little to showcase the splendors of Venice, this comprehensive study laid the groundwork for his later paintings, which celebrated the city's unique cultural history and intriguing urban character (cats. 7 and 8). These works distinguished Carlevaris from previous artists, who generally had used the city as a backdrop for more ambitious civic and religious subjects—as did, for example, Giovanni Bellini in his magnificent *Procession in Piazza San Marco* (1496, Galleria dell'Accademia, Venice).[12] Not incidentally—and to the eventual benefit of

Canaletto—Carlevaris also established the Venetian art market for view painting.

Among the first *vedute* Canaletto produced following his return from Rome were four large-scale paintings (each approximately fifty-five by eighty inches), formerly in the collection of the princes of Liechtenstein, and three of similar dimensions that belonged to the Electors of Saxony in Dresden. There is no evidence linking their purchase directly to Canaletto: the Liechtenstein pictures are not documented as having been in that collection until after the artist's death, and the Dresden paintings were first recorded in 1754. They can, however, be dated to the early 1720s based on their scenographic qualities. Like *The Piazza del Campidoglio,* these works use strongly blocked passages of light and dark and reveal an attention to atmospheric effect. They also show the characteristic oblique perspectival axis, called *scena dell'angolo* (angled scene), with steeply receding rows of repeated architectural elements that draw the eye deep into the pictorial space.

As is evident in *View of Piazza San Marco, Venice* (fig. 4), Canaletto also distorted proportion and scale in his paintings to enhance the overall pictorial effect—another trick borrowed from theatrical design. The Basilica of S. Marco is not nearly as tall nor is the Campanile as slender as the painting suggests, but the exaggeration of scale and topography increases their architectural presence and significantly heightens the dramatic effect.

In addition to pictorial evidence, there are a few extant documents that help illuminate Canaletto's early career. His name appears in a letter from the textile merchant Stefano Conti to his art agent, Alessandro Marchesini.[13] Conti, who was from Lucca, was an avid collector and opened a small gallery for contemporary Venetian art in 1707. He enlisted Marchesini, a Veronese artist living in Venice, to secure works by artists such as Carlevaris, Giuseppe Maria Crespi, and

Giovanni Battista Piazzetta. In 1725 Conti decided to add to his collection and asked Marchesini to purchase more works from Carlevaris; in what may be the most quoted letter in the literature on Canaletto, Marchesini encouraged Conti to consider instead paintings by a younger artist that were similar to those of Carlevaris but with one remarkable difference: "you can see the sun shining in them."[14] The paintings were by a "Sig.r Ant. Canale," he wrote, and "they astonished all who saw them."[15] Marchesini noted that this same man had been attracting a distinguished group of patrons and already had sold works to Zaccaria Sagredo, a member of one of Venice's most illustrious and influential families, as well as to the imperial ambassador, who bought a painting at the annual exhibition at the Scuola Grande di S. Rocco. Undoubtedly impressed, Conti commissioned two views from Canaletto: *The Rialto Bridge from the North* (fig. 5) and *The Grand Canal: Looking North from near the Rialto Bridge* (fig. 6); both were produced in 1725.

Although considerably smaller than the Liechtenstein or Dresden pictures, the paintings made for Conti still reflect Canaletto's roots in the theater. They are similarly inventive—that is, there is no single spot from which the buildings represented can be viewed as depicted here—and they display the same freedom of brushwork, consideration of atmospheric effects, and close attention to animated detail, such as the workers atop construction scaffolding in *The Rialto Bridge from the North*. However, unlike the Liechtenstein or Dresden paintings, the Conti canvases reveal the artist's scrupulous attention to the play of light and shadow, an effect he achieved primarily by varying his underpainting (light to dark gray in the sky and water, warm orange for the buildings). The mechanical repetition of form that created such vertiginous spatial recession in *View of Piazza San Marco, Venice* is absent in these paintings created two years later. Instead, Canaletto describes architectural detail with painterly brushwork, which better captures the textural qualities of the crumbling and decaying Grand Canal palazzos.

At the same time Canaletto was occupied with the Conti commission, he met Owen McSwiney, who would prove to be an important early patron. A charismatic, if somewhat unruly, Irish entrepreneur and theatrical impresario, McSwiney had been living in Venice since 1711, when financial disaster forced him out of London. After his move, he attempted to rehabilitate himself by scouting for emerging Italian opera singers and buying artworks for British collectors. In his role as an art dealer, McSwiney wrote the second Duke of Richmond in March 1726 to describe his latest project—commissioning leading Venetian and Bolognese artists to create a series of allegorical canvases commemorating great men of recent English history.[16] The "tomb paintings," as they have come to be known, were jointly produced by Giovanni Battista Cimaroli, Giovanni Battista Piazzetta, Giovanni Battista Pittoni, Marco and

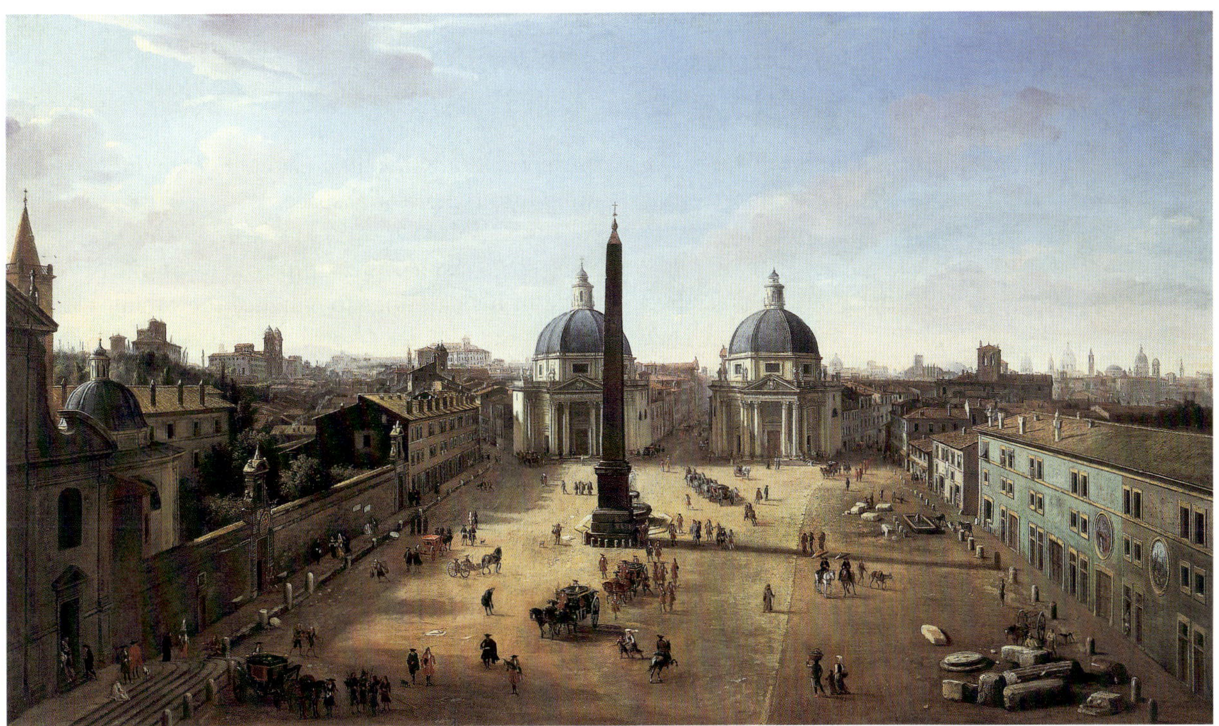

Fig. 3. Gaspar van Wittel (called Vanvitelli) (Dutch, 1653–1736)
Piazza del Popolo, Rome, ca. 1683
Oil on canvas, 28 1/2 x 49 1/2 in. (72.4 x 125.7 cm)
Memphis Brooks Museum of Art; Gift of Mr. and Mrs. Hugo N. Dixon 54.4

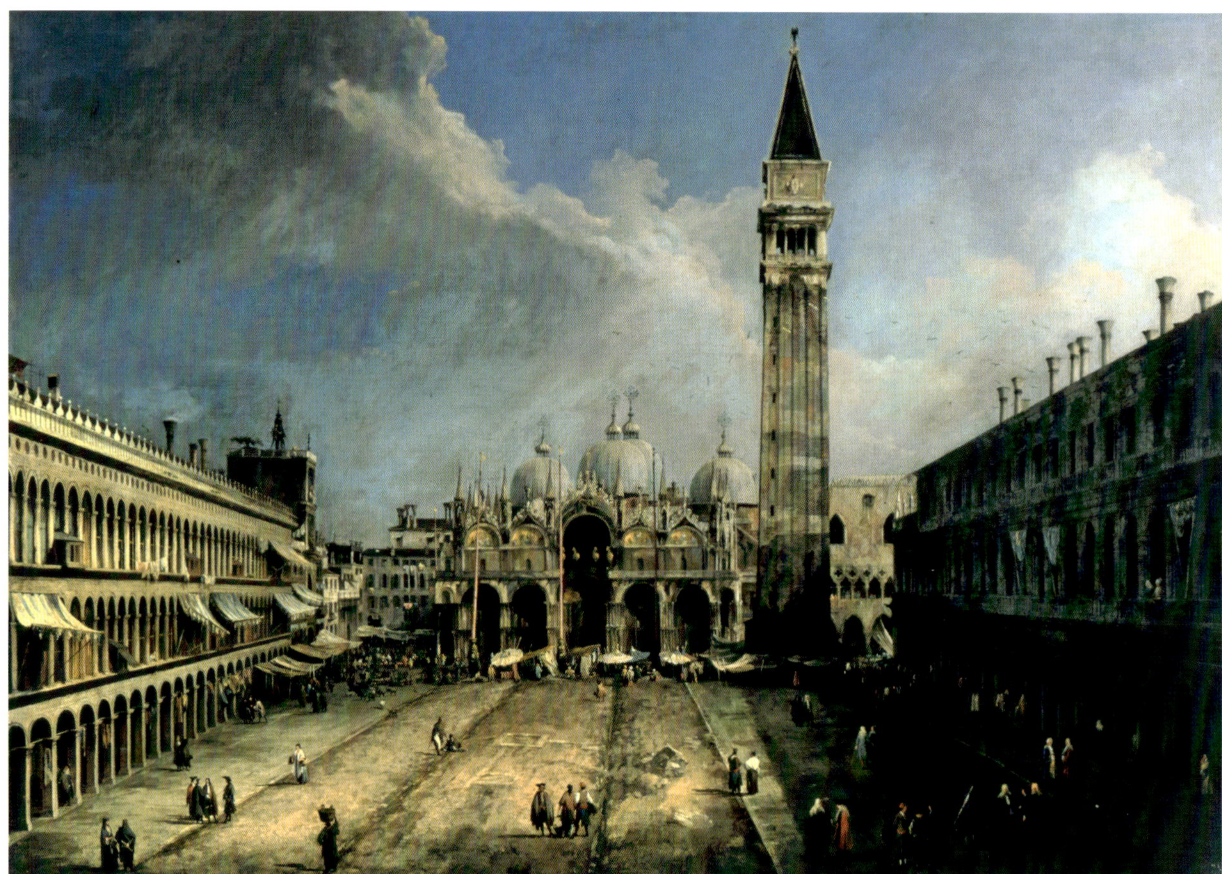

Fig. 4. Canaletto (Giovanni Antonio Canal)
View of Piazza San Marco, Venice, 1723
Oil on canvas, 55 3/4 x 80 1/2 in. (141.5 x 204.5 cm)
Museo Thyssen-Bornemisza, Madrid, 1956.1

Sebastiano Ricci, and Canaletto. In truth, Canaletto's contribution to the project was small, consisting of painting the perspective and landscape for only two of the twenty-four canvases, the *Allegorical Tomb in Honour of Archbishop Tillotson* (1726, private collection) and the *Allegorical Tomb in Honour of John, Lord Somers* (1726, Viscount Windsor collection). Nonetheless, the project was critical to the advancement of his career, as it firmly established his connection to the English clientele he would serve for the next forty years.[17]

In November 1727, the Irishman wrote again to the Duke of Richmond, this time to discuss Canaletto's commissions for him as well as for a Mr. Southwell (evidently an acquaintance of the duke) in England. Further, McSwiney indicated that he had recently shipped the duke two small works on copper, each measuring about forty-five centimeters in height. McSwiney then encouraged Canaletto to adopt this smaller form, recognizing that pleasant, easily portable views would be far more attractive to Grand Tourists visiting Venice than large-scale, dramatic canvases. It was, McSwiney wrote to the duke, "a size he excels in."[18] The letter went on to lament Canaletto's apparent stubbornness in negotiating a price and a timetable, contending, "He has more work than he can doe [sic], in any reasonable time, and well: but

by the assistance of a particular friend of his, I get once in two months a piece sketch'd out, and in a little finish'd, by Force of Bribery." It is worth noting that Marchesini and Conti encountered similar problems with Canaletto.[19]

Despite what is surely an exaggeration of McSwiney's need to coerce Canaletto, the letter is significant for its introduction of the "particular friend," who was almost certainly Joseph Smith (ca. 1674–1770). Born and educated in England, Smith moved to Venice around 1700 and remained there for the rest of his long life. At the time McSwiney was writing to the Duke of Richmond, Smith, a successful banker and merchant, had become one of the most important collectors and connoisseurs in Venice, amassing immense holdings of coins, gems, rare books, prints, drawings, and paintings. He most likely had made Canaletto's acquaintance sometime in the mid-1720s, when McSwiney was living in the Englishman's Venetian residence. Like the Irishman, Smith immediately recognized the artist's commercial potential for the British art market. Soon realizing how to profit from it, he offered a range of services to Canaletto's patrons, including framing, packing, shipping, customs management, and, in some cases, temporary financing. Joseph Smith would become the chief purveyor and most prolific collector of Canaletto's art.

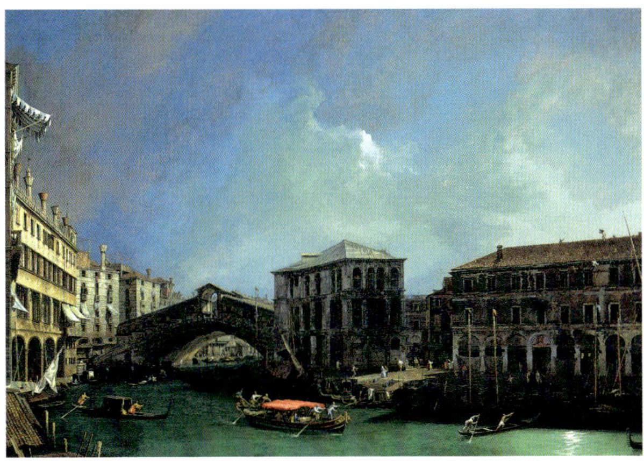

Fig. 5. Canaletto (Giovanni Antonio Canal)
The Rialto Bridge from the North, 1725
Oil on canvas, 36 x 53 1/2 in. (91.4 x 135.8 cm)
Pinacoteca Giovanni e Marella Agnelli, Turin

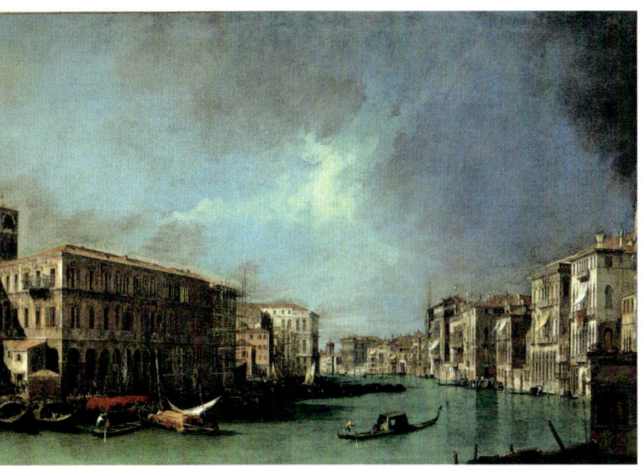

Fig. 6. Canaletto (Giovanni Antonio Canal)
The Grand Canal: Looking North from Near the Rialto Bridge, 1725
Oil on canvas, 35 13/16 x 53 1/8 in. (91 x 135 cm)
Pinacoteca Giovanni e Marella Agnelli, Turin

The first documentary evidence of Smith's negotiating for Canaletto appears in a letter of July 1730. Writing to Samuel Hill of Staffordshire, Smith indicated that the pictures for which the former was waiting—*The Grand Canal, Piazzetta, and Dogana, Venice* (fig. 7) and *The Doge's Palace and Riva degli Schiavoni, Venice* (fig. 8)—would be finished before the end of the year. The subject matter of the pair is typical of the 1730s, when the waterfront area around the Palazzo Ducale, including the Riva degli Schiavoni and the Grand Canal, became especially popular with Grand Tourists for its immediately recognizable views. The busy water promenade was also one of Canaletto's favorite spots, as it provided ample opportunity to observe the details of urban life he loved, from the gondoliers deftly navigating their boats to the street vendors selling their wares.

Although slightly larger than several subsequent works, the two paintings made for Hill reveal many of the technical qualities Canaletto developed during the 1730s. Abandoning the exaggerated contrasts of shadow and light seen in the Conti pictures, which may have seemed ponderous for small-scale works, the artist instead began using a pale beige underpainting that gave the images a lighter feel. Additionally, the Hill pictures demonstrate Canaletto's increasingly refined brushwork; rather than using black ruling for architectural details, he began to favor controlled strokes and impasto when representing stonework, windows, or columns.

Smith's 1730 letter laments Canaletto's slow pace, which seems to have been a constant issue, and concludes by mentioning that "prints of the views and pictures of Venice" were soon to be completed.[20] He was almost certainly referring to the series of fourteen etchings Smith had commissioned from Antonio Visentini after views by Canaletto. By that time, Smith's residence at the Palazzo Magili Valmarana had become an almost obligatory stop for any

wealthy Englishman on the Grand Tour. Here he hung Canaletto's twelve small-format paintings of the Grand Canal and two festival scenes—all of which demonstrated the artist's talents to visitors who might want to commission variations of the works for themselves. Visentini's etchings after the views, which Smith then published through the Giovanni Battista Pasquali Press in 1735 under the title *Prospectus Magni Canalis Venetiarum*, further advertised Canaletto to patrons unable to see the originals or to those who wanted to buy more modestly priced works.

The strategy evidently worked. Between 1729 and 1740, Smith supplied more than eighty views of Venice to British patrons. Besides the two pictures for Samuel Hill were twenty-one paintings for an unknown client that later entered the collection of Sir Robert Grenville Harvey (d. 1931). Likewise, the Duke of Bedford bought twenty-four canvases to hang in Bedford House, and Hugh Howard, whose descendents were the earls of Wicklow, ordered a pair of Grand Canal views. The Earl of Normanton also commissioned views of the Grand Canal from Canaletto; four or more were sent to the Fourth Duke of Leeds, and Sir William Morice and the Earl of Leicester purchased two views apiece. Of course, Smith owned the original fourteen pictures after which the Visentini prints were etched. Canaletto also executed six large canvases for the Englishman's villa at Mogliano. During this time as well, the artist produced several exceptionally beautiful large-scale paintings independently of Smith, including *Venice: The Feast Day of Saint Roch* (ca. 1735, National Gallery, London), the *Riva degli Schiavoni: Looking West* (before 1736, Sir John Soane's Museum, London), and the magnificent *Bacino di San Marco: Looking East* (ca. 1738, Museum of Fine Arts, Boston).

Under Joseph Smith's representation, Canaletto

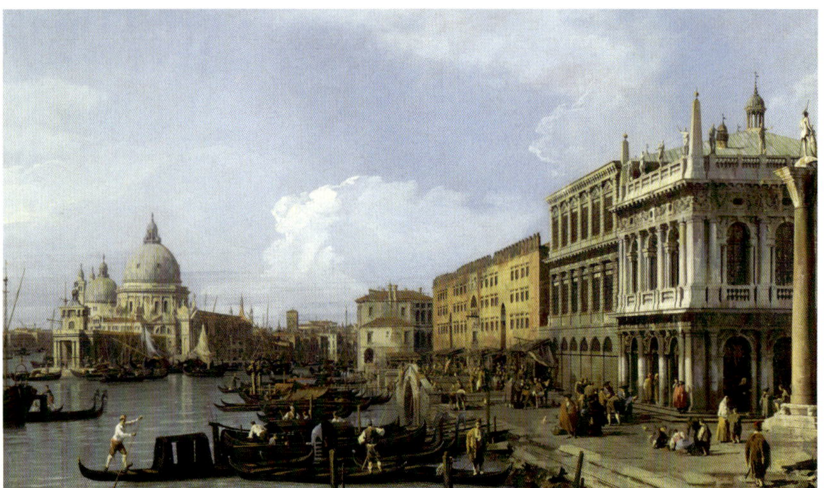

Fig. 7. Canaletto (Giovanni Antonio Canal)
The Grand Canal, Piazzetta, and Dogana, Venice, 1730
Oil on canvas, 23 x 40 in. (58.4 x 101.6 cm)
Tatton Park, The Egerton Collection (The National Trust)

enjoyed great prosperity in the 1730s, but his fortunes shifted considerably during the following decade. In 1741 Italy became involved in the War of Austrian Succession (1740–48), a conflict that curtailed the flow of tourism to Venice and consequently cut off a major source of Canaletto's patronage. Additionally, the artist faced increasing competition from imitators, copyists, and rival view painters who were no doubt encouraged by his success. It has also been suggested that patrons were increasingly impatient with Canaletto because of his apparently fluctuating prices and notoriously slow pace. Writing to his brother Francesco in 1741, Count Bonomo Algarotti indicated that Canaletto not only demanded very high prices but also, "pressed as he was by all too many commissions, would require some *years* to complete them" (emphasis mine).[21] Not all connoisseurs abandoned the *vedutista*, however. Smith continued promoting Canaletto's career, and in 1742 he published a second, expanded edition of the Visentini prints. Retitled *Urbis Venetiarum Prospectus Celebriores*, it boasted an additional twenty-four views of Venice, including churches and *campi* that Canaletto had not previously pictured.[22] Smith also commissioned thirteen *sopraporte* (over-door pieces) for his villa that paid tribute to the great sixteenth-century Venetian architect Andrea Palladio.[23]

Canaletto must have been grateful for Smith's continued support, for sometime after 1744 he published his own set of etchings in a volume titled *Vedute altre prese da i luoghi alrea ideate*, which he dedicated to "Giuseppe Smith."[24] In addition to images of Venice, the portfolio included Roman-flavored capriccios and several topographical views of the Brenta Canal and Padua. The artist and his nephew Bernardo Bellotto had spent several weeks in and around Padua in 1740, and the younger artist may well have assisted with the topographical images. The son of one of Canaletto's three sisters, Bellotto had been working in his uncle's studio since around 1736.[25] Given Canaletto's voluminous output during this time, it is not surprising that he had an atelier. After retiring from scenography, his father also began assisting at the workshop while continuing to paint cityscapes of his own.[26] The impetus for the Brenta trip likely came from Smith, who may have seen Canaletto's diminished activity as an opportunity for the artist to diversify his oeuvre. Both uncle and nephew were highly productive during the tour, making numerous sketches that were later used for engravings and paintings. Smith himself acquired all the drawings, which were extremely lively and demonstrated a freshness of execution that must have derived from the novelty of the material.

Despite the support of his patron and agent, Canaletto no doubt was anxious about the uncertain economic climate and decided, therefore, to visit England, where his work was so highly prized. In May 1746, the English engraver and chronicler George Vertue noted the arrival of "the Famous Painter of Views Canalletti" [sic] in London. He had been recording the contemporary English art scene in preparation for writing a history of eighteenth-century painting to date in his native land. His occasionally

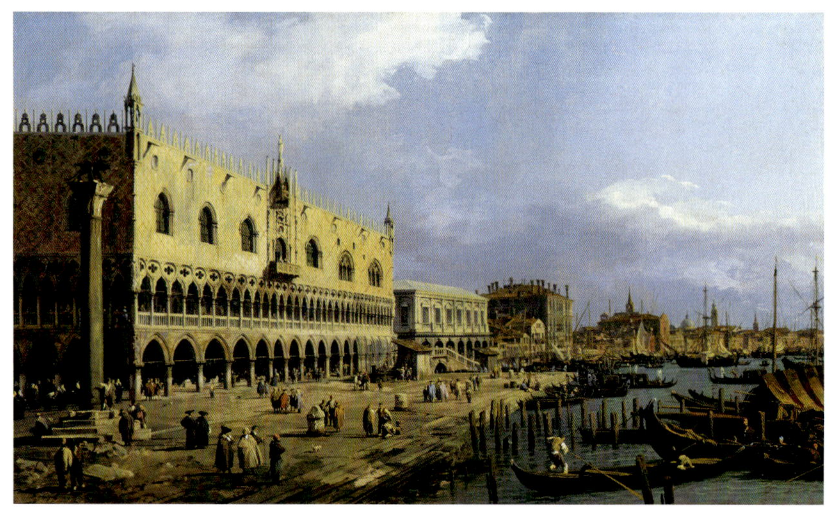

Fig. 8. Canaletto (Giovanni Antonio Canal)
The Doge's Palace and Riva degli Schiavoni, Venice, 1731
Oil on canvas, 23 x 40 in. (58.4 x 101.6 cm)
Tatton Park, The Egerton Collection (The National Trust)

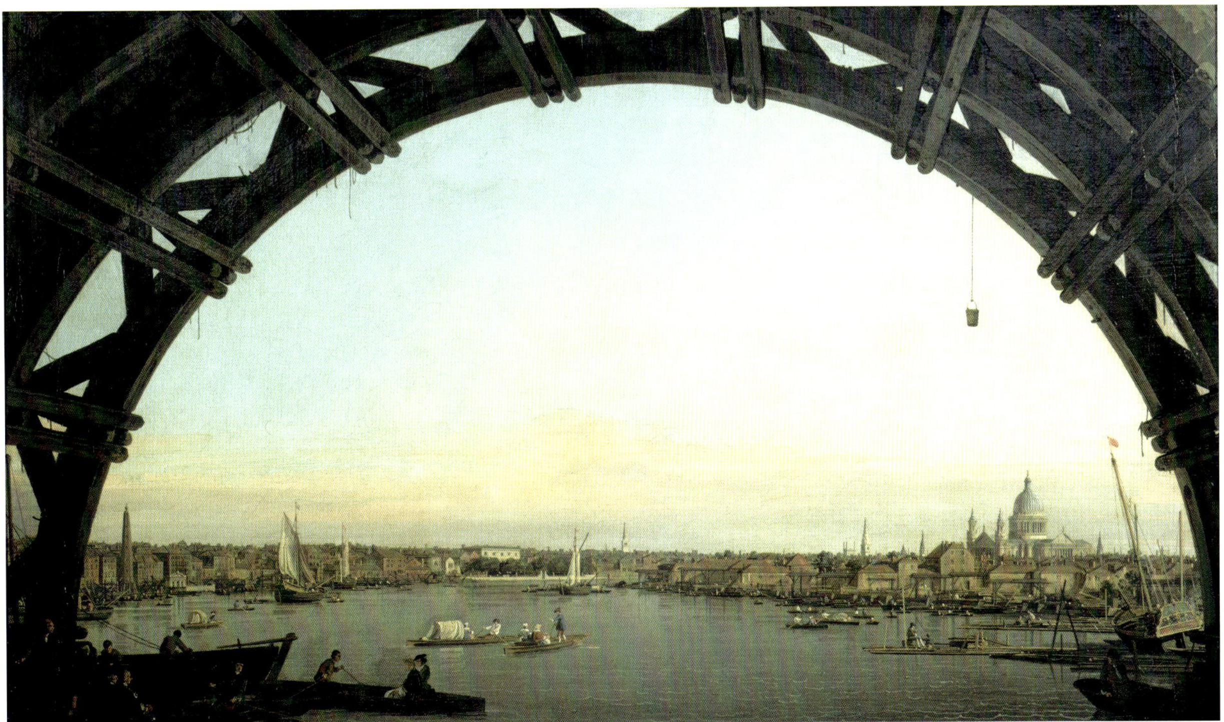

Fig. 9. Canaletto (Giovanni Antonio Canal)
London Seen through an Arch of Westminster Bridge, 1746–47
Oil on canvas, 22 7/16 x 37 7/16 in. (57 x 95 cm)
Syon House, Middlesex, UK/The Bridgeman Art Library

gossipy diaries provide valuable information regarding Canaletto's nearly decade-long English period, beginning with the observation that the artist's arrival was met with great enthusiasm. In particular, Vertue noted "the Multitude of works done abroad for English noblemen & Gentlemen has procured him great reputation," going on to predict his continued success "tho' many persons already have so many of his paintings."[27] To quote the Canaletto connoisseur J. G. Links, "the sting was in the tail,"[28] and though Vertue's concluding caveat that the market was already saturated with Canaletto's work was rather harsh, his words must have rung true. Since all of Canaletto's paintings that passed through Smith's house between 1729 and 1740 went to British patrons, the artist naturally relied on Smith to provide him with letters of introduction. Indeed, the latter wrote to Owen McSwiney, who had been back in London since the 1730s, asking him to arrange a meeting between Canaletto and the Duke of Richmond.

Canaletto's arrival in London auspiciously coincided with the construction of Westminster Bridge. Parliament had first authorized the project in 1736 and both the Duke of Richmond and the Duke of Bedford, two of Canaletto's earliest patrons, supported it. The bridge was a subject of many of his initial endeavors in England. For Sir Hugh Smithson, another supporter of the bridge project, he painted the charming *London Seen through an Arch of Westminster Bridge* (fig. 9), which pictures the Thames from beneath one of the still-unfinished arches. The artist

also created a second view of the span and a beautiful panorama showing Windsor Castle for Smithson, who would become an ardent Canaletto patron. Several other bridge views belong to the artist's first years in England, including an image of it on Lord Mayor's Day, the great panoramas of the Thames done for Prince Lobkowitz of Bohemia, and a picture sent to Joseph Smith in Venice.

In the summer of 1747, with the aid of Owen McSwiney, Canaletto finally met the Duke of Richmond. The nobleman already owned several of the artist's works, including his early collaborative canvas, the *Allegorical Tomb in Honour of John, Lord Somers,* and the pair of Venetian views on copper that McSwiney had mentioned in his November 1727 missive to the duke. In his letter of introduction, Thomas Hill (the duke's former tutor and a friend of McSwiney's) suggested that Canaletto paint from positions inside the duke's London townhouse; this would surely "give him as much reputation as any of his Venetian prospects," Hill asserted.[29] And so it did. *London: The Thames and the City of London from Richmond House* (fig. 10) and *London: Whitehall and the Privy Garden from Richmond House* (fig. 11), both from 1747, are certainly among the most sensitive and beloved works he produced in England. Bathed in a rosy glow reminiscent of Venice's afternoon sunshine, the pictures have often been described as London seen through the eyes of a Venetian. The pair—one observed from a vantage point just above the stables and the other possibly

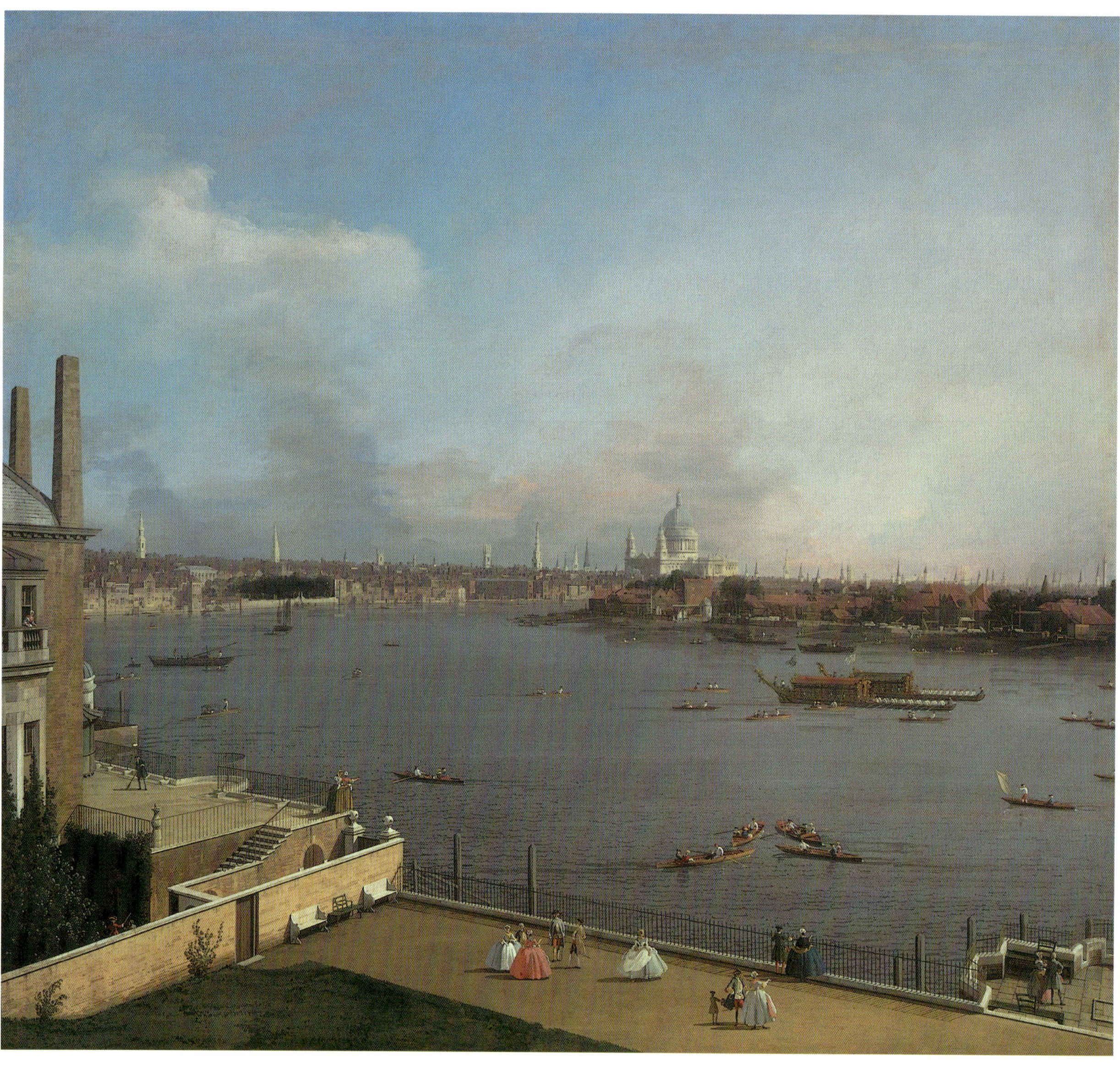

Fig. 10. Canaletto (Giovanni Antonio Canal)
London: The Thames and the City of London from Richmond House, 1747
Oil on canvas, 41 5/16 x 46 1/4 in. (105 x 117.5 cm)
The Trustees of the Goodwood Collection

from the dining room—offers an expansive horizon while simultaneously incorporating intimate, playful vignettes of eighteenth-century high society. Although the panorama of the city skyline stretches out before us in the Whitehall picture (Inigo Jones's Banqueting House and the spire of St. Martin-in-the-Fields are articulated in great detail), the viewer naturally focuses on the modest courtyard of Richmond House. There, a uniformed servant bows to Richmond himself, identified by his blue garter riband, as chickens roam freely near an abandoned workman's ladder.[30] Just through the archway, a man in a tricorn hat greets a visitor, while a soldier standing not far from the duke appears to be urinating against the exterior courtyard wall.

After completing the Richmond pictures, Canaletto painted two depicting Badminton House for the third Duke of Beaufort as well as three paintings and three drawings of Warwick Castle

for Lord Brooke. Ostensibly, the artist was busy during this time, although a July 1749 issue of the *Daily Advertiser* indicates he found this workload unsatisfactorily light. An advertisement reads: "Signor Canaletto hereby invites any Gentleman that will be pleased to come to his house to see a picture done by him being a View of St. James's Park. [sic] which he hopes may in some manner deserve their approbation any morning or afternoon at his lodgings Mr. Wiggan Cabinet maker in Silver street Golden Square."[31] This curious instance of self-promotion may have been Canaletto's response to gossiping dealers; according to Vertue, some were beginning to question the quality of the work (most likely in an effort to devalue it) and even speculating about whether he was in fact "the Famous Painter of Views Canalletti" (as Vertue wrote) or an imposter.[32] Regardless of Canaletto's motive, the ad apparently had scant effect. Indeed, Vertue noted that the painter returned to Venice in

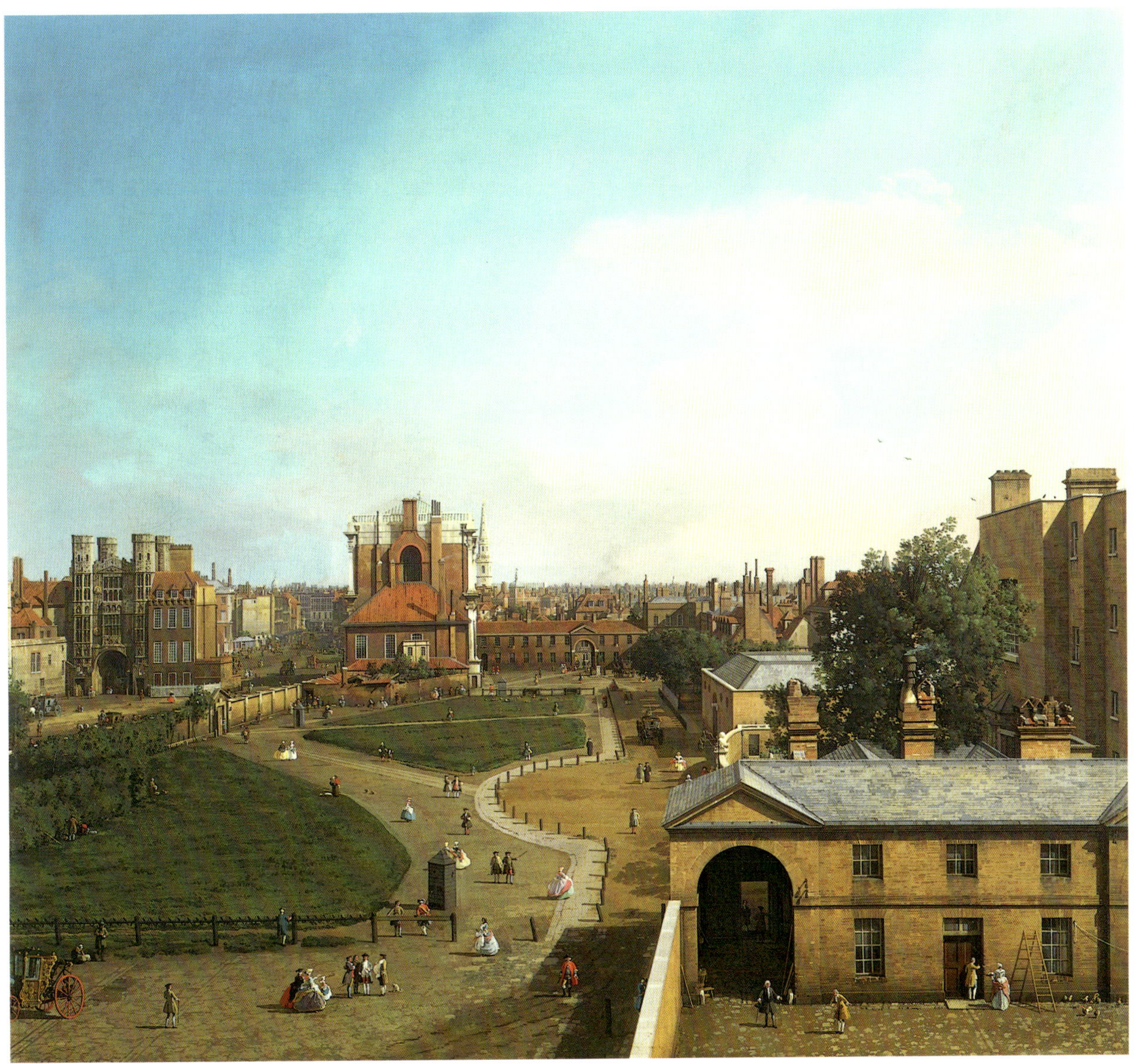

Fig. 11. Canaletto (Giovanni Antonio Canal)
London: Whitehall and the Privy Garden from Richmond House, 1747
Oil on canvas, 42 15/16 x 47 in. (109 x 119.5 cm)
The Trustees of the Goodwood Collection

1750, perhaps hoping to find improved economic conditions. Only eight months later, however, he was back in England.[33]

Unfortunately, little is known of Canaletto's second five-year sojourn there. It appears Lord Brooke invited him to paint two more views of Warwick Castle; these were the first canvases he completed upon his return. Three more paintings are recorded as having been done for Sir Hugh Smithson (now Duke of Northumberland). Six capriccios from the Lovelace Collection can also be dated to this English stay, thanks to the 1754 inscription on the marvelous *Capriccio: A Sluice on a River with a Chapel* (fig. 12). The wealthy eccentric Thomas Hollis commissioned six canvases. A Whig radical known for his strong support of the American colonies (and today best known as the great benefactor of Harvard University), Hollis may have ordered the works at the prompting of his friend Joseph Smith, whom he had met on his Grand Tour in

1750 or 1751.[34] Hardly a cohesive group, the paintings Canaletto made for Hollis vary significantly in subject, ranging from a small Roman view of the Campidoglio, based on one of the artist's old engravings, to the interior of the rotunda at Ranelagh, derived from a drawing he published several years earlier. A third view of St. Paul's Cathedral has been characterized by J. G. Links as "uninspired."[35] This was also true of an imaginary landscape featuring Whitehall. Among these varied creations, however, was the truly charming *Old Walton Bridge over the Thames* (fig. 13). According to an 1809 catalogue of his collection, Hollis himself appears in the foreground of the composition with his friend Thomas Brand, his servant Francisco Giovanni, and his dog Malta.[36] Contemporary descriptions indicate that Hollis was quite tall, so presumably he is the figure in the light yellow jacket framed by the middle arch.

If Canaletto painted *London: The Thames and the City of London from Richmond House* and *London:*

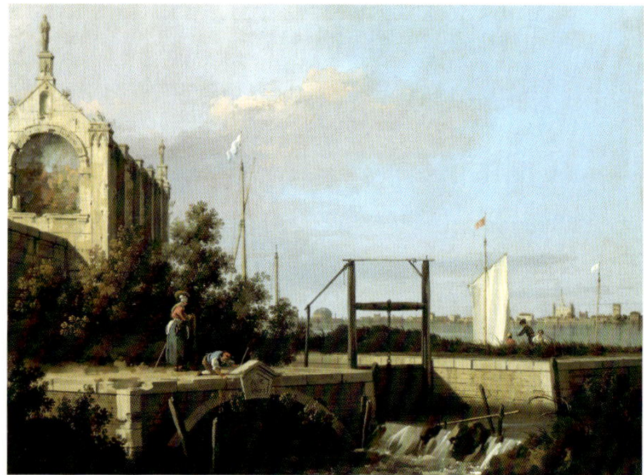

Fig. 12. Canaletto (Giovanni Antonio Canal)
Capriccio: A Sluice on a River with a Chapel, 1754
Oil on canvas, 33 x 46 3/8 in. (83.8 x 117.8 cm)
Museum of Fine Arts, Boston, Bequest of William A. Coolidge, 1993.33

Whitehall and the Privy Garden from Richmond House through the eyes of a Venetian, then *Old Walton Bridge over the Thames* would seem to evoke England as seen through the eyes of an Englishman.[37] Indeed, the painting exceeds topographical accuracy in its representation of the Greater London countryside. Its swirling, dark gray clouds hovering ominously low in the sky capture a sensitivity to local climate not found in Canaletto's other English imagery. In fact, such intensity of feeling and atmosphere had rarely been seen since his earliest masterpieces. The painting's pictorial tension is enhanced by the artist's contrasting brushwork—painterly and textured in the clouds, clean and mathematically precise in the latticed bridge. Among the last canvases Canaletto painted in England, *Old Walton Bridge* also demonstrates the rather mechanical shorthand he adopted toward the end of his career. Using calligraphic touches of paint to indicate heads and hands and depicting clothes with a few quick strokes, he imbues his figures—particularly those in the background—with a doll-like quality that is totally absent in his earlier work.

As he did with all the Hollis pictures, Canaletto inscribed *Old Walton Bridge* in Italian: "Fatto nell'anno 1754 in Londra per la prima ed ultima volta con ogni maggior attentzione ad instanza del Signor cavaliere Hollis" (Painted in 1754 in London for the first and last time with good care for cavaliere Hollis).[38] The inscription is not entirely truthful, however, for Canaletto produced a second, more extensive version just one year later for the bridge's benefactor, Samuel Dicker, a Member of Parliament. This was also inscribed "done for the first and last time . . . in 1755 . . . for Cavaliere Dickers [sic]."[39] Shortly thereafter, he also made a drawing of the same subject for Dicker.[40] The Dicker commission is the last extant record of the painter in England. Sometime in 1755, after a total of nine years in Great Britain, Canaletto returned to Venice.

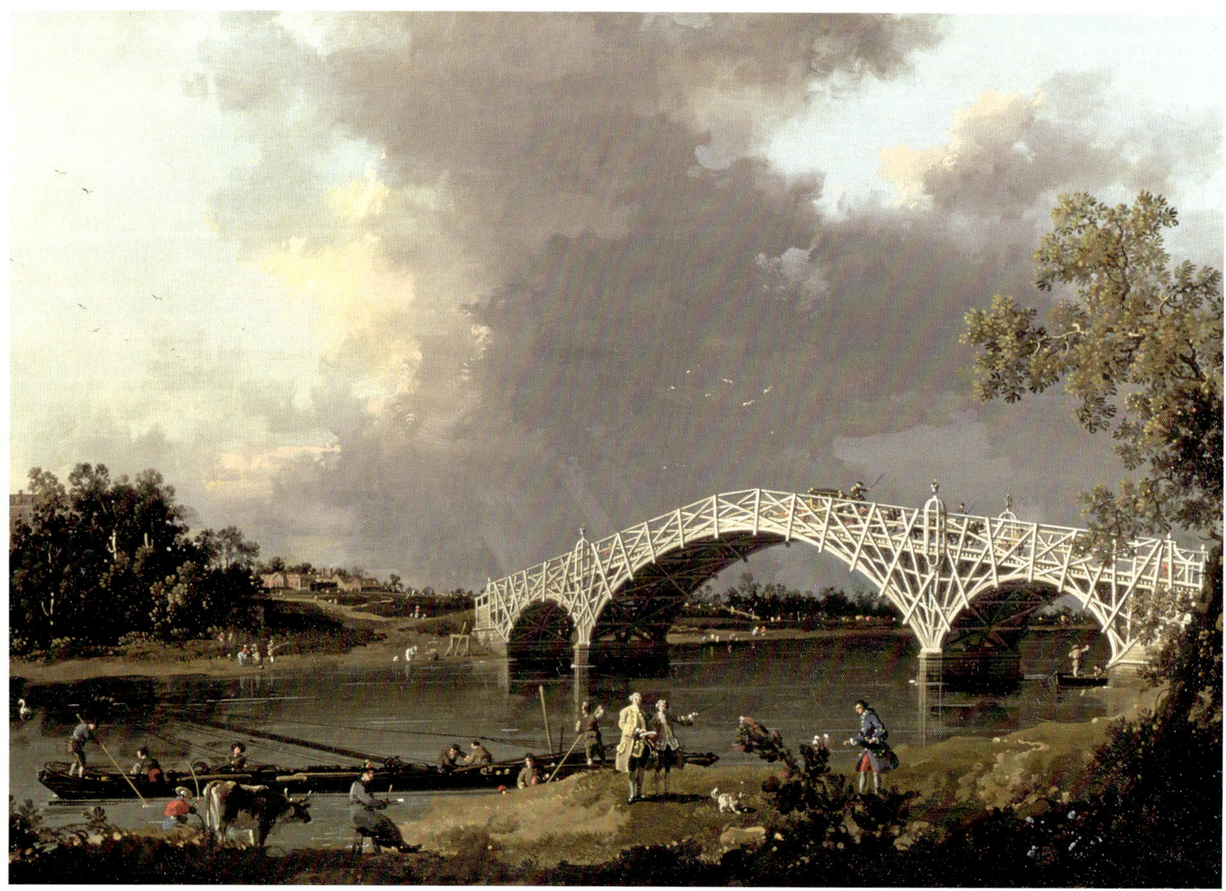

Fig. 13. Canaletto (Giovanni Antonio Canal)
Old Walton Bridge over the Thames, 1754
Oil on canvas, 19 1/4 x 30 1/4 in. (48.9 x 76.8 cm)
Dulwich Picture Gallery, London, UK/The Bridgeman Art Library

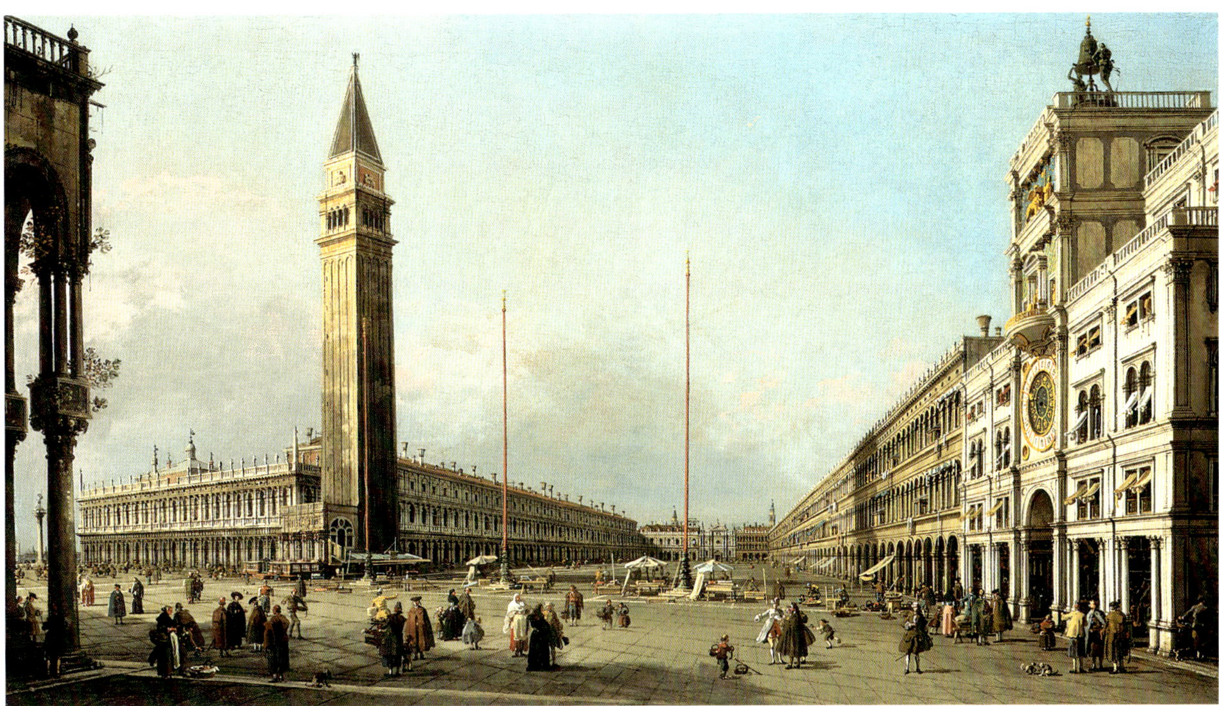

Fig. 14. Canaletto (Giovanni Antonio Canal)
Piazza San Marco: Looking South and West, 1763
Oil on canvas, 23 1/4 x 40 1/2 in. (56.5 x 102.9 cm)
Los Angeles County Museum of Art, Gift of The Ahmanson Foundation M.83.39

J. G. Links has described most of Canaletto's work after his final return to Venice as "that of a tired man whose originality had deserted him."[41] Indeed, the painter's later pieces are marked by a certain mechanical lifelessness, and they rarely display the imagination and invention of his early works. The post–1755 paintings rely heavily on the compositional formulas Canaletto had developed over the preceding three decades. They tend to be small, with dark contours, and employ even more painterly shorthand in the delineation of figures than do his late English works (see cats. 22 and 23).

By that time—the late 1750s—Joseph Smith, then well into his eighties, was doubtless less energetic as well. Furthermore, according to the diaries of the Scottish architect James Adam, Smith's financial affairs were in turmoil. After a visit to Mogliano, Adam described Smith as "devilish poor and should he live a few years longer, which he may do, he will die a Bankrupt."[42] Over a nearly thirty-year period, Smith had acquired an unrivaled collection of Canaletto's work, and in 1760 he began negotiating the sale of the best pieces he owned to King George III. Included in this transaction, which finally occurred in 1762, were fifty-two paintings, more than 140 drawings, and forty-six etchings (including a set of thirty-one plates from *Vedute altre prese da i luoghi alrea ideate*).[43]

In 1763 Canaletto was finally elected to the Venetian Academy, having been passed over earlier that year due to his status as a painter of *vedute*—an inferior genre, according to academic standards. That same year, he depicted *Piazza San Marco: Looking South and West* (fig. 14), a view considered to be the last he rendered of this subject. The picture is essentially a capriccio, as it takes an impossibly wide view of the place. It includes Mauro Coducci's Torre dell'Orologio (clock tower) on the near right; then, moving backward, toward the Procuratie Vecchie, it sweeps north to the Campanile; and it concludes with a glimpse of the lagoon. Though dizzying, the perspective is handled masterfully and incorporates many of the buildings Canaletto had portrayed during his forty-year career. This, along with the painting's distinctive luminosity and its masterful shorthand depictions of the piazza's inhabitants, has led some to hypothesize that because the piece seems almost a summation of Canaletto's life's work, it may have been the one he submitted for admission to the Academy.[44]

Little is known about Canaletto's activities between 1763 and 1768, the last five years of his life. He did produce one drawing, inscribed: "Io Zuane Antonio da Canal, Hò fatto il presente disegnio, delle Musici che Canta nella Chiesa Ducal di San Marco in Venezia in ettá de- / Anni 68 Cenzza Ochiali, Lanno 1766" (I, Zuane Antonio da Canal, made the present drawing of the musicians who sing in the ducal church of San Marco at the age of / 68, without spectacles, in the year 1766)."[45] Then, in April 1768, the artist died of a fever caused by a bladder inflammation. He was buried in the parish Church of S. Lio, where he had been baptized, leaving his three sisters some old clothes, a small bed, a meager investment property, and twenty-eight paintings.

In a career lasting some forty-five years, Canaletto produced more than 500 paintings and an even larger number of drawings. He worked for the most eminent collectors and connoisseurs of his day, and his influence extended throughout Venice and across Europe. Given the fame he enjoyed while alive, it is curious that so little is known about his character or the facts of his life. The few extant documents containing any personal information about him come from agents and dealers who primarily focused on his slow pace and fluctuating prices. Regardless, the artist's contemporaries never disputed his creativity or achievements, and his technique and style significantly influenced the work of his immediate successors Bernardo Bellotto, Francesco Guardi, and Samuel Scott. Although they, too, achieved fame in the field of *vedute* painting, it was Canaletto who decisively contributed to the myth of Venice, which, as the art historian Michael Levey has written, continues to affect both "those who have not seen it—and those who have."[46]

NOTES

1. This is according to baptism records of the Church of S. Lio for October 30, 1697. See Constable and Links 1989, 1: xxi.

2. Antonio Visentini, *Prospectus Magni Canalis: Venetiarum addito Certamine Nautico et Nundinis Venetis* (Venice: Giovanni Battista Pasquali Press, 1735).

3. See Orlandi 1753, Zanetti 1771, and Mariette 1851–60.

4. J. G. Links, "Canaletto: A Biographical Sketch" in New York 1989, 3; Constable and Links 1989, 1: 9; Terpitz 1998; and Pedrocco 2002, 71–73. For more on Scarlatti, see Dent 1905 and Pagaro 2006.

5. Nicoletti 1890. See also Constable and Links 1989, 1: xxii, 11.

6. The drawings are numbered 1 through 23. All but one of them are in the British Museum, London. The other is in the Hessisches Landesmuseum, Darmstadt. The British Museum's Web site (www.britishmuseum.org) provides a concise summary of the provenance and scholarship surrounding the drawings.

7. Canaletto scholars Baron Detlev von Hadeln (1929), K. T. Parker (1948), and Vittorio Moschini (1954) all rejected the drawings as originals. W. G. Constable (1962) remained noncommittal on the issue. James Byam Shaw (1962) and Alessandro Bettagno (1989) accepted them as original, and, more recently, Hugo Chapman wrote persuasively on their behalf. See Chapman, "I disegni giovanili di Canaletto" in Venice 2001, 19–21.

8. Several scholars consider this picture, along with *The Temple of Antoninus and Faustina* (ca. 1720, Szépmüvészeti Mùzeum, Budapest), to be Canaletto's earliest extant paintings. Charles Beddington provides compelling critical analysis in favor of dating it to around 1720. See Beddington, "L'uso dei disegni romani di Canaletto," in Venice 2001, 23. Francis Russell echoes Beddington's assessment of the two paintings and suggests they may have been executed while the artist was still in Rome. Russell 2001, 654–57.

9. Constable and Links 1989, 60–61.

10. For more on Marco Ricci's influence on Canaletto (particularly in relation to the theater), see Pedrocco 2002, 71–77.

11. Luca Carlevaris, *Le fabriche, e vedute di Venetia disegnate: poste in prospettiva, et intagliate da Luca Carlevariis con priveliegii* (Venice: Giovanni Battista Finazzi, 1703).

12. For more on the background of eighteenth-century view painting, see Pedrocco 2002, 29–42.

13. Haskell 1956, 296–97.

14. About Canaletto, Marchesini wrote, "[C]he fa in questo paese stordir universalmente ognuno che vede Le sue opera, che consiste sul ordine di Carlevari [sic] ma vi si vede Lucer entro il sole." ([H]e is astonishing everyone in this town who sees his works, which are on the order of Carlevaris's but you can see the sun shining in them.) For a transcription of the Marchesini-Conti correspondence, see Haskell 1956, 297–99.

15. Ibid., 297.

16. The letter is dated "March 8th 1725/6 N.S." The "1725" refers to the old method of ending the year on March 31, while the "/6" and "N.S." indicate the new method, i.e., the year ending on December 31. See Constable and Links 1989 1: xxiv. For more on this paintings project, see Mazza 1976, 79–102; Haskell 1980, 287–91; and Baetjer and Links in New York 1989, 99.

17. J. G. Links found Canaletto's limited participation in this project curious and suggested that an artist of his growing repute would have been insulted by being given so little responsibility. He further posited that Canaletto only agreed to take part as the project provided him the opportunity to work with many other successful and famous artists. Baetjer and Links in New York 1989, 99–103.

18. W. G. Constable first transcribed the extant letters from McSwiney to the second Duke of Richmond in Constable 1962, 1: 173–76.

19. According to their correspondence, the first Conti paintings were ordered in July 1725 and though a letter dating to August indicates Canaletto intended to begin work promptly, it was not until September that he put brush to canvas and November that he finished. The two additional views Conti commissioned were not ready until the following May. For a transcription of the correspondence between Marchesini and Conti, see Haskell 1956, 297–99.

20. Smith quoted in Chaloner 1950, 164.

21. Algarotti quoted in Haskell 1963, 356, n.1.

22. Antonio Visentini, *Urbis Venetiarum Prospectus Celebriores: Antonii Canal Tabulis XXXVIII; Aere Expressi ab Antonio Visentini in Partes Tres Distribuiti* (Venice: Giovanni Battista Pasquali Press, 1742). For more on both the 1735 and 1742 Visentini print portfolios, see the essay by Johnson and Johnson (p. 33).

23. Eleven of the thirteen *sopraporte* are accounted for; whether the other two are extant is not known. For a discussion of the paintings' subjects and locations, see Constable and Links 1989, 2: 432–33 (cat. 451).

24. Giovanni Antonio Canal, *Vedute altre prese da i luoghi altre ideate da Antonio Canal e da esso intagliate poste in prospetiva* (Venice: n.p., after 1744). M. J. H. Liversidge suggests that Smith might also have sponsored the project in order to profit from the print market, which recently had been expanding in both London and Venice. Liversidge and Farrington in Birmingham 1993a, 15–16.

25. See Edgar Peters Brown, "Bernardo Bellotto" in London and Washington, D.C. 1994, 361–75; and Bożena Anna Kowalczyk, "Canaletto e Bellotto: l'arte della veduta" in Turin 2008, 13–22.

26. There is a handful of view paintings signed by Bernardo Cesare Canal in Venetian private collections. Evidence that he worked in his son's atelier is found in the letter Canaletto received in 1735 from the Collegio dei Pittori (Painters Guild) rejecting his application for membership; it states that if father (already a member) and son are collaborating, only one of them is qualified to join. See Terpitz 1998, 70–71.

27. Finberg 1934, 130; quoted in Links 1977, 64; idem 1982, 147; and idem in New York 1989, 10.

28. Links 1977, 64.

29. Hill quoted in Links 1977, 33. See also March 1911, 2: 602.

30. For identification of the duke, see Baetjer and Links in New York 1989, 233; and Farrington in Birmingham 1993, 68–70 (cat. 9 and 10).

31. Finberg 1921, 21–76; quoted in Constable 1962, 1: 37–38.

32. This was likely an attempt by those dealers to devalue Canaletto's paintings so they could better promote the copyists and imitators. Vertue reported that "on the whole of [Canaletto] something is obscure or strange. [H]e dos [sic] not produce works so well done as those of Venice or other parts of Italy . . . especially his figures in his works done here are apparently much inferior to those done abroad. . . . [This] has much strengthened a conjecture that he is not the veritable Canalletti [sic] of Venice." Finberg 1934, 149; and Constable 1962, 1: 34–38.

33. Finberg 1920, 29–36; Finberg 1934, 151, 158; and Baetjer and Links in New York 1989, 241.

34. Constable and Links 1989, 1: 40 and Liversidge in Birmingham 1993a, 25. See also Blackburn 1780.

35. Links 1982, 173.

36. Whitley 1928, 118–19, quotes an old, privately printed catalogue that identifies the figures in *Old Walton Bridge over the Thames* and dates the painting to 1754. The work is also included in Baetjer and Links in New York 1989, 254 (cat. 73); Farrington in Birmingham 1993a, 96 (cat. 35); and Beddington in New Haven and London 2006, 130 (cat. 37).

37. Ross 1993, 124.

38. Constable and Links 1989, 2: 427–28 (cat. 441).

39. Constable 1962, 2: 428–29 (cat. 442).

40. The drawing was also inscribed "Disegnato da me Antonio Canal detto il Canaleto appresso il mio dippinto in Londra 1755/per il Signore Cavaliere Dickers." (Drawn by me Antonio Canal called Canaleto after my painting in London 1755/for Cavaliere Dickers.) Constable and Links 1989, 2: 582–83 (cat. 755).

41. J. G. Links, "Canaletto" in London and Washington, D.C. 1994, 240.

42. Adam quoted in Links 1982, 200.

43. For the sale of Smith's collection to George III, see Vivian in Frankfurt et al. 1989; and Liversidge in Birmingham 1993a, 14.

44. The painting that Canaletto finally presented to the academy, *Capriccio with a Colonnade, Galleria dell'Accademia, Venice* (Galleria dell'Accademia, Venice), is signed and dated 1765. It is curious that the canvas would have been presented two years after his election in 1763. Links suggests this may have been because he was executing ten drawings of the Festivals of the Doges during that period. Links in London and Washington, D.C. 1994, 244.

45. Constable 1962, 453-54, no. 558.

46. Levey 1980, 96.

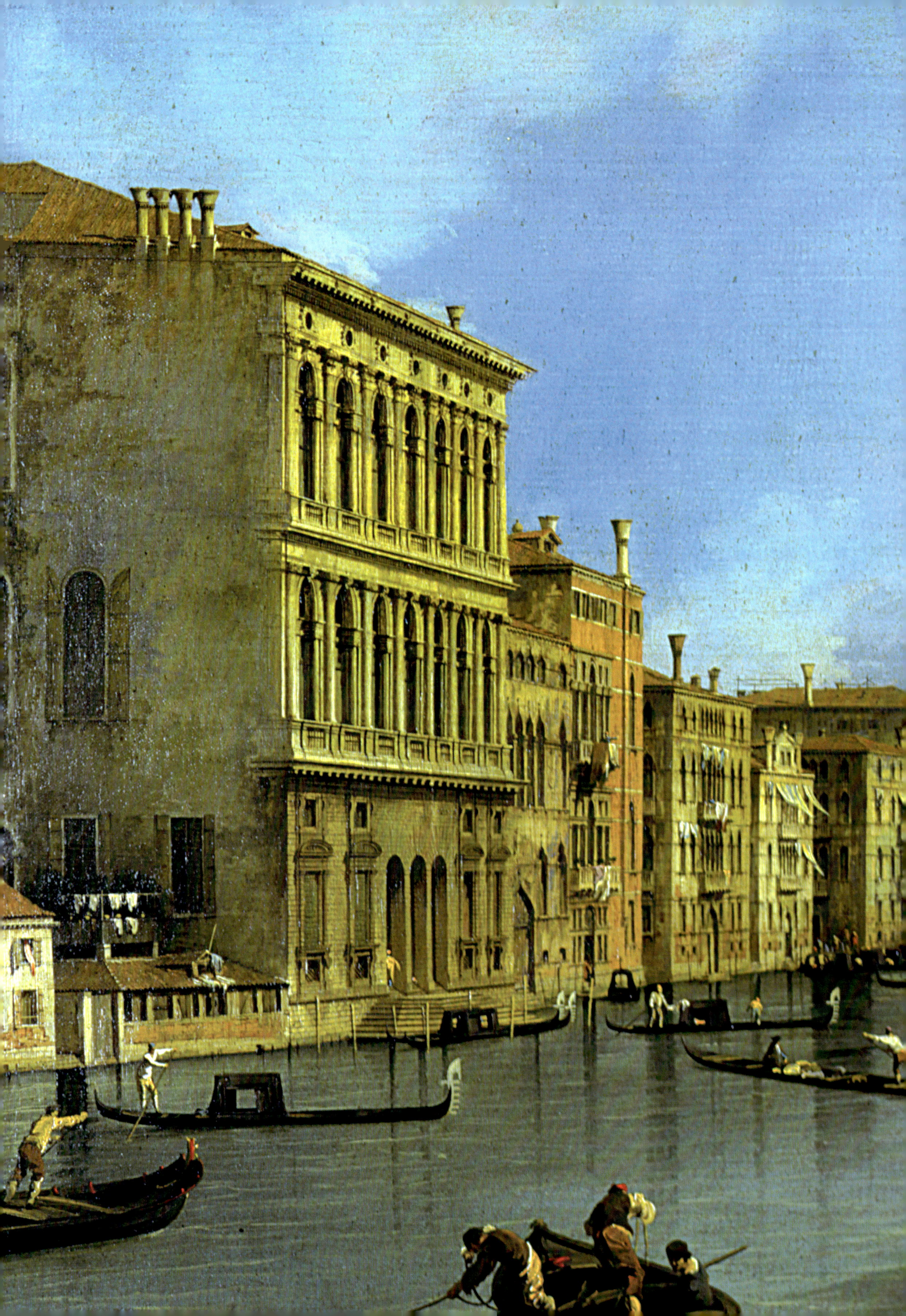

George Proctor: Merchant, Then Gentleman, and the English Taste for Canaletto

STANTON THOMAS

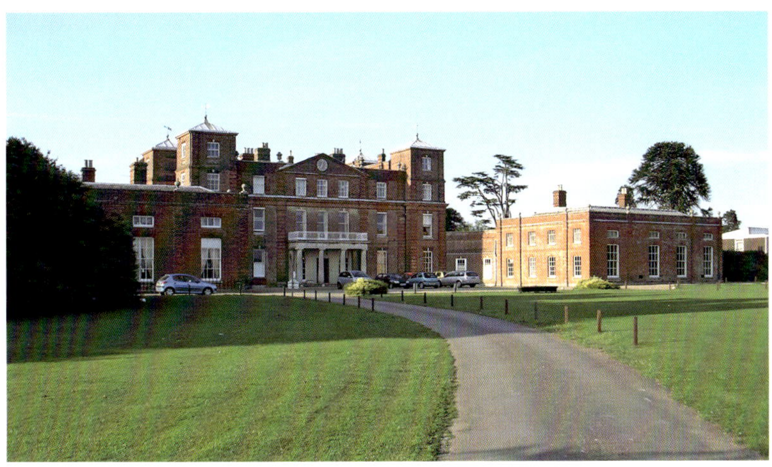

Fig. 1. Matthew Brettingham (English, 1699–1769) and others
Langley Park (now *Langley School*), south façade, begun ca. 1737
Loddon, Norfolk, England

In 1742 the successful merchant and entrepreneur George Proctor retired from the trade and, upon purchasing the estate of Langley Park near Norwich, took up the life of a country gentleman (fig. 1). Although little is known about the personal affairs of Proctor, who was born around 1670, surviving documents record both his financial ventures and wide mercantile interests—which particularly focused on foodstuffs—as well as his acquisition of works of fine art, including Canaletto's *The Grand Canal from the Campo San Vio* (cat. 20) and its pendant, *View of the Molo* (cat. 21), both from about 1740. Tracing Proctor's collecting activities over the years gives one a sense of the factors that shaped not only his aesthetic tastes but also his social ambitions. In particular, his acquisition of these two paintings by Canaletto reflects the English fascination with both Venice and the artist during that period and, in turn, suggests how British taste almost certainly influenced the direction of that painter's work.

Proctor was able to enjoy his Canalettos at Langley Park for just a short time. He died in 1744, two years after purchasing the estate, which was then unfinished but apparently habitable.[1] Matthew Brettingham, who was one of England's most successful Palladian architects, designed and built Langley Park. At the same time, he was collaborating with Lord Burlington and William Kent on Holkham Hall, a splendid and expansive country house in the vicinity.[2] When it was

completed—for Thomas Coke, first Earl of Leicester—Holkham Hall contained a remarkable collection of pictures, sculptures, and manuscripts, many of which Coke had purchased during a six-year Grand Tour of Europe. Proctor's acquisition of a house also designed by Brettingham suggests his ambition to own a grand Palladian-style manor, one worthy of a group of artworks that would form "the core of a collection which was to rival those of many of his Norfolk contemporaries."[3] Langley Park housed works by major Dutch, French, and Italian masters, including Jacob van Ruisdael, Claude Lorrain, and Salvator Rosa.

Proctor's paintings and sculptures—including the two Canalettos—remained at the estate for generations. Although most of the collection was dispersed after World War II, some idea of what it contained can be reconstructed, at least partially,

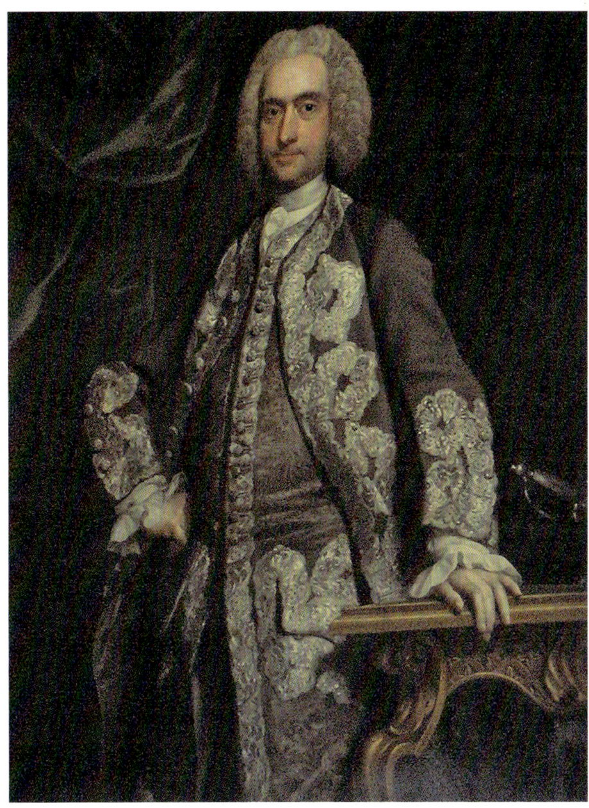

Fig. 2. Unknown Venetian artist
George Proctor, ca. 1740
Oil on canvas, 49 x 39 1/4 in. (125 x 100 cm)
Langley School, Loddon, Norfolk, England

from surviving business accounts, early guidebooks, and auction records. Of the works comprising the Langley Park holdings, several are listed in guides and inventories of the early nineteenth century as having been made specifically for Proctor in Venice or acquired by him there. These include a portrait of him by an anonymous Venetian artist (fig. 2) as well as "Two Greyhounds in veined Marble, [and] the Proctor crest, executed at Venice, 1740."[4] Presumably, he also purchased other pictures, such as a series of six small landscapes by Marco Ricci and a pair of small Canaletto *vedute*, or view paintings, while in the city.[5]

The Grand Canal from the Campo San Vio and *View of the Molo* (cats. 20 and 21) are, however, the most significant works associated with Proctor. According to family tradition and an inventory of 1815 (the earliest known record of them), these large canvases—each measuring about four by five feet— were "painted for G. Proctor Esq. when resident at Venice."[6] More than any other paintings he owned, they indicate Proctor's serious interest in acquiring art. While the handful of works mentioned here establishes Proctor's presence in Venice, his personal records detail his mercantile ventures and offer evidence about his collecting activities.

Proctor's "Day Book," written in London and preserved today in the Norfolk Record Office, comprises the accounts of his London–based business dealings. It also clarifies his ties to Venice, a city he mentions repeatedly as the site of many commodities transactions. Spanning the years 1728 through 1739, these accounts—filled with references to his shares in bags of peppercorns or barrels of herring, to complicated financial investments and dealings with associates in regard to profits and losses—offer a fascinating glimpse into the life of a flourishing London merchant during the early decades of the eighteenth century.

Proctor details payment for a painting in an entry dated September 3, 1729: "Acco^t: of Expenses D^r. To Messrs: Cooper & Lefroy my acco^t: to [?] them £75:5:8 vallue [sic] of [?]347:8:10 @52^s p y being for vallue [sic] of 8300 rem.^{d} Sr Fran Imperiale of Rome for Cost of a picture sent me p y. Peasle ... 75 5"8."[7] The canvas was almost certainly by Francesco Fernandi (called Imperiali, 1679–1740), a Milanese whose oeuvre ranged from grand still lifes to allegorical scenes. Imperiali had clients throughout Europe and enjoyed considerable patronage in England, too; Thomas Coke of Holkham Hall acquired at least two paintings by the artist.[8] He also operated a thriving workshop in Rome. During the first decades of the eighteenth century, the master was much sought after and was especially renowned for training not only visiting British painters but also Italian ones, including the portraitist Pompeo Batoni.[9] The fact that Proctor paid more than £75 for the Imperiali is noteworthy, even if some of that amount very likely included the costs of framing, crating, shipping, and customs duties. By comparison, during the 1730s, Canaletto, whose works were considered rather expensive, sold a pair of small pictures for a total of about £18. Likewise, in 1734, another of Canaletto's patrons purchased four paintings from the artist; including frames and other charges, these works cost a bit more than £54.[10] The amount Proctor spent to buy the Imperiali suggests that he sought out works by popular and important artists rather than lesser-known ones, and that he was willing to part with large sums in order to obtain them.

Unfortunately, no other artworks are mentioned in the "Day Book."[11] But two of its entries, dated August 12 and September 30, 1730, supply a bit of evidence indirectly linking Proctor to Canaletto.[12] These record financial transactions involving "Joseph Smith of Venice" and his brother John, a London banker.[13] Again, although neither entry includes a reference to pictures, and indeed the sums—amounting to several hundred pounds per transaction—are so large that they probably preclude any relationship to payment for paintings, the document clearly establishes that there was at least a business relationship between Proctor and Smith, Canaletto's patron and de facto dealer. By extension, it indicates a probable link between Proctor and the painter. It also bolsters the possibility that Proctor saw Joseph Smith's extraordinary collection while in Venice. Indeed, Smith's home on the Grand Canal, the Palazzo Magili Valmarana, was a prime stop for affluent visiting Englishmen and held the largest and most easily accessible group of Canaletto's work in the city.[14]

There are several reasons why Proctor would have wanted to own paintings by Canaletto. As various scholars have noted, the artist's works were intended to serve as vividly evocative souvenirs of a visit to Venice. The views they offered were not just familiar but also depicted the city most enticingly, "under blue skies and in perpetual spring."[15] As the art historian J. G. Links pithily observed, Canaletto's canvases "appealed to the most unsophisticated tourist as mementoes of the wonders he had seen in Venice while still recognisable as great art by the connoisseur."[16] Furthermore, Proctor no doubt realized that acquiring Canalettos, along with other works, comprised tangible proof of his considerable wealth.

During the eighteenth century, Norfolk was home not only to the extraordinary holdings of the Coke family at Holkham Hall but also to the vast paintings collection of the statesman Sir Robert Walpole at

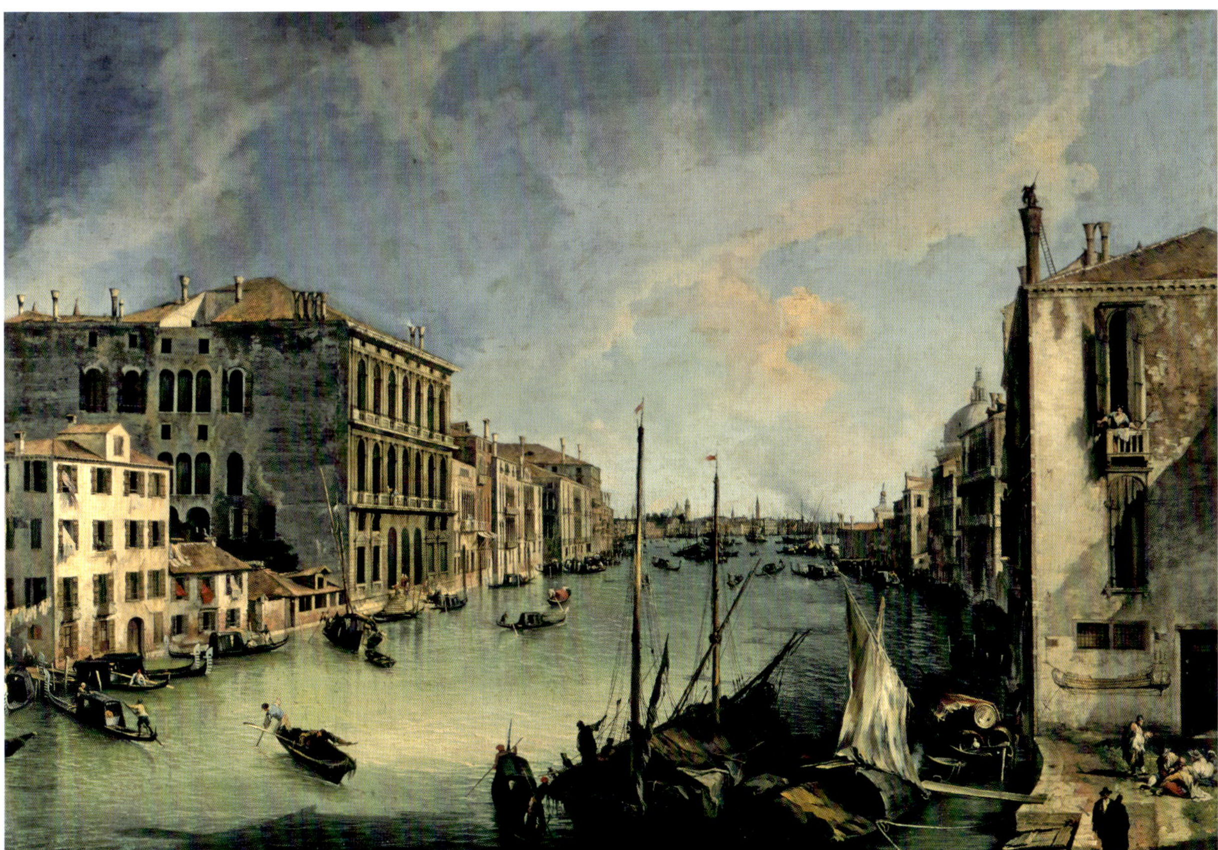

Fig. 3. Canaletto (Giovanni Antonio Canal)
View of Canal Grande from San Vio, Venice, ca. 1723–24
Oil on canvas, 55 1/4 x 80 1/2 in. (140.5 x 204.5 cm)
Museo Thyssen–Bornemisza, Madrid, 1958.8

Houghton Hall. The ownership of prized artworks suggested refined tastes and advanced education as well as substantial affluence. This is particularly true regarding Proctor's acquisition of *The Grand Canal from the Campo San Vio* and *View of the Molo*, which hinted at wide-ranging leisurely travel. Proctor's descendents, even after several generations, remembered and recorded in inventories—in 1815 and later—the fact that the erstwhile merchant had commissioned the works during a stay in Venice. These notations indicate the significance associated with visiting the city as part of the Grand Tour.

It seems clear that Proctor, a self-made businessman, had not experienced that rite of passage, which traditionally was a privilege that upper-class and wealthy young men enjoyed. Typically accompanied by a trusted guide—sometimes a gentleman who specialized in the Grand Tour, an older male family member, or perhaps a mentor or tutor—these youths would travel the Continent, visiting key cities and countries and expanding their knowledge of various cultures and governments. Bruce Redford, in his groundbreaking 1996 study of Venice and the culture of the Grand Tour, notes the important way the tour "not only conferred prestige but also supplied models for negotiation between classical past and British present, the gentlemanly values of humanism and the

practical necessities of politics."[17]

The storied city of Venice was a paramount destination on every Grand Tour, and perhaps the most convincing evidence of a stop there was possession of a work by Canaletto. This was especially true of immediately recognizable images by the artist, who was by far the most popular of the Venetian *vedute* painters, particularly in England. Although Proctor stayed in Venice and commissioned works from the famed artist, his association with the city lacked the cachet of a Grand Tour visit there. Significantly, Proctor's will stipulated that his nephew William Beauchamp, to whom he left almost his entire estate, "as soon as conveniently may be after my death be sent to Travel abroad into some fforeign [sic] parts . . . with a sober lay man[,] a man of learning and manners."[18] In providing his nephew with the privileged lifestyle and education he himself had not enjoyed as a young man, Proctor underscored the importance of the Grand Tour in the molding of upper-class English identity and taste.

The Grand Canal from the Campo San Vio and *View of the Molo* typify the "decorative and evocative views" Canaletto made for British tourists during the 1730s and 1740s.[19] Such paintings record, with what appears to be almost photographic fidelity, famous Venetian settings. The subject matter of the pair was hardly unique: the artist had produced versions of both scenes since the mid-1720s.[20] In fact, the Campo S. Vio view, painted around 1740, is one of at least ten known variations of that vista. Its precise brushwork, light palette, and pale ground—all capturing the summery skies so appealing to tourists—typify the striking shift in Canaletto's style that occurred during the late 1720s and the 1730s.

That shift is beautifully illustrated by comparing this work, in the Memphis Brooks Museum of Art collection (cat. 20), to earlier renderings of the subject, particularly two now in Madrid and Britain's Royal Collection. The Madrid canvas, which is in the collection of the Museo Thyssen-Bornemisza and dates to around 1723–24 (fig. 3), is filled with rich contrasts of color, form, and texture—particularly in its juxtaposition of fast-moving clouds and dusky shadows with the luminous water and sunny walls. At that point in his career, as the noted scholar W. G. Constable observed, Canaletto "was still a man of the theatre."[21] The canvas shows a loose, painterly approach and uses fading light to delineate softly the stone and brick buildings as well as to suggest the city's watery atmosphere. In some cases, the very material of the structures, such as the Palazzo Corner della Cà Grande, which dominates the left side of the composition, seems to dissolve into water itself.

The Madrid painting stands in sharp contrast to the version in the Royal Collection, produced a few years later (fig. 4). Here Canaletto has softened the sharp contrasts of shadows and light, and he has replaced the dramatic sky with a more sedate and sunny one. The canvas also demonstrates

his increasing skill at producing seemingly photographic images of the city. Indeed, although Canaletto famously altered and rearranged elements of the fabric of Venice to suit his needs, here the viewer is captured by what has aptly been termed "the rhetoric of persuasion."[22] That is, although he clearly distorted the breadth of certain views or neighbored buildings in a single painting that in reality cannot be seen together, his reimagined Venice is so compelling that one is seduced into believing it is accurate.

Presumably, Joseph Smith purchased the Royal Collection canvas soon after its completion, around 1728.[23] It hung in his palazzo until King George III acquired it in 1762, so it would have been in Venice during Proctor's sojourn there. With its lighter palette, more controlled execution, and expanses of sunny sky, walls, and water, this work reflects an artistic approach that soon would become more popular with British tourists than Canaletto's earlier and more darkly dramatic pictures.

As the art historians David Bomford and Gabriele Finaldi have pointed out, Canaletto's marked change from his earlier style, with its looser brushstrokes and stronger coloring, to one distinguished by a greater sense of control and blond tonalities must have been the result of a conscious decision—for the later style was "more in keeping with the requirements of the market."[24] This shift may indeed have been the artist's own response to the desires of his patrons; certainly, he would have noticed their enthusiasm for his sunnier vistas of famous Venetian scenery. Also worth noting is the influence of Joseph Smith,

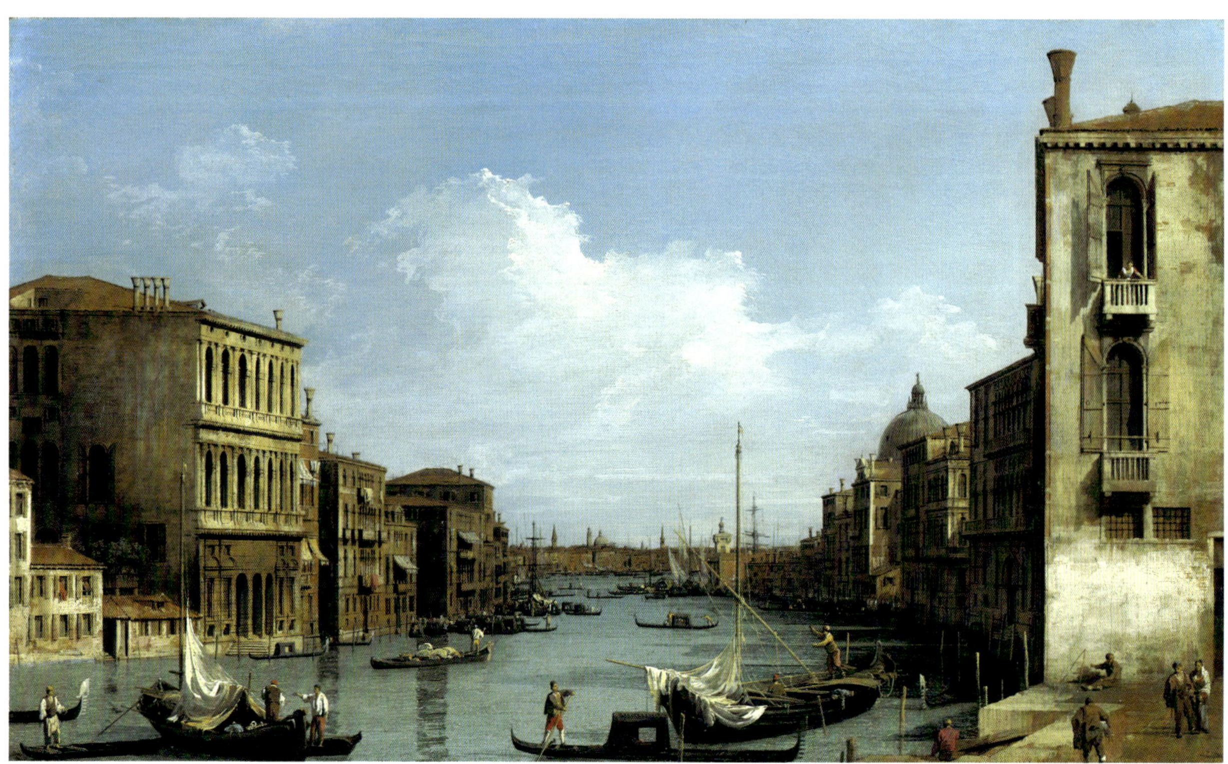

Fig. 4. Canaletto (Giovanni Antonio Canal)
The Grand Canal from Campo San Vio Towards the Bacino, ca. 1727–28
Oil on canvas, 18 1/2 x 31 in. (47 x 79.1 cm)
The Royal Collection, Her Majesty Queen Elizabeth II, RCIN 400518

who, as the art historian John Harris remarked, was "undoubtedly the catalyst for the British *milordi* and Grand tourists in their collecting."[25] Unfortunately, almost nothing survives to show the exact nature of Canaletto's relationship with Smith other than a business arrangement of some sort; after all, Smith's home served as a sort of gallery where visitors—and prospective buyers, such as Proctor—could view Canaletto's works.[26] Furthermore, it is well documented that Smith also provided financing to those who bought art through him as well as help with packing, shipping, and customs.[27]

What is unknown is whether Smith exerted some influence on the artist, not only through his commissions—which were many, ranging from complete series of paintings and etchings to finished drawings—but also through advice to Canaletto about his approach to subject matter. For instance, the scholar Filippo Pedrocco notes the likelihood that Smith exposed Canaletto to recently published theories on light and color.[28] Some idea of the artist's appeal for the English market can be gained by comparing his *vedute* to those of contemporaries such as the Venetian painter Michele Marieschi.[29] While both artists were able to capture beautiful and immediately recognizable images of Venice, Marieschi employed a softer touch to evoke the watery environment of the lagoon and the inexorable decay of the city. Noting the distinct differences between the two artists' approaches to *vedute*, John Harris surmised that "a connoisseur of [Joseph Smith's] discrimination cannot have failed to detect a certain stylized, manufactured look in Canaletto's painting technique, a hard-edged quality absent in Marieschi, whose views are at once authentic, natural, and accurately atmospheric."[30] While at least one scholar attributes the more mechanical appearance of many Canaletto pictures from this period to the artist's need to turn out paintings quickly, the continued demand for such works suggests they were appreciated for their qualities of clarity, light effects, and draftsmanlike precision.[31]

It is the artist's sense of topical accuracy—of the very bricks and stones of the city, of tangible and sunny surfaces—blending seamlessly into the illusion of physical reality that distinguishes Canaletto's work from that of other *vedute* painters. Many of his local compatriots, especially Francesco Guardi, approached the Venetian cityscape with a distinctly Rococo sensibility—filling canvases with flickering brushwork, soft lines, and subdued colors. By contrast, Canaletto often enhances the underlying geometric and linear qualities of buildings and plazas, using the sharp lines of corners and cornices to convey a sense of regularity and control. In addition, he frequently employs

orthogonals, sometimes subtly hidden in rows of windows or boldly incorporated into paving stones, to reinforce the feeling of ordered, rational space. This is particularly evident in many of the paintings acquired by British tourists, including *The Grand Canal from the Campo San Vio*. Canaletto's crisp lines and carefully placed buildings give that work a pleasing and subtle rhythm, as if a grid underlies it, while the glassy, opaque surface of the canal and rough wall surfaces impart a reassuringly tactile quality to the painting.

The increasing sense of order and harmony apparent in Canaletto's works may have been a response to the renewed interest in Andrea Palladio (1508–1580) during the first decades of the eighteenth century. Several art historians have commented upon the English fascination with that sixteenth-century architect, whose designs came to be associated with particular political and social movements in Britain. For instance, in his study of the Palladian revival of that period, Francis Haskell pointed out the propensity of British Whigs not only to build country houses in that style but also to have them decorated by Venetian artists.[32] These structures—such as Proctor's own manor—were English interpretations of Palladio's famous villas scattered throughout the Veneto. As Bruce Redford noted, English people of the eighteenth century were intrigued by the notion of living in homes that, in their eyes, could be traced back in a direct line to Roman villas.[33] Although it would be simplistic to equate works by Canaletto with Palladianism, considering them within the wider context of English taste for the great Venetian architect may help explain both the look and the popularity of his paintings.

Canaletto would have been aware of Palladio's immense importance from his exposure to the man's work—both in Venice and around the Veneto—and through Joseph Smith, a man who "played a crucial role in reassessing the architecture of Palladio."[34] Indeed, around 1734 Smith commissioned the artist to paint a series of thirteen *sopraporte*, or over-door pictures, celebrating the architect; these were installed in the Englishman's villa at Mogliano. And in 1762, he asked Canaletto to produce an edition of the architect's *Quattro libri dell'archittetura* (*The Four Doors of Architecture*, 1570). This treatise on design had a profound affect on European architecture for generations and was especially influential in eighteenth-century England.[35] Seeing Canaletto's work as a reflection of the British and Venetian fascination with Palladio helps explain the artist's canvases within the otherwise ebulliently Rococo environment of his compatriots. He produced pictures for selective and critical patrons who, like Proctor, appreciated the restrained harmony and subdued, if not severe, lines of Andrea Palladio. With their sense of restraint and detachment—somewhat surprising, given that they were images of a city famed for its festive, sensuous, and even licentious way of life—Canaletto's paintings were eminently suitable for the houses they adorned.

NOTES

1. Proctor had been buying properties in the area for some time prior to 1742, evidently in preparation for his move to Norfolk and acquisition of a country house there. An entry in his "Day Book" for September 19, 1738, notes the purchase of several properties of the late Richard Berney (life dates unknown), who had started construction of the manor house of Langley Park. George Proctor, "Day Book," 1728–39, Norfolk Record Office, Norwich, England, BEA (Beauchamp) 278, 436x, n.p. (Hereafter cited as Proctor, "Day Book.")

2. Lord Burlington—as Richard Boyle (1694–1753), the third Earl of Burlington and fourth Earl of Cork, was known—was the preeminent proponent of Palladianism in England. A highly important architect and designer, he worked both with his protégé William Kent (1685–1748) and with Matthew Brettingham. The trio participated in the design and construction of Holkham Hall, although it is unclear what their individual roles were. See Hiskey 1997.

3. Andrew W. Moore, "Early Travelers, 1693–1740" in Norwich 1985, 25.

4. Neale 1820, 46. The Proctor portrait now hangs in Langley School, a public-education institution that has occupied the Langley Park buildings since 1946. The locations of the other works are unknown.

5. For Ricci, see Moore in Norwich 1985, 25. J. P. Neale mentioned the pair of small Canaletto *vedute* and noted that Proctor acquired them in Venice but did not date their purchase. Neale 1820, 45.

6. "Descriptive Catalogue of the Pictures and Pieces of Sculpture at Langley Hall, Norfolk, the seat of Sir William Beauchamp-Proctor, Bart.," 1853[?] (copy of 1815 original), handwritten ms., private collection, cat. 13. According to a notation made in the manuscript at a later date, this inventory probably was compiled by George Overton, butler to Sir Reginald Proctor-Beauchamp (1853–1912). (The order of the family surname had been officially changed in 1862.) Overton also signed his name on the last page of the document. The information about Proctor's purchases in Venice is repeated in other inventories of the Langley Park collection dating to 1832[?] and 1840/1858. Both are likewise handwritten manuscripts and in private collections.

7. Proctor, "Day Book." The painting does not appear in any of the Langley Park collection inventories; its location is unknown.

8. Clark 1964, 229.

9. Ford 1958, 316.

10. For the sale of the pair of small pictures, see Links 1977, 33–34. For the 1734 sale, see London 1981, 16, n. 5.

11. Further references to Proctor's collecting can be found in his "Small Day Book." This document, apparently in his own hand, records his personal and household expenses from 1732 to 1736. In it he notes the purchase of six prints on May 6, 1732, and an entry for September 9, 1736, reads, "Given Belt for 4 pictures – 37.16. _" (£37 and 6 shillings). He also records paying "West for picture frames 12.4.6." (£12, 4 shillings, and 6 pence) on October 1, 1736, and paying a "M^r. Warelst[?] for Small Picture .10.10. –" (£10 and 10 shillings). George Proctor, "Small Day Book," Norfolk Record Office, Norwich, England, BEA (Beauchamp) 305/3, n.p.

12. Proctor, "Day Book." These entries read: "In Lond^o y 12th. August 1730 / Bills Rem^d: D^r. To Messrs: Cooper & Lefroy my Acco^t: to. them £481:14; . . . being for 4 bills rem^d. me for £140 £126:14:–£115 & £100 all drawn by Joseph Smith of Venice on John Smith and endorsed to me & negotiated as at (illegible, crossed out)," and "[In London] 20th D^o: (September 20, 1730) Cash is D^r To Bills Rem^d: £481:14: . . . for 4 bills drawn by Jos. Smith of Venice on Jno. Smith rem^d. me by mess^r Cooper £140 £126:14 – – £115 & £100."

13. London 1993, 8.

14. For more about Smith, his business ventures, and his art collection, see the essays by Libby (p. 11) and Johnson and Johnson (p. 33). See also Liversidge and Farrington in Birmingham 1993a, 13–15; and Links 1977, 33–36.

15. Bomford and Finaldi in London et al. 1998, 55. For a discussion of Canaletto's paintings as aide-mémoire, see Constable in Toronto et al. 1964, 18–19.

16. J. G. Links, "Canaletto" in London and Washington, D.C. 1994, 219.

17. Redford 1996, 66.

18. George Proctor will, proved July 1, 1744, Public Record Office, National Archives (London), catalogue reference: prob[ate] 11/735; image reference: 231.

19. Links 1977, 46.

20. Constable and Links 1989, 2: 227–28 (*View of the Molo*, cat. 88) and 276–77 (*The Grand Canal from the Campo San Vio*, cat. 187). The authors note that the pairing of these works as pendants is documented in at least one other collection, a private one in Paris.

21. Constable quoted in Links 1977, 26.

22. Bomford and Finaldi in London et al. 1998, 12.

23. Constable and Links 1989, 2: 261 (cat. 184).

24. Bomford and Finaldi in London et al. 1998, 55.

25. John Harris, "The Neo-Palladians and Mid-Century Landscape" in London and Washington, D.C. 1994, 247.

26. Pedrocco 2002, 96.

27. Links 1977, 33.

28. Pedrocco 2002, 85.

29. Perhaps the most compelling comparison to Canaletto's *The Grand Canal from the Campo San Vio* is found in Marieschi's *The Grand Canal*, (ca. 1740?) in Sukachev's Fine Arts Museum, Irkutsk, Russia. The composition of the two paintings is nearly identical.

30. Harris in London and Washington, D.C. 1994, 259.

31. Constable and Links 1989, 2: 117.

32. Haskell 1980, 278.

33. Redford 1996, 66.

34. Harris in London and Washington, D.C. 1994, 247. See also Barcham 1977, 383–93 (esp. 387–93).

35. Harris in London and Washington, D.C. 1994, 247–49.

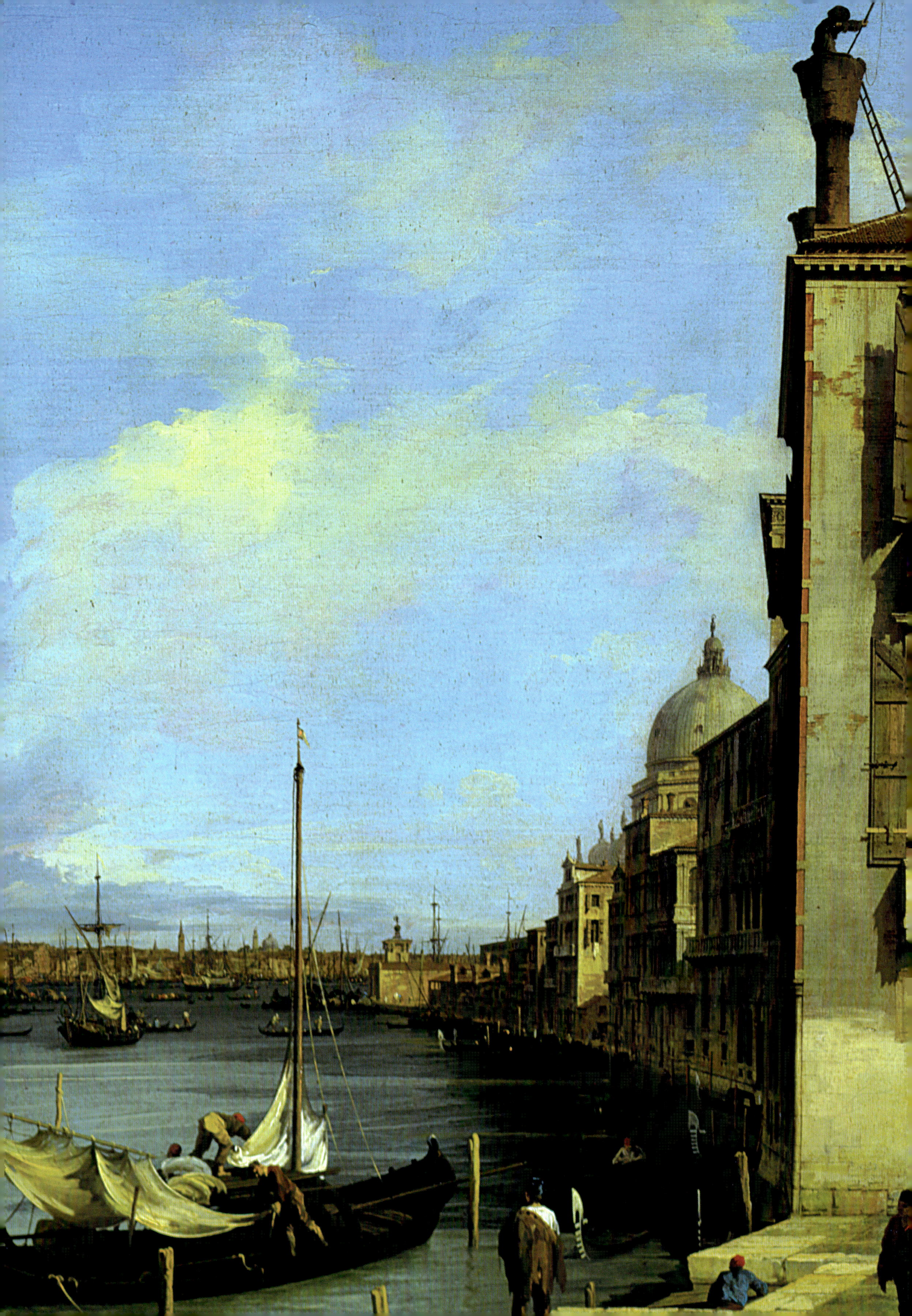

EUGENE J. JOHNSON AND LESLIE N. JOHNSON

Now we began to distinguish Murano, St. Michele, St. Giorgio in Alga, and several other islands, detached from the grand cluster which I hailed as old acquaintances; innumerable prints and drawings having long since made their shapes familiar.[1]

So did the wealthy and cultured Englishman William Beckford in 1783 recall his first view of Venice from the waters of the Venetian lagoon. By the late eighteenth century, travelers could arrive in that city prepared for its marvels by the spate of printed views of Venice that had appeared in previous decades. Not the least of these was a set of twelve views of the Grand Canal plus two scenes of important Venetian festivals, etched by Antonio Visentini (1688–1782) after paintings by Giovanni Antonio Canal, better known as Canaletto, and published in Venice in 1735 under the title *Prospectus Magni Canalis Venetiarum.*[2] English travelers to Venice in the eighteenth century, their numbers increasing every decade,[3] eagerly bought views of the city to take home, and Englishmen such as Beckford took advantage of these visual records to educate themselves before actually going to Italy.[4]

One of the principal destinations of the Grand Tour, Venice presented not only the spectacle of architecture that miraculously seemed to float on water but also a governmental form close to the one the British themselves were developing. For a thousand years and more, Venice had been the home of merchants who plied their trade on the sea; Britain in the eighteenth century was becoming the greatest maritime mercantile power in the world. The Venetian government was controlled by an oligarchy of wealthy families who elected the doge as a titular head of state with clearly circumscribed powers. This arrangement resembled what the Whigs sought to create in England, where they, as wealthy landowners,

would run the government under a monarch whose powers were limited. For these reasons, English visitors could feel at home in Venice, even if there were other aspects of the city that were utterly strange to their northern culture.[5]

An exceptionally wealthy traveler like the fourth Duke of Bedford could literally cover the walls of Bedford House in London with twenty-four Venetian scenes by Canaletto. (Those pictures now hang in the dining room at Woburn Abbey, the country estate of the dukes of Bedford.)[6] Others, less well off, might acquire a single Canaletto, such as the one seen hanging behind the Strode family in their portrait by William Hogarth (fig. 1).[7] The inclusion of this picture in the portrait makes clear that owning even one Canaletto was a great symbol of status. Acquiring a set of printed views of Venice, on the other hand, was within the range of almost anyone with enough money to embark on the Grand Tour. Prints had come into wide circulation in Europe beginning in the late fifteenth century as an affordable means of acquiring works of art. By the

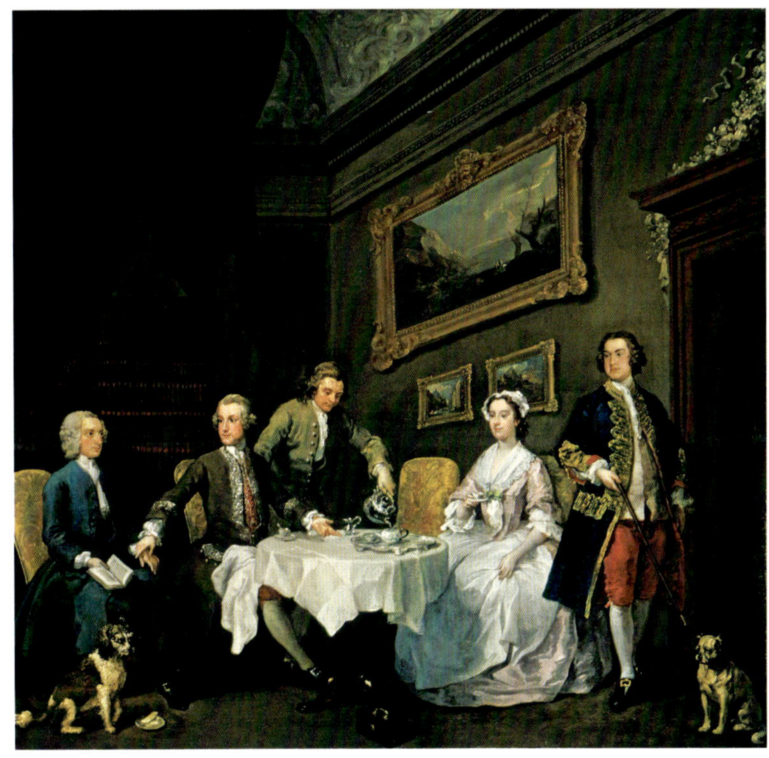

Fig. 1. William Hogarth (English, 1697–1764)
The Strode Family, ca. 1738
Oil on canvas, 34 3/10 x 36 in. (87 x 91.5 cm)
Tate Gallery, London, Bequeathed by Rev. William Finch, 1880

1730s and 1740s, the presses of Venice, which had been a major center of printing since the late fifteenth century, were producing them in large quantities.[8]

Presumably, the commercial possibilities inherent in selling such a set of prints to British visitors lay behind the decision of an English businessman, Joseph Smith (ca. 1674–1770)—whom Horace Walpole sneeringly labeled "The Merchant of Venice"—to commission Antonio Visentini to make a volume of etchings after fourteen Canaletto paintings he owned; twelve of these were Grand Canal views, while the other two depicted Venetian festivals.[9] Smith kept these paintings in his house and showed them to visitors from his homeland, who in turn could commission copies of them from Canaletto. Smith took his cut of the purchase price.

The Englishman in Venice to whom almost all British travelers turned, Smith was a remarkable character who put together a fine art collection that included Vermeer's *The Music Lesson* (ca. 1662–65, Royal Collection, Windsor Castle) and pictures by Rubens and Rembrandt.[10] In addition, he had the works of Sir Isaac Newton translated into Italian and saw to their publication. An astute merchant, banker, and publisher, Smith was sufficiently successful to afford the purchase, in 1740, of the small palazzo on the Grand Canal in which he had lived since his arrival in the city around 1700. He served as British Consul in Venice from 1744 to 1760.[11]

The first twelve etchings in Visentini's *Prospectus Magni Canalis Venetiarum*, published under Smith's auspices, are views of the Grand Canal arranged in two sets of six, each set starting from the Rialto Bridge at the center of the city and moving sequentially, first downstream to the Piazza S. Marco and then upstream to the northern end of the canal, toward the mainland (see map p. 50). Etchings after Smith's two Canaletto canvases of Venetian festivals, not part of the suite of twelve canal paintings, complete the volume.[12] Also included are two elegant pages in front—one bearing portraits of Canaletto and Visentini in elaborate Rococo frames (cat. 13a) and the other a title page bristling with allegorical references to the city.[13] The publication was a clear success. In 1742 a second edition, expanded to include thirty-eight plates, appeared; that same edition was reprinted in 1751 and 1754.[14]

In Plate I of the 1735 edition (cat. 13b), the viewer looks south from the center of the Rialto Bridge toward the point where the canal bends to the left, just beyond two very large late-Gothic palaces of the fifteenth century, Cà (Venetian for "house") Foscari and Cà Giustiniani. Cà Foscari, partly hidden behind the mast of a boat, faces the canal, just right of center on the print. Plate II (cat. 13c) shows those two palaces in the right foreground and then looks down the canal toward the Convento di Sta. Maria della Carità, whose sharply pointed Gothic gables appear just left of center.

That façade, in turn, occupies the right foreground of Plate III (cat. 13d), as one looks downstream toward the great dome of the Church of Sta. Maria della Salute. Just to the left of the Carità's tower one sees a shuttered window on the top floor of the Palazzo Barbarigo, located on the Campo S. Vio. That is the palazzo in the right foreground of Plate IV (cat. 13e)—now with two windows—the shutters of the upper window opened to reveal a figure looking out. Again one sees the dome of the Salute, but one can look past that to the end of the canal where it empties into the Bacino di S. Marco, the body of water directly in front of the Piazzetta and the Doge's Palace. In Plate V (cat. 13f) that palace comes partially into view on the left. The Salute dominates the right foreground, and beyond it emerges the tower of the Dogana del Mar, or customs house, with its figure of Fortune atop a gilded globe. The vantage point in Plate VI (cat. 13g) is from the center of the mouth of the canal but looking back upstream, with the Dogana and the Salute on the left. At the end of the view up the canal are the backs of the gables of the Carità.

All the views seem to have been taken from slightly elevated positions on land, with the exception of Plate VI, which Canaletto must have sketched from a boat. The suggestion of the latter image is that a gondola bearing visitors down the canal has turned to offer a look back at what the passengers have just passed. The first six plates, then, present a continuous sequence of views of the lower half of the Grand Canal that would allow someone who had been in Venice to reconstruct the experience of floating down its waters.

With Plate VII (cat. 13h) we return to the Rialto Bridge, but here look *at* it rather than *from* it. In Plate VIII (cat. 13i) we turn our eyes upstream, with the Mercato Nuovo on the left side of the canal and our view terminated by the great mass of Cà Vendramin-Calergi in the distance. Four houses in from the right is Joseph Smith's small Gothic palazzo, which Visentini, who was an architect by trade, later remodeled. Plate IX (cat. 13j) brings the Cà Vendramin-Calergi into the right foreground, recalling the way the Cà Foscari moves from the background to the foreground in Plates I and II. The flank of the Church of S. Geremia appears in the distance, its tall tower capped by an octagon. That structure, the tallest one in Plate X (cat. 13k), stands to the left of the entrance to the Canareggio Canal. This print offers the only view in the set that looks to the side, down another canal. In the distance are the tall, multistoried structures of the Ghetto, the quarter to which Venetian Jews were confined after dark. Because Plate X fails to provide a view down the Grand Canal, the logical progression of leading the viewer from one monument to another—characteristic of the previous plates—is interrupted at this point. Indeed, Plates X, XI, and XII are not linked by buildings that appear in two consecutively numbered prints.

Plate XI (cat. 13l) does not show S. Geremia but moves down the canal to a point just below the Church of the Scalzi, whose Baroque façade dominates the right margin. Beyond the Scalzi, and still on the right, is the largely undecorated exterior of Palladio's Church of Sta. Lucia, destroyed in the nineteenth century to make way for the railroad station that finally provided a land connection, via causeway, from the city to the mainland. On the left is the tall dome of the Church of S. Simeone Piccola, and in the distance one sees the flank, marked by three windows, of the now-demolished Church of Sta. Croce. Beyond that small structure are the relatively modest houses that characterized this less monumental end of the canal. Plate XII (cat. 13m), the last in the series, does not include Sta. Croce. Rather, the viewer stands at a point beyond that church to look at a row of houses on the left, while the horizon line is marked by the mountains on the mainland that were much easier to make out in the smog-free air of the eighteenth century than they are today. This was likely the last view of Venice for visitors leaving the city on their homeward journey. Thus as they leafed through the prints back home, this plate would have reminded them of their own departures.

Scholars who have studied these prints have noted that they offer a sequential trip up and down the Grand Canal that starts at, and then returns to, Rialto.[15] An explanation of why this arrangement was adopted (as opposed, say, to moving downstream from the beginning of the canal, toward the mainland, to the Bacino) seems clear. Rialto is the original core of the city, founded on the highest bank—Rivus Altus, or Rialto—of the Grand Canal, which is an ancient riverbed. When visitors first came to Venice, they often began exploring it from that point. Such was the case with Johann Wolfgang von Goethe, who visited in 1786. He reported that after settling into his lodgings, he made his way there through the maze of streets: "I easily found the Grand Canal and the Rialto Bridge, the principal bridge—the view down from it is grand—lively and very beautiful."[16] This is the view in Plate I (cat. 13b).

Publication of the prints put the Canaletto paintings in a fixed sequence. The information that allowed this arrangement was already contained in the paintings themselves, but that sequence does not follow the order in which they were executed. Although we cannot be sure of the precise chronology, it seems clear that they were painted neither in the order in which they appear in the *Prospectus Magni Canalis Venetiarum* nor in one that corresponds to the series of spaces that unfolds in the city.[17] Moreover, we have no idea how they were hung in Smith's house. Most scholars agree that the earliest painting is the one Visentini reproduced in Plate XII [cat. 13m]—the last of the sequence as published. Datable on the basis of style and technique to about 1723–24, the canvas showed the view from the end of the canal toward the mainland.[18] That work does not, however, necessarily

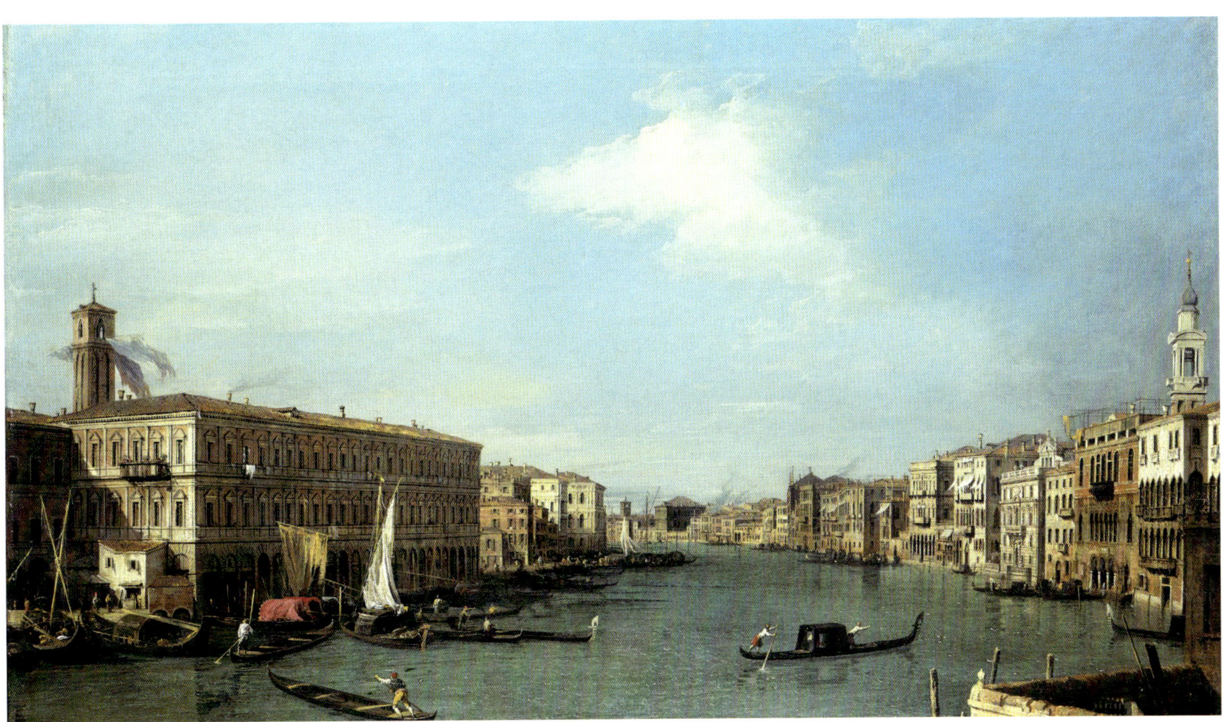

Fig. 2. Canaletto (Giovanni Antonio Canal)
The Grand Canal Looking Northwest from near the Rialto, ca. 1726–27
Oil on canvas, 18 3/4 x 31 1/2 in. (47.6 x 80 cm)
The Royal Collection, Her Majesty Queen Elizabeth II, RCIN 406017

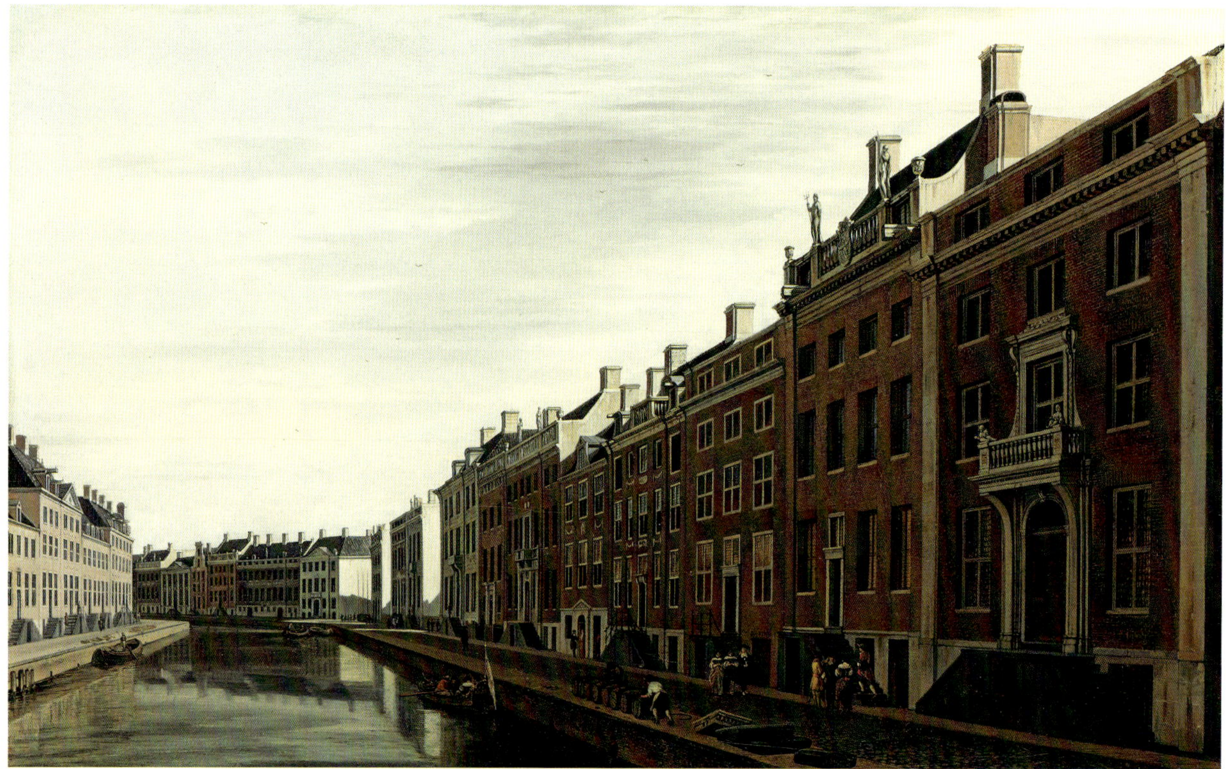

Fig. 3. Gerrit Adriaensz. Berckheyde (Dutch, 1638–1698)
The Bend in the Herengracht near the Nieuwe Spiegelstraat in Amsterdam, 1672
Oil on panel, 15 15/16 x 24 13/16 in. (40.5 x 63 cm)
Rijksmuseum, Amsterdam, SK-A-4750

imply that a sequence of Grand Canal views would follow.[19] Indeed, the three paintings showing the upstream end of the canal (on which Plates X, XI, and XII are based) are not connected by consecutively shown buildings. Thus they do not seem to constitute parts of a continuous sequence, whereas the other paintings Visentini reproduced do.

At some point while the pictures were being painted, Canaletto and/or Smith apparently decided that the set would show sequentially linked views. The Grand Canal is unique among European urban spaces. Even Amsterdam, with its concentric rings of canals, does not have one major waterway bisecting the city and forming the principal means of circulation through an aqueous environment. The inimitable experience of fluidly gliding along the canal may even have suggested the arrangement that appears in Canaletto's paintings and in Visentini's etchings after them. To the best of our knowledge, no earlier published set of printed views of a city provides a similar re-creation of the sequential spatial experience of moving through an urban setting. The prints provided the possibility of armchair reminiscences of the Venice that travelers had once visited.

The paintings of the canal upon which the etchings are based are actually divided between seven pictures looking downstream and five looking in the opposite direction. The place where they divide is located just downstream from Joseph Smith's own house, so

that the paintings themselves show movement up and down the canal from the starting point of his neighborhood. If one imagines a visitor's gondola trip downstream departing from Cà Smith, then the view of the Rialto Bridge in Plate VII (cat. 13h) would serve well as the first of the twelve views. To present Venice as it was experienced from his residence, however, might have been too bold an act of hubris even for the notoriously proud Smith, and it would also have destroyed the symmetrical division of the views as published. Whatever the case, Plate VII recalls the fact that many English visitors began their exploration of the city by visiting the home of their countryman Smith, who could guide their choices of sites to visit, introduce them to important Venetians, and perhaps even sell them a memento of their stay.

Smith's palazzo plays something of a role in the Canaletto paintings of Venice he owned as well as in the Visentini etchings. It appears, as we have noted, toward the right-hand margin of Plate VIII (cat. 13i). One of the two earliest-documented Canaletto pictures of the Grand Canal—a painting commissioned in 1725 by Stefano Conti of Lucca— shows the same view; however, a structure in the right foreground obscures all but the upper part of the Smith residence (fig. 6, p. 15). The house comes into full view in the Canaletto painting later executed for Smith, and it remains in full view in the etching. After Visentini completed remodeling the façade in a classical style in 1751,[20] Smith had Canaletto repaint the house in the canvas that depicted it (fig. 2).[21] Curiously, the etching was never modified to show the new façade.[22]

If the Visentini works indeed comprised the first attempt to replicate, in a series of prints, the experience of moving sequentially through a specific urban space, what precedents might there have been for such a novel undertaking? It seems likely that the idea originated in seventeenth-century Holland, where a kind of armchair visual travel had been created by inventive printmakers. According to David Freedberg, Dutch artists of that period made prints that recalled the experience of walks in the countryside.[23] Walter S. Gibson analyzed *Plaisante Plaetsen* (*Pleasant Places*, ca. 1611–12), a set of prints by Claes Jansz. Visscher showing well-known sites walkers visited in the rural areas around Haarlem; the importance of these images was widely recognized.[24] Catherine Levesque observed that, in the late seventeenth century, writers noted "the usefulness of prints in presenting absent and distant things as if they were before our eyes, [and] in facilitating the recollection of matters that have escaped our memory."[25] None of the sets of Dutch prints, however, shows a sequenced ordering in which a building or object in the background of one scene is incorporated into the foreground of the next. Although Dutch painters such as Gerrit Adriaensz. Berckheyde produced single images of canals, such as *The Bend in the Herengracht near the Nieuwe Spiegelstraat, Amsterdam* (fig. 3), they did not create sequential pictures like those Canaletto produced. We do not know what Dutch works might have been available to the Italian painter, but we can say that his patron Joseph Smith had a significant interest in seventeenth-century Dutch painting: witness the Rembrandts and the Vermeer in his collection.

Urban views produced in Rome in the late sixteenth and seventeenth centuries may bring us somewhat closer to home. Pope Sixtus V, during his brief papacy (1585-1590) undertook an extraordinary reordering of Rome to make the city more readily understandable to pilgrims wishing to visit its most important shrines. To that end he set up four ancient obelisks as markers of important moments in the urban fabric, and he capped the still-standing triumphal columns of the emperors Trajan and Marcus Aurelius with statues of St. Peter and St. Paul respectively, to proclaim the triumph of Christianity over paganism. Sixtus also built in the Vatican Palace a library wing whose walls he has decorated with views of the obelisks and triumphal columns. In one view, which shows the obelisk he placed before the apse of Sta. Maria

Maggiore, one can also make out in the far distance, to the left of the Colosseum, the obelisk he placed in front of the transept of S. Giovanni in Laterano, the cathedral of Rome. That obelisk appears in the foreground of a second fresco in the library that focuses on the Lateran. In the fresco of Piazza Colonna that shows the column of Marcus Aurelius, the column of Trajan can be found in the background. That column is also represented, closer up, in another fresco.[26] In these pairs of views of Rome, then, we can find the artistic device later exploited by Canaletto, of leading the viewer from one site to another by showing in one scene a distant object that becomes a foreground object in a second. When the young Canaletto was in Rome in 1719–20, he could have seen the frescoes in the Vatican library.

Illustrated guidebooks to Rome, published in ever-increasing quantities from the sixteenth century on, offer at least one interesting parallel to what the Visentini etchings provide—a set of sequential views. For example, on facing pages in one guide of 1725 are a view of the Pantheon and its portico and a view of the Piazza della Rotonda, the open space in front of the ancient temple. These sights cannot be seen simultaneously in the piazza; the visitor has to turn around 180 degrees to experience both. Moving the eye from one page to the next re-creates that experience in the imagination.[27]

Compared with a set of 103 etchings of Venice by the painter Luca Carlevaris published in 1703, Canaletto's dozen sequential views of the Grand Canal collected in the 1735 portfolio seem remarkably original.[28] In the Carlevaris images the same buildings appear more than once, but the views are not arranged in sequence. For example, the Convento di Sta. Maria della Carità is the subject of Plate 22, and it appears in the background much later, in Plate 69. Plates 70 and 71 contain views of the same group of palaces along the Grand Canal, but looking upstream in 70 and downstream in 71. Clearly, the Visentini prints were intended to compete with and outstrip the Carlevaris etchings.[29] Equally clear is that one of Canaletto's major contributions to the history of cityscape painting was his exhaustive documentation of the entire fabric of a city, not just its major monuments.[30]

Smith, Canaletto, and Visentini reunited in 1742 to produce an expanded second edition of etchings of Venice. The new volume consisted of three sections: Part 1, the original fourteen prints published in 1735; Part 2, additional views of the Grand Canal; and Part 3, views of other areas of the city. The opening plates of Part 2 begin at the upstream end of the canal, as seen from the vantage point of a visitor entering it from the mainland.

Plate 1 (cat. 13n) shows the small Church of Sta. Croce in the background. In Plate 2 (cat. 13o), the church occupies the foreground—and so on down the canal.[31] The nonsequential arrangement of views of the upstream end of the canal in Plates X–XII in the 1735 edition is now corrected by a careful unfolding of views that move downstream, as if one had just come into town by boat from the mainland. As J. G. Links has pointed out, both the last plate of Part 1 (cat. 13m) and the first plate of Part 2 (cat.13n) show the house in which the British Resident lived. (It is the second complete house on the left in Plate I of Part 1 and the first complete house on the right in Plate 1 of Part 2.) The Resident was the equivalent of an ambassador representing the government, whereas the Consul (the position Smith held) represented England's economic interests. The prominence of the house in both prints would have reminded British visitors of a building they likely had come to know and to which they had probably been welcomed— like the people at the door in both images.

Generally, visitors from northern Europe would approach and leave Venice on the *Burchiello*, a boat that plied the Brenta River between Venice and Padua on a regular basis. Goethe described the *Burchiello* as a "public ship" on which he encountered "mannerly company."[32] "[W]e had come down the beautiful Brenta, passing many a magnificent garden, many a magnificent palace, viewing with a hasty glance the wealthy, busy towns along the shore."[33]

In 1747, five years after the Visentini prints appeared for the second time, another Venetian artist, Gianfrancesco Costa (1711–1772), published a set of 140 sequential views of the journey up the Brenta, *Le delizie del fiume Brenta* (*The Delights of the Brenta River*).[34] Costa seems to have taken the sequential manner in which the Smith/Canaletto/Visentini team had arranged views of the Grand Canal as the organizing principle of his own work. Like the 1735 *Prospectus,* Costa's set is divided into two parts, separated by a storm scene at Plate 70. The series begins at the mouth of the Brenta and ends in a landscape, with Padua seen from the point where the voyage of the *Burchiello* ended. The curious vessel, with its flat-roofed cabin and rectangular windows, pops in and out of Costa's scenes, which record the life and sites along the Brenta that Goethe so vividly described.

Le delizie del fiume Brenta offers a geographical and conceptual sequel to the *Prospectus Magni Canalis Venetiarum*—geographical in that Costa's views continue the progress toward home of the departing traveler, and conceptual in that they expand upon the number of views and upon the depiction of everyday life along the way. The presence of the *Burchiello* also suggests that Costa intended his work as a sequel to

Visentini's Grand Canal etchings. The *Burchiello* makes an appearance in Plates 1 and 2 (cats. 13n and 13o) of Visentini's etchings of 1742, which show the upper end of the canal and feature the Church of Sta. Croce. The craft is seen in the background of Plate 1, bearing visitors on the first leg of their homeward journey. In Plate 2 the *Burchiello* is in the foreground, bringing visitors into Venice. Costa's 140 sequential views suggest the possibilities of film in the way they narrate the experience of space. Could the works of Costa, Canaletto, and Visentini be precursors of that fluid art?

NOTES

1. Beckford 1834, 1: 100.

2. Antonio Visentini, *Prospectus Magni Canalis Venetiarum addito Certamine Nautico et Nundinis Venetis* (Venice: Giovanni Battista Pasquali Press, 1735).

3. Black 1992, 6.

4. Some travelers were disappointed by the actual city after having come to know it through paintings and prints. See Eglin 2001, 94–95.

5. Eglin studies the relationship between Venice and England. Ibid.

6. Links 1977, 44–45.

7. Eglin 2001, 110–11.

8. The earliest set of printed views of Venice is Luca Carlevaris, *Le fabriche, e vedute di Venetia disegnate: poste in prospettiva, et intagliate da Luca Carlevariis con priveliegii* (Venice: Giovanni Battista Finazzi, 1703). The Visentini set of 1735 was followed in 1741 by the publication of Michele Marieschi's *Magnificentiores Selectioresque Urbis Venetiarum Prospectus.*

9. Although many scholars refer to these prints as engravings, they are in fact etchings—as revealed by the characteristic bluntly rounded ends of their lines. Engraved lines, in contrast, have pointed ends. The most recent study of the paintings after which Visentini's etchings were made is Clayton 2005, 24ff. Smith sold the paintings to King George III in 1762, and they remain in the Royal Collection.

10. For a list of the northern paintings Smith owned, see Vivian 1971, Appendix B.

11. The most detailed study of Smith is Vivian, ibid.

12. British travelers were particularly keen on Venetian festivals and often would arrange their itineraries so as to be in the city on the days of great public celebrations. Eglin 2001, 70.

13. The title page is analyzed in Corboz 1985, 2: 464–65.

14. Antonio Visentini, *Urbis Venetiarum Prospectus Celebriores: Antonii Canal Tabulis XXXVIII; Aere Expressi ab Antonio Visentini in Partes Tres Distribuiti* (Venice: Giovanni Battista Pasquali Press, 1742). The new title takes into account the fact that the third part of the publication contains views of major Venetian buildings and open spaces that are not located on the Grand Canal. A facsimile of the 1742 edition is in Links 1971.

15. Dario Succi, "La svolta: le quattordici vedute veneziane di Canaletto per Smith e la traduzione incisoria di Visentini. Osservazioni sulla cronologia" in Venice 1986, 36, makes the point clearly. Clayton (2005, 25) is puzzled by the organization, but he does not seem to have been aware of Succi's work, which is not included in his bibliography.

16. Goethe 1989, 59.

17. None of the pictures in this group bears a date. Succi (in Venice 1986, 33–45) makes a convincing argument for dating the paintings, contending that the increasing ease with the etching medium one finds in the first state of the Visentini etchings, published in 1735, can be corroborated with the changes in Canaletto's style one observes in the twelve paintings. Clayton (2005, 28–72) offers the latest attempt to put the pictures in chronological order, but unfortunately his analysis does not make use of Succi's work.

18. On the primacy of this painting in the series Succi and Clayton agree.

19. Succi (in Venice 1986, 37) believes it does imply such a sequence.

20. Dario Succi, "Un misterioso disegno preparato per un'acquaforte mai incisa per Smith" in Venice 1986, 160, points out that remodeling of the house, the new façade of which was unveiled in 1751, began shortly after Smith bought it in 1740.

21. Levey 1962, 338.

22. In an unfinished drawing of the canal closely related to Plate VIII, Visentini anchored the right margin with the Smith palazzo as he had remodeled it. The purpose of the drawing is not known, but Dario Succi believes its size suggests that it was a preparatory drawing for a new etching that would accompany the four large views of the Piazza S. Marco after Canaletto that Visentini had also produced for Smith. Succi in Venice 1986, l60–62, n. 17 (cat. 176).

23. Freedberg 1980, 16. We are grateful to Zirka Filipczak for leading us to Freedberg's book.

24. Gibson 2000, 93: "Both landscape images and maps were frequently touted as a convenient means of vicarious travel." We are grateful to Walter Gibson for his advice on this essay.

25. Levesque 1994, 10.

26. The Vatican Library frescoes are well illustrated in D'Onofrio 1967, figs. 61, 71, 83, and 85. For a more recent discussion, with bibliography, of the activities of Sixtus V in Rome, see Charles Burroughs, "Absolutism and the Rhetoric of Topography: Streets in the Rome of Sixtus V," in Çelik et al. 1994, 189–202.

27. Franzini 1725. See also Zorach 2008, 152.

28. See note 8.

29. The long and distinguished history of Venetian *vedute* is sketched out by Aikema and Bakker in Amsterdam 1990, 19–46. The most recent work on this subject, Pavanello 2008, was published too recently for evaluation here.

30. Dario Succi, "L'edizione completa delle 'Prospettive di Venezia': Canaletto e Visentini, Joseph Smith regista" in Venice 1986, 48.

31. Links (1971, 44) points out that nine of the twenty-four etchings in Part 2 are based on known views of Venice by Canaletto that in great probability also belonged to Smith. No original painting is known to be the source for Plate 1 of Part 2, however. Of the seven views of the upstream half of the canal in Part 2, six look downstream.

32. Goethe 1989, 56.

33. Ibid., 58.

34. Costa 1747. See Calabi 1915, 226–33.

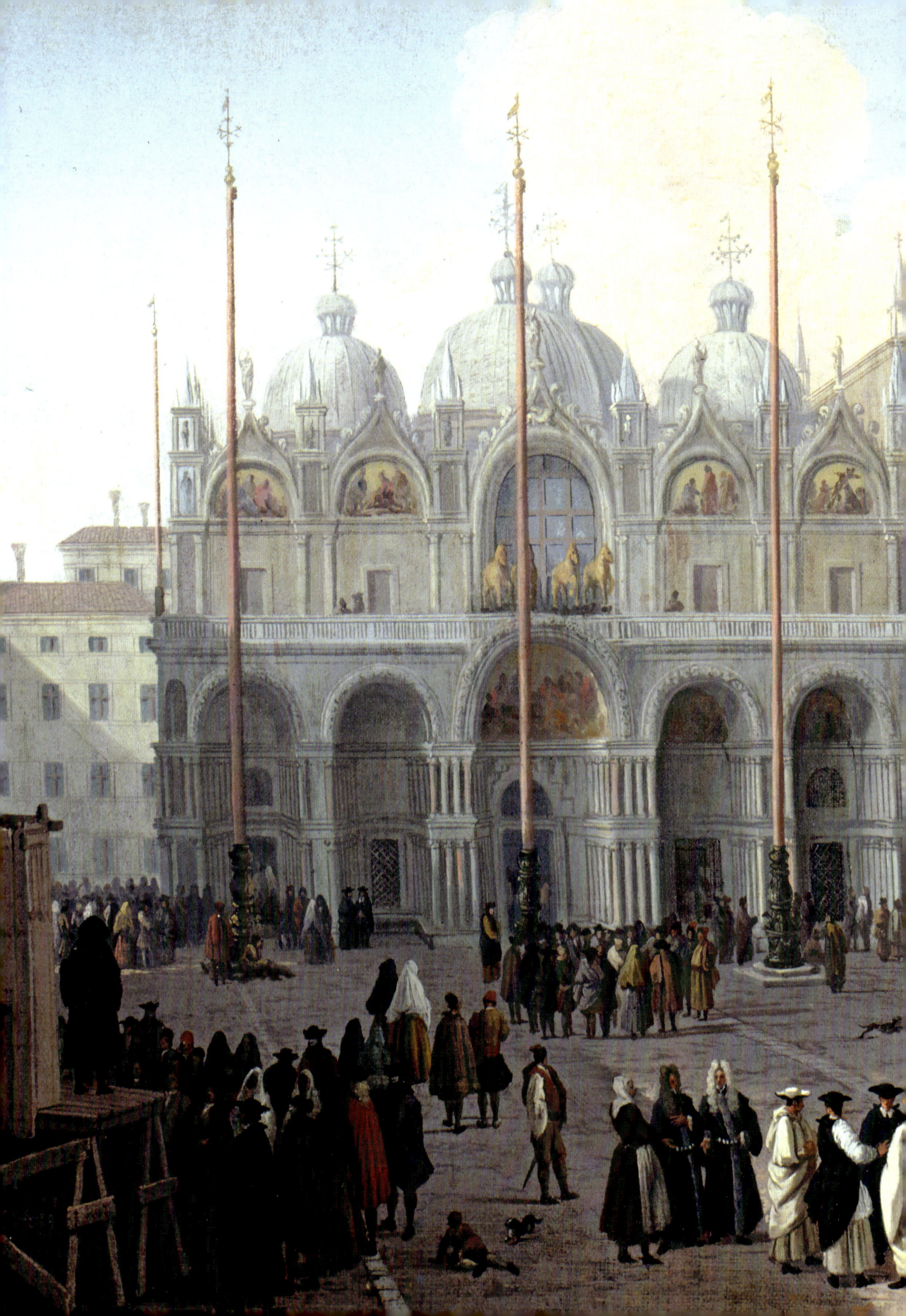

Private Images for Public Spaces:
Religious Art in Eighteenth-Century Venice

WILLIAM BARCHAM

This essay raises a set of questions regarding the cultural role and artistic vigor of religious imagery in eighteeth-century Venice. What kinds of economic forces shaped the patronage of altarpieces and small devotional paintings at the time? Can pious art be private if it adorns public spaces? Was Venice truly a devout city, despite its appeal to gamblers and those seeking the services of courtesans? How does our modern perception of Venice as an arena for the debaucheries of libertines such as Giovanni Casanova and Lorenzo da Ponte conform to life as it was actually lived there? Finally, what did famous Venetian artists paint when they worked in Protestant churches abroad where neither altarpieces nor great fresco cycles were permitted?

For more than 400 years, Venice was famed for its wealth, power, and international clout. With its virtually unlimited mercantile and financial resources and vast territorial reach, the Venetian republic reigned supreme between the twelfth and sixteenth centuries. Yet by 1600, the *secolo d'oro*, or Golden Age, was over. Venice's empire diminished in size, especially after the loss of two wars fought against the Ottoman Empire between around 1650 and 1690, and mercantile shipping subsequently declined. The resulting economic failure and lack of fiscal confidence affected both individuals and the state. Either because of poverty or self-absorption, members of the governing patrician class often refused to fulfill their political responsibilities, at times declining ambassadorial appointments or turning down official administrative positions. Anxious for an infusion of new capital into governmental coffers and desperate for bureaucrats ready to serve the homeland, the Venetian state sold membership into the patriciate to merchants who, though they lacked a distinguished genealogy, were able and willing to pay lordly sums of money.[1]

Despite Venice's reduced role in European diplomacy by 1700 and its economic stagnation, the city undertook impressive public and private works. For example, the government built *murazzi*, or water barriers, along the outer shore of the Lido—the sandbar or barrier reef separating Venice from the Adriatic Sea—in order to protect the city and its tenuous lagoon existence from periodic flooding. The entire surface of the Piazza S. Marco was paved with a striking geometrical stone design that survives today; the interlocking rectangles and bands, which included small slots cut into the pattern, allowed the canals flowing beneath the open square to bubble gently upward at high tide. In the private sector, many of the new patrician families erected great palaces along the Grand Canal, investing sizable portions of their fortunes to sink foundation pilings underwater and designing lavish interiors that would at once confirm their recently acquired power and outdo the old moneyed class.

Corresponding with the practical urban projects was the building of grandiose churches; between 1700 and the end of the century, Venice witnessed the construction and decoration of more than twenty-four such structures.[2] Already standing in the city were more than seventy-five Renaissance churches as well as many even older houses of worship surviving from the late Middle Ages. When at mid-century Venice's Christian population was about 140,000 souls, the ratio of citizenry to clergy ranged between fifty and 100 people per priest.[3] Preaching in Venice was renowned throughout the Italian peninsula; this was likely a result of the city's preeminence in the printing and publishing of doctrinal orations and homilies. More religious books, tracts, and panegyrics saw the light of day there than almost anywhere else in Europe at the time. Often, the men celebrating Mass were the sons of impoverished patricians with few other career choices. And though it has been said that the churches of Venice were filled with eager and rapt worshipers, it is of course impossible to assess the piety and spiritual commitment of the citizenry as a whole.[4]

Venice was unmistakably a city with a vibrant religious life, one insistently and sonorously punctuated throughout the day by the ringing of church bells in every parish. However, its chief reputation abroad was one of decadence and profligacy, a notoriousness that flourishes anecdotally to this day. It stems in part from the bawdy escapades

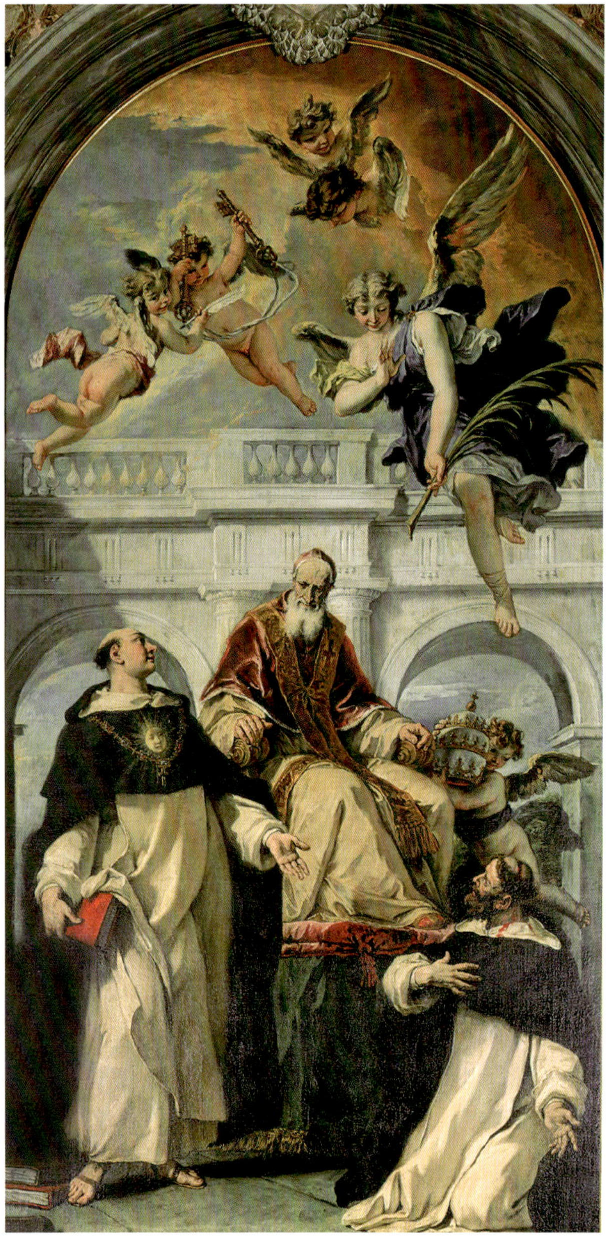

Fig. 1. Sebastiano Ricci (Italian, 1659–1734)
Pope Pius IV, St. Thomas and St. Peter the Martyr, ca. 1730–33
Oil on canvas, 135 x 66 1/2 in. (343 x 169 cm)
Sta. Maria del Rosario, Venice

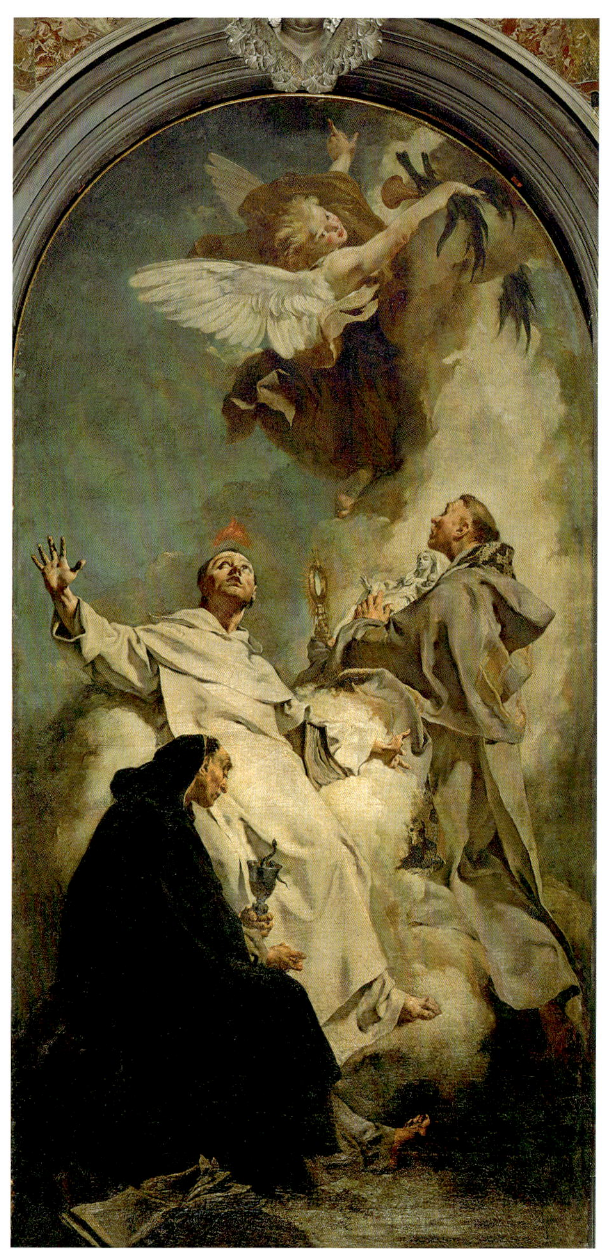

Fig. 2. Giovanni Battista Piazzetta (Italian, 1683–1754)
The Three Dominican Saints: Vincent Ferrer, Ludovico Bertrand, and Hyacinth, 1738
Oil on canvas, 135 x 66 1/2 in. (343 x 169 cm)
Sta. Maria del Rosario, Venice

Casanova recounted in his autobiography. And in Voltaire's bitingly satirical *Candide* (1759), the young and naive eponymous protagonist arrives in Venice to enjoy the worldly delights of its palaces and taverns but never sets foot in a church. To emphasize the city's unsavory aspects, Voltaire has Candide meet ten monarchs who, down on their luck and sorely tried by Providence, seek Carnival and carnal pleasures with disreputable women and in local casinos. But if Casanova's bordellos and Voltaire's gambling houses exemplified Venetian corruption, the city's myriad churches reflected its piety. In fact, the number of consecrated altars far exceeded that of the gaming tables.[5]

Despite the financial woes Venetian society faced during the eighteenth century, nearly all churches were quickly completed, including those with lavish interior ornamentation.[6] Whereas patrician support previously had financed ecclesiastical building, civic outreach proved to be successful in the 1700s. The construction of the Franciscan Church of S. Francesco della Vigna in the mid-sixteenth century and of the Dominican Church of Sta. Maria del Rosario (familiarly called the Gesuati) in the 1720s and 1730s illustrates this difference.

Doge Andrea Gritti, one of the most powerful heads of government in the history of the Venetian republic, supervised the S. Francesco project, with Cardinal Giovanni Grimani, patriarch of the ancient bishopric of Aquileia, being responsible for the church façade. Hailing from two of Venice's great patrician families, Gritti and Grimani provided authoritative

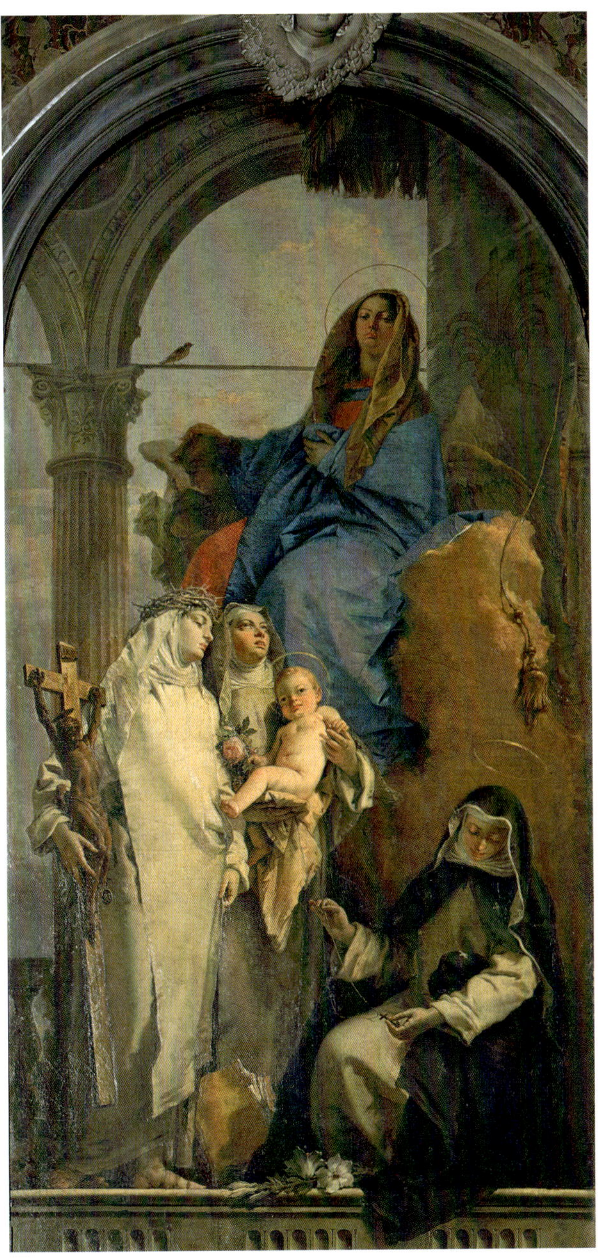

Fig. 3. Giambattista Tiepolo (Italian, 1696–1770)
Virgin and Child with Three Dominican Saints: Rosa da Lima, Catarina da Siena,
and Agnese da Montepulciano, 1747–48
Oil on canvas, 134 x 66 in. (340 x 168 cm)
Sta. Maria del Rosario, Venice

and aristocratic leadership, which encouraged other members of their class to participate. Famous clans, such as the Badoer, Barbaro, Bragadin, Contarini, and Giustiniani, sponsored side chapels in the church, commissioning ornate altars and costly altarpieces. A sense of patrician privilege still permeates S. Francesco's interior, where contemporary visitors appreciate the opulence of the chapels and the way the imposing grillwork separates private spaces from public ones.

Almost two centuries later, the Gesuati church—in which no division between public and private exists—was erected under quite different circumstances. Intent upon increasing its sway in Venice in the late seventeenth century, the Observant branch of the Dominican order bought

at auction an abandoned church far across the city from its motherhouse of SS. Giovanni e Paolo. The vacant building and its grounds were in a neighborhood that for several hundred years had been dominated by the Franciscans, traditional rivals of the Dominicans. Nevertheless, the Dominicans received a warm welcome from their new parishioners. Heartened by this apparent acceptance, the Observants dedicated an altar in 1691 to the Madonna of the Rosary, a Dominican devotion since the 1570s, and soon decided to replace the old church with a grander one. The Dominican prior directing the building project quickly realized the harsh economic realities of the day and petitioned the government for authorization to seek public funds. Once that was granted, he asked each guild in the city to plead the Dominican cause before its membership. The largest guild of all, the ironmongers, initiated the enterprise by parading through Venice, calling out for funds and bearing banners depicting Thomas Aquinas, a patron saint of the order and one of the most influential figures in Dominican history. This public appeal was astonishingly successful. As money poured in, other guilds joined the undertaking, and in 1729 even the *salumieri*, or salami makers, got involved.

Sta. Maria del Rosario was completed in 1736, and by the end of the next decade—only half a century after the Dominicans had moved into the neighborhood—the church boasted numerous altars dressed in precious Sicilian jasper, altarpieces by Venice's greatest contemporary painters, and a magnificent ceiling fresco by Giambattista Tiepolo. The Dominicans understood the tenor of the times and no longer counted on patrician patronage, as the Franciscans had two centuries earlier for the Church of S. Francesco della Vigna. Similarly, because the artistic geniuses of the *secolo d'oro*—Jacopo Tintoretto, Paolo Veronese, and Titian—were long deceased, the eighteenth-century Observants commissioned another brilliant trio: Giovanni Battista Piazzetta, Sebastiano Ricci, and Tiepolo painted splendid altarpieces in Sta. Maria del Rosario that captured the spiritual fervor animating Venice during the early decades of the eighteenth century (figs. 1–3).[7]

Boundaries that separate private from public in houses of worship often are barely visible, if they exist at all. Private and public, moreover, can identify not only the physical spaces in church but can also characterize approaches, attitudes, thoughts, and actions that imperceptibly merge when considering ecclesiastical patronage and Christian worship. For instance, large sums of money and numerous approvals were required to initiate a work of art in a church, but ultimately the work reflected the talent and sensibility of the artist. Indeed, although the production of sacred art was an expression of communal will, it was individuals, in the end, who transformed these spaces: one attends a church to join with a community, but the individual worshiper undergoes a personal, spiritual experience there.

Unlike the side chapels in S. Francesco della Vigna, the three chapels in Sta. Maria del Rosario containing the altarpieces by Piazzetta, Ricci, and Tiepolo were never gated, and they project only slightly from the nave. As a result, each painting is clearly visible from the main sanctuary. Furthermore, the works privilege neither private cults nor family devotions but instead depict a *sacra conversazione*, or holy conversation, with Dominican saints. First appearing above altars in the late thirteenth century, the *sacra conversazione* shows a gathering of saints usually positioned on either side of the Virgin Mary and Christ Child, although other figures may replace them in the center. In the trio of works in Sta. Maria del Rosario, three Dominicans stand or sit in prayer or contemplation, although a few talk or read scripture. The purpose of these paintings was to focus attention on the consecrated altar. The paintings also encouraged the devotee to meditate and converse with Christ through Dominican intercession. Although the *sacra conversazione* had been highly popular during the Renaissance, it was less so by the seventeenth century, when most European artists favored renderings of dramatic narratives. However, in Venice, a traditional society where the local artistic heritage endured, the static *sacra conversazione* retained its appeal.

Not surprisingly, Ricci, Piazzetta, and Tiepolo approached their commissions for Sta. Maria del Rosario in markedly individual ways. Ricci, the oldest of the trio and the first one chosen to create a work, painted *Pope Pius V, St. Thomas and St. Peter the Martyr* (fig. 1), which is distinctive for its depiction of figures actually conversing. On the left, the learned Thomas Aquinas holds a tome while engaging in a serious doctrinal discussion with Pope Pius IV, who is seated on a massive throne at center. On the right, the kneeling and bloodstained St. Peter the Martyr (also called Peter of Verona) asserts his willingness to die in the fight against heresy.[8] A great arcade in the background monumentalizes this solemn encounter, whose tone is gainsaid by the presence of two bare-bottomed cherubs aloft above Aquinas and the pope and of a long-legged angel hovering over Peter.

Adorning the chapel altar across the nave but closer to the chancel is Piazzetta's *The Three Dominican Saints: Vincent Ferrer, Ludovico Bertrand, and Hyacinth* (fig. 2), a solemn expression of Christian revelation and individual rapture.[9] Vincent Ferrer and Hyacinth sit upon thick clouds,

which descend onto a bare terrain from the heavens. Like Ricci, Piazzetta introduced an angel, but the figure is unmistakably seraphic and otherworldly. Piazzetta turned his saints in different directions, and they occupy separate portions of pictorial space. Each is absorbed in personal ecstasy. In striking contrast to Ricci's solid composition, weighty forms, conversational character, and coloristic splendor, Piazzetta conveys zigzagging movement, blissful spirituality, and monochromatic sobriety.

Ten years after Piazzetta's work was unveiled, Tiepolo completed *Virgin and Child with Three Dominican Saints: Rosa da Lima, Catarina da Siena, and Agnese da Montepulciano* (fig. 3) for the chapel altar directly opposite Ricci's painting. Responding to, or possibly reacting against, the works of his two older colleagues, Tiepolo included in his *sacra conversazione* the Virgin Mary and Christ Child, neither of whom Ricci or Piazzetta had depicted.[10] Like Ricci, however, Tiepolo placed his three saints in an architectural setting, and, like Piazzetta, he portrayed a golden cloud—this one enthroning Mary—descending to Earth. A canary perched on the tie rod of the arch at the upper left alludes to a biblical anecdote: drops of Jesus' blood fell on the tiny bird after it plucked a thorn from his forehead on the road to Calvary. The crown of thorns atop Catherine's head also alludes to this encounter. The lily at Rose's feet refers to Mary, the saints, and Dominican vows. And the shimmering brocade behind Mary with a radiant tassel resting on the cloud to the far right points up the Virgin's role as Queen of Heaven. Tiepolo insisted upon such material reality in order to encourage worshipers to picture themselves as St. Rose holding the Christ Child. Like Ricci and Piazzetta, he urged the devout to participate in what they witnessed and thereby open themselves to spiritual renewal under the guidance of Dominican saints.

Sebastiano Ricci, the senior artist of the three great religious painters of eighteenth-century Venice, is credited with forging, early in the century, the Rococo style, which he subsequently popularized elsewhere on the Continent. Despite the discomforts and inconveniences of travel at that time, Ricci toured extensively, enjoying success first in Italy and later in London, where from 1711 to 1716 he painted mostly mythological subjects for cultivated aristocrats.[11] He also undertook two religious projects there, but—not surprisingly, in a Protestant country—neither one included images of Roman Catholic saints. As the Scottish philosopher and historian David Hume scathingly wrote in "The Natural History of Religion" (1757), Catholicism had transformed ordinary humans into supernatural idols:

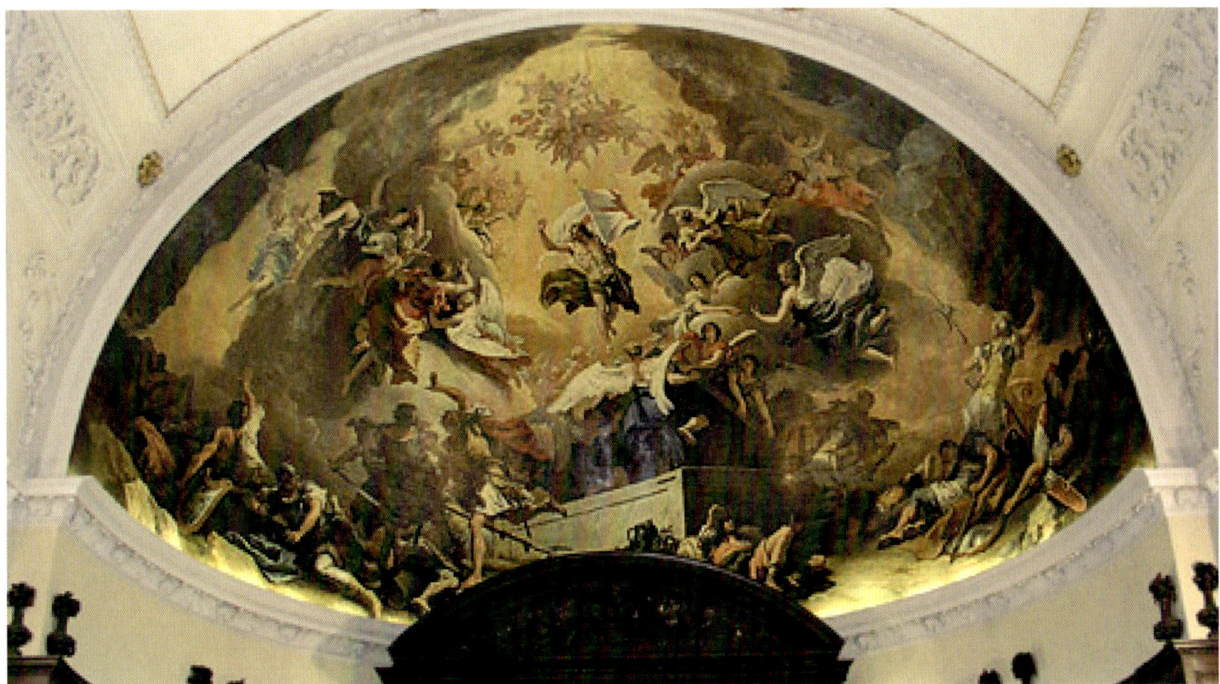

Fig. 4. Sebastiano Ricci (Italian, 1659–1734)
The Resurrection, 1714
Oil on plaster, dimensions unavailable
The Royal Hospital Chelsea, London

The heroes in paganism correspond exactly to the saints in popery. . . . The place of HERCULES, THESEUS, HECTOR, [and] ROMULUS, *is now supplied by* DOMINIC, FRANCIS, ANTHONY, AND BENEDICT . . . *whippings and fastings, cowardice and humility, abject submission and slavish obedience, are become the means of obtaining celestial honours among mankind.*[12]

Unable to honor Catholic saints on English soil, Ricci responded to his two requests by portraying key moments in Christ's life.

Ricci was asked to decorate two Protestant chapels, one private and the other semipublic. At Bulstrode House in Buckinghamshire, the seat of Henry Bentinck, first Duke of Portland, he created depictions of the Baptism, Last Supper, and Ascension; because the original Bulstrode structures no longer stand, these works are known today only through extant oil sketches.[13] Ricci's second English undertaking was *The Resurrection* (fig. 4), painted for the apse of the chapel at the Royal Hospital in Chelsea. King George I had commissioned this work to commemorate his predecessor, the recently deceased Queen Anne, whose father and uncle—Charles II and James II, respectively—had initiated construction of the hospital complex in the 1680s. Ricci executed a powerfully dramatic piece, undoubtedly recognizing the importance of the Royal Hospital, not to mention his own significance as the first representative of the Venetian artistic tradition to work at the English court.

The Resurrection vividly demonstrates Ricci's thorough knowledge of Italian art, gained from his earlier itinerant career and enriched by the brilliant brushwork typical of Venetian painting. He based his composition on Annibale Carracci's 1593 altarpiece in Bologna of the same subject, in which Christ,

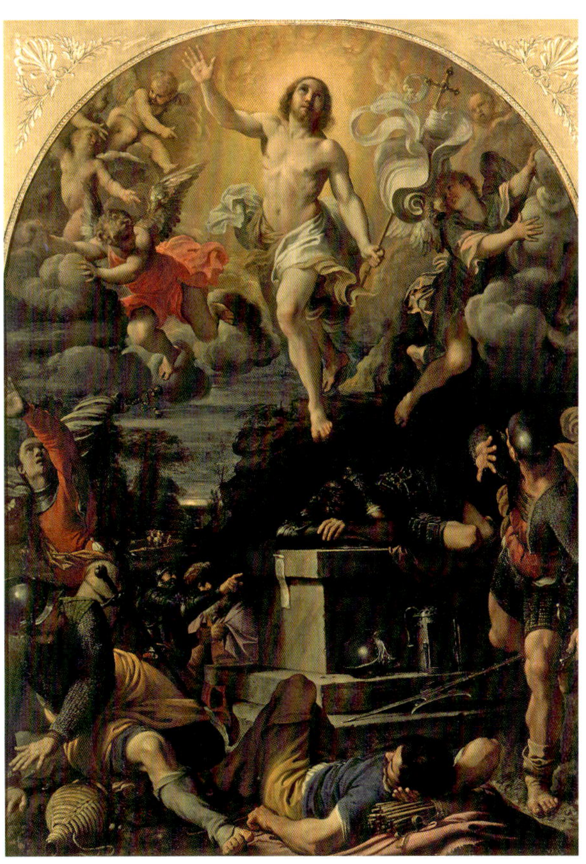

Fig. 5. Annibale Carracci (Italian, 1560–1609)
The Resurrection of Christ, 1593
Oil on canvas, 85 x 63 in. (217 x 160 cm)
Musée du Louvre, Paris

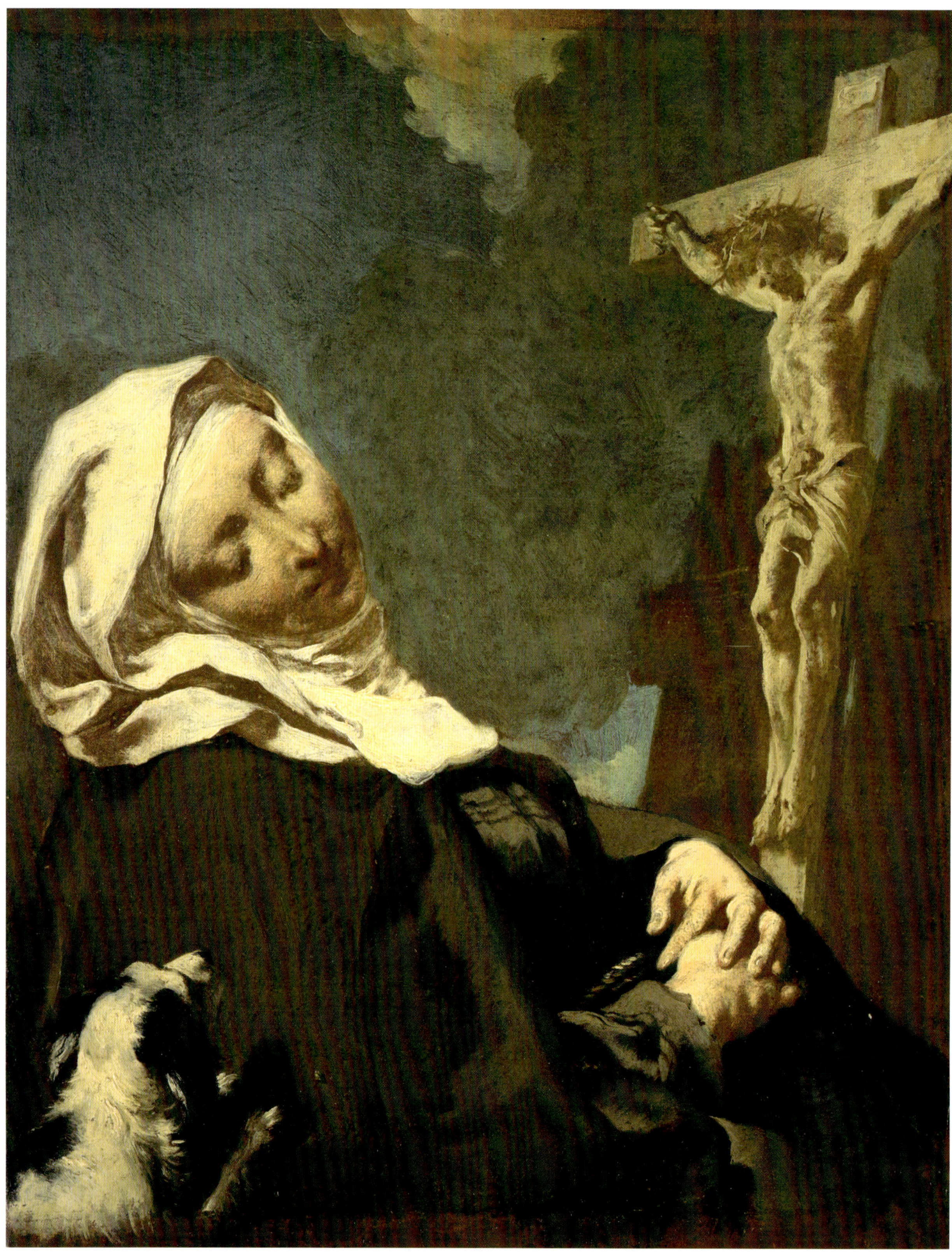

Fig. 6. Giovanni Battista Piazzetta (Italian, 1683–1754)
Saint Margaret of Cortona, 1737
Oil on canvas, 15 1/4 x 12 1/8 in. (38.7 x 30.8 cm)
Bequest of Lore Heinemann in memory of her husband, Dr. Rudolf J. Heinemann, National Gallery of Art, Washington, 1997.57.9

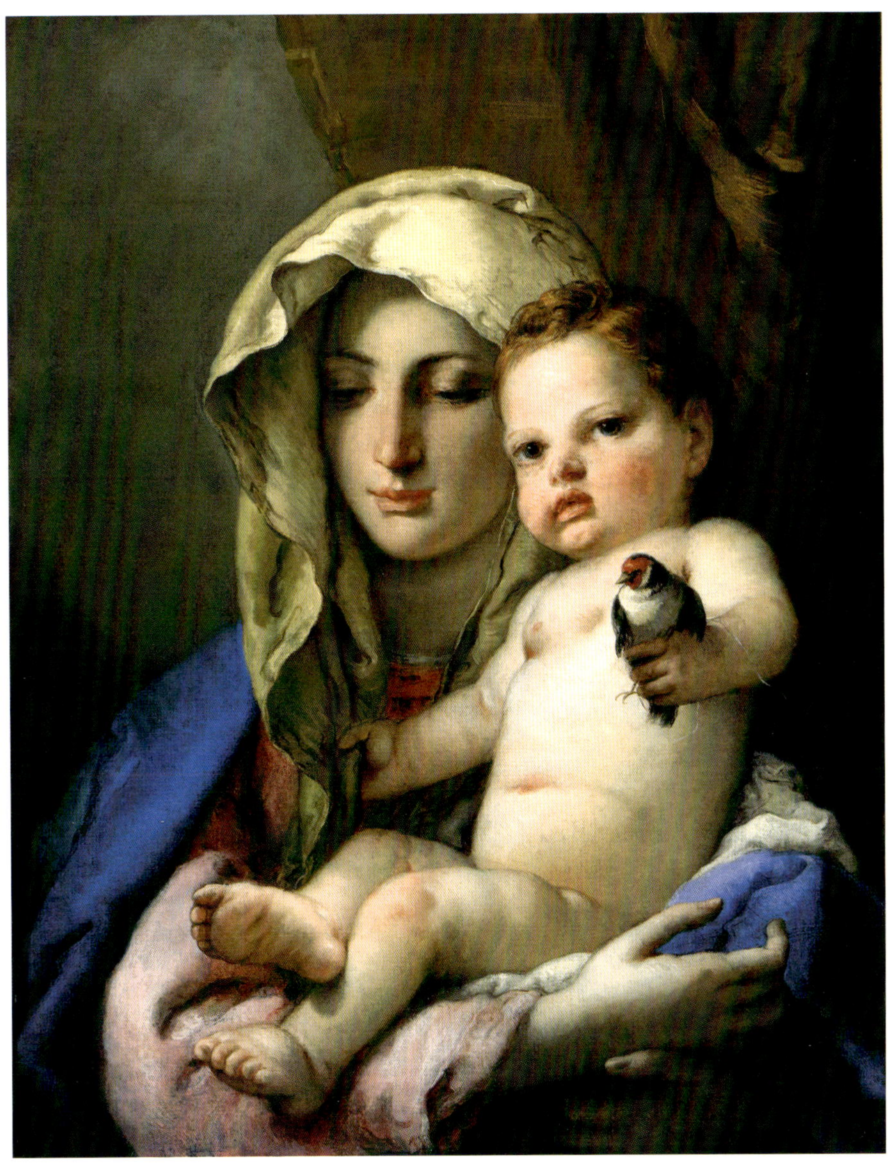

Fig. 7. Giambattista Tiepolo (Italian, 1696–1770)
Madonna of the Goldfinch, ca. 1767-70
Oil on canvas, 24 7/8 x 19 13/16 in. (63.1 x 50.3 cm)
Samuel H. Kress Collection, National Gallery of Art, Washington, 1943.4.40

surrounded by angels, ascends above five soldiers who form a U-like arrangement (fig. 5).[14] Rather than emulating the vertical thrust of Carracci's work, Ricci envisioned a broad scene bursting horizontally over the altar area.[15] *The Resurrection* posed both a social and an artistic challenge, because the chapel in Chelsea served not ordinary parishioners but wounded and handicapped war veterans supported by the British Crown. Ricci honored their presence by animating the composition with numerous military figures witnessing Jesus' miraculous return to life. This conceit enabled worshipers to appreciate divine redemption, made visible through Christ's resurrection, while also observing the portrayed soldiers watching the miracle as it happened. Ricci effected his striking concept and dramatic composition with brushwork that sweeps across the architectural surface, creating an artistic whirlwind typical of his great Catholic works but

never previously seen in London.

Neither Piazzetta nor Tiepolo ever worked for Protestant patrons, although the latter did paint outside Italy—in Bavaria and Spain.[16] As artists who typically articulated Catholic piety, both executed small works meant for intimate domestic contemplation as well as large altarpieces for churches such as Sta. Maria del Rosario. A painting of private devotion, Piazzetta's *St. Margaret of Cortona* (fig. 6) represents a thirteenth-century Tuscan woman who lived out of wedlock with a young nobleman and bore his child. News of his murder, and her consequent release from sin, came first with the unexpected return of his hunting dog, shown at the bottom left of the canvas.[17] She subsequently renounced all her possessions, became a Franciscan tertiary, and mortified her flesh. After Pope Benedict XIII canonized Margaret in 1728, a female Franciscan tertiary presumably commissioned Piazzetta to portray the newly sanctified woman. The artist shows Margaret falling backward as if overcome by a vision of the Crucifixion, her clasped hands signifying that prayer and meditation have brought her to spiritual rapture.[18] Within a constricted space, Piazzetta contrasted the saint's obliquely inclined figure with the upright cross that bears her Savior; Margaret's Franciscan habit and the simple fence on the right attest to her ascetic life. A golden cloud descending across the blue sky suggests Margaret's spiritual freedom and her intention to transcend the material world. Whoever commissioned the work unquestionably found it a powerful aid in personal devotion.

Tiepolo has been called "the presiding genius" of eighteenth-century Venetian art.[19] Although such a characterization is simplistic, his art does, in fact, combine the best elements found in the paintings of his two older colleagues—joining the rich coloration and seductive beauty of Ricci's canvases with the emotional depth and intense drama of Piazzetta's imagery. Tiepolo's *Madonna of the Goldfinch* (fig. 7) is, like Piazzetta's *St. Margaret of Cortona*, a work of private devotion.[20] The title refers to the bird in the Christ Child's hand; in Christian iconography, this is an emblem for the crown of thorns. The goldfinch reputedly eats thistles, an act that denotes Christ's Passion and his willingness to sacrifice himself for mankind. Cradled in the arms of his wistful mother, the infant gravely proffers the symbol of his earthly suffering. Tiepolo captures a somber moment but does so by conjoining delicate pinks and rich reds with the dazzling fold and precious blue of Mary's veil and robe. The radiantly colored mother and son likewise contrast with the darkened world behind them, thus suggesting both the possibility and the mystery of Christian salvation.

By the eighteenth century, Venice's formidable affluence, might, and international influence had all but disappeared. Yet foreigners still flocked to the fabled city to sample the worldly pleasures available there. Most Venetians, however, continued to be wholeheartedly committed to their Catholic religion—its rituals, dogma, and saints. Numerous ecclesiastical construction sites throughout the city and the abundance of exquisite works of art adorning church altars were tangible signs of its residents' piety. Devout Venetians responded to calls for alms to finance the beautification of church interiors, and their more affluent contemporaries, following time-honored Catholic custom, commissioned private works of art for personal devotion. Indeed, the question of whether eighteenth-century Venice was a devout city must be answered not by recalling the notorious and infamous

but by walking its streets, entering its churches, and contemplating its religious imagery.

NOTES

1. Two fundamental histories of Venice written in English are Lane 1973 and Norwich 1982.

2. This number is derived from the lists in Lewis 1979, 3–10.

3. Tivaroni 1888, 32–33, wrote that religious personnel in Venice (including Conventuals) numbered 37,910 in a total population of 139,095. Préclin and Jarry 1955–56, 85, noted that in the whole of the Veneto in 1766 there were 22,307 priests in a population of 2,334,972. And Georgelin 1978, 740, reported that in that same year Venice had one priest for every fifty-four inhabitants.

4. The assertion about Venice's eager and rapt worshipers was made by both Francesco Zanotto 1989, 322, and da Nembro 1958, 117–30.

5. Two books focusing on life in eighteenth-century Venice are Andrieux 1972 and Georgelin 1978.

6. One exception was the façade of Sta. Maria della Visitazione, also called the Church of the Pietà (located on the Riva degli Schiavoni near the Hotel Danieli), which was not finished until the twentieth century.

7. For Piazzetta, Ricci, and Tiepolo and their works in this church, see Niero and Rugolo 2006.

8. The Italian Thomas Aquinas (1225–1274) was the great Dominican theologian of the late Middle Ages (Farmer 1983, 375–76); Pius V (1504–1572) was a Dominican friar who was elevated to the papacy in 1565 (idem, 330–31); and Peter of Verona was a Dominican friar and priest who, after his murder for persecuting members of the Manichaean heresy, became revered as the first martyr of the Dominican order (idem, 326).

9. Vincent Ferrer (1350–1419) was a renowned Dominican friar and missionary (also famous for his anti-Semitism) who worked to breach the Great Schism between the Roman Catholic and Eastern Orthodox churches (Farmer 1983, 392–93). The Spaniard Louis Bertrand (1526–1581) was a Dominican missionary who worked in what is now Colombia (www.newadvent.org/cathen/09376b.htm). The Polish-born Hyacinth (1185–1257) knew St. Dominic and received the habit of his order from Dominic's own hands (www.newadvent.org/cathen/07591b.htm).

10. It should be noted that Ricci, Piazzetta, and Tiepolo were almost certainly following requests made by their Dominican patrons regarding the saints who would appear in each altarpiece. Catherine of Siena (ca. 1340–1380) belonged to the Dominicans' third order and was famed for her involvement in Church politics (Farmer 1983, 370–72). Rose of Lima (1586–1617) joined the third order, taking Catherine of Siena as her model and becoming the first saint of the New World (idem, 349 and www.newadvent.org/cathen/13192c.htm). Agnes of Montepulciano (ca. 1268–1317) established a convent

for Dominican nuns in her Tuscan hometown (www.newadvent.org/cathen/01213c.htm).

11. Returning to Venice from London in 1716, Ricci stopped in Paris and was inducted into the French Royal Academy.

12. David Hume, "The Natural History of Religion" in Wollheim 1964, 68.

13. For the Bulstrode House commission, see Garberson in De Grazia and Garberson 1996, 230–36.

14. Posner 1971, 2: 31–32 (cat. 73 and fig. 73).

15. Two Ricci preparatory oil sketches for the Chelsea commission are in the collections of the Dulwich Picture Gallery, London, and the Columbia (South Carolina) Museum of Art (see cat. 6). Since they are quite similar to each other and to the completed painting, it is not possible to trace a linear progression from one sketch to another or to the work in the hospital chapel. There are several possible explanations for these virtually duplicate pictorial drafts: 1) Ricci had to satisfy several patrons (in the case of Chelsea, he might have had to submit sketches both to a hospital committee and to a representative of the Crown); 2) he planned to sell one of them; or 3) he intended to carry one back to Venice as a *ricordo*, or recollection, of the English commission.

16. Tiepolo worked for the Prince-Archbishop of Würzburg in Bavaria between December 1750 and 1753, and for the Spanish royal family in Madrid between spring 1762 and his death there in March 1770.

17. Mariuz and Pallucchini 1982, 93 (cat. 74, as formerly in the Tommasi Collection); the painting entered the collection of the National Gallery of Art, Washington, D.C., in 1997. For St. Margaret, see www.newadvent.org/cathen/09653b.htm.

18. Piazzetta configured the saint somewhat in the manner of Gianlorenzo Bernini's *Blessed Ludovica Albertoni* (ca. 1675), which is in the Church of S. Francesco della Ripa, Rome.

19. This term is the title of the final chapter of Levey 1994. Levey uses it in order to characterize Tiepolo historically.

20. Garberson in De Grazia and Garberson 1996, 285–89.

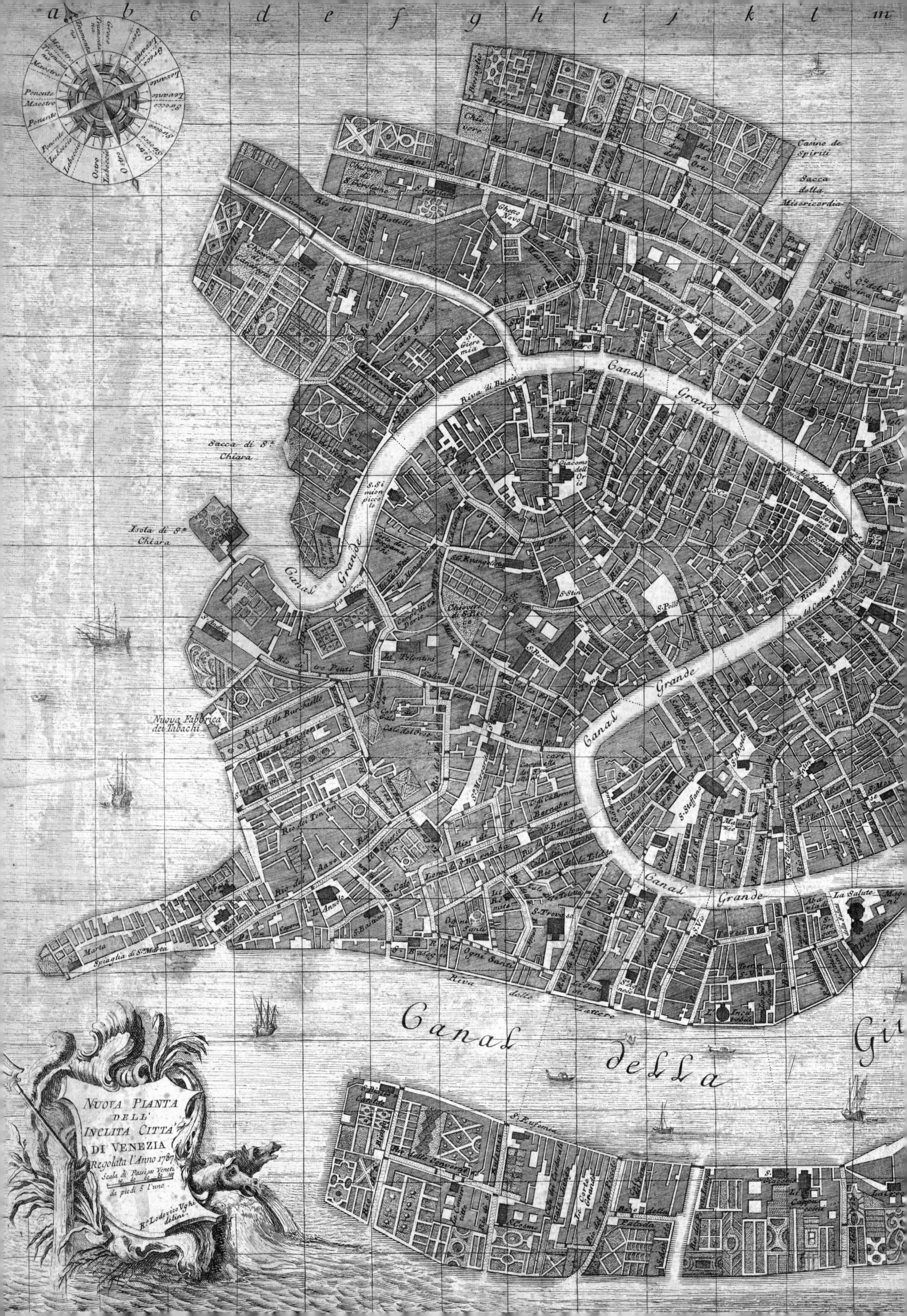

a b c d e f g h i l k l m
Tramontana
Greco Levante
Maestro
Ponente Maestro
Ponente
Ponente Ostro
Ostro
Casino de Spiriti
Sacca della Misericordia
Ghetto Novo
Canal Grande
Rio del
Sacca di S.ta Chiara
Isola di S.ta Chiara
Canal Grande
Riva di Biasio
S. Simon picolo
S. Giacomo dell'Orio
S. Stin
S. Polo
S. Rocco
Canal Grande
Nuova Fabbrica dei Tabachi
Rio delle Burchielle
Il Tolentini
Canal Grande
S. Angelo
S. Stefano
Rio del Tentori
S. Bernaba
Rio di S. Barnaba
Longo di S. Barnaba
Canal Grande
L'Anzolo
S. Trovaso
La Salute
Marta
Spiaglia di S.ta Marta
Riva delle Zattere
Canal della Giu
S. Eufemia
Canal della
NUOVA PIANTA DELL' INCLITA CITTA' DI VENEZIA
Regolata l'Anno 1787
Scala di Passi 500 Veneti da piedi 5 l'uno
F. Lodovico Ughi delin.

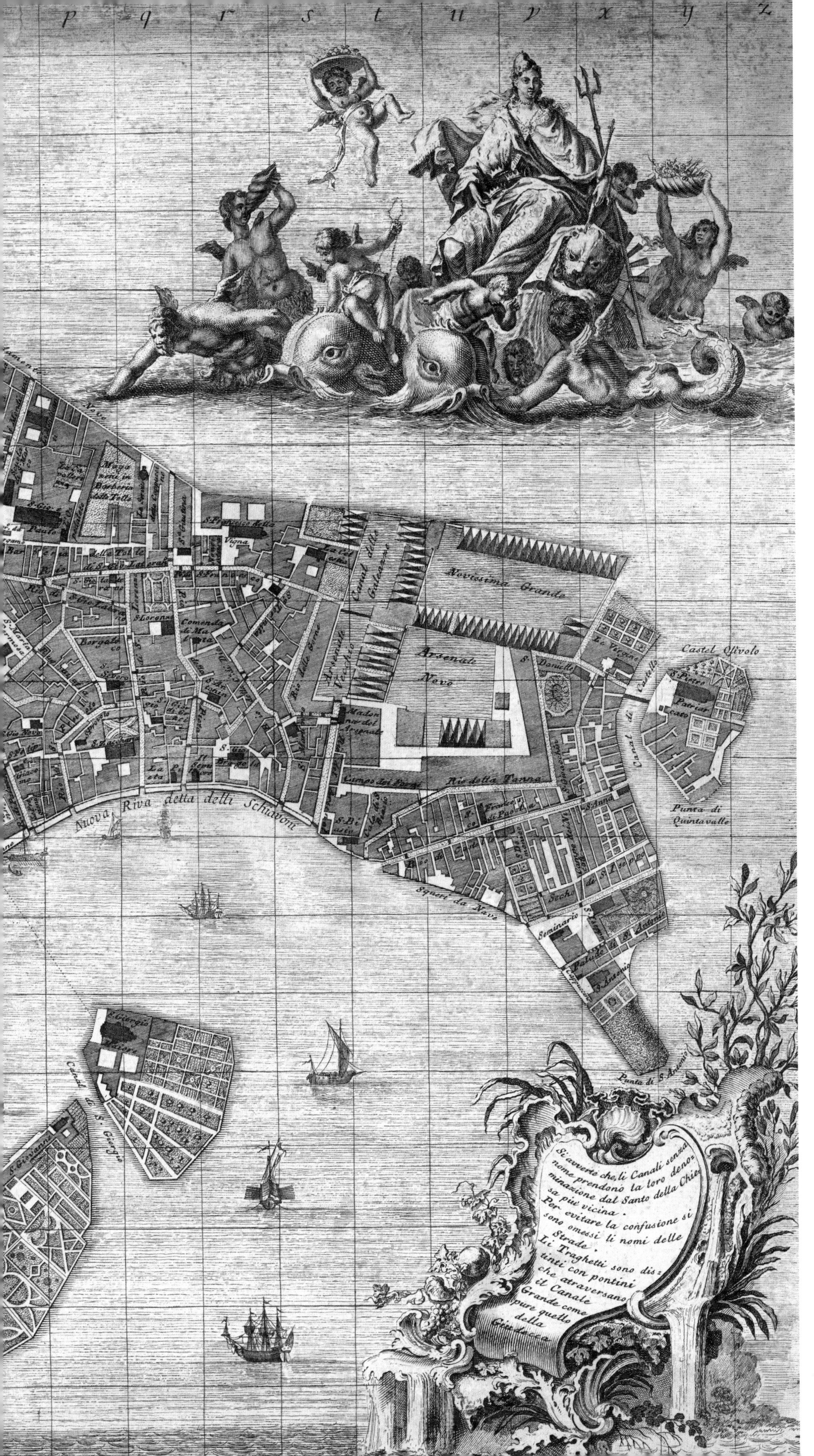

Ludovico Ughi
Nuova pianta dell'inclita citta di Venezia recolata l'anno 1787
(Venice: Ludovico Lurlanetto Press, 1787)
19 ½ x 26 ¾ in. (49.5 x 68 cm)
Image Courtesy of The American Philosophical Society, Philadelphia

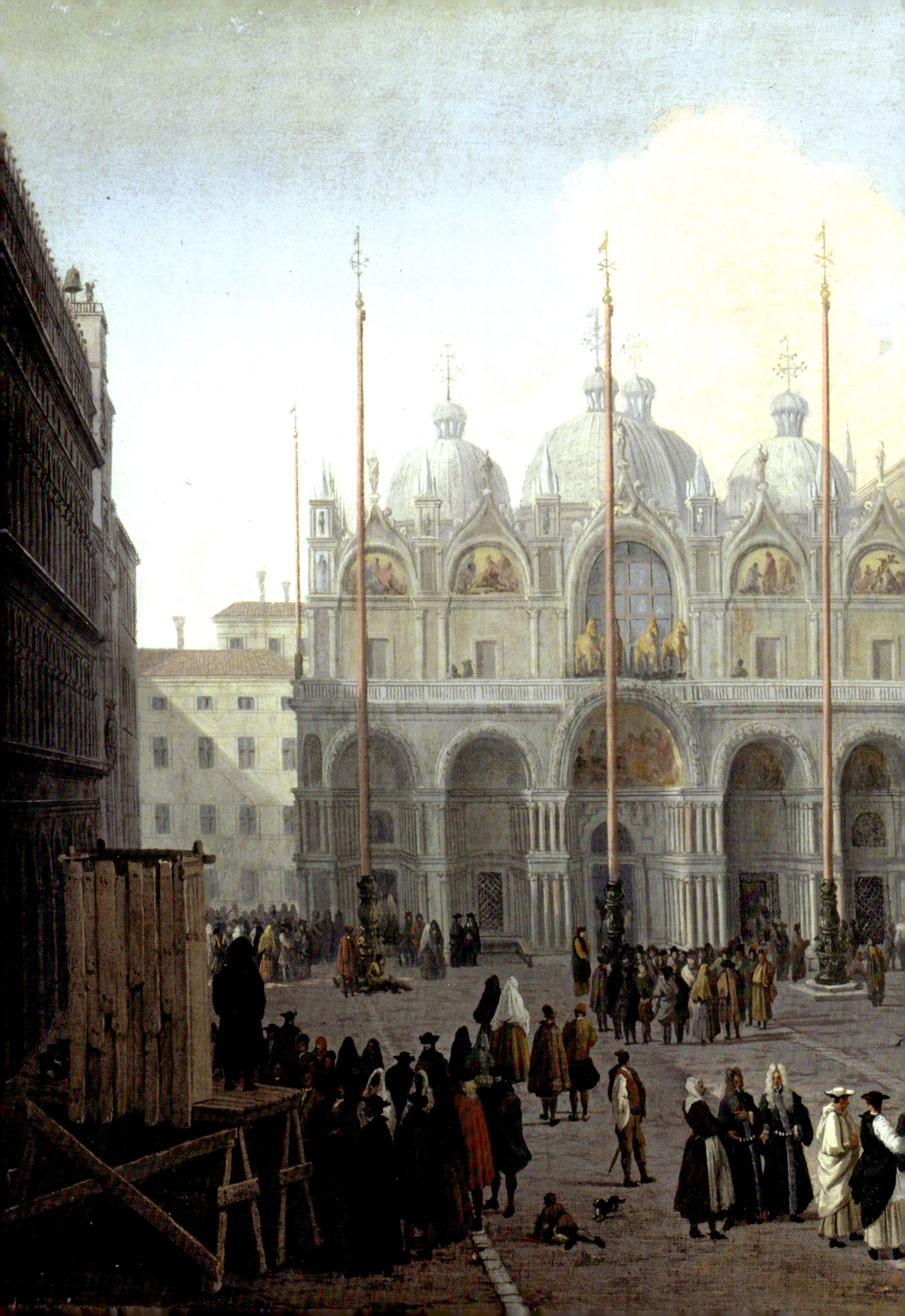

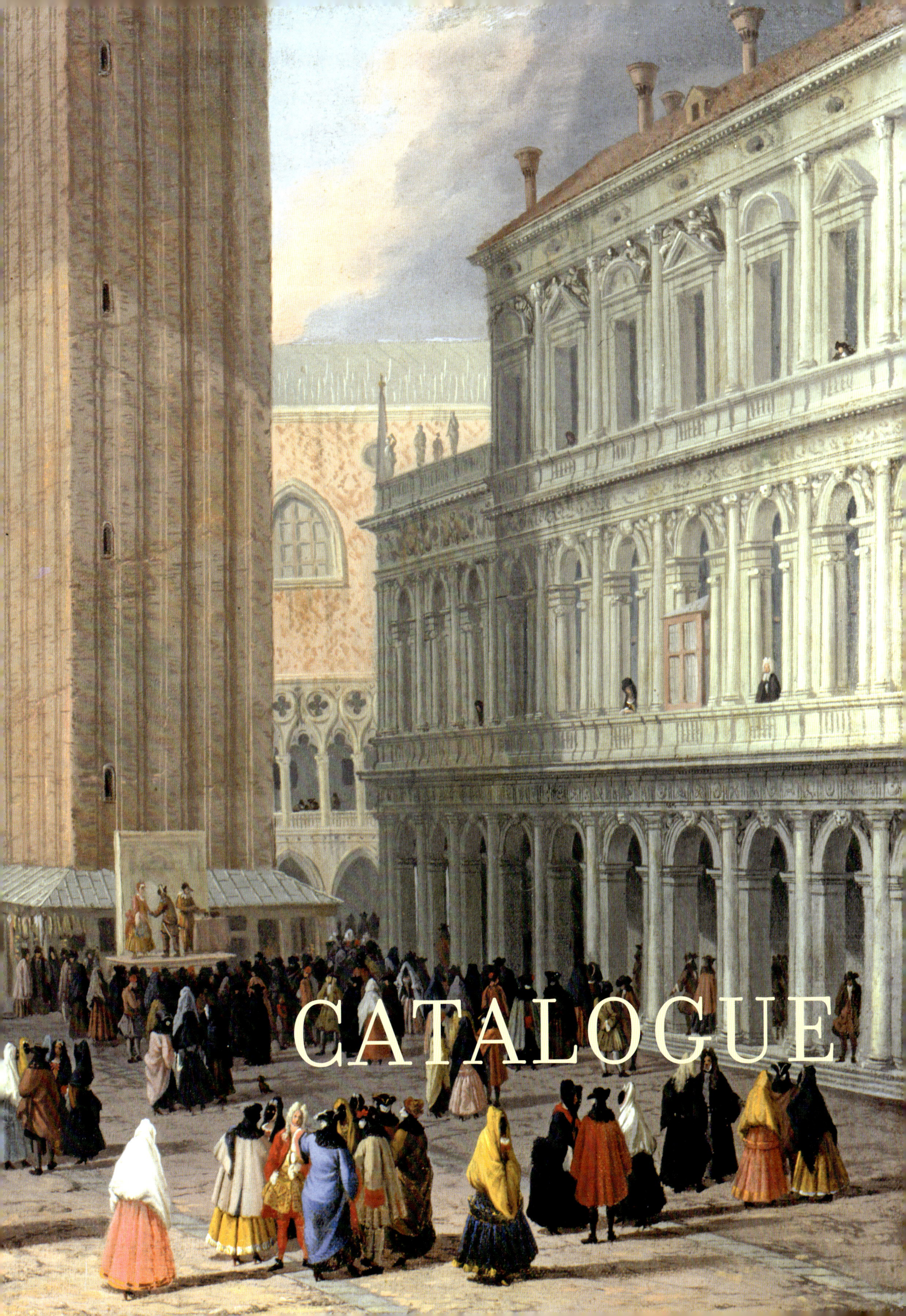
CATALOGUE

1. Sebastiano Ricci, 1659–1734
   The Battle of the Lapiths and Centaurs, ca. 1705
   Oil on canvas, 54 1/2 x 69 5/8 in. (138.4 x 176.8 cm)
   High Museum of Art, Atlanta; Gift of the Samuel H. Kress Foundation, 58.55

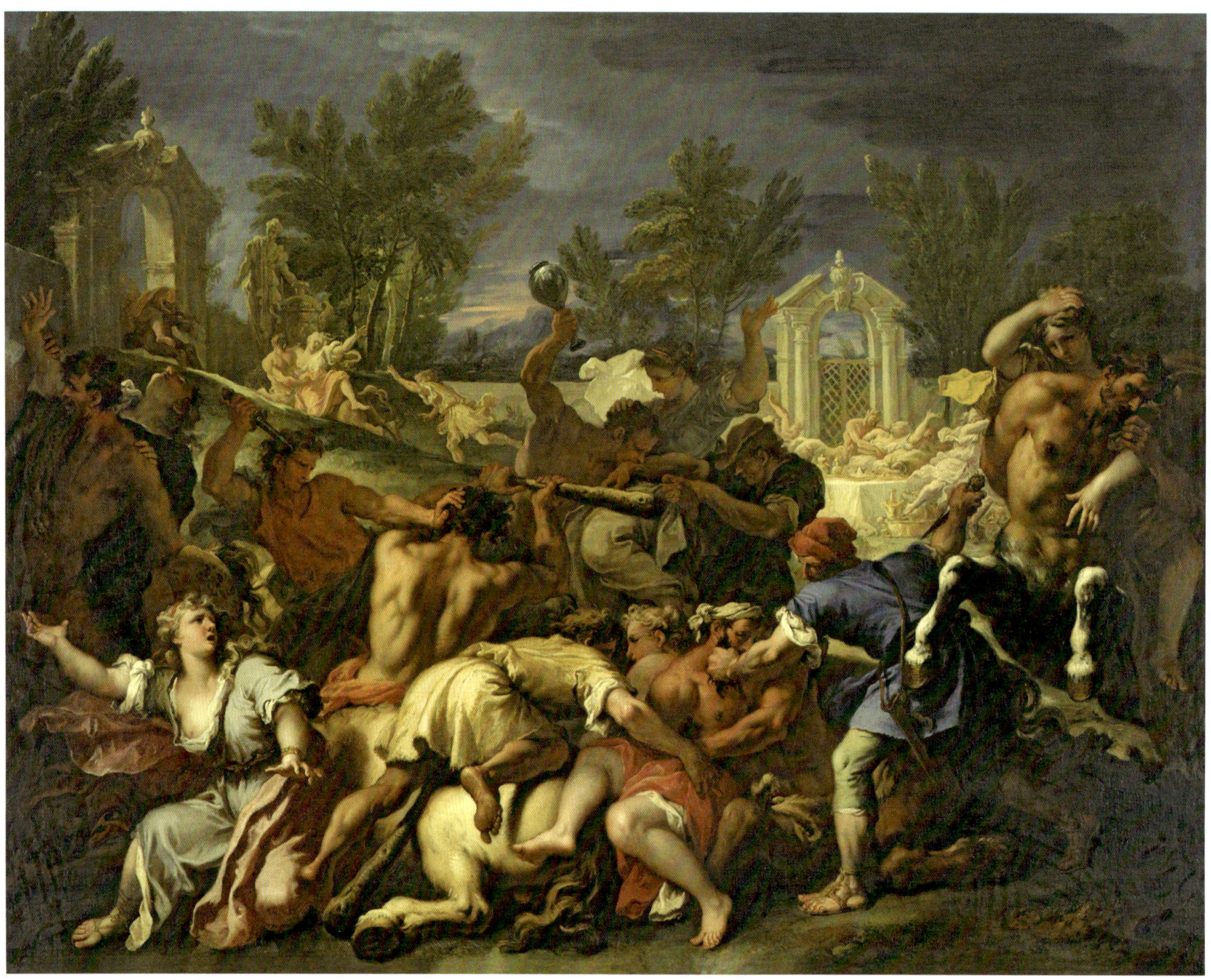

In classical mythology, Centaurs—creatures half horse and half man—symbolized the tension between more bestial carnal desires and the power of the mind to reason and thus exercise moral control. More grandly, the battle of the Lapiths and Centaurs, an episode best known from book twelve of Ovid's *Metamorphoses*, reflects the age-old conflict between civilization and barbarity. In this tale, the Lapiths, a peaceful people of Thessaly, invite the Centaurs to celebrate the marriage of their king, Pirithous, to the maiden Hippodamia. During the wedding feast, Eurytus, one of the Centaurs, becomes drunk and lustily attempts to carry off the bride. A savage battle ensues, and the Centaurs are finally driven off with the help of the Greek hero Theseus.

Rather than focusing on blood and gore, as many of his artistic predecessors had done, Ricci interprets the event as an epic clash of heroic figures, their bodies contorted and straining amid an idyllic landscape. An emphatic diagonal divides the canvas into scenes taking place in the background and the foreground. The battle itself rages in the center foreground. To the right, a Centaur abducts a Lapith woman, while, on the left, another woman withdraws in terror. She gestures toward escape with one hand and, with the other, reaches out and draws the viewer into the scene. The main protagonists struggle in the background. On the right, Eurytus abducts Hippodamia, and on the left, Theseus pursues—ready to strike at the villainous Centaur.

This erudite painting contains many artistic references, especially to the overwrought poses of Hellenistic statuary and straining figures of Michelangelo as well as to the colors and compositional strategies of Venetian masters such as Tintoretto and Titian. Here, too, Ricci seeks to rival the Baroque splendor of the Neapolitan Luca Giordano (1632–1705), who exerted a strong influence upon his style.

The Battle of the Lapiths and Centaurs may be a pendant to Ricci's *The Contest Between Apollo and Pan Judged by King Midas* (fig. 1.1), which is based on another tale in Ovid's *Metamorphoses*. Both paintings are stylistically close to early works by Ricci, such as *The Rape of the Sabine Women* (1699), in the Palazzo Barbaro-Curtis, Venice. Indeed, the High Museum of Art picture is youthful and delightfully brazen compared to Ricci's more mature works of the 1720s. This early dating also highlights links to certain other influences, such as Pietro da Cortona (1596–1669).[1]

The Battle of the Lapiths and Centaurs is an outstanding example of a precocious artist absorbing the influences of various artistic forebears and displaying a unique style through his interpretation of a familiar classical subject. Ricci revels in the dramatic telling of the story and in using sensational color and dynamic composition to generate a sense of spectacle and awe.

AVC

Note

1. *The Contest Between Apollo and Pan Judged by King Midas*, which is in the collection of the Chrysler Museum of Art, Norfolk, Virginia, has recently been dated to this earlier period in Ricci's career. Its pairing with *The Battle of the Lapiths and Centaurs* is supported by the two paintings' evident stylistic similarities, nearly identical dimensions, and the fact that both of them were in Sir Richard Colthurst's collection before being separated on the art market. They were once thought to date to 1723, rather late in Ricci's career, based on presumed similarities to two paintings in Dresden. The earlier dating is now preferred. See Scarpa 2006, 143.

Provenance: Sir Richard Colthurst [1928–2003], Blarney Castle, County Cork, Ireland; David M. Koetser, New York, by 1953; Kress acquisition, 1953.

References: Suida 1958b, 53–55; Washington, D.C. 1961, 78; San Francisco 1964, no. 216; Milkovich in Memphis and Lexington 1965, no. 14; Suida 1965, 55; Shapley 1973, 128, K1955; Daniels 1976a, 1–2, no. 5; Daniels 1976b, no. 176; Scarpa 2006, 142–43, no. 6.

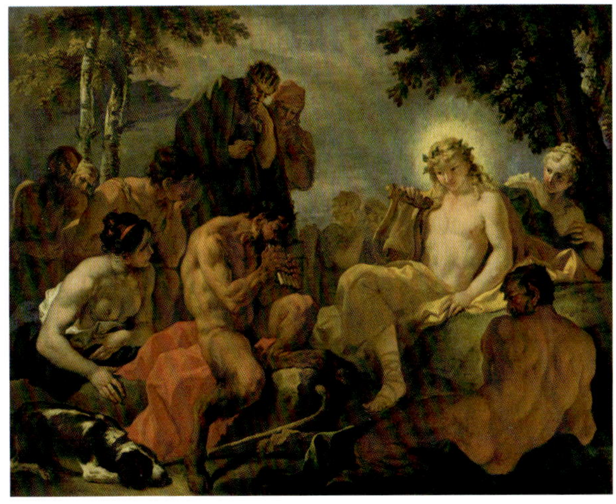

Fig. 1.1. Sebastiano Ricci
The Contest Between Apollo and Pan Judged by King Midas, ca. 1685 – 87
Oil on canvas, 53 1/2 x 68 1/4 in. (135.9 x 173.3 cm)
Gift of Walter P. Chrysler, Jr., Chrysler Museum of Art, Norfolk 71.696

2. Sebastiano Ricci, 1659–1734
   The Finding of Moses, ca. 1705–10
   Oil on canvas, 51 7/8 x 42 in. (131.8 x 106.7 cm)
   Memphis Brooks Museum of Art; Gift of the Samuel H. Kress Foundation, 61.204

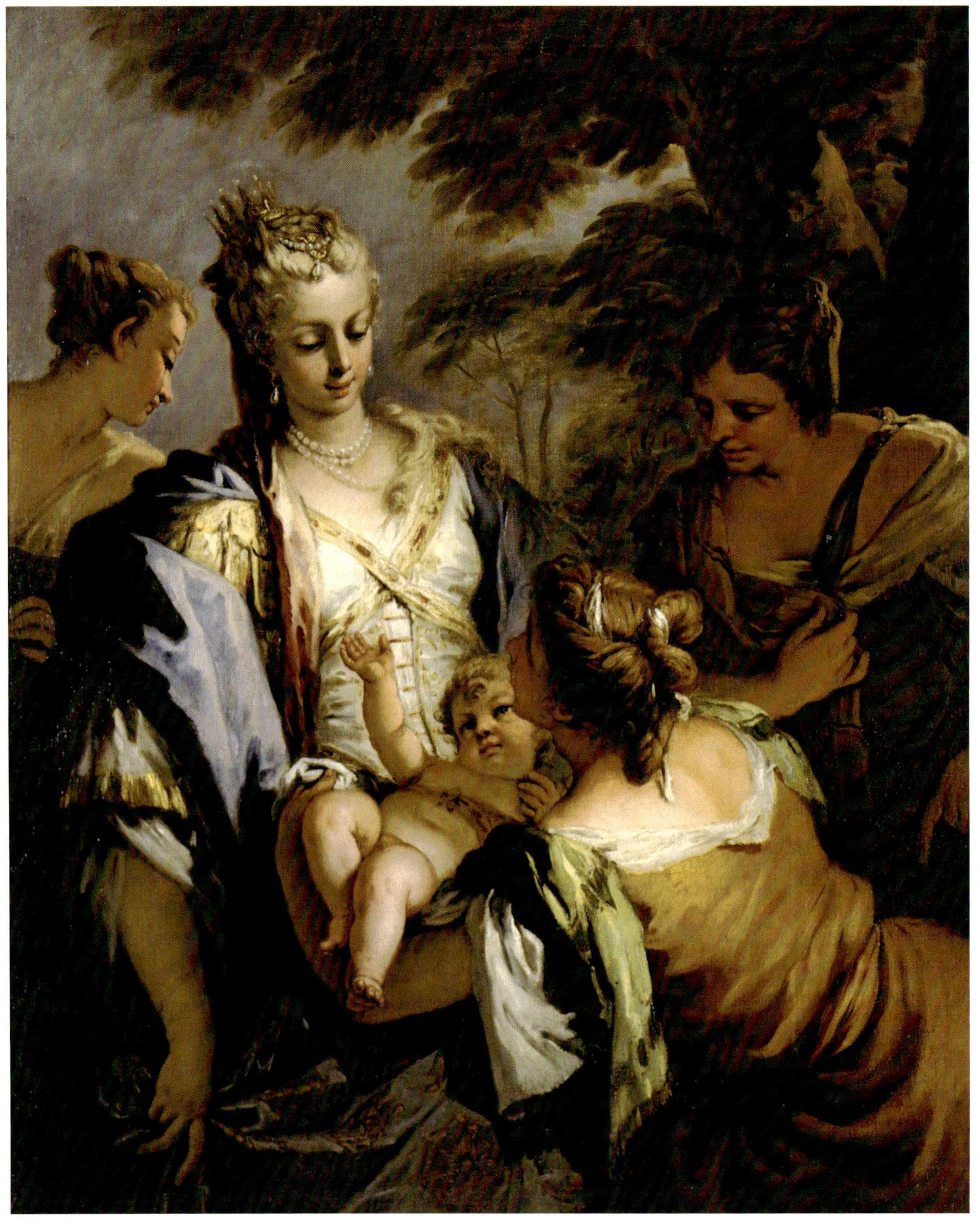

This familiar story is from the Old Testament book of Exodus, whose early chapters trace the Hebrews' long captivity in Egypt and their ultimate liberation from bondage. Fearing the growing numbers of Hebrews in his kingdom, the pharaoh orders that all their newborn sons be slain. To save her child from this fate, the mother of the infant Moses places him in a basket and sets it afloat on the Nile. The pharaoh's daughter discovers the baby as she approaches the river with her handmaids to bathe. Ricci's painting depicts the moment when, having sought a nursemaid, she unwittingly returns Moses to his own mother.

Ricci shows the pharaoh's daughter admiring the child. As befits her royal status, her neck, ears, and blond hair are adorned with splendid pearls, and she wears a golden crown. She is attired in sumptuous robes of marvelous blues, whites, and gold. In contrast, Moses' mother, shown receiving the child, is humbly dressed, primarily in yellow—a color often associated with Jews during the eighteenth century—and her hair is bound with a simple ribbon. Two attendants accompanying the ruler's daughter are coiffed similarly to each other, readying themselves to bathe, and wear garb indicating their status as handmaids. One of them appears to study the child with both wonder and a hint of trepidation. The other stands behind the princess, glancing back toward the Nile—a suggestion of nostalgia for the immediate past, from which the event unfolding here will irretrievably separate them all.

The Finding of Moses demonstrates how Ricci, with seeming effortlessness, could imbue a familiar biblical event with unusual majesty and drama. In part, the painting is a virtuoso essay in color and texture, displaying the artist's ability to capture the essence of cloth, hair, and flesh, here set against a sketchy yet beautiful Venetian landscape. Strong diagonals lend movement to the composition, complementing the rich tonalities and textures and guiding the viewer among the faces of its five characters.

Both this work and its presumed pendant, *Jephthah and His Daughter* (cat. 3), reflect Ricci's deep admiration for the sixteenth-century Venetian master Paolo Veronese, who executed several depictions of the same subject. One of these may have inspired Ricci's interpretation, especially the canvas now in Dresden that came from the Casa Grimaldi de' Servi, Venice, or a similar version that is now in the Museo Nacional del Prado (fig. 2.1). In particular, the pose of the princess in the latter painting and its subtle harmonies of whites, greens, and gold are echoed in the present canvas. However, Ricci's *The Finding of Moses* is neither a copy nor a variant of the earlier artist's work. Instead it is a fresh interpretation, which at once

respects and rivals that of his Venetian predecessor in its dramatic telling of the biblical tale. Whereas Veronese's composition is expansive, Ricci's is closely cropped and more focused. This tighter format, free of tangential figures and details, allows Ricci to explore the emotional aspects of the story, which centers on revelation and acceptance. Indeed, although Ricci himself painted several versions of this subject, none is as poignantly dramatic as the Memphis Brooks Museum of Art's picture.[1]

Scholars have assigned *The Finding of Moses* and *Jephthah and His Daughter* a range of dates between 1705 and 1710.[2] The question of dating cannot be securely resolved, but based on their style the works assuredly belong to this period, which coincided with Christopher Crowe's consulship at Livorno (Leghorn) and was a time of rich artistic activity for Ricci. During these years he was painting principally in Venice and Florence, and his works were becoming known across Europe.

AVC

Notes

1. Other versions attributed to Ricci are in the collection of General E. Caviglia, Genoa; the Royal Collection, London; the National Gallery of Australia, Melbourne; the Palazzo Taverna, Rome; and the Palazzo Reale, Turin. All these works include several additional figures and extensive landscapes and settings.

2. The pair of paintings in the Memphis Brooks Museum of Art collection are probably contemporary with a group of canvases from the collection of Don Carlo Pannizza that are now in the Galleria Nazionale, Parma, dated to around 1705. See Scarpa 2006, 271–75, nos. 363–71.

Provenance: Possibly Christopher Crowe [1682–1749], Kiplin Hall, Richmond, North Yorkshire; possibly by descent to Sarah Talbot Carpenter [1876-1957]; thence to her husband Christopher Turnor [1873-1940], Stoke Rochford Hall, Grantham, Lincolnshire; Arturo Grassi, New York, 1947–50; Ars Antiqua, New York, 1950; Kress acquisition 1950.

References: Louisville 1948, no. 20; Suida 1950, 18, no. 18; Suida 1958a, 44; *Connoisseur* 1961, 286, ill.; Milkovich in Memphis and Lexington 1965, 13, no. 10; Pilo 1966, 305; Shapley 1973, 126, no. K1703; Daniels 1976a, 70–71, 223a; Daniels 1976b, no. 187; Memphis 1984, 66; Raleigh et al. 1994, 211, no. 37; Memphis 2004, 85; Scarpa 2006, 236–37 no. 267.

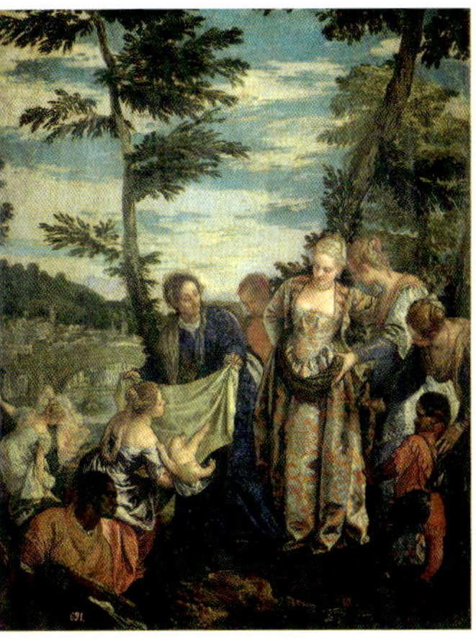

Fig. 2.1. Paolo Veronese
Moses Saved from the Waters, ca. 1575–85
Oil on canvas, 22 7/16 x 16 15/16 in. (57 x 43 cm)
Museo Nacional del Prado, Madrid

3. Sebastiano Ricci, 1659–1734
Jephthah and His Daughter, ca. 1705–10
Oil on canvas, 52 5/8 x 43 1/8 in. (133.7 x 109.5 cm)
Memphis Brooks Museum of Art; Gift of the Samuel H. Kress Foundation, 61.205

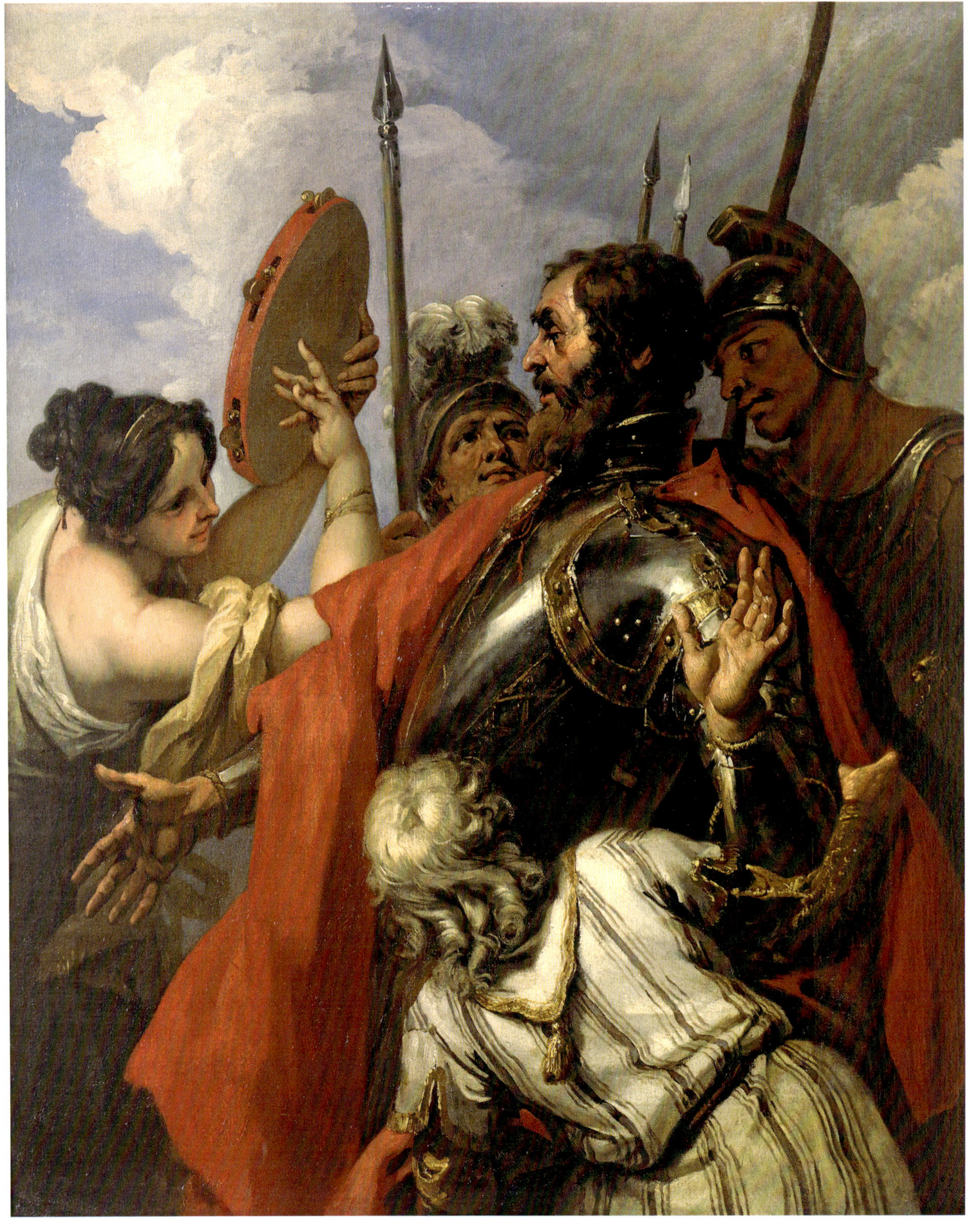

The Old Testament tale of Jephthah, set during a time of war between the Israelites and the Ammonites, is told in the book of Judges. Preparing to do battle, Jephthah vows to the Lord that, if triumphant, he will offer up the first living creature to emerge from his house as a burnt sacrifice. He routs the enemy, but the cost of this victory soon becomes apparent on his homecoming:

> *When Jephthah arrived at his home at Mizpah, there was his daughter coming out to meet him, with timbrel and dance! She was an only child; he had no other son or daughter* (Judges 11:34).

Ricci depicts the heartrending moment when the triumphant warrior, still clad in armor, sees his daughter joyfully rush out to greet him. Throwing up his hands, he recoils upon realizing the consequence of his promise to God.

The meticulously rendered facial expressions reinforce the unfolding tragedy. Ricci contrasts Jephthah's shocked visage with the joyous innocence of his daughter's. As in *The Finding of Moses* (cat. 2), which is almost certainly the pendant to this picture, ancillary figures play an important role in helping to focus the viewer's attention and underscore the drama of the scene. In this case, two soldiers stoically gaze at their leader, not at his daughter, since they know of his vow and await his decision whether or not to honor it. Similarly, an attendant—depicted foreshortened and with his back toward the viewer— looks up at Jephthah in anticipation of the warrior's reaction.

Jephthah and His Daughter serves as a mournful counterpoint to the fortuitous outcome of the story depicted in *The Finding of Moses*.[1] Both works involve moral choices by adults that determine the fate of children: Jephthah will honor his, even though it means sacrificing his only child, while the pharaoh's daughter will defy her father's decree in order to save an infant. Their pairing prompts the viewer to consider the implications of faith, family, and fate.

Although nothing is known of the original setting for these works, or who may have commissioned them, tradition holds that they belonged to Christopher Crowe. The British consul in Livorno (Leghorn) from 1705 to 1716, Crowe acted as an agent for collectors in England and amassed an impressive group of paintings himself that he later displayed at Kiplin Hall in North Yorkshire.[2] These rather large pictures may have been intended to adorn either side of a window or doorway or perhaps a space in a private chapel.

Their similar compositional devices and use of color strengthen the supposition that *Jephthah and His Daughter* and *The Finding of Moses* are pendant works.

For example, each picture includes five individuals, four of whom focus their attentions on a single, central protagonist—one male and the other female. In addition, Jephthah and the pharaoh's daughter counterbalance each other in their respective movements and reactions. Also, the warrior's attendant and Moses' mother share similar poses, and both emerge from the lower-right-hand corner of each picture. The predominant colors of the two canvases are contrasting rather than complementary. For instance, Ricci sets a rich, saturated red against metallic grays in his portrayal of Jephthah but relies on a palette of rich browns, blues, and greens in *The Finding of Moses*. His use of color underscores the themes of each painting—for example, vivid red to suggest the bloody fate of Jephthah's daughter but cool, tranquil tonalities to capture the story of the baby Moses' rescue.

Although this is Ricci's only known depiction of the Jephthah story, a rare theme in the eighteenth century, the figure of its protagonist is closely related to the artist's circa 1700 image of Mars in a nine-panel ceiling decoration he created for the Palazzo Mecenigo-Robilant, Venice, that is now in the Gemäldegalerie, Berlin (fig. 3.1).[3] Ricci's likeness of the Roman god of war is practically a mirror image of Jephthah—both are clad in armor and gesture with open arms—and it offers a classical thematic counterpart to the biblical warrior.

AVC

Notes

1. Although *Jephthah and His Daughter* and *The Finding of Moses* (cat. 2) were likely created as a pair, it is also possible they were part of a larger decorative scheme. In particular, Daniels (1976a, 70, nos. 223a, 223b) noted that the two canvases might have been over-door paintings, adding that they were "probably painted as pendants."

2. For a biographical sketch of Crowe and brief history of Kiplin Hall, see Museums, Libraries, and Archives Council 2008, 12.

3. For Ricci's *The Olympian Gods: Mars*, see Scarpa 2006, 156, no. 43; and Daniels 1976, 16, no. 51. The facial expression in a bust-length painting now in a Swiss private collection is, in expression, less evocative than Jephthah but similar in physiognomy; the work could have easily served as a *modello*, or detailed study, for the completed figure. See Scarpa 2006, 236, no. 268 and fig. 269.

Provenance: Possibly Christopher Crowe [1682–1749], Kiplin Hall, Richmond, North Yorkshire; possibly by descent to Sarah Talbot Carpenter [1876-1957]; thence to her husband Christopher Turnor [1873-1940], Stoke Rochford Hall, Grantham, Lincolnshire; Arturo Grassi, New York, 1947–50; Ars Antiqua, New York, 1950; Kress acquisition, 1950.

References: Louisville 1948, no. 21 (as *The Greeting of Saul*); Suida 1950, 19, no. 19; Suida 1958a, 46; Milkovich in Memphis and Lexington 1965, 14, no. 11; Pilo 1966, 305; Shapley 1973, 126; Daniels 1976a, 70, no. 223b; Daniels 1976b, no. 188; Memphis 1984, 66; Raleigh et al. 1994, 211, no. 38; Memphis 2004, 85; Scarpa 2006, 236–37, no. 268.

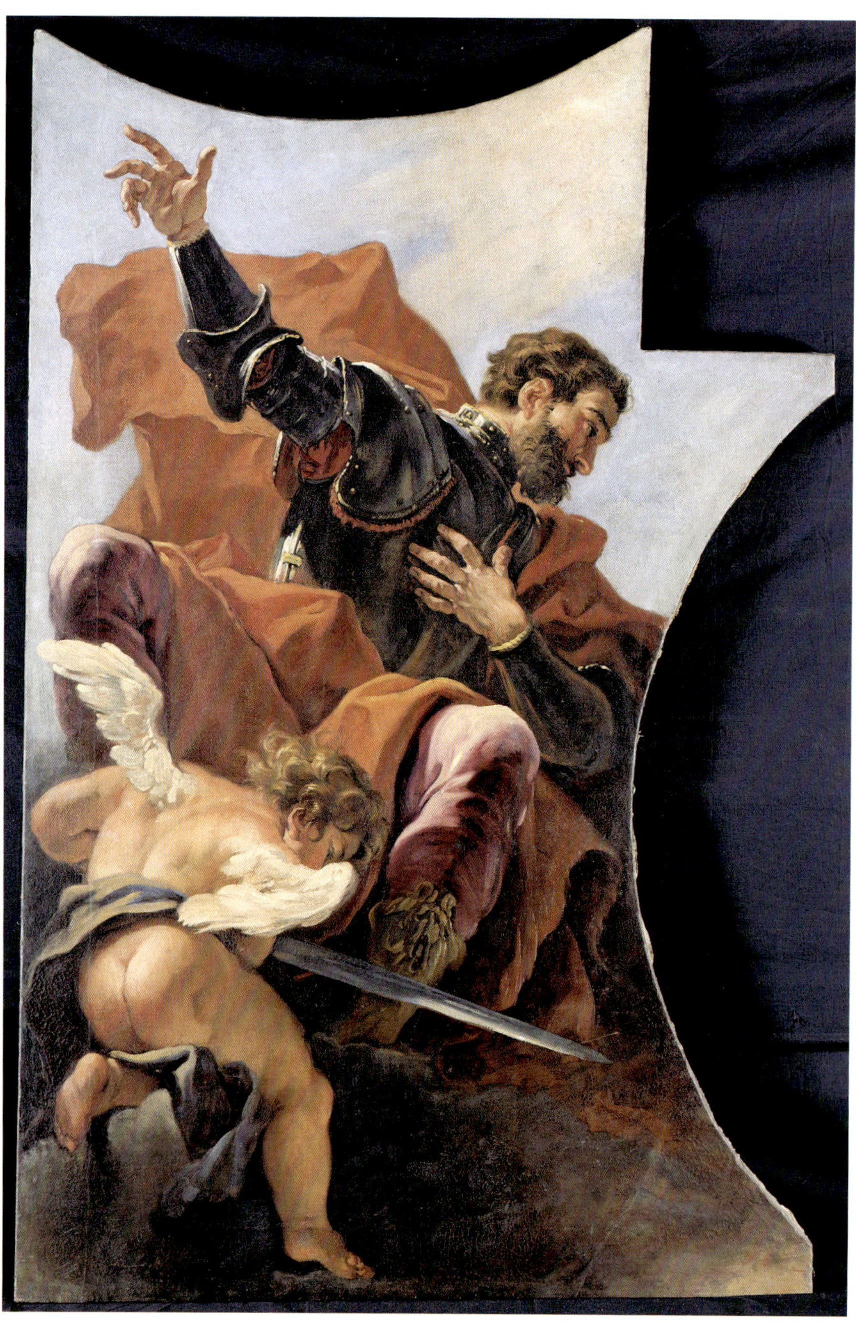

Fig. 3.1
Sebastiano Ricci
The Olympian Gods: Mars, ca. 1700
Oil on canvas, 68 5/16 x 46 1/2 in. (173.5 x 118 cm)
Gemäldegalerie, Staatliche Museen zu Berlin

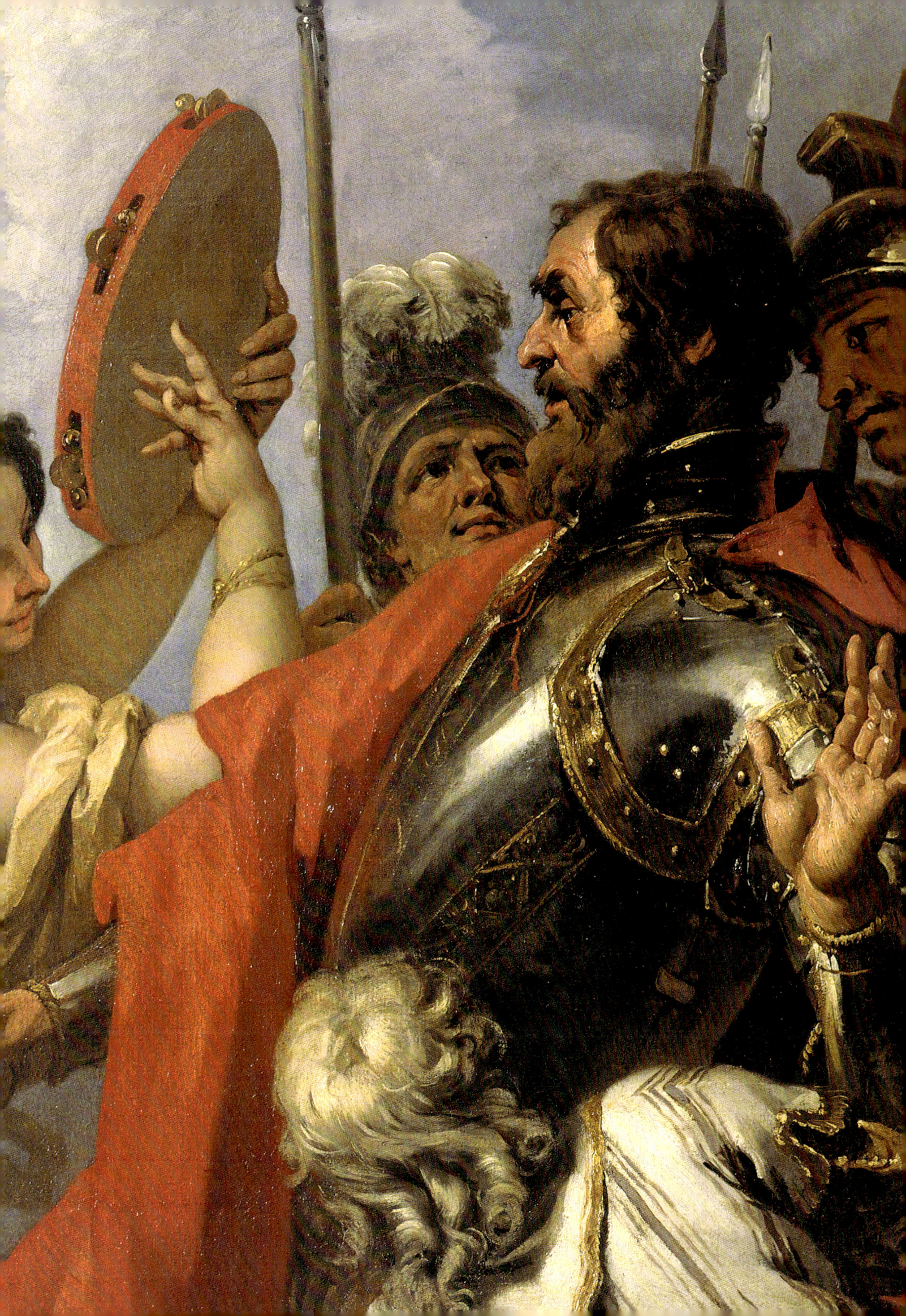

4. Sebastiano Ricci, 1659–1734
   Flora, ca. 1712–16
   Oil on canvas, 49 5/16 x 60 1/2 in. (125.3 x 153.7 cm)
   Blanton Museum of Art, The University of Texas at Austin, The Suida-Manning Collection,
   with support from The Cain Foundation in memory of Effie Marie Cain, 494.1999

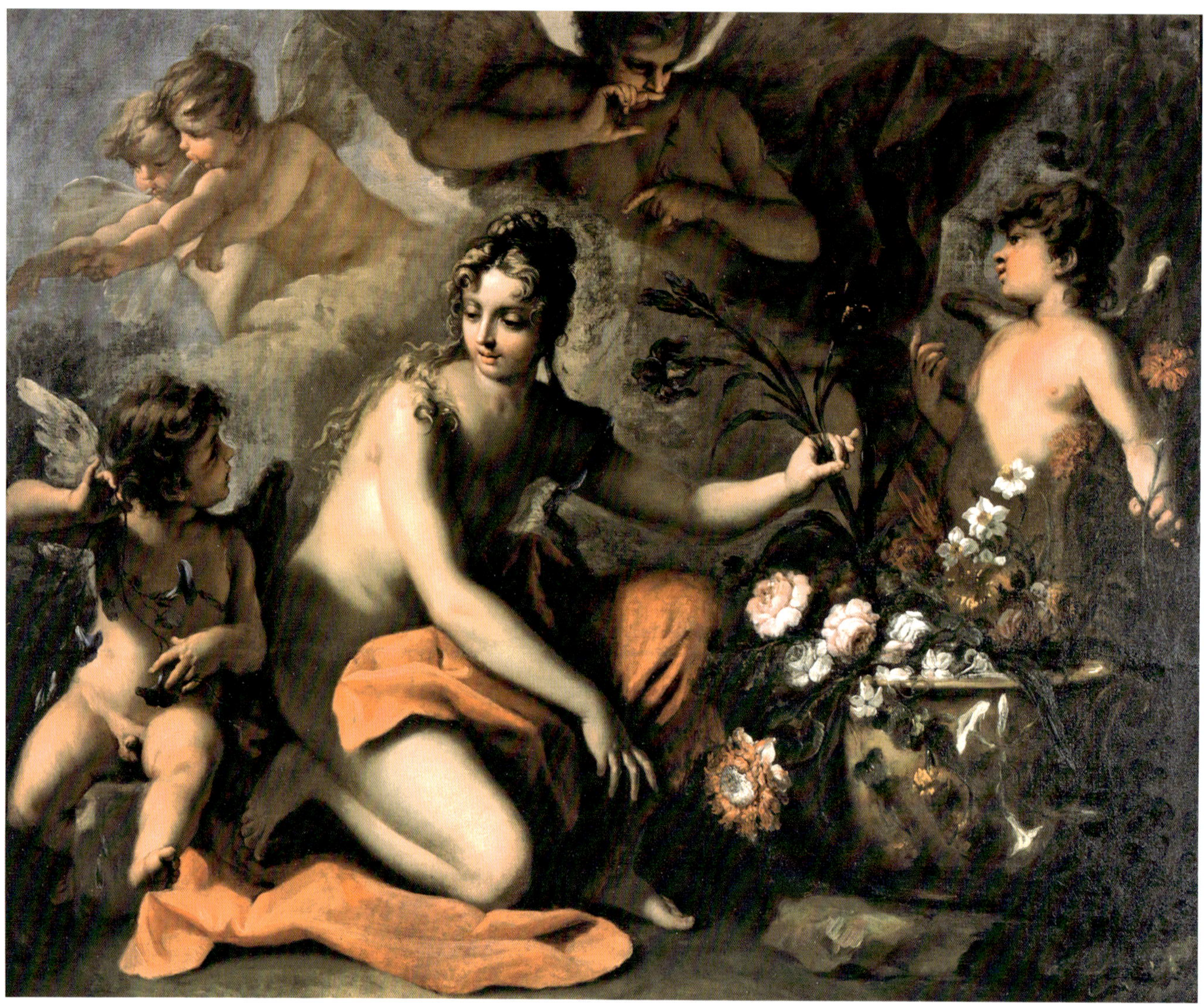

The ancient classical myth of Flora is best known from book five of *Fasti* by the Roman poet Ovid. Zephyr, god of the west wind, seduces and marries the nymph Chloris, who metamorphoses into Flora, the goddess of flowers and personification of spring.[1] In *Fasti*, she describes herself thus:

I enjoy perpetual spring: the season's always bright,
The trees have leaves: the ground is always green. I've
a fruitful garden in the fields that were my dower,
Fanned by the breeze, and watered by a flowing
spring. My husband stocked it with flowers, richly,
And said: "Goddess, be mistress of the flowers."

Although Ricci's painting is titled *Flora*, it in fact depicts Chloris in a calm but portentous moment, just before Zephyr's violent seduction. Zephyr emerges from a cloud blown by two floating putti and points to his prey with his left hand while holding a right finger to his lips, entreating a standing putto to be a silent accomplice. Chloris, unaware of Zephyr's intentions, looks with innocent attentiveness toward another seated companion and continues arranging her flowers.

Hints of eroticism are employed in a witty and teasing manner, from the suggestive way Chloris grasps an iris, to the unabashed display of the seated figure's genitalia, to the complicity of Zephyr and the standing putto. Ricci's picture is a confident foray into the intellectual and artistic challenges of the Venetian *paragone*, or relative superiority of the arts. Ricci seeks to rival the power of Ovid's poetry in visual form, while also posing Chloris in a softened variant of a classical statue, the crouching Venus (Aphrodite), in order to suggest the primacy of painting over sculpture. Several versions of this famed statue were well known and an especially notable Roman example from the late-second-century A.D. was in England during Ricci's sojourn there (fig. 4.1).[2] This statue had been admired and copied by Rubens in Mantua before being sold to England's King Charles I. In England, the distinguished portraitist Sir Peter Lely owned it for a time; after his death, it returned to the Royal Collection. Ricci's British patrons would have readily recognized his allusion to the statue. Indeed, *Flora* is normally dated to Ricci's stay in England (from the winter of 1711–12 until 1716), where he finished many pictures in a similar vein, including three classically themed canvases for Burlington House in London: *Bacchus and Ariadne, Venus and Cupid,* and *Diana and Endymion.*[3]

Other artistic references abound in this painting, especially to the sensuality of Titian's nudes and to the soft seductiveness of Correggio in the figures among the clouds. Ricci's graceful and virtuoso handling of paint recalls that of two earlier Baroque masters, Pietro da Cortona and Luca Giordano. Ricci probably employed a specialist in floral imagery to help him paint the urn of flowers. Overall, this evocative, lighthearted example of Venetian Baroque classicism is justly considered one of Ricci's most elegant masterpieces, universally lauded for its successful handling of color, light, and sensuous form.

AVC

Notes

1. Ovid 2004.

2. The sculpture remains part of the Royal Collection and is currently on loan to the British Museum. See Bober and Rubenstein 1986, no. 18; and Scott-Elliot 1959, 214, 218.

3. See Scarpa 2006, 209–10, nos. 192–94. The authorship of a fourth painting associated with the three canvases executed for Burlington House—titled *Cupid with Flowers*—has been questioned. See Scarpa 2006, 210, no. 195.

Provenance: Savoy Auction Gallery, London; Robert Manning [1924–1996] and Bertina Suida-Manning [1922–1992].

References: Manning 1961, no. 37; Milkovich in Memphis and Lexington 1965, no. 5; Daniels 1976a, 82, no. 274; Daniels 1976b, no. 306; Spike in Princeton 1980, no. 38; Bober 1999, 451; Bober 2001, 126–27, no. 3, 13; Austin 2006, 82; Scarpa 2006, 143, no. 8.

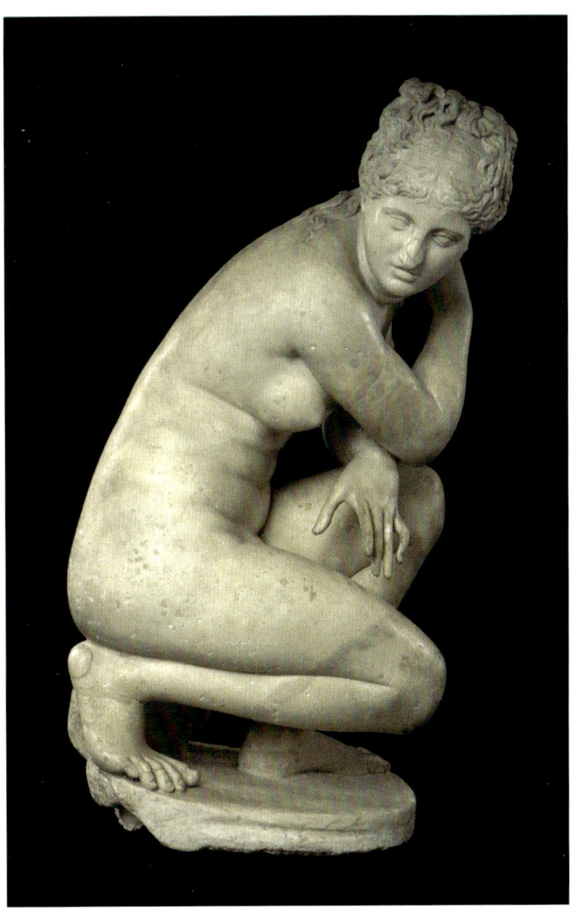

Fig. 4.1. Roman, 2nd century A.D.
A Naked Aphrodite Crouching at Her Bath
Marble, h.: 44 1/8 in. (112 cm)
The British Museum, London; On loan from Her Majesty the Queen, GR 1963.10-29.1

5. Sebastiano Ricci, 1659–1734
   The Last Supper, ca. 1713–14
   Oil on canvas, 26 1/2 x 40 7/8 in. (67.3 x 103.8 cm)
   Samuel H. Kress Collection, National Gallery of Art, Washington, 1943.4.32

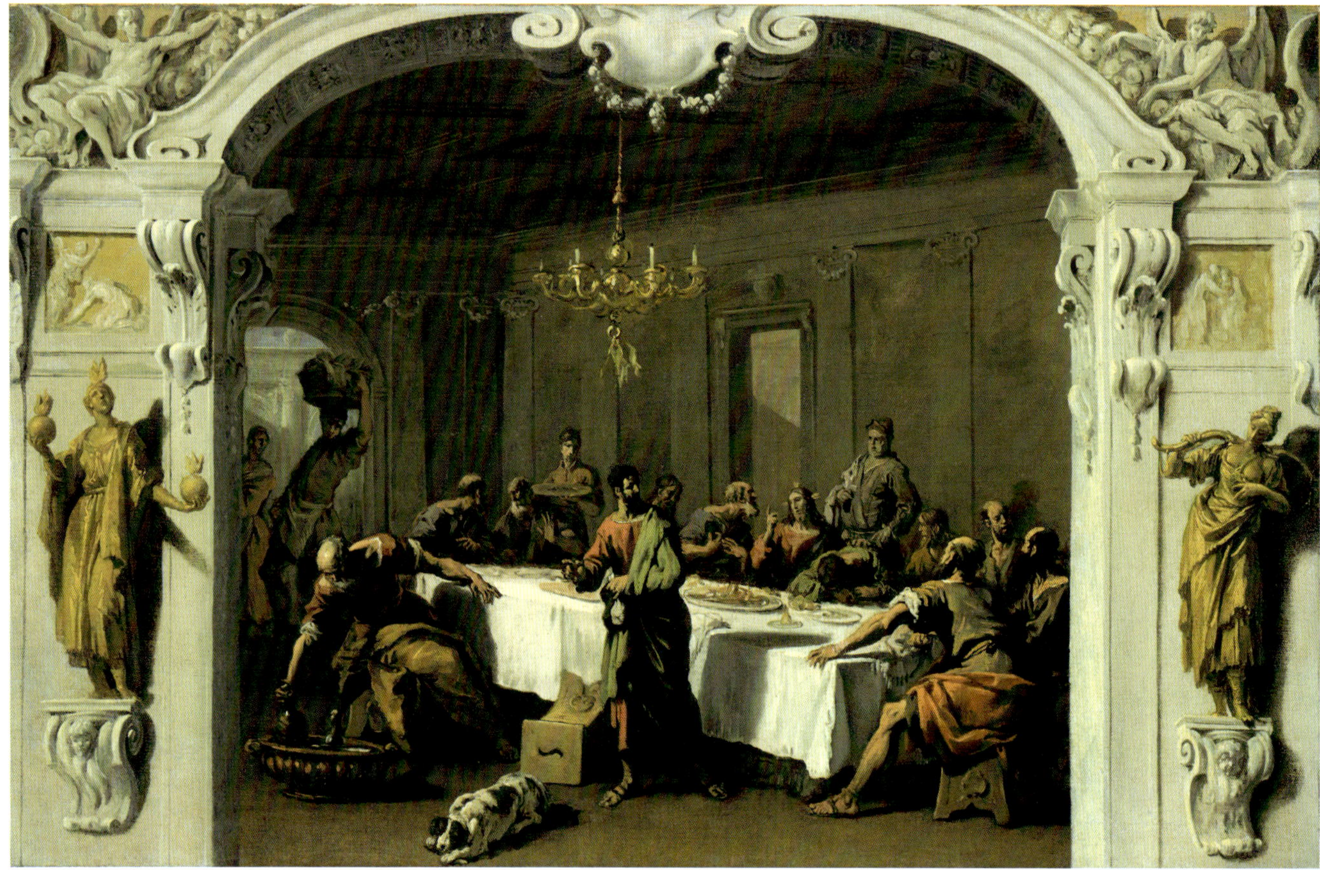

Sebastiano Ricci was a peripatetic artist who, before settling in Venice, worked extensively in Italy and spent considerable time abroad, executing commissions in Paris and Vienna, among other cities. He went to London in the winter of 1711–12, accompanied by his nephew Marco (1676–1730), who had already completed a productive two-year stay in the British capital (from 1708 to 1710). Both artists left the country for good in 1716.

During his sojourn in England, Sebastiano worked for some of that country's most prominent figures. The present painting likely served as a *modello*, or detailed study, for the chapel decoration commissioned by Henry Bentinck, the first Duke of Portland, for Bulstrode House in Buckinghamshire.[1] Unfortunately, the original structure and chapel no longer stand, and thus Ricci's work there has been lost. However, George Vertue, the famous engraver and chronicler of British art, visited there on more than one occasion and wrote an account of his experiences in 1733 in which he described the chapel decoration. He noted that there was an Ascension on the chapel ceiling and a "Salutation" (probably either an Annunciation or a Visitation), a Baptism, and a Last Supper on its walls.[2] The present canvas, along with three extant versions of the Baptism, are believed to comprise a visual record of part of the Bulstrode House commission.[3]

In *The Last Supper*, Ricci depicts the moment when Christ announces that one of his apostles will betray him. Judas, in the center foreground, leaves the table, moneybag in hand, while the others remain seated, displaying a range of emotions. Though there seem to be only eleven apostles (including Judas) in the composition, technical analysis of this *modello* has revealed that the architecture framing

the scene was painted after the central image and obscures an additional seated figure on the right.[4] Naturally, this would have been corrected in the completed chapel painting.

Historically, there has been much interest in identifying the background figures. Vertue believed the servant standing behind Christ was Sebastiano Ricci's self-portrait. Artists of the day commonly incorporated images of themselves as ancillary figures in paintings that showed groups of people; Ricci did so in several works. More recently, the servant on the left has been plausibly identified as Marco Ricci, who assisted his uncle on most of his major English commissions, including the one for Bulstrode House.[5] These two portraits would have served as a type of "signature" by the two artists and their identifications are likely to be correct. More speculative, but still plausible, is the suggestion that the woman in the background doorway is one of Sebastiano Ricci's mistresses.

Marco is credited with *The Last Supper*'s architectural surrounds, in which trompe l'oeil sculptures and reliefs provide complementary imagery to the main scene; however, because they are so sketchy, their themes are only tentatively identifiable.[6] The female figure on the left holding flaming orbs probably represents divinity or divine inspiration. Above her is a scene that is thought to be either the Annunciation to Joachim or, more plausibly, Christ's Agony in the Garden. On the right stands a personification of Obedience, identifiable by her customary attribute—the yoke. The scene above her most likely depicts Judas's kiss, although it has also been said to show the meeting of Joachim and Anna at the Golden Gate. Together the Christological scenes complement the Last Supper

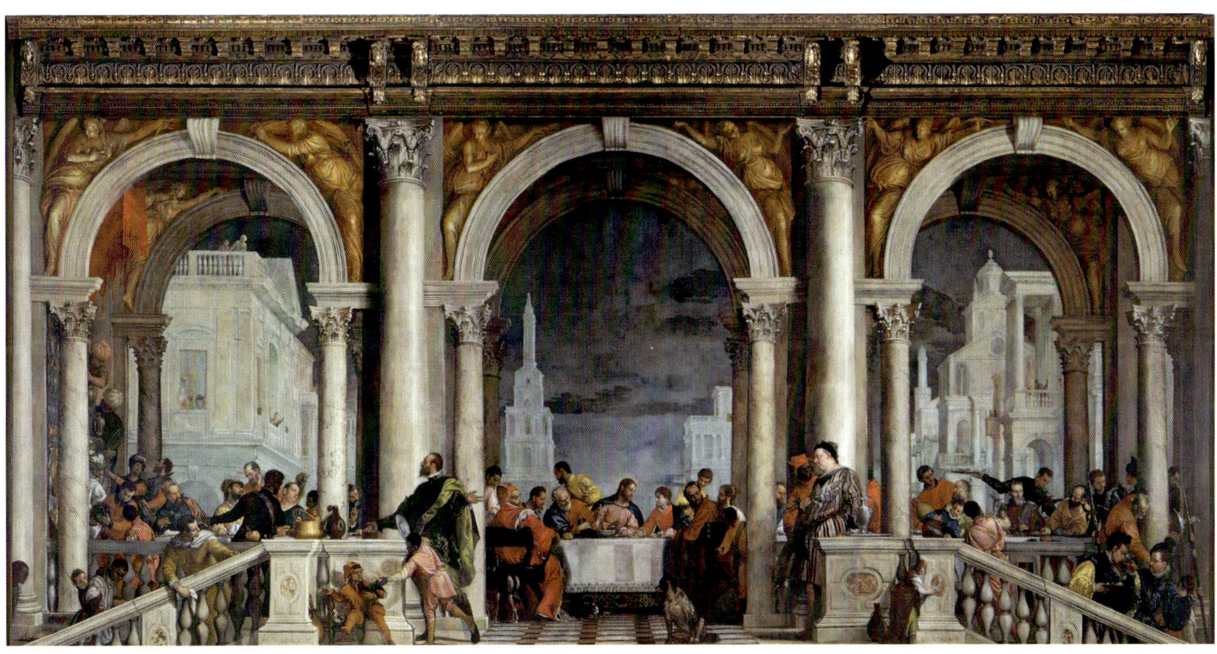

Fig. 5.1 . Paolo Veronese
Feast in the House of Levi, 1573
Oil on canvas, 218 1/2 x 503 15/16 in. (555 x 1,280 cm)
Galleria dell' Accademia, Venice

by showing episodes that immediately followed this central event.

In composition and technique, the painting clearly reflects the influence of Ricci's Venetian predecessors Paolo Veronese and Jacopo Tintoretto. Like Veronese, in works such as the *Feast in the House of Levi* (fig. 5.1), Ricci presents his subject theatrically, as if it were a stage performance mounted in a contemporary setting. The abundance of genre-like details, such as serving vessels and the dog in the foreground, further encourages viewers to imagine themselves present at the historic moment. Ricci's debt to Tintoretto, who painted the Last Supper no fewer than nine times, is likewise evident. The compositional hallmarks of Tintoretto's renderings of this subject, such as the one in the Scuola Grande di S. Rocco, Venice (fig. 5.2), include dynamic diagonals and bold juxtapositions of light and shadow. Tintoretto's influence here can be seen in Ricci's diagonal placement of the table and dramatic contrasting of light and shadow to emphasize key elements in the composition.

Ingeniously inventive and supremely confident, Sebastiano Ricci employed a wide range of styles, here relying strongly on Venetian predecessors but also updating them with virtuoso Baroque flourishes, to create a compelling Last Supper for his eminent British patron.

AVC

Notes

1. Bulstrode House (later also known as Gerrard's Cross) and its chapel were built around 1676–85 for George Jeffreys, the first Baron Jeffreys of Wem. Hans William Bentinck, the first Earl of Portland, acquired the house, and his son Henry, who commissioned Ricci, inherited it. See *The Country House Companion,* www.dicamillocompanion.com (accessed April 30, 2009).

2. Finberg 1936, 47–48.

3. See Daniels 1976a, 153, no. 530; and Scarpa 2006, 343, no. 557.

4. See Scarpa 2006, 313, no. 557.

5. Vertue was the first to identify Sebastiano Ricci in this work. Garberson (De Grazia and Garberson 1996, 235, n. 12) concurred with Vertue and noted that Georgiana, Duchess of Devonshire, writing in 1785, was the first to propose the identification of Ricci's mistresses. Garberson discounts the possibility that one of Sebastiano's mistresses appears in the completed chapel painting, but the identification as such of the woman looking through the door in that work remains a possibility. In her description of the Bulstrode chapel, the duchess wrote, "[Ricci] has put his own figure in a full bottom'd wig, and his mistresses peeping through ye door at ye Lords supper." See *Anglo-Saxon Review* 1899, 81. A woman appears in the same spot in the present work (to the left of the servant bearing a basket on his head). Although identification of her as one of Ricci's mistresses is a matter of conjecture, it is not an implausible one given the painter's colorful reputation. In addition to Garberson, see Daniels 1976a, 40–41, no. 115 and n. 8; and Scarpa 2006, 343, no. 557.

6. See Scarpa 2006, 343, no. 557; and Garberson in De Grazia and Garberson 1996, 230–36.

Provenance: Possibly Manfrin Collection, Palazzo Venier, Venice; Count Alessandro Contini-Bonacossi [1878–1955], Florence, by 1937; Kress acquisition, 1939.

References: Washington, D.C. 1941, 169; Osti 1950, 123, no. 1; Pallucchini 1952, 77–78; Watson 1954, 174; Ghidiglia Quintavalle 1956–57, 85; Whinney and Millar 1957, 310; Croft-Murray 1962–70, 2: 15, 266; Garas 1964, 131; Martini 1964, 161, no. 46; Washington, D.C. 1965, 114; Zampetti 1969, 28; Fredericksen and Zeri 1972, 175; D'Arcais 1973, 10–11, 13; Shapley 1973, 127–28; Twickenham 1974, no. 71; Washington, D.C. 1975, 306; Daniels 1976a, 40, no. 115 and 153, no. 530; Daniels 1976b, 118, no. 325; Daniels 1976c, 72; Pilo 1976, 98–99, nos. 156, 159; London 1978, no. 1; Shapley 1979, 1: 400–2; Christiansen 1982, 42; Aikema 1984, 95; Daniels 1984, 109; Washington, D.C. 1985, 351; Rizzi 1989, 128–29; Scarpa 1991, 22–25; Düsseldorf and Hannover 1991, 224–25, no. 68; Pallucchini 1995, 38; Garberson in De Grazia and Garberson 1996, 230–36; Scarpa 2006, 343, no. 557.

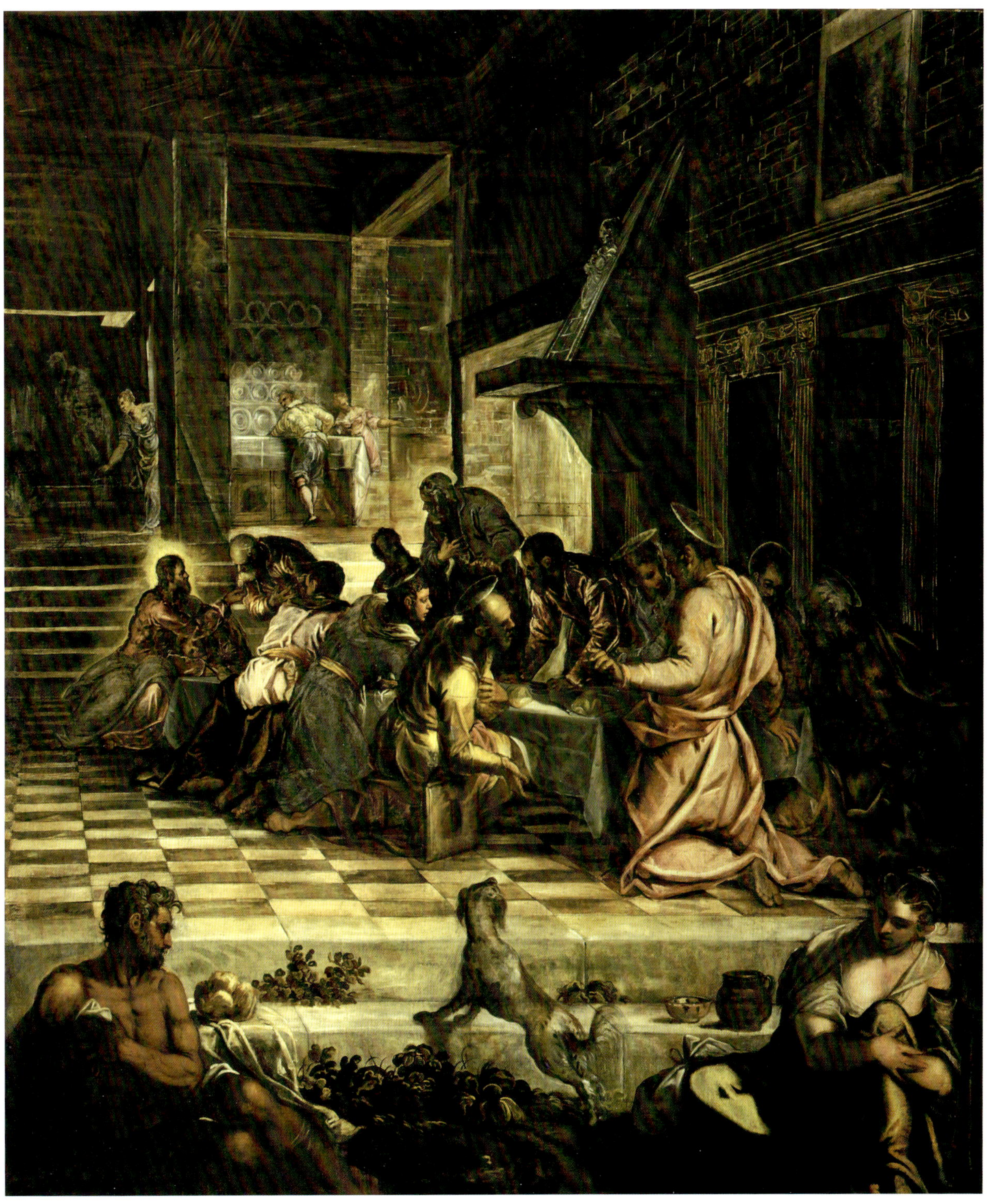

Fig. 5.2
Jacopo Tintoretto
The Last Supper, 1579–81
Oil on canvas, 211 13/16 x 191 3/4 in. (538 x 487 cm)
Scuola Grande di San Rocco, Venice

6. Sebastiano Ricci, 1659–1734
   Christ Resurrected Surrounded by Angels, ca. 1712–16
   Oil on canvas, 39 5/8 x 49 5/8 in. (100.6 cm x 126 cm)
   Columbia Museum of Art, Columbia; Gift of the Samuel H. Kress Foundation, CMA 1954.41

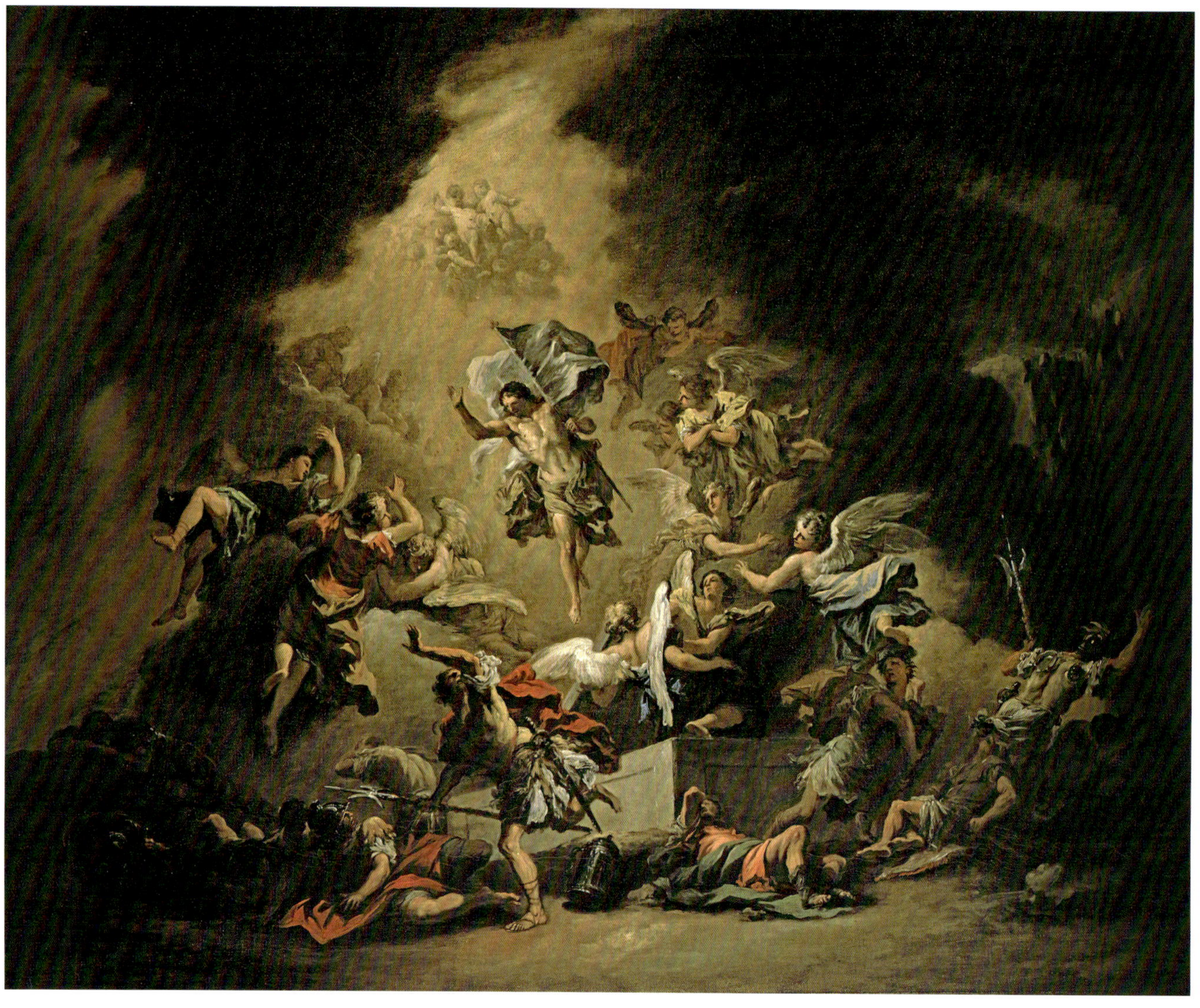

This painting derives from Ricci's last major undertaking in England, a mural for the apse of the chapel at the Royal Hospital in Chelsea (see fig. 4, p. 45). Established by King Charles II (1630–1685) for aged and injured soldiers, the hospital was built in stages by Christopher Wren between 1689 and 1702. The chapel was consecrated in 1691. When George I was crowned in 1714, it was he, in consultation with Charles Talbot, first Duke of Shrewsbury (one of Ricci's chief English patrons), who likely commissioned the Italian artist to decorate the apse.

The present work is one of two *modelli*, or detailed studies, prepared for the chapel mural; the other is now in the Dulwich Picture Gallery, London.[1] Considering the year of the commission, it was probably intended to honor Queen Anne, who died on August 1, 1714.[2] The Columbia Museum of Art *modello* is the slightly larger of the two and is considered sketchier in style. There are few major compositional differences among the three versions, though the trompe l'oeil effects are substantially heightened in the concave mural, which remains in situ and in good condition despite damage to the chapel during World War II.

The theme of the Resurrection was an appropriate one for a hospital setting, as it offered—depending on one's condition and perspective—the hope of a miraculous recovery or an inspiring promise of life after death under the care of the risen Christ. It also had ample precedents in European painting.[3] Notable in Ricci's imagery are the emphatic nature of Christ's emergence from his tomb and the boisterous spectacle that attends this miracle. Roman soldiers flee from Christ while angels flock toward him. The pyramidal composition forces the viewer's eye toward the heavenly glow of divine presence. Ricci used contrasting colors to underscore the drama and emotions of the event, starting with a rather somber brown background and punctuating it with fully saturated bursts of red, blue, white, and yellow.

Christ Resurrected Surrounded by Angels reflects the culmination of an exuberant vein of Baroque painting that led directly to the Rococo. Indeed, it represents the epitome of Ricci's mature style, which has been summed up as "characterized by fluid brushwork, luxuriant *colorito*, and theatrical monumentality."[4] Although his nephew Marco Ricci assisted on the Royal Hospital mural and received some credit and payment for his efforts, this *modello* is considered to be entirely Sebastiano's work.

The most direct forerunner of Ricci's Royal Hospital commission is the Resurrection painted by Annibale Carracci (1560–1609) in 1593, now in the Musée du Louvre (see fig. 5, p. 45).[5] Carracci was among the first Italian Baroque artists. As the two *modelli* and finished mural demonstrate, Ricci carefully studied his approach to composition, color, and dramatic gesture. Additionally, the angels opening the tomb are reminiscent of those in a Resurrection painted by the sixteenth-century Venetian master Paolo Veronese for the Church of S. Giacomo on Murano (now in Westminster Hospital, London). Furthermore, Ricci infuses his figures with a sensuousness and fleshiness that recall the work of Correggio, whose early-sixteenth-century ceiling paintings became models for making the ethereal concretely visual and were a particular influence upon the final version of Ricci's work for the semidome ceiling of the chapel apse.

AVC

Notes

1. Scarpa 2006, 219–20, no. 220.

2. Ibid., 221–22, no. 224; and Daniels 1974, 422.

3. Among the more famous earlier examples of this subject created for a hospital setting is Matthias Grünewald's *Isenheim Altarpiece* (1512–16, now in the Musée d'Unterlinden, Colmar, France).

4. Worcester 2005, 247.

5. Originally painted in 1593 for the Palazzo Luchini, Bologna, it was displayed in the Church of the Corpus Domini, Bologna, as early as 1689.

Provenance: Possibly William Pleydell-Bouverie [1895–1968], seventh Earl of Radnor, (sold, Christie's, London, July 27, 1945, lot 45, to Weil); Count Alessandro Contini Bonacossi [1878–1955], Florence; Kress acquisition, 1950.

References: Suida 1954, 53, no. 22; Pallucchini 1960, 14; Bonacossi 1962, 119; Milkovich in Memphis and Lexington 1965, no. 13; Pilo 1966, 305; Daniels 1969, 6; Shapley 1973, 126–27; Daniels 1976a, 23, no. 74; Daniels 1976b, no. 329; D'Arcais 1976, 256; Rizzi 1989, 130; Pallucchini 1995, 43; Bailey and Barker in Worcester 2005, 35; Scarpa 2006, 176–77, no. 88.

7. Luca Carlevaris, 1663–1729
Piazza San Marco Towards San Marco, before 1723
Oil on canvas, 33 1/2 x 48 1/2 in. (85.09 x 123.19 cm)
The John and Mable Ringling Museum of Art, Sarasota; Museum Purchase, 1953, SN669

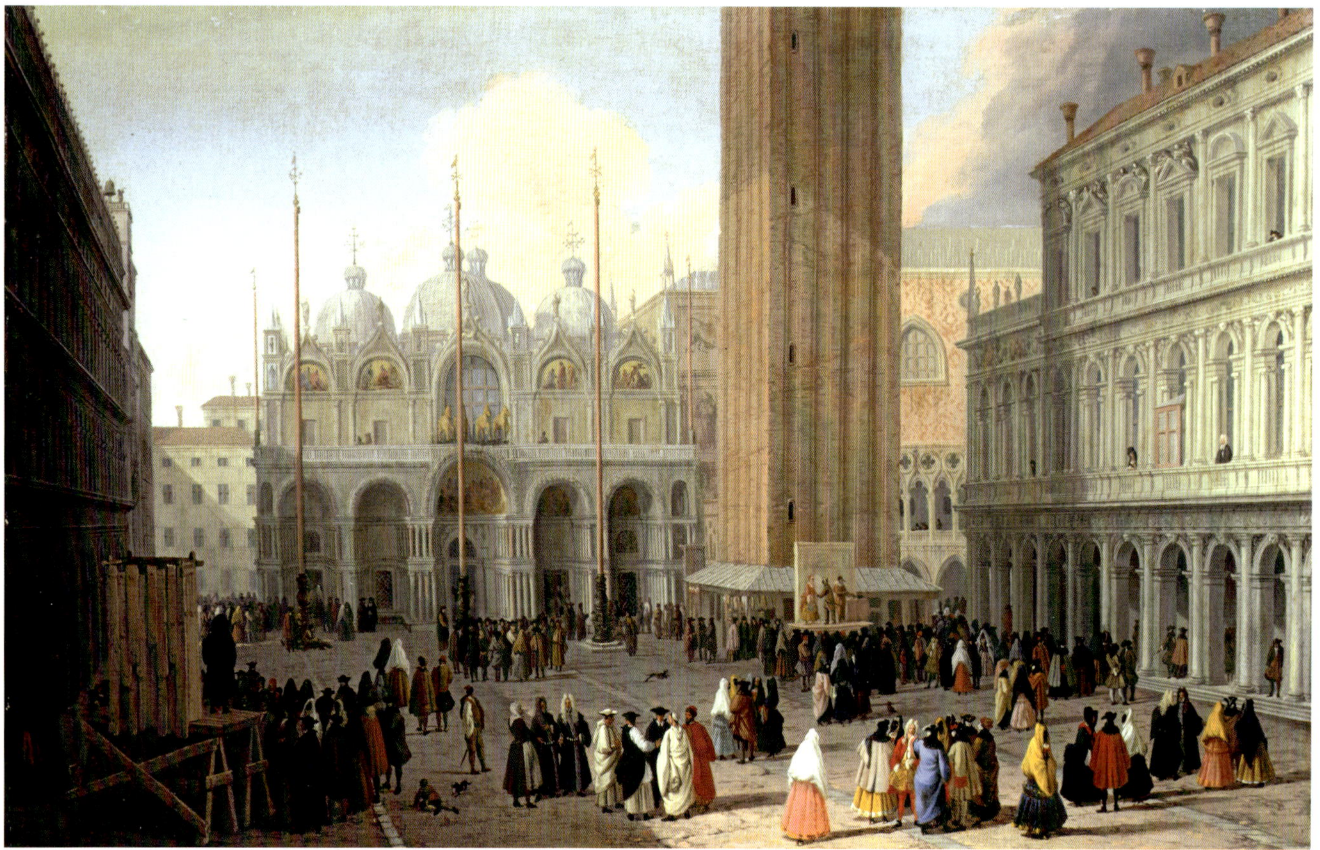

Luca Carlevaris was born in the small city of Udine in the northern Veneto and at age thirteen settled in Venice, where he remained for the rest of his life. Although he was a young boy when his father, Giovanni Leonardo, a noted painter, architect, and mathematician, died in 1669, he seems to have inherited the senior Carlevaris's artistic inclination. Today Luca Carlevaris is best known as the "father" of the Venetian *veduta* (view painting), although he was certainly not the first artist there to specialize in it. He was, however, the first to approach view painting in a relatively systematic way (in part because of his sustained focus on mathematics and geography) and to base his reputation upon it. As such—and because he established the Venetian art market for *vedute*—he can be seen as Canaletto's most significant predecessor.

In the late 1690s Carlevaris visited Rome, where the views and capriccios of the Dutchman Gaspar van Wittel (called Vanvitelli, 1653–1736) captured his attention and inspired him to paint fanciful architectural and topographical images of his own. With the publication in 1703 of his compendious survey of Venetian architecture, *Le fabriche, e vedute di Venetia disegnate*, Carlevaris decisively declared himself a *vedutista*, or view painter.[1] Possessing a comprehensive knowledge of the cityscape, he transformed Venice into an intriguing artistic subject, producing large-scale paintings that celebrated its rich history and singular beauty. Unlike any work then locally available, these urban views were instantly popular, and *vedute* painting quickly became an independent, highly valued genre.

In subject and execution, *Piazza San Marco Towards San Marco* is typical of Carlevaris's *vedute*. His compositions rarely show areas outside the piazza, and almost all are executed in high-key colors, with strong contrasts of light and shadow and a precise handling of architectural detail.[2] In addition, his skies generally are rendered in pale blue with notes of rose while his buildings are characteristically veiled in pale gray shadow. The latter quality, unfortunately, might have led to his decline in favor, as suggested by correspondence between the Lucchese collector Stefano Conti and his Venetian agent, Alessandro Marchesini, in 1725. When Conti requested pictures by Carlevaris, Marchesini advised him to reconsider. As the agent explained, an artist by the name of "Sig.r Ant. Canale" painted *vedute* like those of Carlevaris but with one striking difference: "you can see the sun shining in them."[3]

Indeed, virtually the entire composition of the Ringling canvas falls under the shade of the Procuratie Vecchie, and the bustling figures cast long shadows on the unpaved piazza.[4] For a time, Carlevaris enjoyed success painting views such as this not only for Venetian patrons but also for foreign ones.[5] However, he was not an especially prolific artist, and by the mid-1720s the much younger and more energetic Canaletto surpassed him in terms of output, not to mention popularity.

AL

Notes

1. *Le fabriche, e vedute di Venetia disegnate: poste in prospettiva, et intagliate da Luca Carlevariis con priveliegii* (Venice: Giovanni Battista Finazzi, 1703) was a detailed graphic survey that consisted of 103 plates representing the churches, palaces, and other buildings of Venice as well as its bridges, canals, and *campi*.

2. William Barcham, "Townscapes and Landscapes," in London and Washington, D.C. 1994, 99.

3. Marchesini wrote, "[C]he fa in questo paese stordire universalmente ognuno che vede Le sue opera, che consiste sul ordine di Carlevari [sic] ma vi si vede Lucer entro il sole." ([H]e is astonishing everyone in this town who sees his works, which are on the order of Carlevaris's but you can see the sun shining in them.) As transcribed in Haskell 1956, 297. For this exchange of letters, see also Links 1977, 1–8; and Constable and Links 1989, 1: xxv–xxvii.

4. Until 1723 the piazza was surfaced in brick, with several drainage channels running east to west. That year, it was paved with white marble. Thus this painting cannot have been executed after 1723.

5. Conti's first commissions of Carlevaris, in 1707, probably did the most to help make his work known; following those, he received commissions from the Earl of Manchester and Count Colloredo, the imperial ambassador. See W. G. Constable 1962, 1: 51–76; and J. G. Links, "Canaletto: A Biographical Sketch" in New York 1989, 14–19.

Provenance: Henry Pelham-Clinton [1834–1879], sixth Duke of Newcastle-under-Lyne, Clumber Park, Nottingham, by 1879; by inheritance to Henry Pelham-Clinton [1864–1928], called Lord Lincoln, seventh Duke of Newcastle-under-Lyne; by inheritance to Francis Pelham-Clinton-Hope [1866–1941], eighth Duke of Newcastle-under-Lyne; probably sold by Francis Pelham-Clinton-Hope to D. A. Hoogendijk, Amsterdam, 1938; (with D. A. Hoogendijk, Amsterdam, 1938–39?); Louis Dignus [1881–1945], Baron van der Goes van Dirxland, before 1939–53; (with D. A. Hoogendijk, Amsterdam, by 1953).

References: Richardson and Grigaut 1953, 253–54, fig. 7; Martin-Méry in Bordeaux 1956, xix, 4, pl. 18, no. 6; Rizzi 1967, 94, pl. 164; Fredericksen and Zeri 1972, 45, 637; Tomory 1976, 86–87, no. 83; Sutton in New York and Tampa 1981, 15, 69, fig. 37, no. 9; Janson 1986, 108, no. 34; Merling 2002, 154, ill.; Borys 2008, 100.

8. Luca Carlevaris, 1663–1729
Piazza San Marco Towards the Piazzetta, before 1723
Oil on canvas, 25 x 39 1/8 in. (63.5 x 99.4 cm)
The John and Mable Ringling Museum of Art, Sarasota; Museum Purchase, 1953, SN670

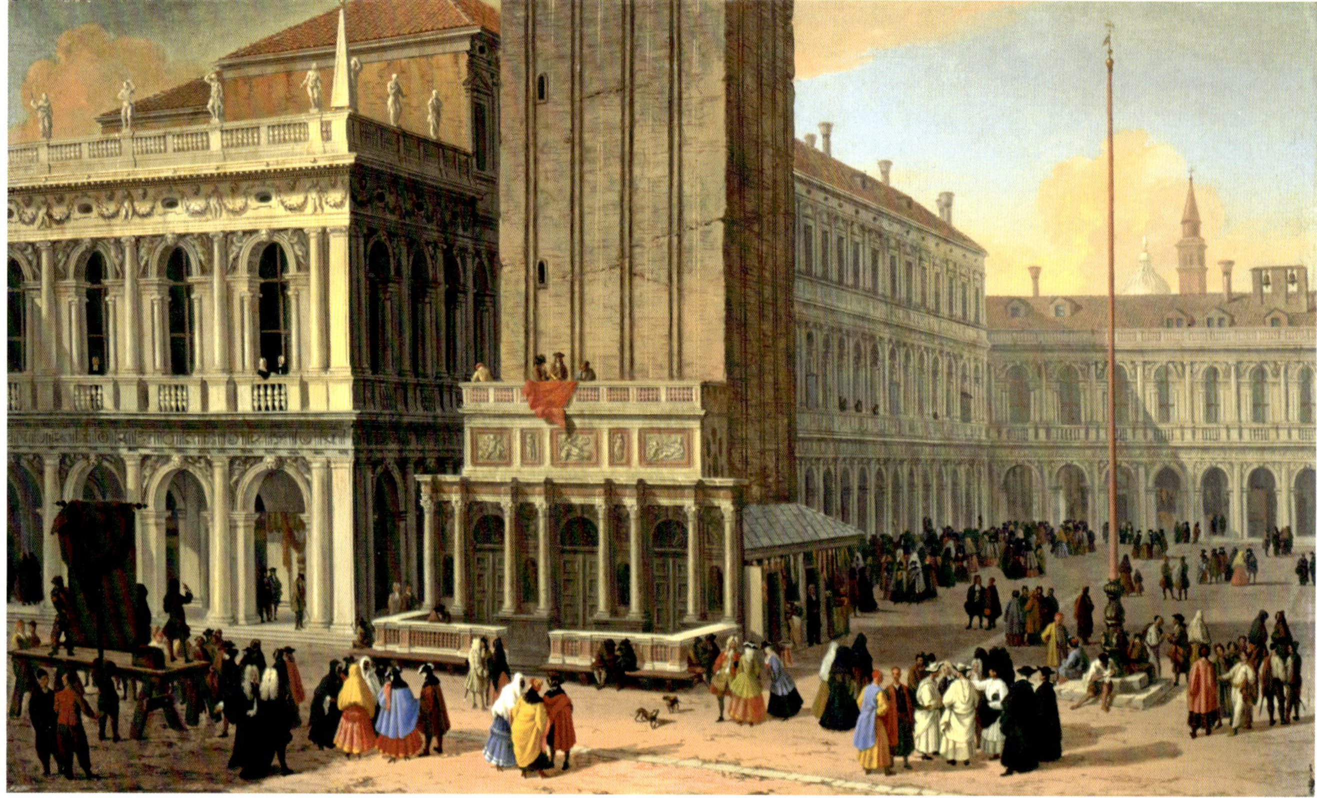

Carlevaris is widely regarded as the founding father of Venetian view painting, but a portrait of him in the Ashmolean Museum, Oxford, indicates that he probably saw himself as a mathematician and scientist above all (fig. 8.1).[1] Indeed, his first large-scale "artistic" endeavor, *Le fabriche, e vedute di Venetia disegnate*, suggests a proclivity for precise, scientifically derived detail.[2] By including little embellishment and few inventive flourishes in the 103 etchings that comprise this survey of Venetian architecture, Carlevaris presented a remarkable visual record. However, as at least one scholar lamented, he did "little to make known [the city's] splendors to strangers."[3] Consequently, it is often supposed that while the *vedute* of the younger Canaletto were artful constructions, those of Luca Carlevaris were literal and unbiased translations.

Contrary to these assumptions, Carlevaris was well aware of the beauty of the Venetian cityscape and was undoubtedly willing to mold it to suit his pictorial needs. In *Piazza San Marco Towards the Piazzetta*, for example, spatial depth and proportion accord only loosely with reality. Depicted from a relatively elevated perspective—roughly the same height as the figures that overlook the Piazzetta from the balcony of Jacopo Sansovino's *loggetta* above the entrance to the Campanile—the piazza appears to be crowded into the space.[4] Greatly compressed and foreshortened in other parts of the composition as well, such as the representations of the Procuratie Nuove, the entire scene bears the feeling of a stage set.

Seen against this backdrop, Carlevaris's figures assume a certain theatrical quality, thereby enlivening and animating the painting. The noblemen engrossed in conversation, masked ladies promenading, passersby pausing to view comedians who perform on makeshift stages, and others represent the wide range of individuals who frequented the Piazza S. Marco and reveal the artist's profound interest in urban life. Just as he systematically documented Venice's architecture in *Le fabriche, e vedute di Venetia disegnate*, Carlevaris portrayed its populace with such care that one might even consider his figural works as *vedute* themselves (fig. 8.2).[5]

AL

Notes

1. In "Townscapes and Landscapes" in London and Washington, D.C. 1994, William Barcham wrote that Carlevaris's father was "an architect of sorts as well as a mathematician" (111, n. 7). It is highly unlikely that he trained his son, as he died when Luca was a young boy. For Carlevaris and his father, see Levey 1980, 104–78; Links 1967, 453; idem 1982, 14–19; William Barcham in London and Washington, D.C. 1994, 96–99; and Succi in Padua 1994, 15–20.

2. *Le fabriche, e vedute di Venetia disegnate: poste in prospettiva, et intagliate da Luca Carlevariis con priveliegii* (Venice: Giovanni Battista Finazzi, 1703). For a photographic reproduction of the volume, see Fiorani 1980. For more on the encyclopedic spirit that characterized eighteenth-century Venice, see Reale in Padua 1994, 91–106.

3. Links 1982, 14.

4. The elevated perspective is unusual in that Carlevaris tended to keep his viewpoints close to the ground, thereby imitating the actual urban experience.

5. A prolific draftsman, Carlevaris produced a great many figure sketches. Important examples can be found in the British Museum and Victoria and Albert Museum, London, and the Museo Correr, Venice. For more on Carlevaris's draftsmanship, see William Barcham in London and Washington, D.C. 1994, 92–100. For the artist's portrayals of Venetians, see Reale in Padua 1994, 99.

Provenance: Henry Pelham-Clinton [1834–1879], sixth Duke of Newcastle-under-Lyne, Clumber Park, Nottingham, by 1879; by inheritance to Henry Pelham-Clinton [1864–1928], called Lord Lincoln, seventh Duke of Newcastle-under-Lyne; by inheritance to Francis Pelham-Clinton-Hope [1866–1941], eighth Duke of Newcastle-under-Lyne; probably sold by Francis Pelham-Clinton-Hope to D. A. Hoogendijk, Amsterdam, 1938; (with D. A. Hoogendijk, Amsterdam, 1938–39?); Louis Dignus [1881–1945], Baron van der Goes van Dirxland, before 1939–53; (with D. A. Hoogendijk, Amsterdam, by 1953).

References: Richardson and Grigaut 1953, 253; Rizzi in Udine and Rome 1963, 92, pl. 30, no. 73; Rizzi 1967, 95, pl. 165; Fredericksen and Zeri 1972, 45, 637; Tomory 1976, 87, no. 84; Janson 1986, 108, no. 35; Merling 2002, 154, ill.; Pedrocco 2002, 60; Borys 2008, 100.

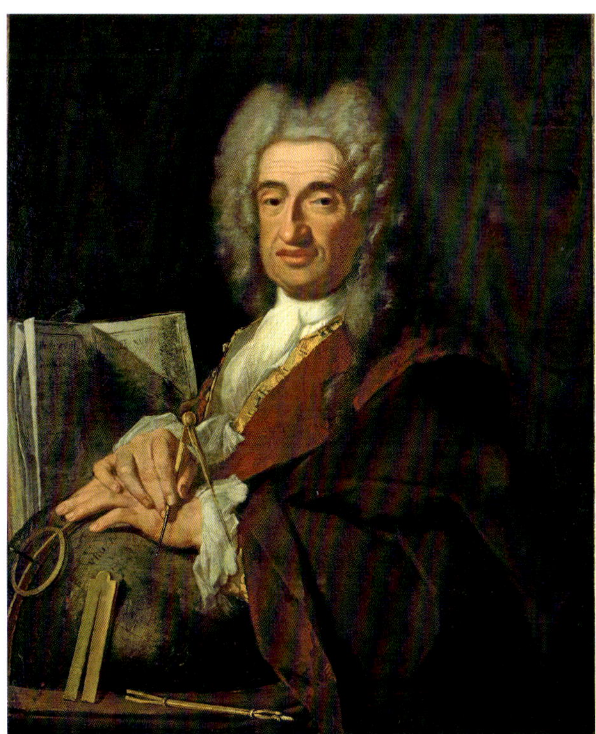

Fig. 8.1. Bartolomeo Nazari
Luca Carlevaris, ca. 1724
Oil on canvas, 38 3/16 x 31 5/16 in. (97 x 79.5 cm)
Ashmolean Museum, University of Oxford; Presented by friends of C. F. Bell, first Keeper of the Department of Fine Art, 1931; WA1931.18

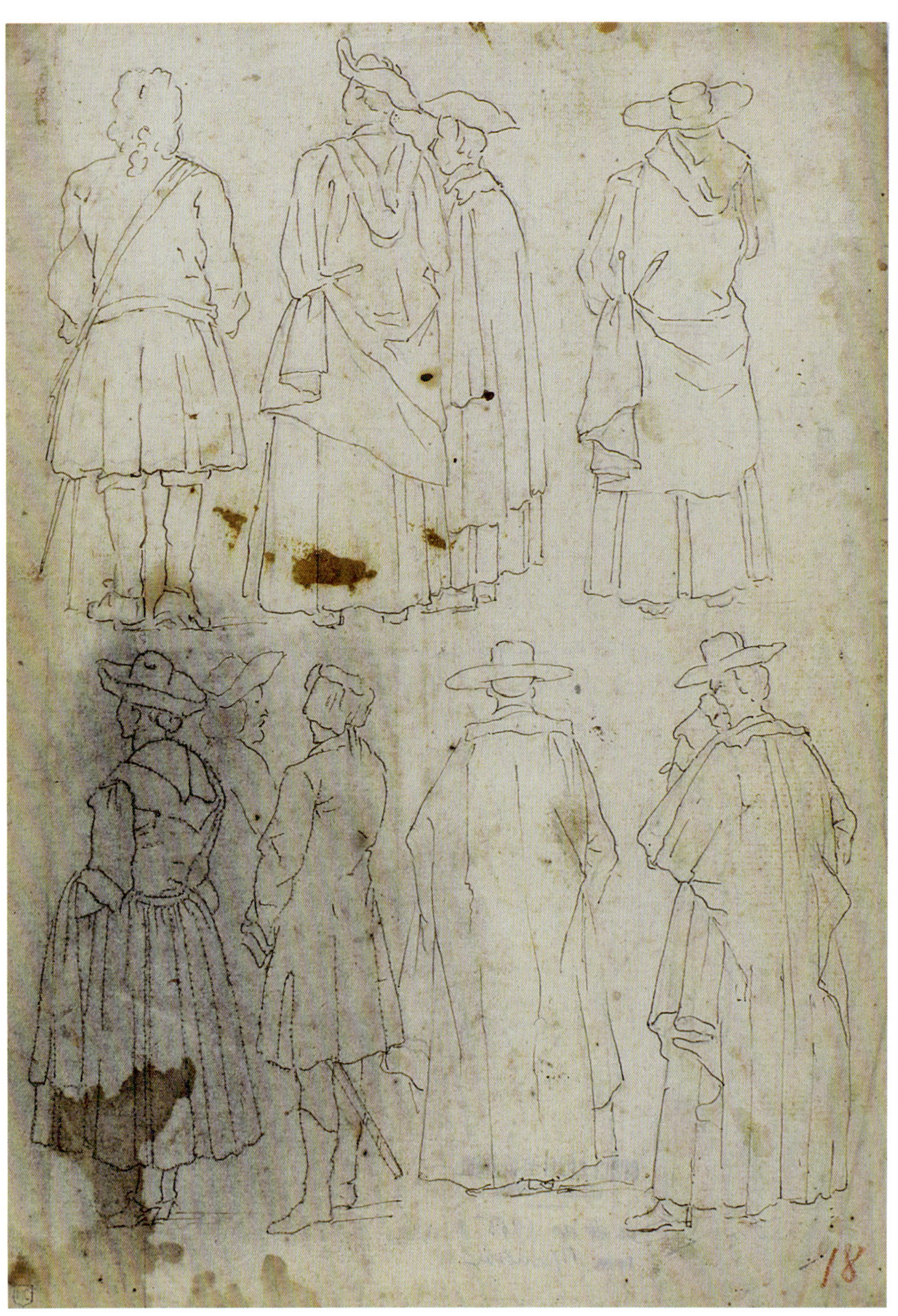

Fig. 8.2. Luca Carlevaris
Soldati religiosi e popolari, n.d.
Drawing, dimensions unavailable
Fondazione Musei Civici di Venezia, Museo Correr, Venice

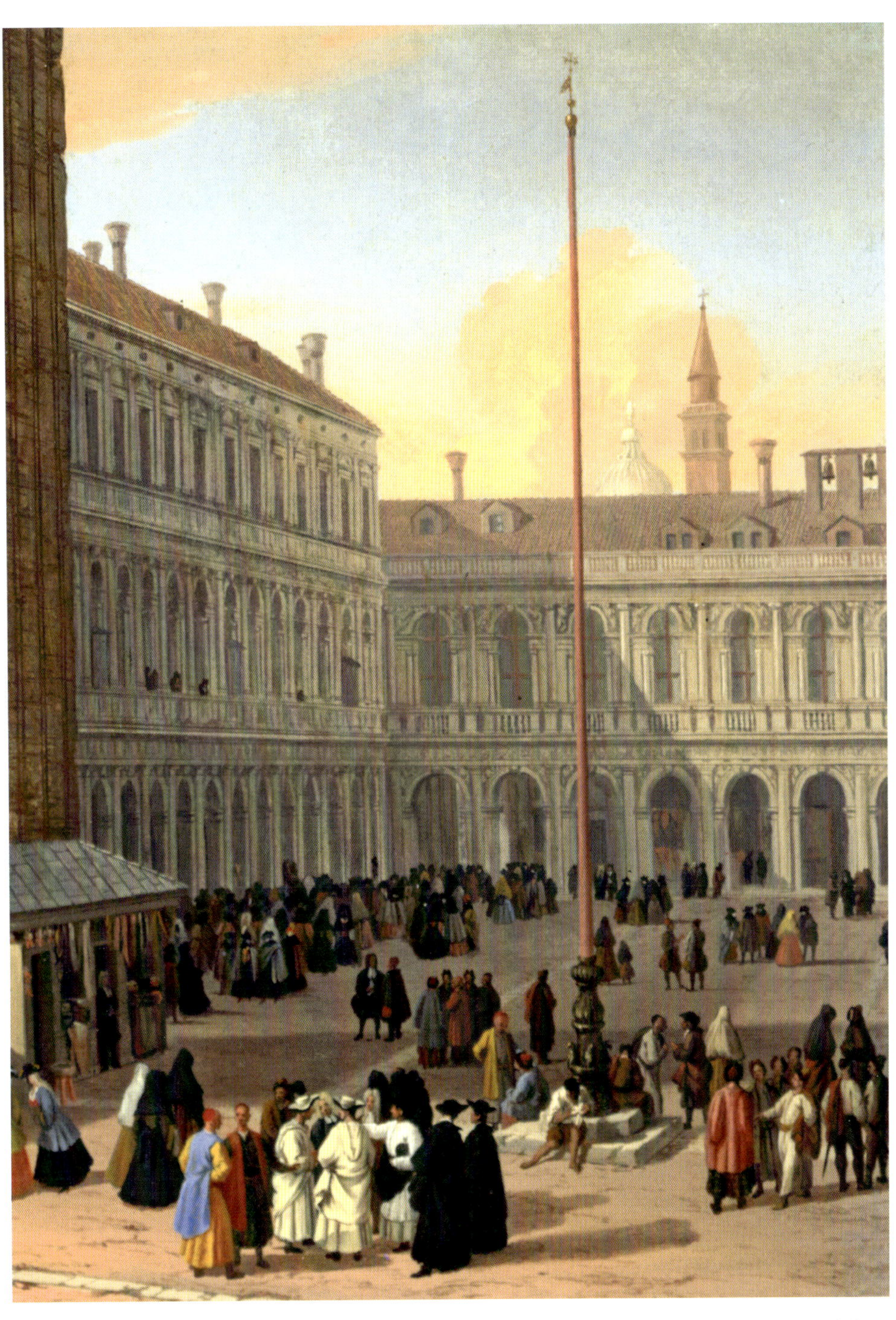

Luca Carlevaris
Piazza San Marco Towards the Piazzetta (det.), before 1723
Oil on canvas, 25 x 39 1/8 in (63.5 x 99.4 cm)
The John and Mable Ringling Museum of Art, Sarasota; Museum Purchase, 1953, SN670

9. Giovanni Giuliani, 1663–1744
Pair of Seated Blackamoor Figures, ca. 1722–28
Polychromed and gilded terra-cotta with wooden base, each 35 1/2 x 15 1/2 in. (90.2 x 39.4 cm)
The John and Mable Ringling Museum of Art, Sarasota; Museum Purchase, 1949, SN7270 and SN7271

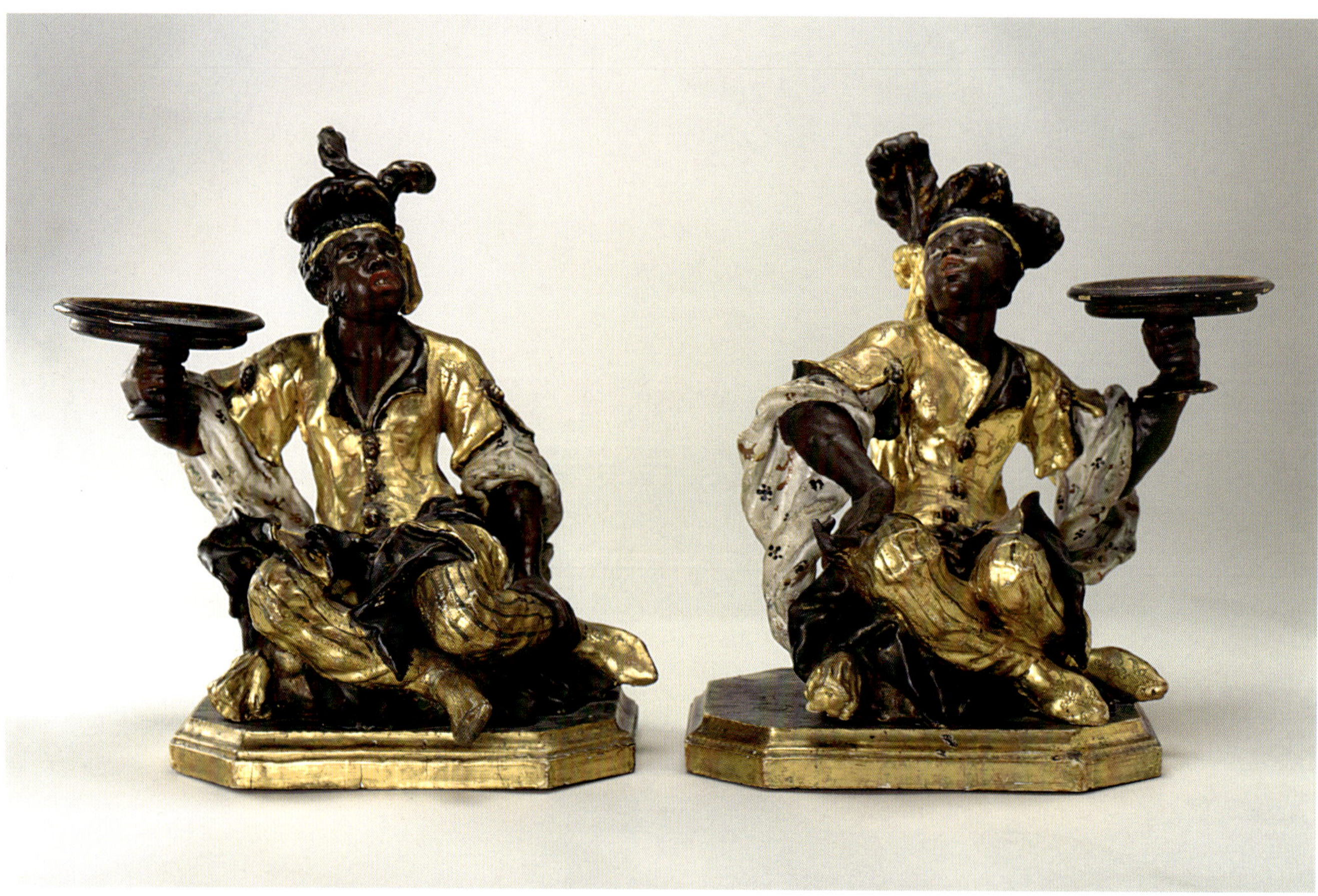

Exotic subjects fascinated Rococo artists. Fancifully dressed slave figures, called Blackamoors, were especially popular in the decorative arts and were fashioned into vases and stands. Here the artist has created striking designs for two figures that probably were meant to hold candles. With their full red lips, short broad noses, and tightly curled hair, the sculptures represent stereotypes of Africans in eighteenth-century European art. They wear plumed headbands tied at the neck and model elaborate gold costumes—characteristics also commonly found in portrayals of Africans at that time.[1] This style of dress is perhaps more accurately termed *à la Turque*; however, artists tended to conflate the image of the Moor (a Muslim from Spain or North Africa) with that of the Turk, given the affinities between the two cultures and Venice's long-standing trade connections (and fascination) with the Near East.[2] It is for these reasons, as well as the widely held belief that Africans were synonymous with exoticism, that Blackamoor sculpture enjoyed such popularity in the Venetian decorative arts.

The Ringling Blackamoors were sculpted by the Venetian-born Giovanni Giuliani, who trained in both Venice and Munich before moving to Vienna in 1689. It is believed he made them for the imperial apartments in the Cistercian abbey of Heiligenkreuz. A pair of terra-cotta Blackamoor figures also hailing from that abbey (now in the Stiftsmuseum, Heiligenkreuz im Wienerwald) provide valuable circumstantial evidence for a proposed dating of the Ringling pieces to circa 1722–28 (fig. 9.1).

After joining the Heiligenkreuz abbey as a lay brother in 1711, Giuliani became involved in the renovation and decoration of its church. He constructed a new funerary chapel and choir stalls, and he produced sculpture for the cloister, courtyard, and high altar. In addition, he was asked to design the interiors of the emperor's apartments, and it appears that the Stiftsmuseum terra-cottas were *bozzetti* (small-scale models) for sculpture decorating the apartments' elaborate furnace, which was completed in 1722.[3] After the death of the abbot, Gerhard Weixelberger, in 1728, the furnace was dismantled, evidently because his successor found the presence of Blackamoors there indecorous. It was reinstalled in 1737 and remains there today—bearing no sign of the figures.[4]

Although the Ringling Blackamoors are nearly twice the size of the Stiftsmuseum terra-cotta *bozzetti*, the two pairs share many stylistic similarities, particularly in their description of the sleeves and buttons and the modeling of the faces and limbs. Given these likenesses as well as their common origin, it is interesting to hypothesize that they simply evolved from the 1722 furnace decoration. Yet the significant discrepancy in size and the postural difference between the figures and the *bozzetti*—the figures sit with tucked legs on their bases, whereas the terra-cottas are designed to sit on a ledge with legs dangling—make it more likely that the Ringling Blackamoors were intended to be freestanding objects. The strong resemblance between the pairs may therefore simply reflect the consistency with which Giuliani executed his overall vision for the emperor's room before the stylistic regime change of 1728.

AL

Notes

1. In the first edition of *Iconologia*, Cesare Ripa's popular sourcebook of symbolic images, figures wearing feathered dress personify America—not Africa. According to the art historian Lorenz Seelig, comparable feathered attire was first used in theatrical portrayals of Africans during the late Renaissance and early Baroque, as feathers were by then considered synonymous with "exotic origin or exotic appearance." Lorenz Seelig, "Christopher Jamnitzer's 'Moor's Head': A Late Renaissance Drinking Vessel" in Earle and Lowe 2005, 208, n. 70. For representations of Africans in late Renaissance and Baroque Europe, see Veit 1976; and Seelig in Earle and Lowe 2005, 207.

2. For more on the European fascination with Turkish culture during the eighteenth century, see Devisse and Mollat 1979, 154–60.

3. An inventory of the emperor's rooms at Heiligenkreuz compiled in 1927 lists six Blackamoor figures: two sitting pairs and one large standing pair. These have been identified as the Stiftsmuseum terra-cottas, the Ringling Blackamoors, and another pair of Blackamoors that are also in the Stiftsmuseum, respectively. For this inventory, see Ronzoni in Vienna 2005, 232, n. 5.

4. Ibid., n. 2.

Provenance: Stift Heiligenkreuz, Austria; Oscar Bondy [1870–1944], Vienna and New York, by 1938; seized by Nazi forces, 1938*; restituted to Elisabeth (Mrs. Oscar) Bondy, New York, 1948; probably sold by Mrs. Bondy to the Blumka Gallery, New York; (with Blumka Gallery, New York, 1949).

* The sculptures are identified in the Nazi-generated inventory of Bondy's collection (July 4, 1938; Vienna, BDA-Archiv, Restitutions-Materialen, K 8/1, p. 11) as nos. OB (Oscar Bondy) 190 and 191, "Sitzender Mohr mit Tonschale [bemalt und teilw. Vergeldet (Giuliani?] H = 39 cm, um 1740." Also, Allied forces in Austria charged with restituting stolen art after the war list the sculptures as having passed through one of their collecting sites, the monastery of Kremsmünster, as "nos. 375 and 376." Each is described as "Giuliani, Ceramic, seated negro, painted and gilded, wooden pedestal, [dimensions] 36/39." National Archives and Records Administration, College Park, Md., National Archives Record Group R6260, entry USACA-USFA, file Rep and Rest, box 158. I am grateful to Victoria Reed, Museum of Fine Arts, Boston, for locating this information and sharing it with me.

References: Sarasota 1953, n.p., no. 40; Lawrence 1955, n.p., no. 4; Sobotik in Sarasota 1972, 46–47, no. 123; Duval in Sarasota 1982, 78, nos. 62, 63; Merling 2002, 140; Ronzoni in Vienna 2005, 232–33, ill.

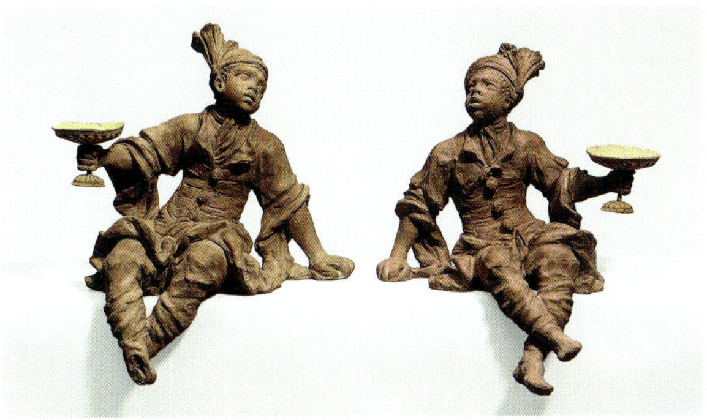

Fig. 9.1. Giovanni Giuliani
Pair of Seated Blackamoors, 1722–25
Terra-cotta, each 15 1/2 x 14 in. (40.8 x 35.5 cm)
Stift Heiligenkreuz, Stiftsmuseum, Heiligenkreuz im Wienerwald

10. Giovanni Antonio Pellegrini, 1675–1741
   Justice Fulminating the Vices, 1717
   Oil on canvas, 13 5/8 x 12 11/16 in. (34.6 x 32.3 cm)
   Blanton Museum of Art, The University of Texas at Austin, The Suida-Manning Collection 443.1999

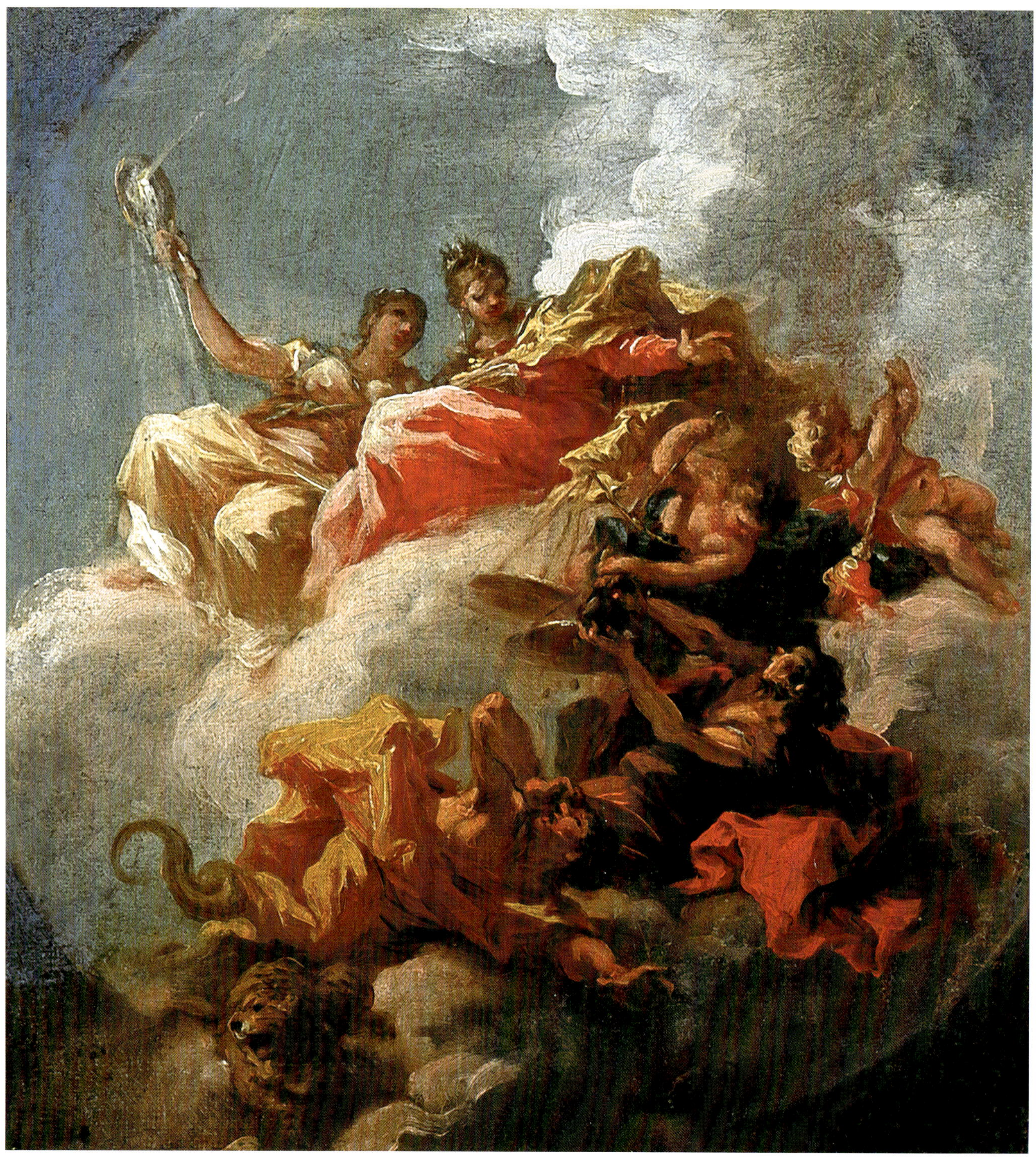

This is an oil sketch for Pellegrini's painting *Wisdom and Justice Battling the Vices*, commissioned in 1716 as part of the elaborate ceiling decorations in the Collegezaal, or aldermen's chamber, of the Antwerp city hall.[1] In 1769 the French artist and historian Jean-Baptiste Descamps cited the painting in his travel book about the southern Low Countries, praising Pellegrini's fluid style and apparent ease with the medium.[2] Descamps's comments could also be applied to the present image, which the Antwerp canvas closely resembles. The two works share the same bold composition, and the sketch bears a clearly indicated outline for the circular format used in the final painting.

Fittingly for a room devoted to discussions of civic concerns, *Justice Fulminating the Vices* focuses upon the victory of righteousness and wisdom over corruption and immorality. In conceiving the Blanton oil sketch, Pellegrini drew freely from *Iconologia*, Cesare Ripa's perennially popular sourcebook of symbolic images, a copy of which he owned.[3] The focal point of the composition is the personification of Justice, who appears in rich pink and gold garments near the center of the canvas. Seated on clouds, the figure roughly corresponds to Ripa's personification of Divine Justice as a young woman wearing a crown.[4] As in *Iconologia*, the diadem represents her worldly power, including the right to mete out punishment.

Prudence is seated at her side, holding a mirror, a device that, according to Ripa, allows her to know herself—including her defects—better.[5] The rays shining from the looking glass, evidently omitted from the finished painting, reflect the sketch's title. Descending from heaven, divine lightning fulminates, or blasts, at personifications of corruption. Justice and Prudence are aided by two putti, one using a torch as a weapon and the other holding a pair of scales, both of which are also attributes of Justice in her different guises.[6] The figure with whom they grapple is probably Avarice, personified as a greedy old woman carrying a bag or purse; she tries to alter the balance of the scales with the coins falling from this receptacle.[7] Beneath her, shielding his face from Justice's divine light, is the personification of Deceit. He corresponds to some details in *Iconologia*, which characterizes that vice as a male figure with serpents' tails (although Pellegrini shows only one) who is accompanied by a leopard.[8] The former probably refers to the deceiving snake in the Garden of Eden. Leopards also bore a negative connotation; Ripa notes that their spots served to lure unsuspecting victims.

Pellegrini, like several other eighteenth-century Venetian artists, especially Sebastiano Ricci and Giambattista Tiepolo, worked internationally and enjoyed great popularity across Europe. Although best remembered for his work in England, where he lived from 1708 to 1713, Pellegrini also traveled in Austria, Bohemia, France, the Netherlands, and Saxony. His loose, painterly style and extraordinary sense of color—balancing rich, deep tones with warm pastels—mark him among the most important originators of the Rococo style.

ST

Notes

1. For discussions of the Antwerp commission, see Knox 1995, 132–33; and Smekens 1973, 74–78.

2. Descamps 1772, 203.

3. It was included in an inventory of Pellegrini's books made after his death. That inventory, which is reproduced in an article by Frances Vivian in *Burlington Magazine*, lists the book only as *La Iconologia del Ripa*, and does not indicate its publication date. See Vivian 1962, 328, n. 48. Ripa's *Iconologia* appeared in numerous editions over several hundred years and was translated into several languages. For the present entry, I have made use of an early English edition, *Iconologia: Or, Moral Emblems* (1709), which predates Pellegrini's painting by only a few years.

4. Ripa 1709, 36.

5. Ibid., 63.

6. Ripa personifies Justice in several forms. For his simplest incarnation of her—and with the torch as her attribute—see Ripa 1709, 47. For Divine Justice, which seems to have been the main source for Pellegrini's painting, see idem, 36.

7. Ripa 1709, 8.

8. Ibid., 42. The Antwerp painting also includes a mask falling from the hands of Deceit. This motif, which corresponds to Ripa's description, is not readily apparent in the Blanton Museum oil sketch.

Provenance: Probably acquired by Robert Manning [1924–1996] and Bertina Suida [1922–1992].

Reference: Austin 2006, 83.

11. (a, b) Follower of Marco Ricci, 1676–1730
   Landscape with Tobias and the Angel, ca. 1715
   Landscape with Boaz and Ruth, ca. 1715
   Oil on canvas, each 29 3/4 x 36 3/4 in. (75.6 x 93.3 cm)
   The John and Mable Ringling Museum of Art, Sarasota; Bequest of John Ringling, 1936, SN179 and
   SN180

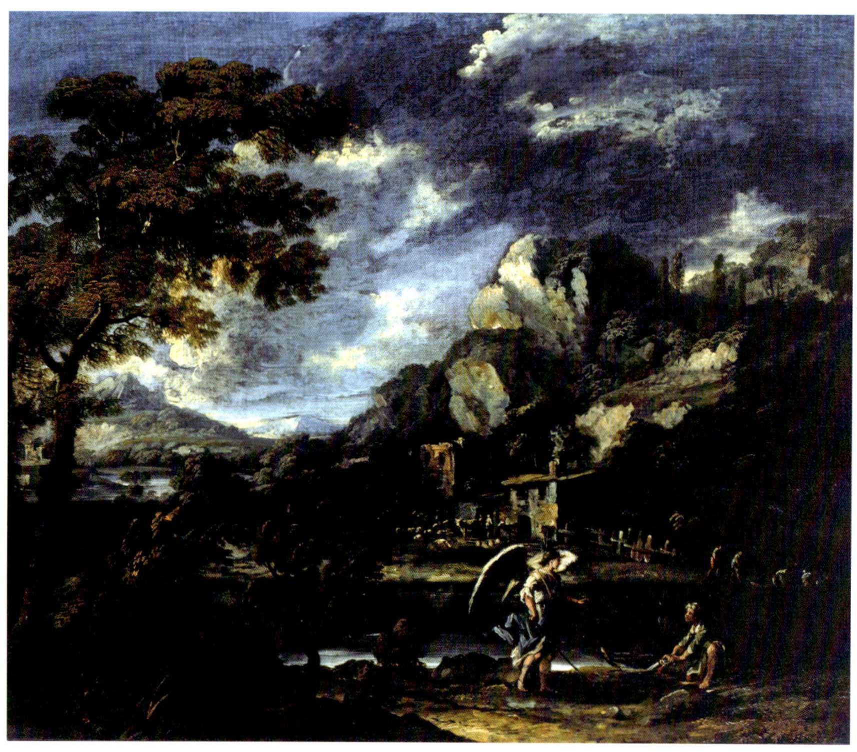

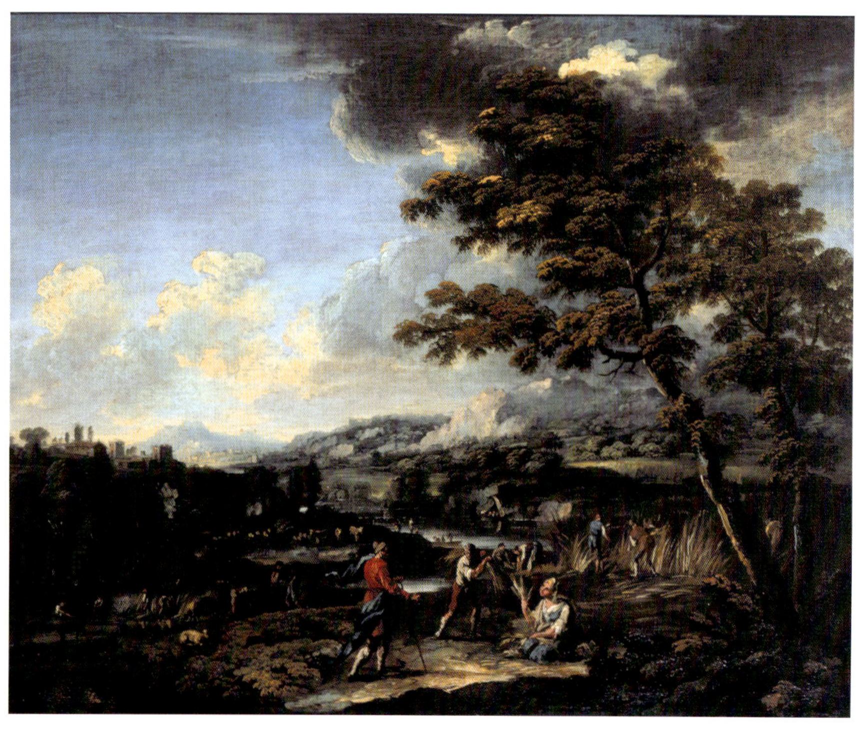

Marco Ricci's greatest contribution to eighteenth-century Venetian art lies in his poetic landscape imagery. Ranging from bucolic pastoral views to wild mountainous vistas, his paintings draw upon the work of great French seventeenth-century landscape artists such as Gaspard Dughet (also known as Gaspard Poussin) and Claude Gellée (called Claude Lorrain). The present pair of canvases by an unknown adherent of Ricci's style—their broad valley views highlighted by pastel hills and romantically twisted trees—are very much in keeping with this tradition. Another influence on Ricci was the Neapolitan painter Salvator Rosa, whose picturesque, anecdotal landscapes were widely popular in Italy during the seventeenth and eighteenth centuries. A narrative component also figures in the Ringling paintings—both of which depict episodes from the Old Testament—though that seems to have been a pretext for the artist's true focus, the landscape itself.

Ricci's pictorial vision of nature was one he likely developed while working as a theatrical-scene designer in England with Giovanni Antonio Pellegrini between 1708 and 1712.[1] Up to that time, scenography had relied upon the decorative, heavily Baroque models popularized by the Bibienas, a family of Bolognese stage designers and architects who were active across Europe from the 1670s to the 1780s. Beginning in the early 1700s, the field underwent a significant stylistic change as artists began producing backdrops that were more closely related to "naturalistic" landscape and capriccio painting.[2] Ricci became a leading Venetian proponent of this change. His successful theatrical work and canvases alike influenced a new generation of view and landscape painters, including Canaletto, Francesco Guardi, and Michele Marieschi, and spawned a host of imitators and followers, such as the artist who made the present pendants.

These landscapes draw upon Ricci's example in both style and technique. The staccato brushstrokes of thickly layered oil paint, called *macchie*, or marks, were a trademark of the artist. They are particularly visible in the voluminous, peach-tinted clouds and golden shafts of wheat used to accent the biblical story of Boaz meeting his future wife, Ruth, for the first time. Ricci's free brushwork likewise finds imitation in the articulation of foliage and rendering of the Archangel Raphael's wings in the pendant image, which depicts the apocryphal story of Tobias and the Angel. Another sign of the artist's influence in the Ringling canvases is the use of a reddish-brown ground to enhance the dramatic play of light and shadow.

AL

Notes

1. For Ricci in England, see Constable and Links 1989, 58–59; and Pedrocco 2002, 73.

2. For eighteenth-century Venetian theater, see Povoledo 1951, 126

Provenance: Private collection, New York, by 1909; John Ringling [1866–1936], Sarasota, after 1909–36.

References: Detroit and Indianapolis 1952, no. 56 (SN180 only); Miami Beach 1953; Milkovich in Memphis and Lexington 1965, 17, nos. 27, 28; Fredericksen and Zeri 1972, 174, 637; Tomory 1976, 108–9, nos. 106, 107; Sarasota 1979, 12, no. 13; Janson 1986, 107, nos. 31, 32; Borys 2008, 96.

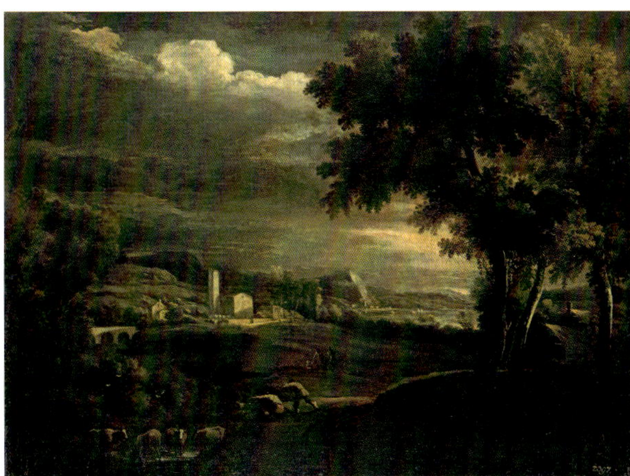

Fig. 11.1. Marco Ricci
At the Mountain Lake (Am Bergsee), n.d.
Oil on canvas, 37 13/16 x 50 3/4 in. (96 x 129 cm)
Gemäldegalerie Alte Meister, Staatliche Kunstsammlungen, Dresden, Gal. Nr. 562

12. Giovanni Battista Piazzetta, 1683–1754
   Madonna and Child Appearing to Saint Philip Neri, probably 1725 or after
   Oil on canvas, 44 1/4 x 25 in. (112.4 x 63.5 cm)
   Samuel H. Kress Collection, National Gallery of Art, Washington, 1961.9.82

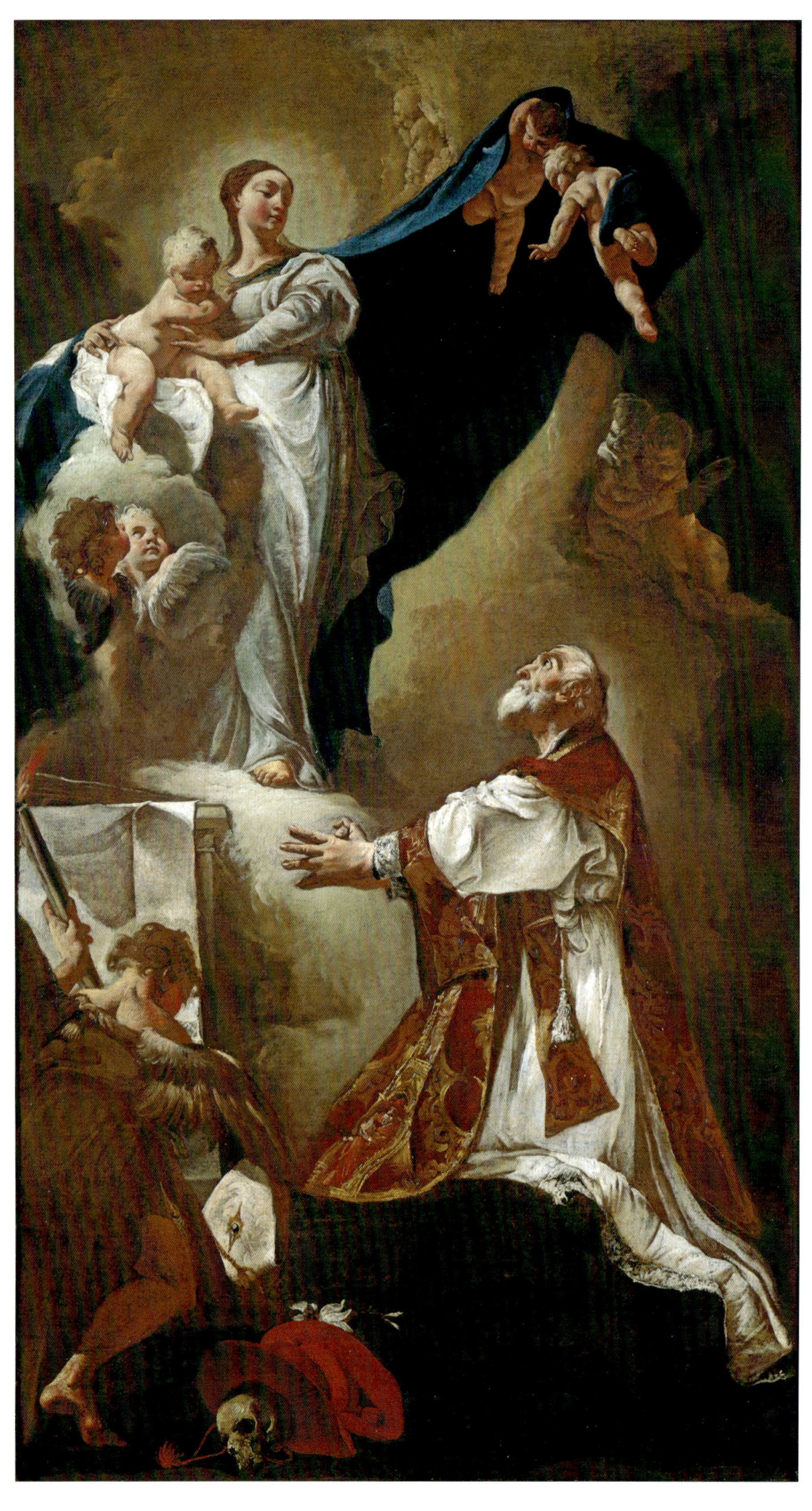

Renowned for his intelligence, piety, and humility as well as his remarkable ability to make Roman Catholic doctrine accessible in simple, appealing terms, St. Philip Neri (1515–1595) ranks among the most influential figures of the Counter-Reformation. In addition to addressing both the spiritual and physical needs of poor Romans, he hosted groups of the faithful for intellectual discussions of spirituality; these initiatives led him, in 1575, to found the order of the Congregation of the Oratory.[1] Biographies of Neri, who was canonized in 1621, include accounts of his devotion to the Virgin Mary, which was rewarded by numerous visions of her and the infant Jesus. The nature of these experiences is reflected in Piazzetta's painting.

As Philip kneels before an altar, the Virgin, holding Jesus and surrounded by cherubs, appears before him. Piazzetta masterfully blurs the earthly and heavenly realms: while the altar, floor, and steps seem solid and tangible, the rest of the space evokes an otherworldly apparition. Lost in his contemplation of this vision, he seems unaware of the candle-bearing angel alongside him. The placement of the Virgin's mantle, pulled upward by cherubs and partially covering them, is an allusion to the Madonna della Misericordia, who shelters and protects the faithful with her cloak.[2] The stem of lilies on the altar steps suggests Philip's purity and sanctity. The red cardinal's hats, miter, and skull at the lower left have been interpreted as symbols of worldly temptations that Philip rejected.[3] The skull, which typically appears in images of the Crucifixion, refers both to Christ's triumph over death and to his direct link with Adam and the Garden of Eden.[4] Piazzetta may have included it here to reinforce the message of salvation offered by the Virgin and Christ Child.

As the art historian Eric Garberson noted, Piazzetta's image of the saint relies to some extent upon a 1614 altarpiece of the same subject by Guido Reni (fig. 12.1).[5] In both works, the elaborately dressed saint, a stem of lilies at his feet, kneels in prayer before the altar, above which is an apparition of the Virgin Mary and Jesus. Probably the most striking difference between the two images is how each artist has depicted the experience. In the earlier altarpiece, the apparition appears behind the main figure and thus outside his view, as if Reni were offering a glimpse into Philip's psyche. In contrast, Piazzetta, painting more than a century later, portrays the saint actually seeing the miracle occur.

The Virgin Appearing to Saint Philip Neri is one of two copies by Piazzetta's hand of his altarpiece in the Church of Sta. Maria della Consolazione, Venice.[6] Because the National Gallery of Art painting is less than one-third the size of the original, scholars initially thought it was a *modello*, or detailed study, made for the altarpiece's patrons.[7] Despite Piazzetta's loose handling of paint in this canvas, its rich details and fine finish suggest that it is actually a *ricordo*, or smaller-scale copy, by him; until the nineteenth century, patrons commonly ordered such replicas of famous paintings from major artists.[8]

ST

Notes

1. Bibliotheca Sanctorum 1987, 759–90.

2. For the Madonna della Misericordia, see Schiller 1966, 198.

3. Jones (1981, 2: 182) noted the objects' relationship to earthly temptations.

4. For skull symbolism as related to the Crucifixion, see Schiller, 169.

5. Garberson in De Grazia and Garberson 1996, 208–9.

6. The other version is in the Residenzgalerie, Salzburg. Measuring 36 5/8 x 21 in. (93 x 53.3 cm) it, too, is small compared to the final painting. See Salzburger Residenzgalerie 1975, 87.

7. For a brief review of scholarly opinions about the National Gallery of Art picture, see Garberson in De Grazia and Garberson 1996, 208.

8. For a discussion of the altarpiece, see Jones 1981, 2: 140–41, 223–24.

Provenance: Private collection, Rome, by 1941; Adolph Loewi, Los Angeles; Kress acquisition, 1950.

References: Arslan 1942, 206; Pallucchini 1942a, 10; Pallucchini 1942b, 49; Pallucchini 1956, 18, 20; Haskell 1963, 273; Washington, D.C. 1965, 264; Zampetti 1969, 128; Fredricksen and Zeri 1972, 163; Shapley 1973, 137–38; Residenzgalerie 1975, 87; Shapley 1979, 2: 365–66; Jones 1981, 2: 223–24, no. 73; Mariuz and Pallucchini 1982, 85, no. 43; Washington, D.C. 1985, 304; Knox 1992, 102; Martineau and Robinson 1994, 476, no. 73; Garberson in De Grazia and Garberson 1996, 207–12.

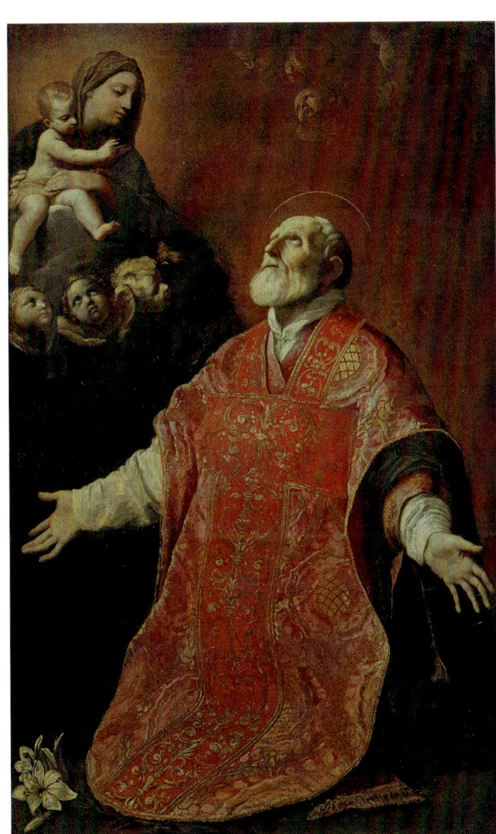

Fig. 12.1. Guido Reni
Saint Philip Neri, 1614
Oil on canvas, 70 7/8 x 43 5/16 in. (180 x 110 cm)
Sta. Maria in Vallicella, Rome

13. (a – o) Antonio Visentini, 1688–1782

Prospectus Magni Canalis Venetiarum adduti Certamine Nautico et Nundinis Venetis
(Venice: Giovanni Battista Pasquali Press, 1751)
Etchings, each 10 13/16 x 16 7/8 in. (27.5 x 42.8 cm)
Matthew Nimetz Collection, New York

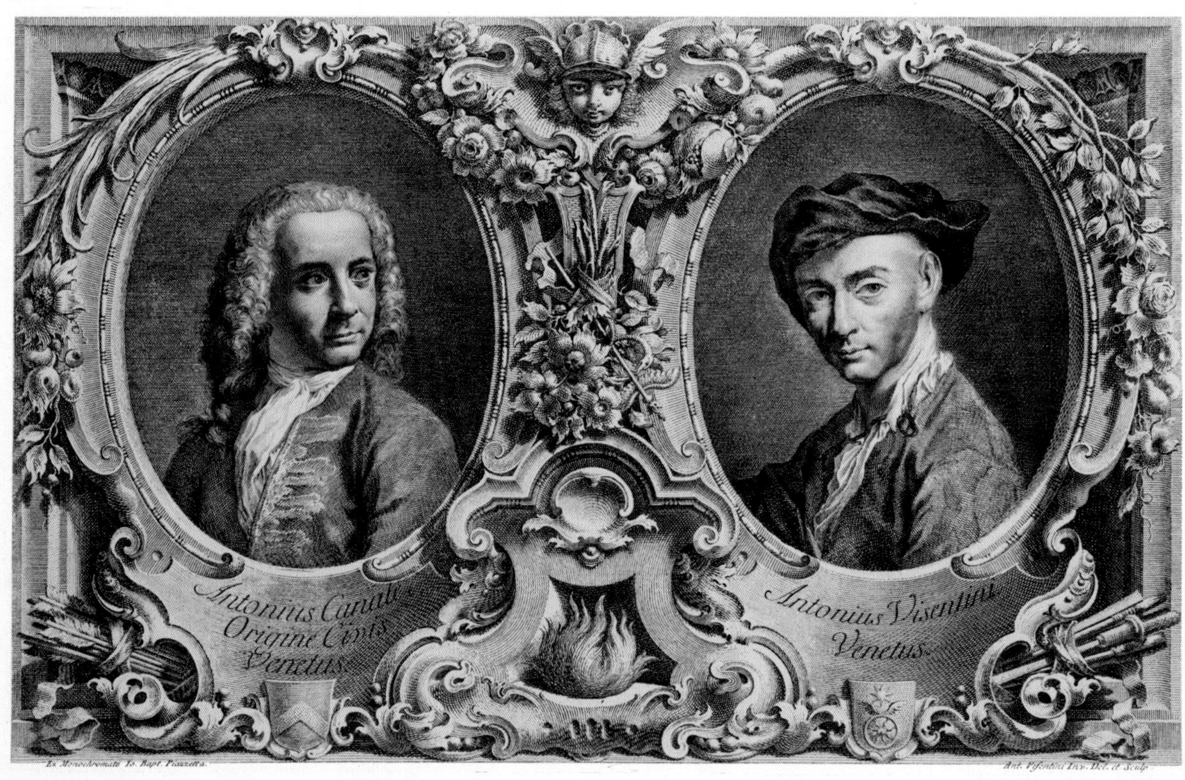

13a. Frontispiece

In 1735 Giovanni Battista Pasquali published a portfolio of fourteen etchings by Antonio Visentini after twelve Grand Canal views and two Venetian festival scenes painted by Canaletto.[1] Titled *Prospectus Magni Canalis Venetiarum*, it was conceived by Joseph Smith, who, besides financing Pasquali's press, had served as Canaletto's de facto agent since about 1730. As a line on the title page reading "in Aedibus Josephi Smith Angli" (in the home of Joseph Smith, Englishman) indicates, the original paintings hung in his Venetian palazzo—where they could be viewed by visiting Grand Tourists who could in turn commission copies or variations from the artist for themselves. Publishing was one of Smith's many enterprises, and the Visentini endeavor was intended to expose Canaletto's work to prospective patrons who were unable to see the originals in person as well as provide a more modestly priced alternative to buyers who could not afford his canvases.

The venture was a great success. Canaletto replicated (and in some cases modified) the paintings for many purchasers, and in 1742 Pasquali produced a second, expanded edition of the Visentini portfolio. It included twenty-four additional plates, also derived from Canaletto paintings that Smith either owned or had handled on the artist's behalf.[2] The words *elegantius recusi* (elegantly recut) on the title page meant that enough copies of the first volume had been sold to necessitate a re-etching of the fourteen plates it contained. The second edition must have sold well, too, as a third edition appeared in 1751 and a fourth in 1754; both of these duplicated the 1742 version. The Nimetz prints, which are in nearly perfect condition, belong to the 1751 reprinting.

By the time the 1751 edition was issued, Canaletto had been living in London for nearly five years. Although he had prospered in Venice in the 1730s under Joseph Smith's wing, Italy's involvement in the War of Austrian Succession (1740–48) severely curtailed the flow of tourism to Venice, thus greatly restricting his patronage. In search of renewed opportunity, he moved to London in 1746. He would stay there until 1755, returning to Venice only once, for eight months in 1750.[3] Given the publication date of the third edition, it is interesting to hypothesize that Canaletto and Smith saw in the artist's brief return home a favorable moment to revive the Visentini prints. Although Visentini would not have needed to work from the original paintings this time (the third edition being identical to the second), there was nothing to indicate who owned the works; the line "in Aedibus Josephi Smith Angli" no longer appeared on the title page.

The first twelve prints depict the cityscape along the Grand Canal. Seven (13b–h) offer contiguous views that begin at the Rialto Bridge and move sequentially downstream toward the Piazza S. Marco, while the other five (13i–m) take us upstream to the northern end of the canal, toward the mainland. As Eugene J. and Leslie N. Johnson write in their essay the prints "reconstruct the experience of floating down" the waters of the canal (see p. 34). Until the mid-nineteenth century, the Rialto was the only bridge to span the Grand Canal, making its neighborhood and surrounding waterways the heart of the city's activities. Consequently, it was from this point that most visitors would begin their exploration of Venice. With its additional twenty-four prints, the 1742 edition (and the identical 1751 and 1754 reissues) expanded upon the sequential arrangement with ten new views of the Grand Canal. The first two plates of Part 2 (13n and 13o) depict the points nearest the entrance of the canal from the mainland— images that doubtless enhanced travelers' "armchair reminiscences" (to use the Johnsons' term) of their arrival in Venice.

AL

Notes

1. Antonio Visentini, *Prospectus Magni Canalis Venetiarum addito Certamine Nautico et Nundinis Venetis* (Venice: Giovanni Battista Pasquali Press, 1735).

2. Smith's sale in 1762 of nearly his entire collection to King George III included only one Canaletto painting reproduced in the 1742 edition of the Visentini prints. The Earl Fitzwilliam bought another three of the twenty-four, and the Duke of Buckingham purchased eight or nine of them; the latter group later became known as the Harvey series.

3. For Canaletto's English period, see Finberg 1920, 29–36; Finberg 1934, 151, 158; and Baetjer and Links in New York 1989, 241.

Provenance: Jeudwine Collection, London (with David Tunick, Inc., New York, by 1972); Nimetz Collection, New York, 1972.

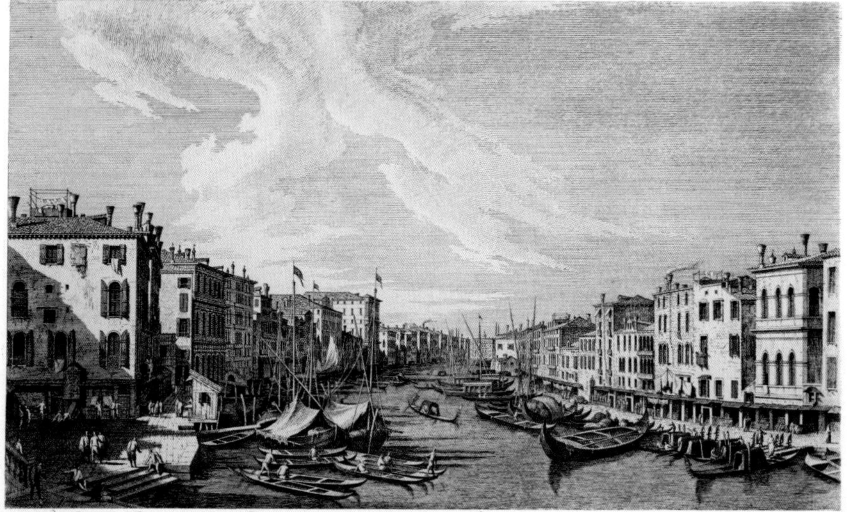

13b. *Ex Ponte Rivoalti ad Orientem, usque ad Aedes Foscarorum, cui respondet Ripa Vinaria*
   (*Grand Canal: Looking Southwest from the Rialto Bridge to the Palazzo Foscari*)

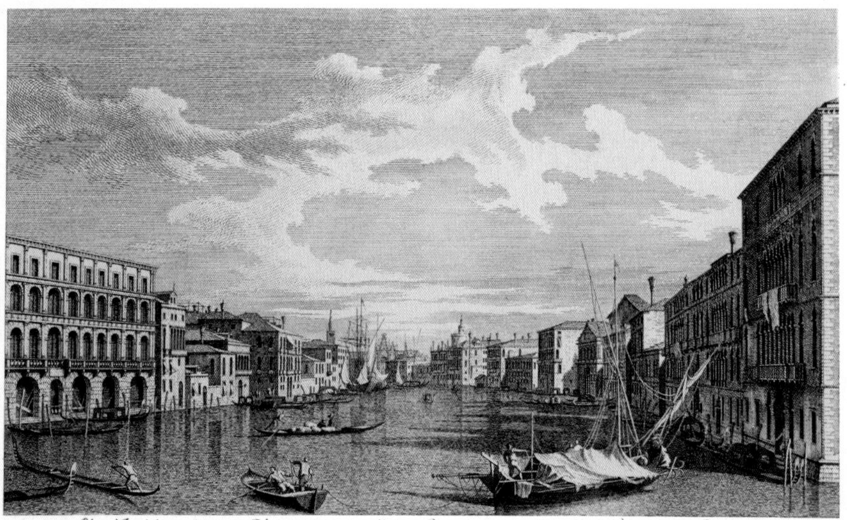

13c. *Ab Aedibus hinc Foscarorum, illinc Linorum, usque ad Templum Charitatis*
   (*Grand Canal: Looking South from the Palazzi Foscari and Moro-Lin to Sta. Maria della Carità*)

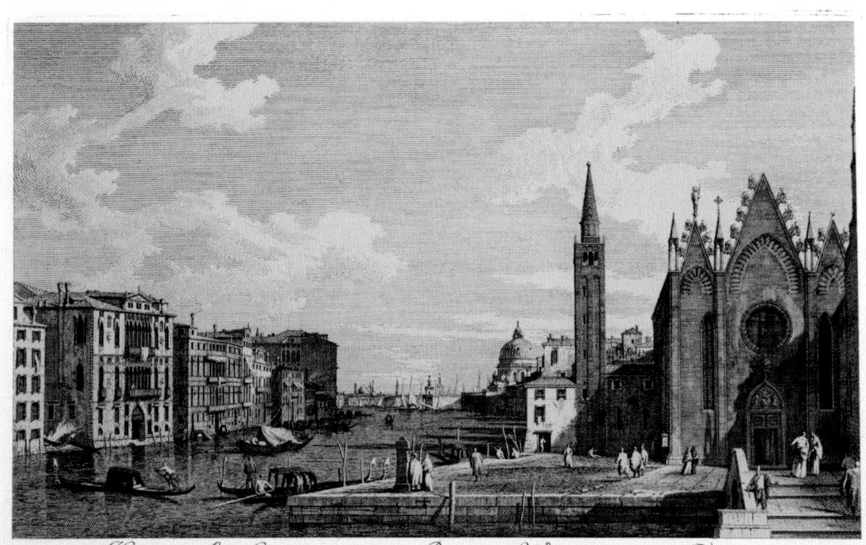

13d. *Hinc ex Aede Charitatis, illinc ex Regione S. Vitalis usque ad Telonium*
   (*Grand Canal: From Sta. Maria della Carità to the Bacino di S. Marco*)

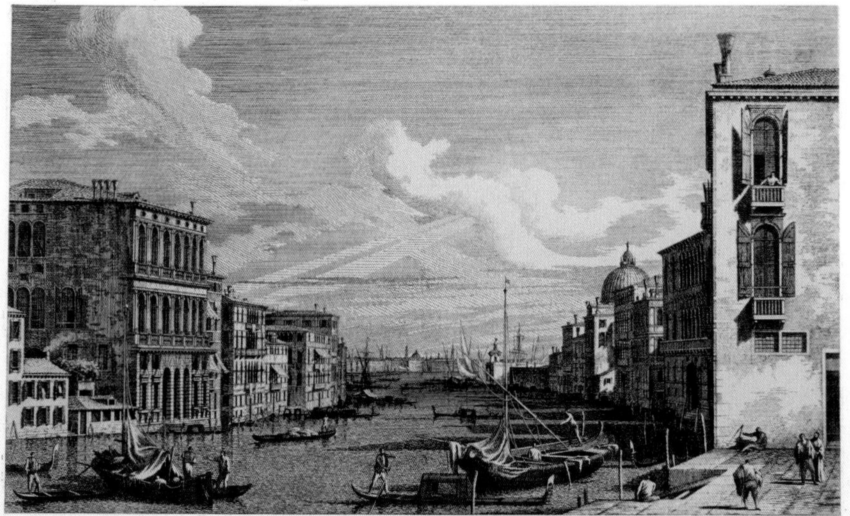

13e. *Hinc ex Platea S. Viti, illinc ex Domo Corneliorum, ad idem Telonium*
(*Grand Canal: Looking East from the Campo S. Vio*)

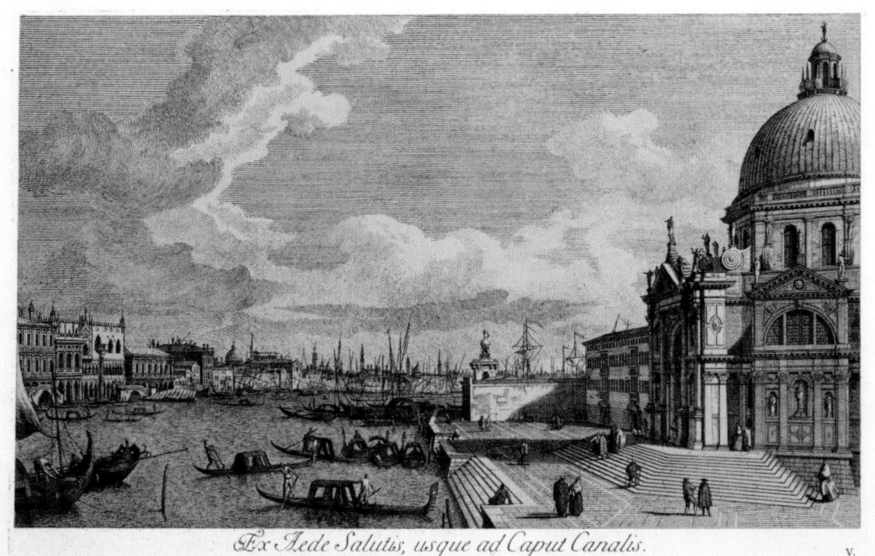

13f. *Ex Aede Salutis, usque ad Caput Canalis*
(*Entrance to the Grand Canal: Looking East*)

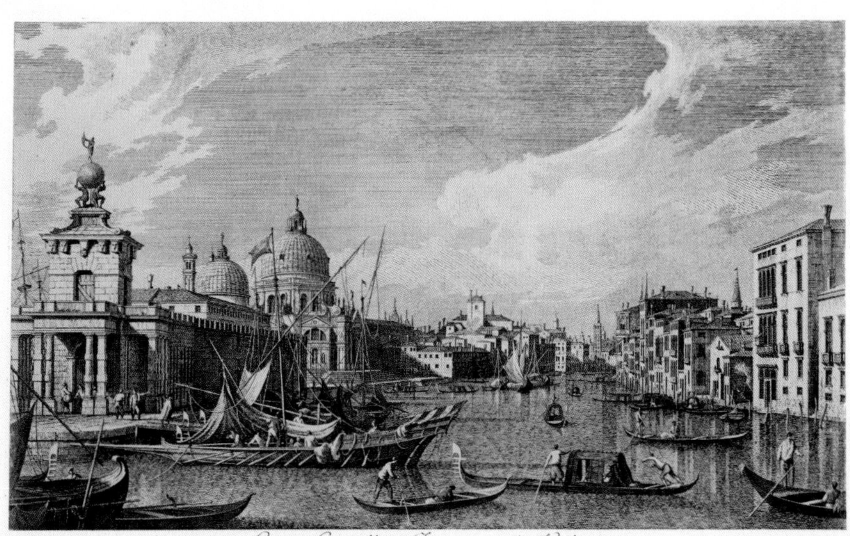

87.

13g. *Caput Canalis et Ingressus in Urbem*
(*Entrance to the Grand Canal: Looking West*)

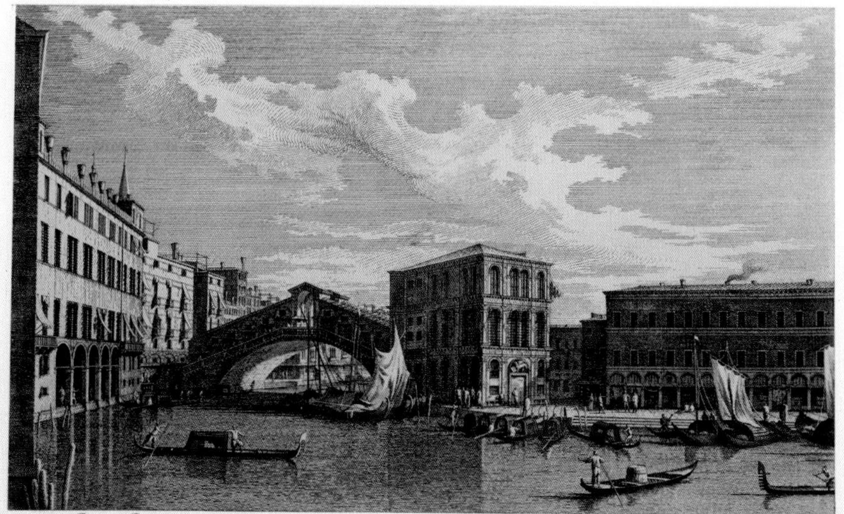

13h. *Pons Rivoalti ad Occidentem, cum Aedibus Publicis utrique Lateri adjectis*
(*Grand Canal: The Rialto Bridge from the North*)

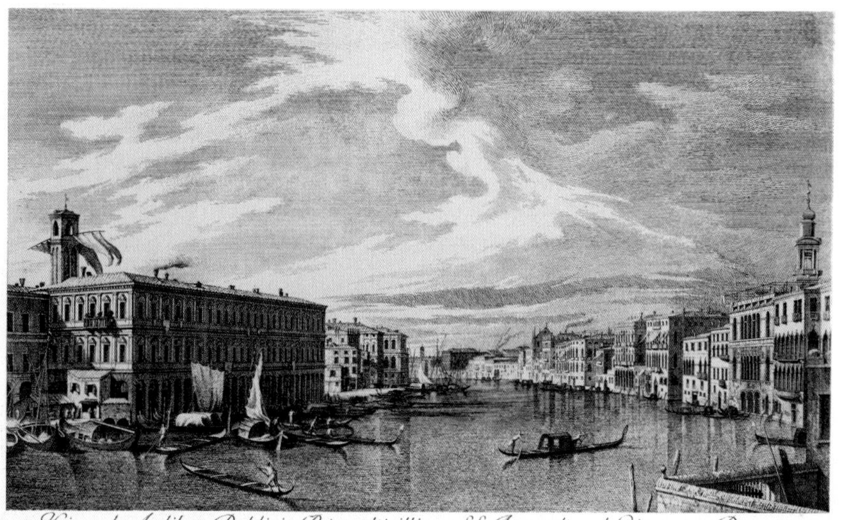

13i. *Hinc ab Aedibus Publicis Rivoalti, illinc a SS. Apostolis ad Grimanam Domum*
(*Grand Canal: Looking North from near the Rialto Bridge*)

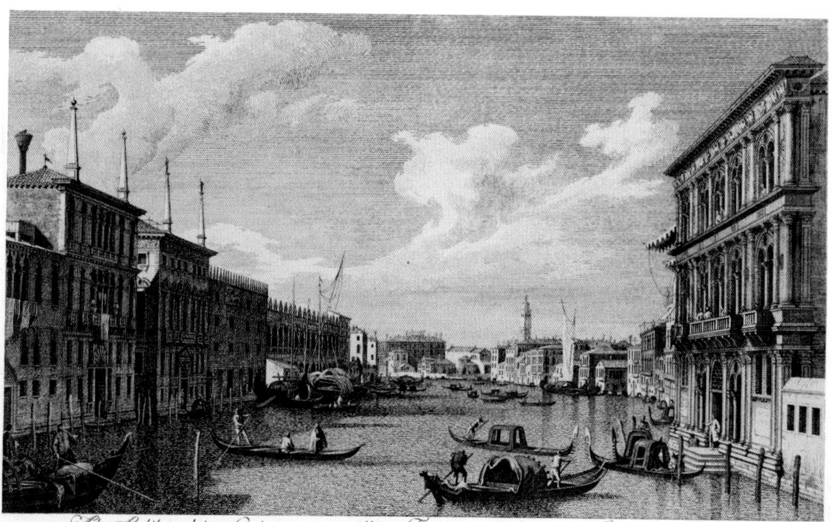

13j. *Ab Aedibus hinc Grimanorum, illinc Thronorum usque ad Canalem Regium*
(*Grand Canal: Looking Northwest from the Palazzo Vendramin-Calergi to S. Geremia and the Palazzo Flangini*)

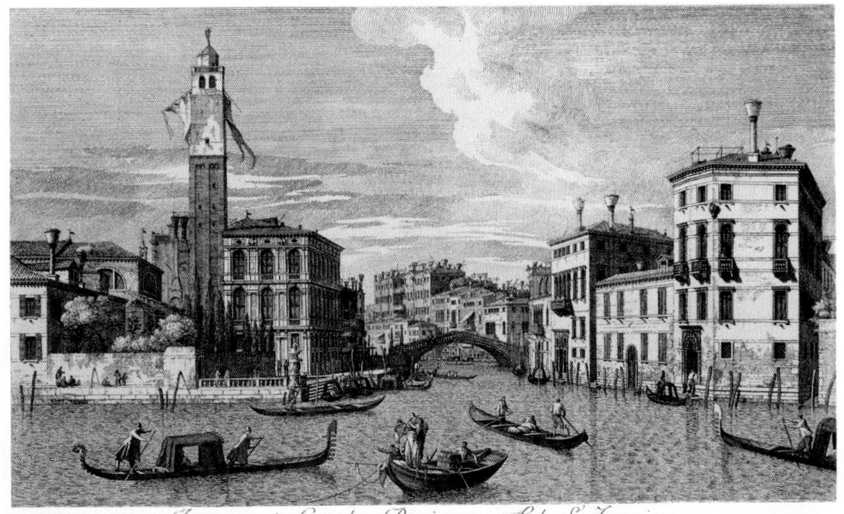

13k. *Ingressus in Canalem Regium ex Aede S. Jeremiae*
  (Grand Canal: S. Geremia and the Entrance to the Cannaregio)

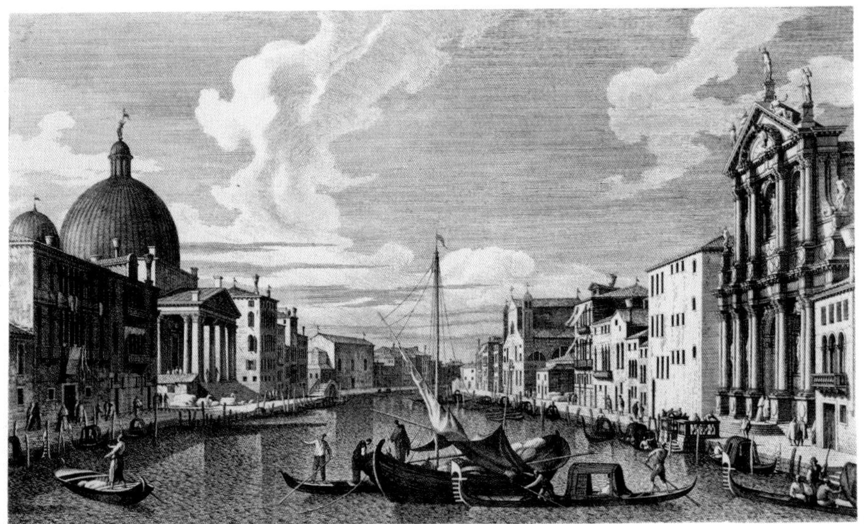

13l. *Hinc ex F. F. Discalceatorum Templo, illinc ex S. Simeone Minore usque ad Fullonium*
  (Grand Canal: Looking Southwest from the Chiesa degli Scalzi to the Fondamenta della Croce, with S. Simeone Piccolo)

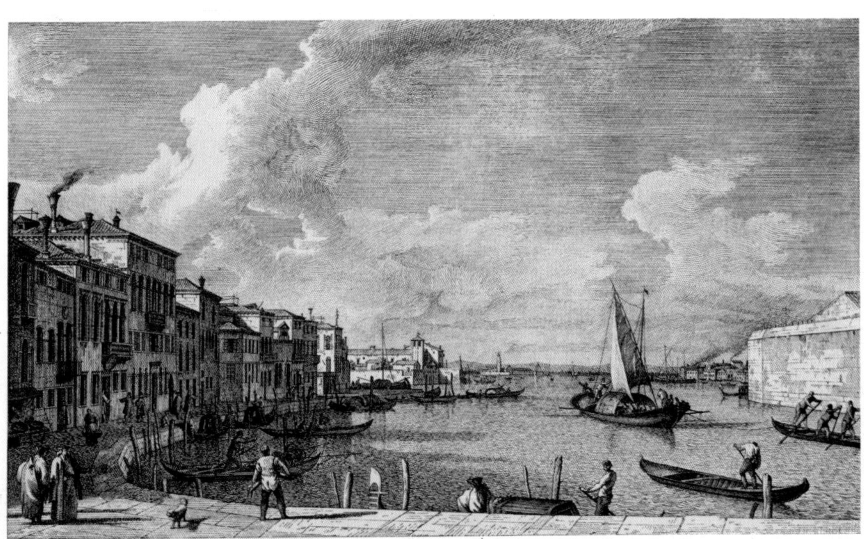

13m. *Ex Fullonio usque ad Aedem S. Clarae ubi Canalis desinit*
  (Canale di Sta. Chiara: Looking Northwest from the Fondamenta della Croce to the Lagoon)

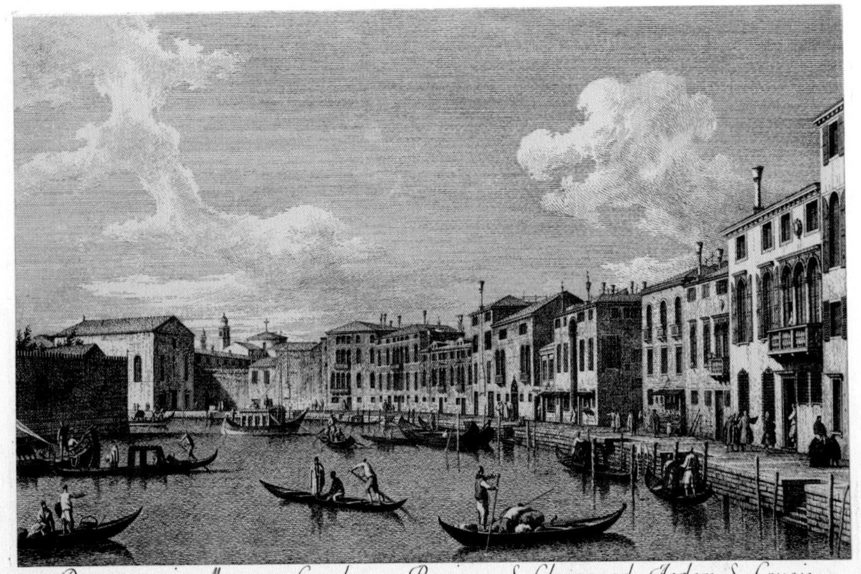

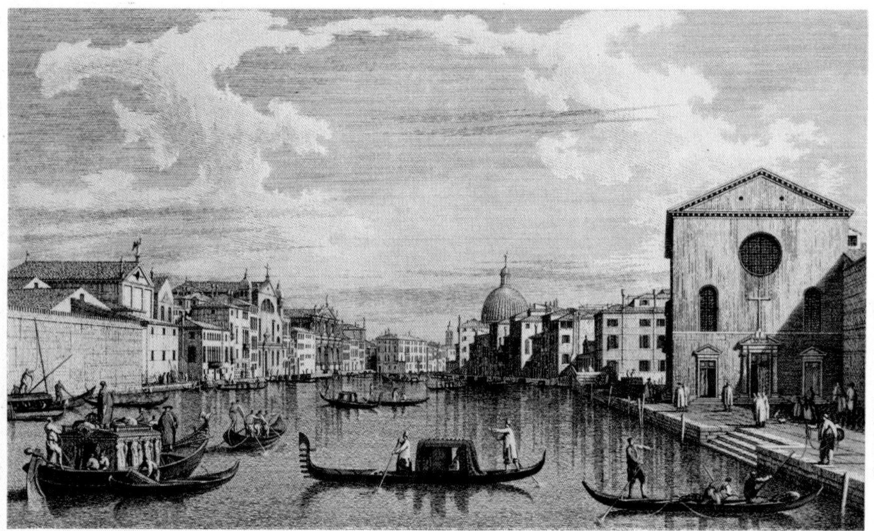

131. *Prospectus in Magnum Canalem e Regione S. Clarae ad Aedem S. Crucis*
   (*Canale di Sta. Chiara: Looking Southeast along the Fondamenta della Croce*)

130. *Prospectus ab Aede S. Crucis ad P. P. Discalceatos*
   (*Grand Canal: Looking Northeast from Sta. Croce to. S. Geremia*)

Antonio Visentin
Prospectus Magni Canalis Venetiarum adduti Certamine Nautico et Nundinis Venetis (det
(Venice: Giovanni Battista Pasquali Press, 175
Etchings, each 10 13/16 x 16 7/8 in. (27.5 x 42.8 cm
Matthew Nimetz Collection, New Yor

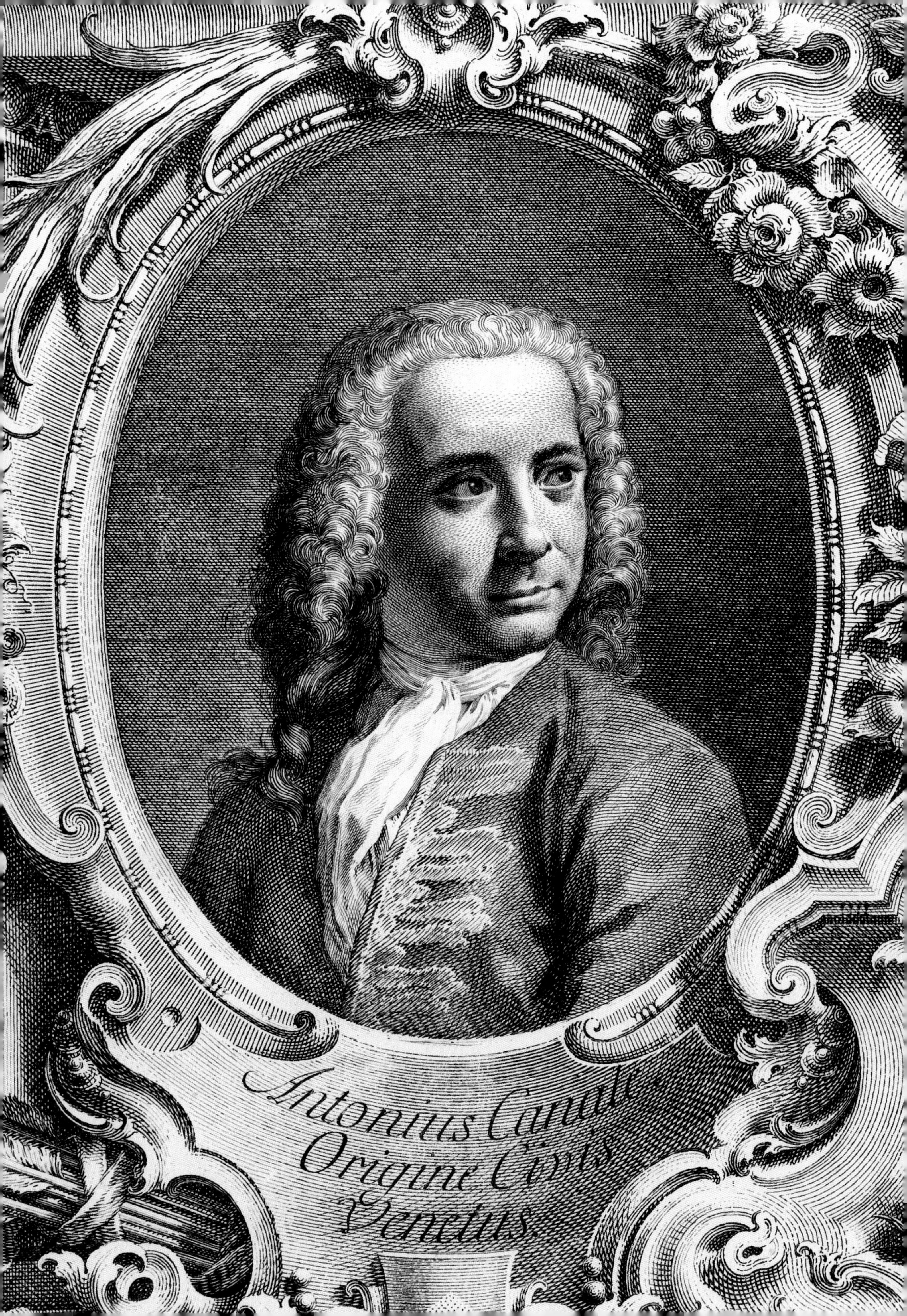
Antonius Canal
Origine Civis
Venetus

14. Giambattista Tiepolo, 1696–1770
   The Miracle of the Holy House of Loreto, 1743
   Oil on canvas, 48 3/8 x 30 3/8 in (122.9 x 77.2 cm)
   The J. Paul Getty Museum, Los Angeles, 94.PA.20

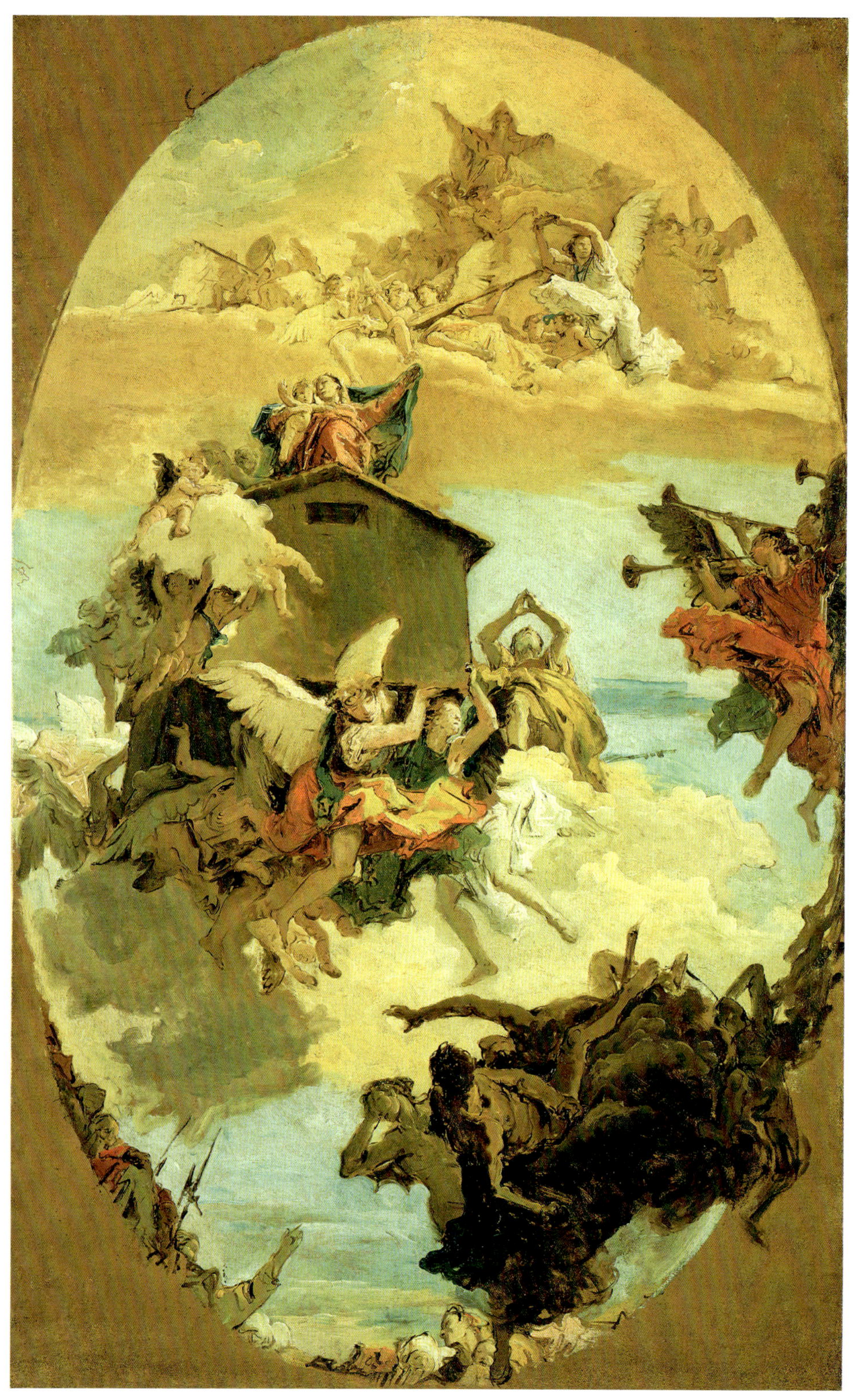

The second of two *modelli*, or detailed studies, for the ceiling fresco (1745, now destroyed) (see fig. 14.2) in the Church of Sta. Maria di Nazareth (or degli Scalzi) in Venice, this canvas depicts the translation, or movement, of the Virgin's Holy House, or Santa Casa. According to legend, the home in which the Virgin Mary had been born, raised, and received the Annunciation was miraculously transported by angels when, in 1291, its safety was threatened by advancing Moslem armies. Flying first to Trsat (in present-day Croatia) and then to Italy, it ultimately landed in Loreto.[1] The Carmelite Order, which had assumed guardianship of the house in Nazareth, was officially entrusted with the Loretan shrine in 1489 and, in 1646, received the Venetian Senate's approval to establish a church in Venice. Sta. Maria di Nazareth was dedicated on the Feast Day of the Translation of the Holy House, December 10, 1650.

Tiepolo began planning the composition in September 1743, producing two *modelli* and a number of preparatory drawings.[2] In the first *modello*, now in the Accademia, Venice (fig. 14.1), the image is crowned by a swiftly descending angel, who bears a lily—a symbol associated with the Annunciation. Below, God the Father and Christ sit enthroned in the heavens, while the Santa Casa—with the Virgin alone at its peak—is borne aloft by angels. Heretical figures occupy space to the left of the visionary scene but are partially obscured by the border of the painting.

Tiepolo, or his patrons, apparently found the first *modello* unsatisfactory. He achieved a clearer pictorial organization in the second one, arranging the composition vertically in three sections. At the apex in near-grisaille, God the Father occupies the farthest distance, presiding alone over the miraculous flight of the Holy House. In the center section, engaging the middle-distance and depicted *di sotto-in-sù* (from below, looking upward) with a complete if subdued palette, trumpeting angels herald the Virgin Mary and infant Christ's journey atop the soaring Santa Casa. And in the bottom section—painted with a brush that is loaded with dark tones—the demons tumble hellward, away from the miraculous event and, breaking the pictorial frame, into the viewer's space.

The changes Tiepolo made in creating the Getty canvas certainly enhanced the clarity of the design, yet they may also be viewed in relation to contemporaneous Church polemics and to Carmelite and Loretan devotional traditions.[3] Although the cult of the Virgin and worship of the Holy House were strong by the decade when this painting was made, few components of Marian theology, including the Immaculate Conception, had yet become established dogma.[4] In fact, many aspects of Mariology were subjects of ecclesiastical controversy.[5] By relocating the Santa Casa to the middle register, Tiepolo gave the house greater presence and the Virgin closer proximity to heaven, underscoring a controversial component of Marian devotion—her association with the Holy Trinity. Tiepolo further enforces this by substituting the Christ Child in the Virgin's arms for the Christ of the Trinity, thus implying their shared seat in heaven and identifying the two as *co*-redeemers and benefactors of humanity. Finally, by giving prominence to the heretical figures, Tiepolo reinforced the Virgin's triumph over Satan—and perhaps even over those who dared to contest her immaculacy.[6]

AL

Notes

1. Fogolari 1931, 18.

2. For documents, see ibid., 30–32; Knox 1968, 397; and Christiansen in Venice and New York 1996, 300. For Tiepolo's preparatory drawings, see Mras 1956, 41–44; and Knox 1968, 394–403.

3. Barcham 1979, 430–47.

4. The Feast Day of the Translation of the Holy House was first celebrated by the Papal States in 1728. Four years later, Pietro Valerio Martorelli published his *Teatro storico della Santa Casas nazarena*, a compendium of the Holy House's history, which he dedicated to Pope Clement XII. See Barcham 1979, 437. The Immaculate Conception, the belief that Mary was born free of the stain of original sin, did not formally become part of Catholic doctrine until 1854.

5. For eighteenth-century Venetian ecclesiastical criticism of Marian devotion, see Barcham 1984, 445–47.

6. On this point, see Christiansen in Venice and New York 1996, 301

Provenance: Probably Cecilia Guardi, by inheritance from her husband, Giambattista Tiepolo, 1770; Edward Cheyney [–1884], London and Badger Hall, Shropshire, ca. 1842/52–84; upon his death, held in trust by the Estate of Edward Cheyney, 1884–85; (sold, Christie's, London, April 29, 1885, lot 160); Archibald Philip Primrose [1847–1929], fifth Earl of Rosebery, Dalmeny House, Lothian, Scotland, 1885–1929; by inheritance to Albert Edward Harry Mayer Archibald Primrose [1882–1974], sixth Earl of Rosebery, Dalmeny House, Lothian, Scotland, and Mentmore, Bucks., England, 1929–74; by inheritance to Eva Isabel Marian Strutt [1892–1987], sixth Countess of Rosebery, Dalmeny House, Lothian, Scotland, 1974; (sold, Sotheby's, London, December 11, 1974, lot 150); British Rail Pension Trustee Company, Ltd., London, 1974–94; (sold, Hazlitt, Gooden and Fox, Ltd., London).

References: Fogolari 1931, 18–32; London 1951, 34, no. 120; Lorenzetti in Venice 1951, 65–67, ill.; Watson 1952, 44; London 1954 143, no. 504; Mras 1956, 41–44, fig. 6; Pallucchini 1960, 88; Crivellato 1962, 53; Morassi 1962, 19, 54, 57; Wescher 1962, 49; Los Angeles et al. 1968, 112–13; Knox 1968, 397; Pallucchini 1968, 108–9, no. 151a; Zampetti in Venice 1969, 378, under no. 175; Rizzi in Udine 1971, 92; Barcham 1979, 433, 438–39; Levey 1986, 112–14, fig. 108; Brunel 1991, 171–73; Scirè 1991, 247; Barcham 1992, 88, fig. 22; Pignatti and Brown in Fort Worth 1993, 33, 108, 228–31, ill.; Alpers and Baxandall 1994, 64, 151, fig. 76; Stein in Fredericksen 1995, no. 15; Christiansen in Venice and New York 1996, no. 486, 8, 10, 22, 147, 193, 194, 288, 295–301; Walsh and Gribbon 1997, 109, 126–27, ill.; Seydl in Los Angeles 2005, n.p.

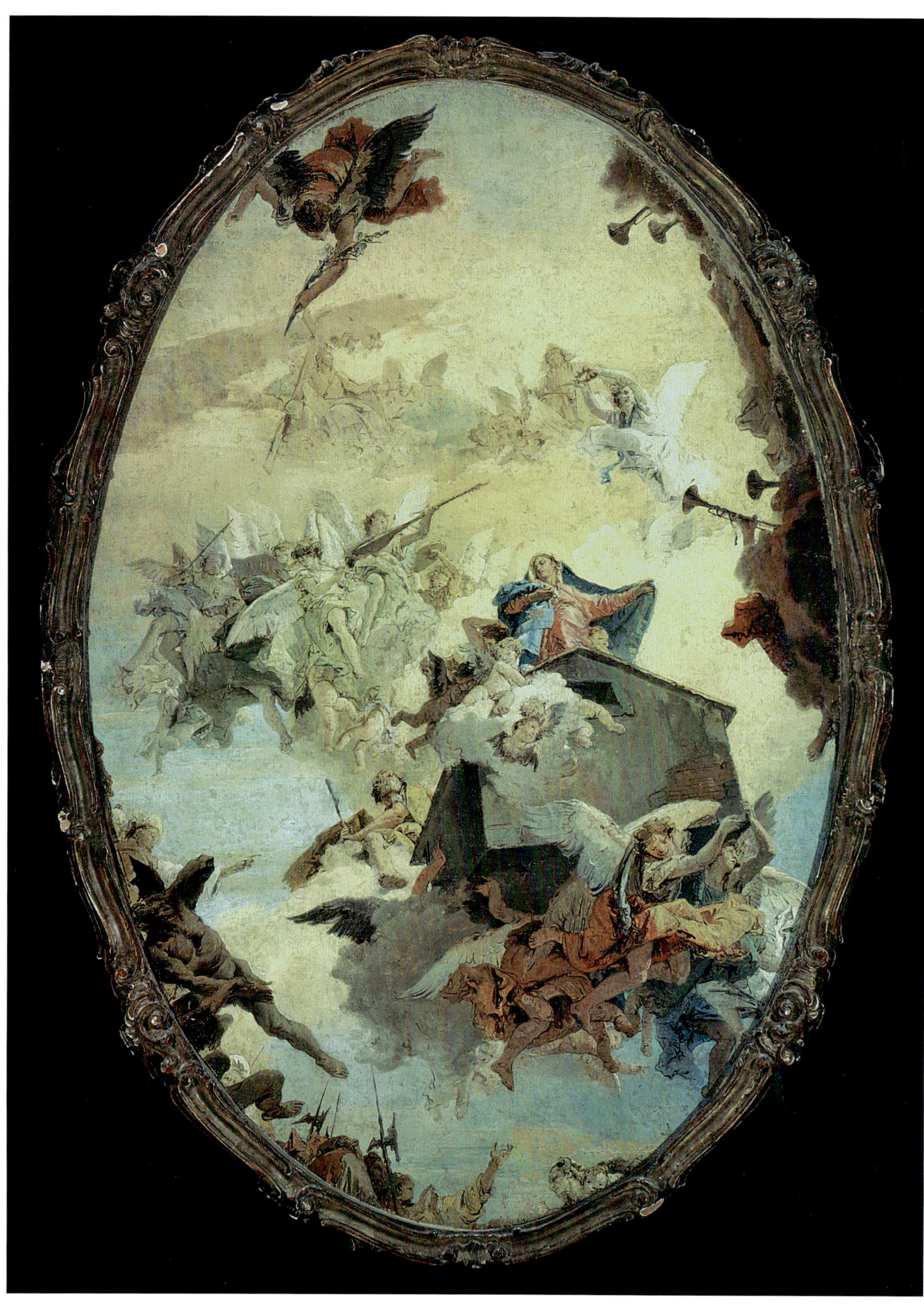

Fig. 14.1
Giambattista Tiepolo
Modello for *The Miracle of the Holy House of Loreto*, 1743
Oil on canvas, 48 13/16 x 33 1/2 in. (124 x 85 cm)
Galleria dell' Accademia, Venice

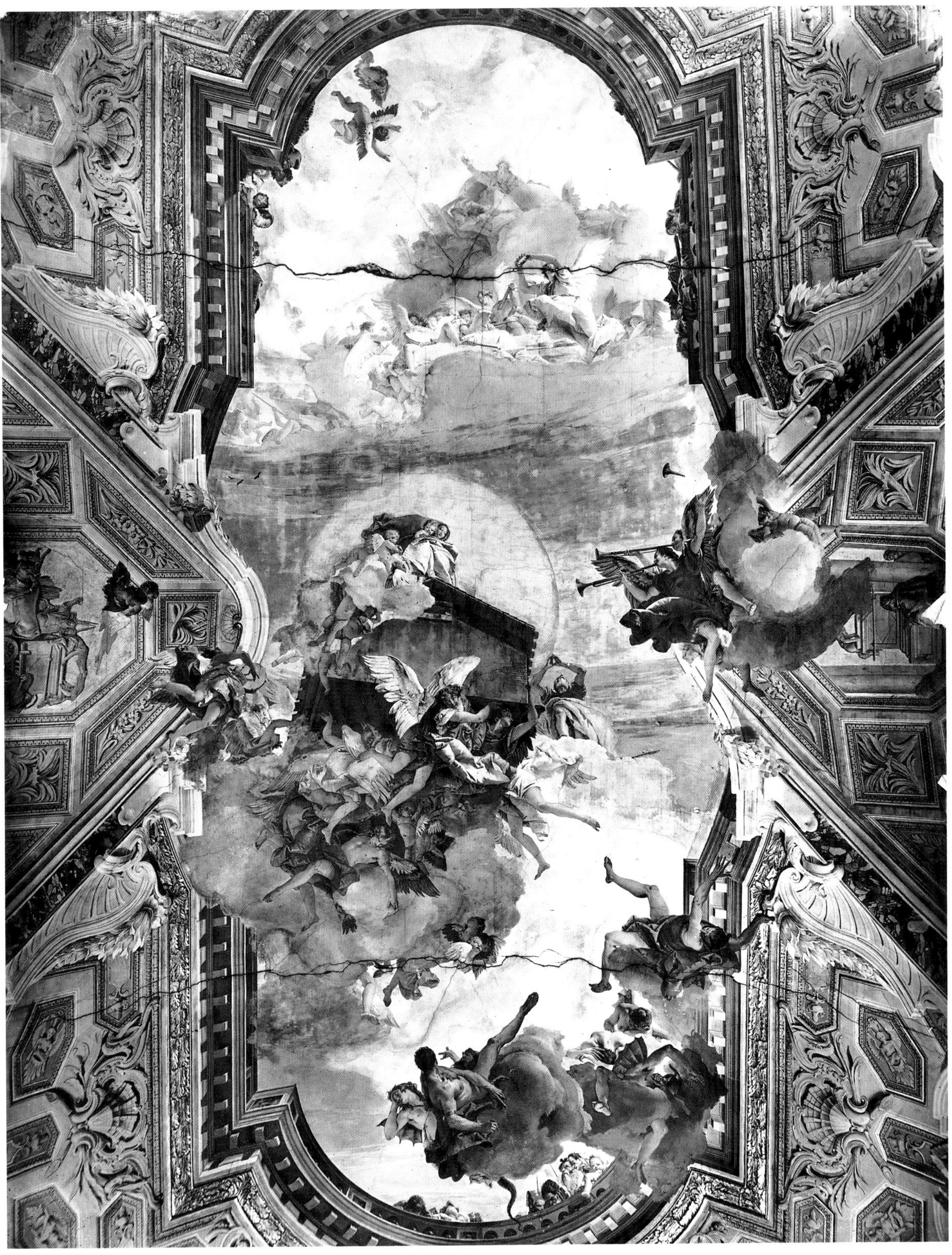

Fig. 14.2
Giambattista Tiepolo
The House of Loreto, 1745
Ceiling fresco, dimensions unavailable
Church of Sta. Maria degli Scalzi, Venice
This fresco was destroyed during World War I

15.[†] Giambattista Tiepolo, 1696–1770
   Allegory: Glory and Magnanimity of Princes, ca. 1757–61
   Fresco, transferred to canvas, 148 x 75 in. (375.9 x 190.5 cm)
   The John and Mable Ringling Museum of Art, Sarasota; Museum Purchase, 1951, SN652

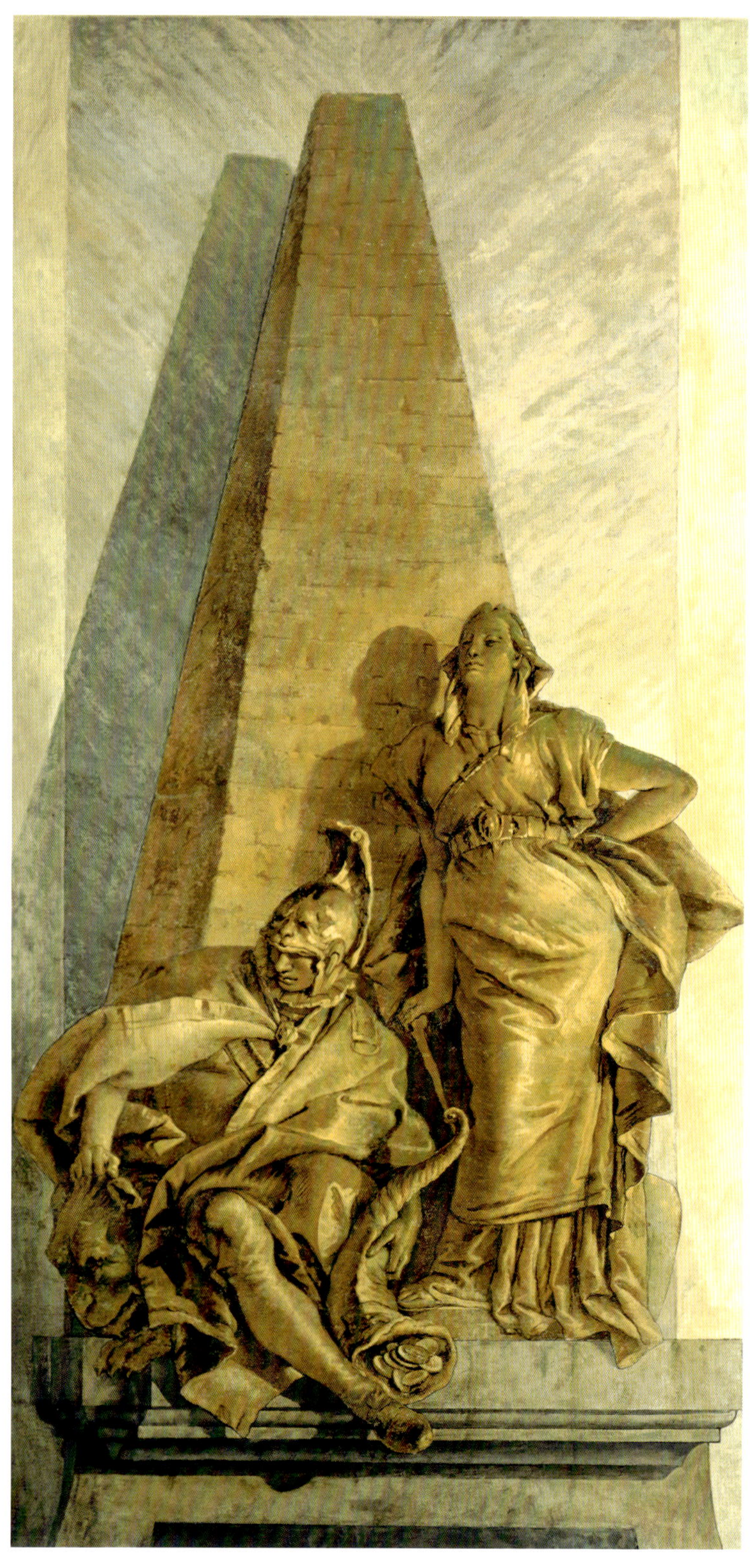

Tiepolo derived the figures in this bold, illusionistic grisaille from *Iconologia*, Cesare Ripa's popular sourcebook of symbolic images, in which they are depicted and described as allegories of princely Glory and Magnanimity. In Ripa's characterization, Magnanimity dresses in splendid gold cloth and abundant jewelry, wears a crown, and holds a scepter. Her forehead is broad and her nose "rotund," and she sits astride a lion, reflecting her power and courage. Behind her, a cornucopia overflows with gold coins, indicating that she generously gives money away without expecting remuneration.[1]

Notably absent from Ripa's text but included in the Ringling Tiepolo are the princely figure and the pyramid—a structure traditionally associated with the East and with the Macedonian conqueror Alexander the Great. Given that Alexander was also known for defeating the lion at Bazaria (a story evoked here), the artist might have found him to be a historical exemplar of nobility and magnanimity and, for that reason, included him to augment and animate the composition.[2]

Tiepolo first augmented Ripa's description of Magnanimity with a pyramid in one of his finest works, the staircase-ceiling fresco *Asia* (fig. 15.1), which was part of the *Apollo and the Continents* cycle he painted between 1750 and 1753 in the Würzburg palace of Prince-Archbishop Carl Philipp von Greiffenclau. He utilized this imagery again on the ceiling of the throne room in the Palacio Real, Madrid (1762–64), a work commissioned by King Charles III of Spain. Disappointingly little is certain about the original location of the Ringling fresco, but it is known to have been painted for a villa somewhere in Vicenza.[3] For a time, it was believed to have been one of the paintings Giambattista and his son Giandomenico (1727–1804) produced to decorate a series of rooms at the Villa Valmarana, near Vicenza, in 1757.[4] Although this remains unsubstantiated, Tiepolo's documented presence in Vicenza before he left for Spain in 1762 provides valuable circumstantial evidence to help date the present work no earlier than 1757.

An over-door grisaille from the nearby Palazzo Canossa, Verona, where Giambattista and Giandomenico Tiepolo worked in 1761, was closely related to the Ringling fresco—providing further key dating information. From what can be determined in photographs—the palazzo was destroyed during World War II—it appears the grisaille was far less rich and lively than the Ringling work, leading several scholars to conclude it was painted by Giandomenico.[5] Often criticized as having lacked inventiveness, he was the principal imitator of his father's style. Thus it is surmised that Giandomenico created the Palazzo Canossa grisaille after Giambattista's original in the unknown villa, meaning that the present fresco was painted no later than 1761.

AL

Notes

1. Ripa 1645, 383.

2. For Alexander the Great in Bazaria, see Rollin 1839, 554.

3. Ripa wrote that the image of Magnanimity was particularly well suited for adorning the homes of nobility. Although the villa for which this fresco was made has yet to be identified, there are three compositions associated with it: a Mars and a Venus (private collection, Turin), each of which is half the size of the fresco; and a small fragment of a Bacchic mask (Tallyrand Collection, Paris).

4. This suggestion was first made in the Simonetti sale catalogue of 1932. Yet in a July 11, 1951, letter written to Rodolfo Pallucchini (acting on behalf of Ringling Museum director A. Everett Austin, Jr.), Tomasso Valmarana asserted that the fresco could not have originated at his family's villa: "So di certo che nessuno di nostri affreschi si trova in commercio, per di più non esistono nè in Foresteria nè in Villa muri con spazi vuoti cioè con pareti senza affreschi." (I am certain that none of our frescoes ever entered the market, as there are no empty spaces either in Foresteria or in the villa [Valmarana], that is, no walls missing frescoes.) (Ringling Museum curatorial files)

5. Maria Santifaller first discovered photographs of the over-door grisaille inside a folio, titled *Affreschi del XVI e XVII secolo: Paolo Veronese, Gian Battista Tiepolo, e Contemporanei*, 1900, in Eduard Sack's archives. See Santifaller 1975, 283. It was she who first suggested attributing this work to Giandomenico, a suggestion later seconded by Antonio Morassi. See Santifaller 1974, 283–84.

Provenance: Unknown villa, Vicenza; Baron Giorgio Franchetti [–1922], possibly in his villa in Cannes, before 1922; Atillio Simonetti [1843–1925], Rome, –1925; by inheritance to his sons, Rome, 1925–32; (sale, Tavazzi, Rome, April 25–May 6, 1932, no. 541); (with Adolph Loewi, Los Angeles, 1932–51).

References: Venice 1929, 68, no. 2, pl. 34 (as *Allegorical Figures*); Pollak 1932, 77, no. 541, fig. 14 (as *Allegoria*); Murray 1951, 26; Morassi 1962, 48, fig. 372 (as *Two Allegorical Figures with an Obelisk*); Fredericksen and Zeri 1972, 197, 637 (as *Two Allegorical Figures*); Santifaller 1974, 283–84, n. 21, fig. 369 (as *Allegorical Composition in Grisaille*); Schmidt 1974, 59–60 (as *Beauty Dominating Strength*); Santifaller 1975, 196, nos. 13, 14, fig. 3; Tomory 1976, 110–13, no. 109 (as *Allegory: Glory and Magnanimity of Princes*); Morse 1979, 255; Janson 1986, 62; Merling 2002, 137; Borys 2008, 106.

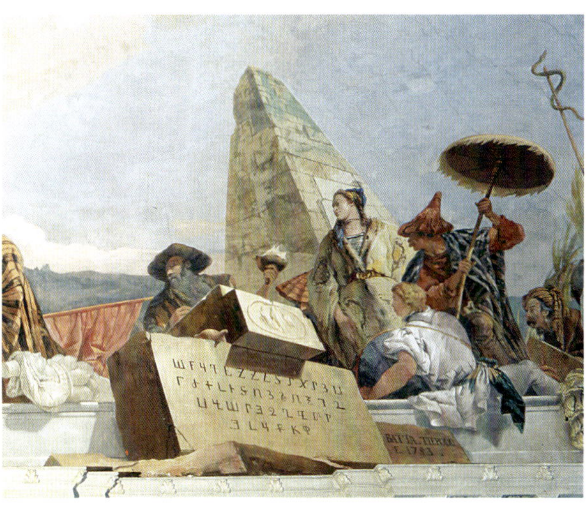

Fig. 15.1. Giambattista Tiepolo
Asia, from the fresco cycle *Apollo and the Continents*, 1753
Ceiling fresco of the staircase (detail), dimensions unavailable
Residenz, Würzburg, Germany

16. Giambattista Tiepolo, 1696–1770
   St. Joseph and the Christ Child, ca. 1735
   Oil on canvas, 36 x 28 3/4 in. (91.4 x 73 cm)
   New Orleans Museum of Art: Gift of Professor W. P. Carr, 56.63

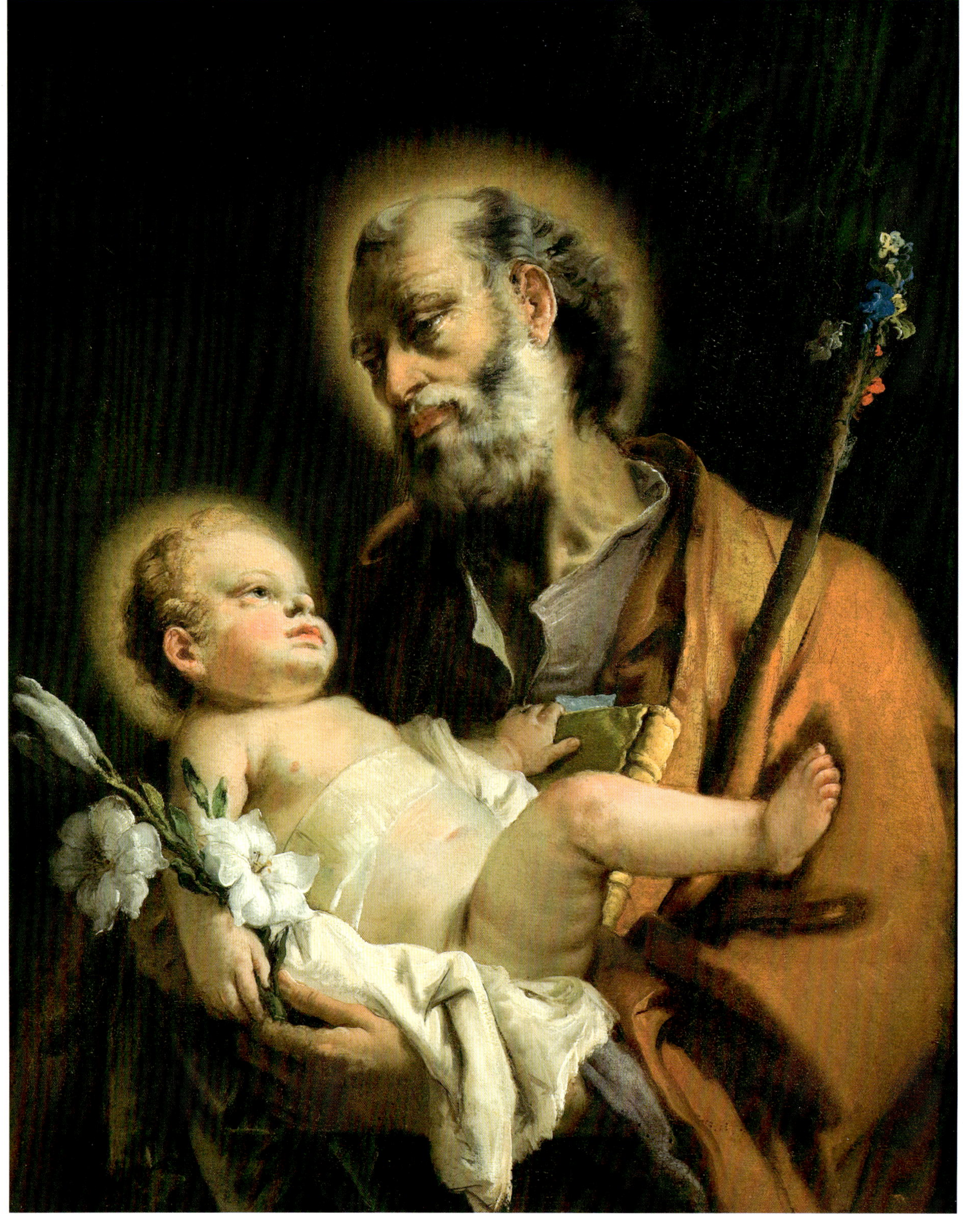

Although perhaps best known for his grand scenes taken from mythology and history, Tiepolo also excelled when working on a smaller scale, whether as a portraitist or as a painter of devotional images. In its palpable sense of intimacy and warmth, *St. Joseph and the Christ Child* reveals his skill in both these genres. The art historian Catherine Whistler noted that this depth of feeling is found in much of the artist's religious imagery, adding that Tiepolo focused often on "the character of saintly individuals and [on] the nature of their spiritual experience."[1] Here, St. Joseph tenderly holds the holy infant, gazing at him with love and reverence. Golden nimbuses, which shine against the dark background, emphasize the sanctity of this pair. Tiepolo contrasts the child's unblemished youth with Joseph's lined visage and gray hair. Underscoring Jesus' innocence and purity is the stem of lilies lying on his right forearm. His left hand touches the top edge of a book, a gesture meant to signify his literal fulfillment of scriptural prophecies. Tiepolo reinforces the notion of Jesus as the embodiment of divine light by placing his radiant form against Joseph's richly colored mantle.

Worth noting, too, are the colorful flowers that adorn the saint's staff and provide contrast with the white lilies. According to early Christian legend, when God was searching for a suitable foster father for Jesus, he caused the staff to blossom as a sign of divine favor.[2] The flowers may also allude to a verse in the book of Isaiah (11:1): "And there shall come forth a shoot out of the stock of Jesse / And a twig shall grow forth out of his roots"—foretelling that the Messiah will be a descendent of the House of David.

In the early seventeenth century, portraitlike images of Joseph holding the infant Jesus became increasingly popular, no doubt in response to contemporary Catholic belief in the saint's role as Christ's foster father.[3] Among the first Italian artists to focus upon the pair was Guido Reni. His *St. Joseph with Christ Child* (fig. 16.1) could well have inspired several of Tiepolo's images of Joseph, including the present one.[4] Like the earlier master, Tiepolo offers an intimate scene of father and son. Yet while he may have borrowed the basic composition from Reni, his interpretation of the subject is his own. In particular, he places Christ and Joseph in an unidentifiable space rather than in a landscape, and he uses light and color to emphasize their otherworldly and visionary aspects.

When *St. Joseph and the Christ Child* first entered the New Orleans Museum of Art collection, it was thought to be by Tiepolo's son Giandomenico (1727–1804). But in 1976, Antonio Morassi, a noted Tiepolo connoisseur, attributed the work to Giambattista. Other scholars agreed, with Maria

Santifaller adding the suggestion that the canvas might also have been Tiepolo's earliest interpretation of the theme.[5]

ST

Notes

1. Catherine Whistler, "Tiepolo as a Religious Artist," in New York 1996, 189–97, esp. 193.

2. This association is traditionally ascribed to St. Jerome (ca. 347–420). See Jameson 1867, 159–60.

3. The cult centering on St. Joseph had been gaining ground since the fifteenth century. During the Baroque period, he was so acclaimed that, in 1621, Pope Gregory XV made church attendance obligatory on the saint's feast day. In 1726 Pope Benedict XIII inserted Joseph's name into the Litany of the Saints. See Herbermann 1913, 7, 506.

4. In addition to the Hermitage picture, there is a painting by Reni and his workshop in the Basilica dei SS. Giovanni e Paolo, Venice, showing Joseph holding Jesus. Several Tiepolo works portray the saint revering the infant, for example, the altarpiece *Adoration of the Christ Child*, in the Sacristy of the Canons, Basilica di S. Marco, Venice; significantly, in that work it is Joseph, rather than the Virgin Mary, who cradles the child. For images of Joseph and Christ alone, see Gemin and Pedrocco 1993, 229, no. 34 and 494, nos. 524, 524a.

5. Morassi's attribution was based on the similarities he noted between the New Orleans painting and a work that was then in a private collection in Bergamo and securely attributed to the senior Tiepolo. He dated the New Orleans picture to about 1730–35. This information is based upon a letter from Morassi, presumably addressed to Maria Santifaller, dated March 29, 1976. She referred to the letter in her discussion of the present painting, further suggesting that this work may have been the same one that was recorded as having been in the Barbisoni Collection, Brescia, in 1760. Santifaller 1976, 80, n. 59.

References: New Orleans Museum of Art 1966, 58, no. 63; Santifaller 1976, 80; Birmingham and Springfield 1978, 54; New Orleans Museum of Art 1980, 36.

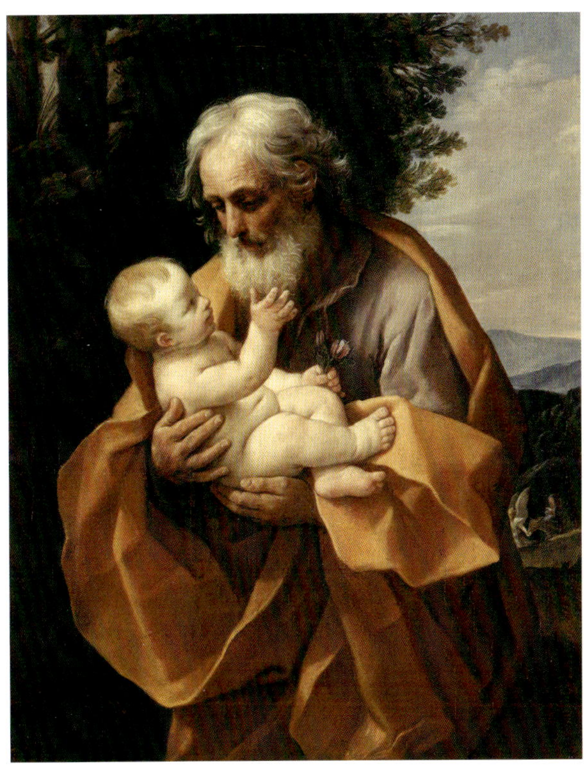

Fig. 16.1. Guido Reni
St. Joseph with Christ Child, ca. 1620
Oil on canvas, 49 1/2 x 39 3/4 in. (126 x 101 cm)
Hermitage, St. Petersburg, Russia

17. Giandomenico Tiepolo, 1727–1804, or his studio
    The Minuet, ca. 1755
    Oil on canvas, 30 3/4 x 42 3/4 in. (78.1 x 108.6 cm)
    New Orleans Museum of Art: The Samuel H. Kress Collection, 61.88

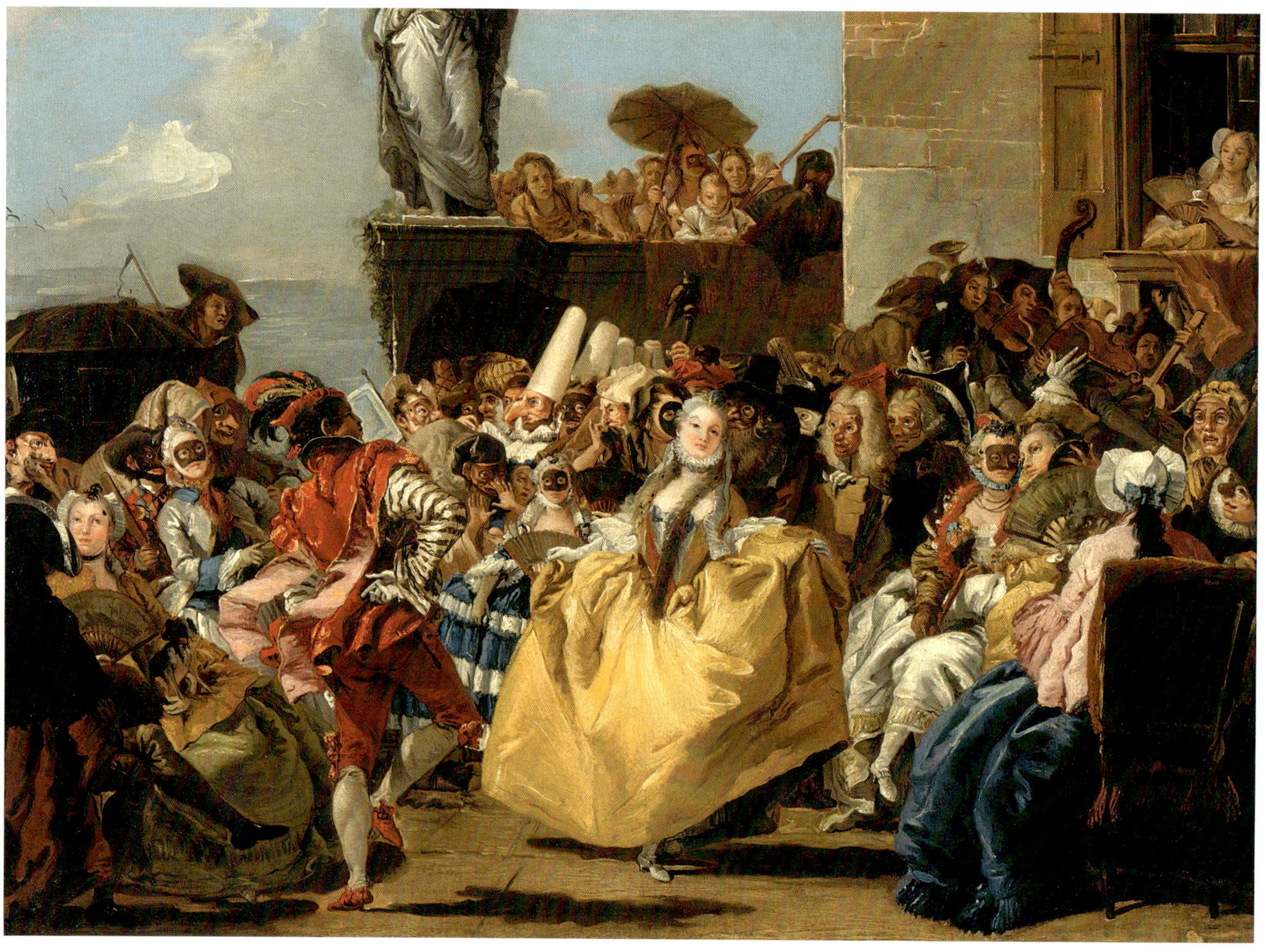

The Minuet depicts a throng of revelers crowded into the garden of a country villa to celebrate the carnival season.[1] The composition is organized around the figure of a young woman and her dancing partner. Resplendent in a rich yellow dress, she dances gracefully, lifting her skirt to reveal the turn of an ankle as she performs. Her partner, wearing a boldly colored costume of scarlet, white, and black, responds with his own refined movements. The painting illustrates a traditional minuet, with two dancers performing alone before a group in order to show that "their exquisite manners, dress, and skill" made them "indeed worthy adornments to society."[2] The lavishly attired revelers surrounding the couple have pulled back their chairs to provide enough space for dancing. A small ensemble of strings and horns plays at the upper right, and conversations and socializing in the crowd further animate the scene.

Many of the onlookers wear types of popular vernacular masks that eventually were adapted for carnival costumes. For instance, the *moretta*, a small oval mask of black velvet that covers the faces of several women here, derives from customs associated with convent-visiting.[3] Most of the mask styles, however, were borrowed from the commedia dell'arte, a theatrical genre of the sixteenth to eighteenth centuries that involved improvisations upon standardized plots and stock characters. For instance, several men behind the dancing woman wear the disguise of Punchinello—beak-nosed masks and tall conical hats; this highly popular commedia character embodied the cruel and deceitful aspects of human nature.[4] The red costume worn by the dancing man suggests the character of Mezzetino, a mischievous fictional lothario.[5] As the art historian Michael Levey noted, images such as *The Minuet* are hardly accurate depictions of carnival life but are intended, instead, to evoke the season when masks and costumes allowed different classes, as well as visitors, to mingle freely and anonymously amid the hedonistic festivities.[6]

The Minuet is one of four versions of roughly the same subject associated with Giandomenico Tiepolo and his studio.[7] Of these, *Carnival Scene* (ca. 1754–55), a work purportedly by the artist that is now in the Musée du Louvre, is closest to the New Orleans Museum of Art painting. It differs only in details, such as the landscape and clouds in the background as well as the handling of faces and drapery.[8] Although *The Minuet* also has been attributed entirely to Giandomenico, the heaviness of certain passages—some of the faces and the rather indistinct landscape—suggest at least some level of workshop participation.[9] Although none of the versions bears a signature nor any indication of when it was made, the pendant to the Louvre painting, titled *The Charlatan* (also known

as *The Tooth Puller*), is signed and dated.[10]

Giandomenico's focus upon elegantly dressed and courtly Venetians dancing outdoors dates to the 1750s, a decade during which he increasingly turned to depicting scenes from daily life. In 1757 he worked with his father, Giambattista Tiepolo, at Count Giustino Valmarana's villa near Vicenza, painting the frescoes decorating the Foresteria, or guesthouse, of this patron, who was a scholar and theater enthusiast.[11] These murals display the younger Tiepolo's concentration upon mundane and earthy themes, in contrast to the grander images—drawn from history, religion, and mythology—that his father primarily produced. Perhaps most important, the present painting and related works confirm Giandomenico's interest in Punchinello; the artist frequently portrayed this character in order to evoke the sorrows and poignancy of human existence. Eventually, he would produce more than a hundred beautiful drawings of Punchinello—works that are numbered among his masterpieces.

ST

Notes

1. Although sometimes identified as a courtyard in Venice, the landscape of hills shows the setting to be the adjoining mainland. The related painting *Carnival Scene* (Musée de Louvre) makes this aspect of the composition clearer.

2. Sutton 1985, 119–52.

3. Mazzarotto 1980, 107–9.

4. Ibid., 110–11.

5. Duchartre and Weaver 1966, 171.

6. Levey 1986, 133.

7. In addition to *Carnival Scene*, noted above, the others are *The Minuet* (Museo de Arte, Barcelona) and *The Country Dance* (Metropolitan Museum of Art, New York).

8. Until the 1950s, many scholars believed the former to be the work of Giambattista Tiepolo, but today most assign the work to his son on stylistic grounds. See Levey 1986, 240–44.

9. In 1950 the art historian W. R. Valentiner evaluated *The Minuet* for the New Orleans Museum of Art (at the time, the painting was on loan there), describing it as an excellent example of Giandomenico's work (New Orleans Museum of Art file notes). Other scholars, notably Antonio Morassi, cited the painting as "one of many copies" of the Louvre picture. In addition, they attributed it to Giandomenico's father, Giambattista Tiepolo. See Morassi 1962, 33, 38ff.; and Shapley 1973, 155, K1948.

10. See Sack 1910, 214. Shapley (1973, 155, no. K1948) notes that scholars have disputed the reading of the signature and date on the Louvre picture.

11. Levey 1986, 240–44.

Provenance: Robert Philip Wyndham Adeane [1905–1979], Babraham Hall, Cambridge, England; (sold Christie's, London, May 13, 1949, no. 45); David Koetser, New York, 1952; Kress acquisition 1953.

References: Suida 1953, 62; Morassi 1962, 33, 38ff.; Wescher 1966, 64; Shapley 1973, 155, no. K1948.

18. Canaletto (Giovanni Antonio Canal), 1697–1768
    View of the Grand Canal, Venice, ca. 1726-30
    Oil on canvas, 24 3/8 x 39 5/8 in. (61.9 x 100.6 cm)
    Birmingham Museum of Art; Gift of the Samuel H. Kress Foundation 1961.121

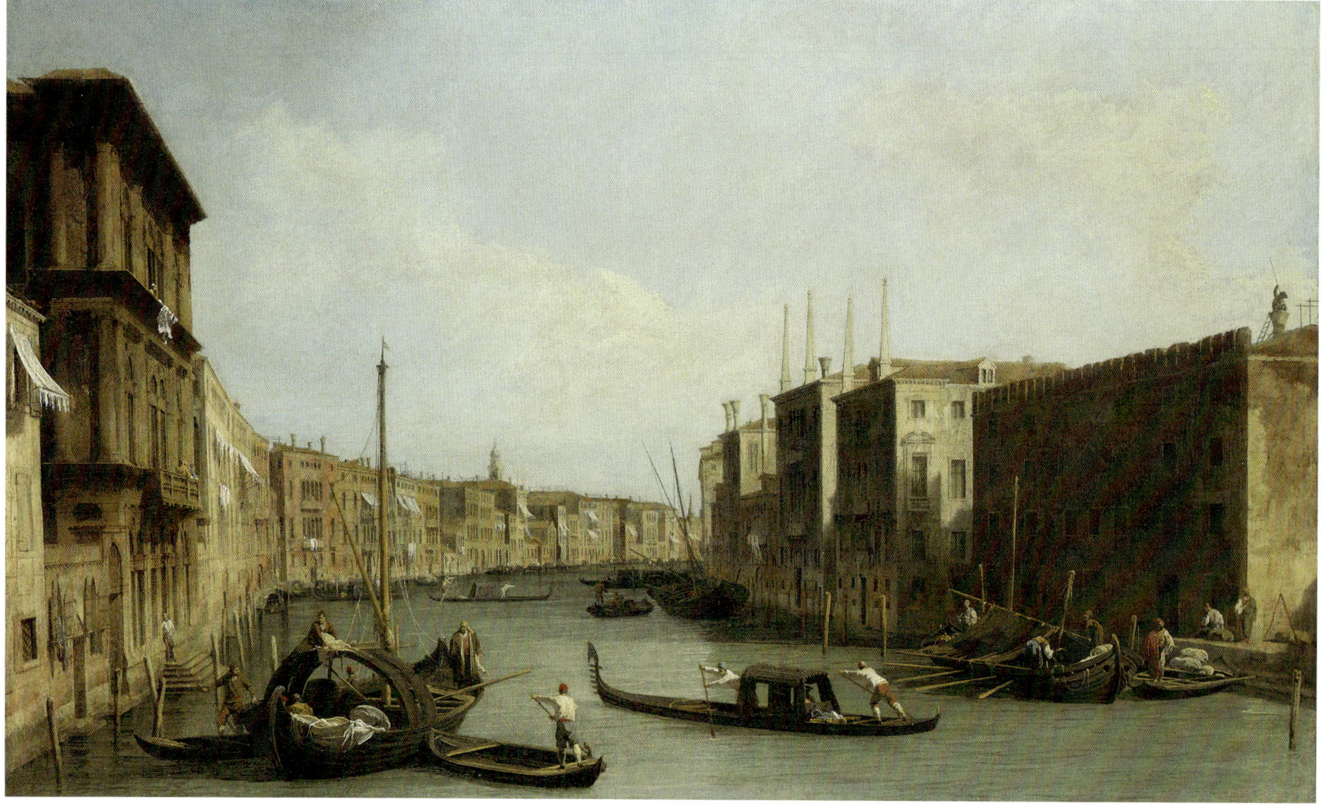

Although Canaletto is generally associated with depictions of immediately recognizable Venetian locales—such as the Piazza S. Marco and the Molo as well as such familiar structures as the Church of Sta. Maria della Salute, the Campanile, and the Doge's Palace—he also frequently captured less notable vistas. The Birmingham Museum of Art painting, in which only private dwellings and a mundane civic building are shown, is one of just three known Canaletto versions of this particular Grand Canal view.[1] Here, he chose a vantage point looking to the southeast, down the waterway toward the Rialto district, which is beyond the curve of the canal and so not visible. The simple brick façade and castellated cornice of the Deposito del Megio, a civic granary built in the 1400s, dominates the right bank. Canaletto included its wide quay, with boats unloading their cargos, and enlivened the scene by including a chimney sweep working on the roof. Immediately beyond the Deposito stand the Palazzo Belloni-Battagia and the Palazzo Tron, each with slender obelisks marking their façades. Today, only the former, presumably designed by Baldassare Longhena, retains its obelisks.

In 1481 the Venetian architect Mauro Coducci was commissioned to design the imposing Palazzo Vendramin-Calergi, which dominates the left side of the painting. Canaletto faithfully recorded its beautifully articulated classical columns and cornice but took considerable liberties with its façade. Specifically, he narrowed the width of the structure by several bays and reduced the size of its balcony. Canaletto often distorted distances and dimensions in order to combine disparate vistas within a single canvas. Beyond the Palazzo Vendramin-Calergi, the other buildings, including the palazzi Michiel dalle Colonne and Michiel del Brusa, seem to dissolve into an anonymous wall of masonry. The campanile of the Church of SS. Apostoli appears in the distance, above this line of structures.

The relatively obscure subject of this painting suggests it originally may have been conceived either as a pendant or as part of a larger series of works. A very similar view—though it adopts a slightly different angle and lacks the chimney sweep—is one of twenty-four canvases that the fourth Duke of Bedford commissioned Canaletto to paint (fig. 18.1).[2] Bedford traveled to Venice at some point before his 1731 marriage and subsequent succession to the dukedom the following year.[3] These paintings, now preserved at Woburn Abbey, the Bedford family's country house, include views of such famous sites as the Piazza S. Marco and the Molo as well as lesser-known vistas. As originally installed—at Bedford House in London—the series would have comprised a remarkable and expansive range of Venetian views,

no doubt prompting pleasant memories of the duke's visit to the city. The circa 1730 dating assigned to the Bedford pictures also accords with the Birmingham Museum painting. As W. G. Constable and J. G. Links noted, its blond tonalities and grayish shadows suggest it belongs to the late 1720s.[4] Likewise, the painting's cool palette and relatively modest size reveal how Canaletto responded to the aesthetic preferences of the English market.

ST

Notes

1. The three versions are discussed in Constable and Links 1989, 2: 310–11, nos. 247, 248, and 249.

2. London 1950, 25. See also Constable and Links 1989, 2: 188–89, no. 4.

3. Scharf 1890, 216–17.

4. Constable and Links 1989, 2: 310–11, no. 249.

Provenance: Private collection, England*; Julius Böhler, Munich, by 1931; Böhler and Steinmeyr, Lucerne**; Kress acquisition 1950; on loan to the Birmingham Museum of Art, 1951.

* According to Munich 1931, 3, no. 12.

** According to Constable 1962: 2, 292, no. 249.

References: Munich 1931, no. 12; Howard 1951; Birmingham 1952, 65; Constable 1962, 2: 292, no. 249; Haydon 1967, 79; Berto and Puppi 1968, 93, no. 46A; Fredericksen and Zeri 1972, 41; Shapley 1973, 160–61, no. K1806; Constable and Links 1989, 2: 310–11, no. 249; Wright 1992, 34; Birmingham 1993b, 95.

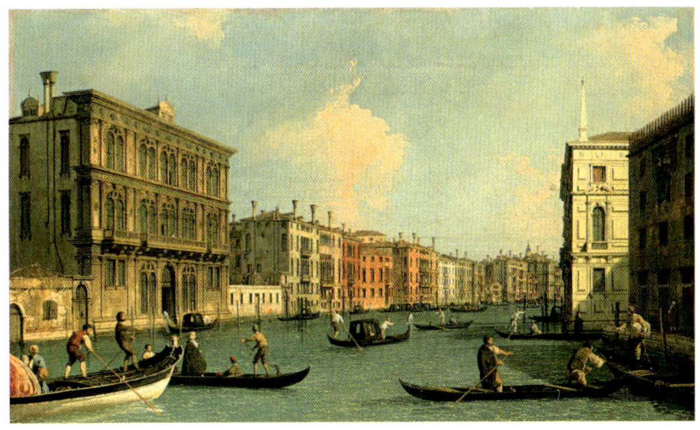

Fig. 18.1. Canaletto (Giovanni Antonio Canal)
A View on the Grand Canal from the Palazzo Vendramin-Calergi to the Traghetto a San Felice, ca. 1730
Oil on canvas, 18 1/2 x 31 1/2 in. (47 x 80 cm)
Collection of Woburn Abbey, Woburn, Bedfordshire; by kind permission of His Grace the Duke of Bedford and the Trustees of the Bedford Estates

19. Canaletto (Giovanni Antonio Canal), 1697–1768
Rialto Bridge, ca. 1730
Oil on canvas, 14 9/16 x 25 11/16 in. (37 x 65.2 cm)
Philadelphia Museum of Art; John G. Johnson Collection, 1917, Inv. 1404

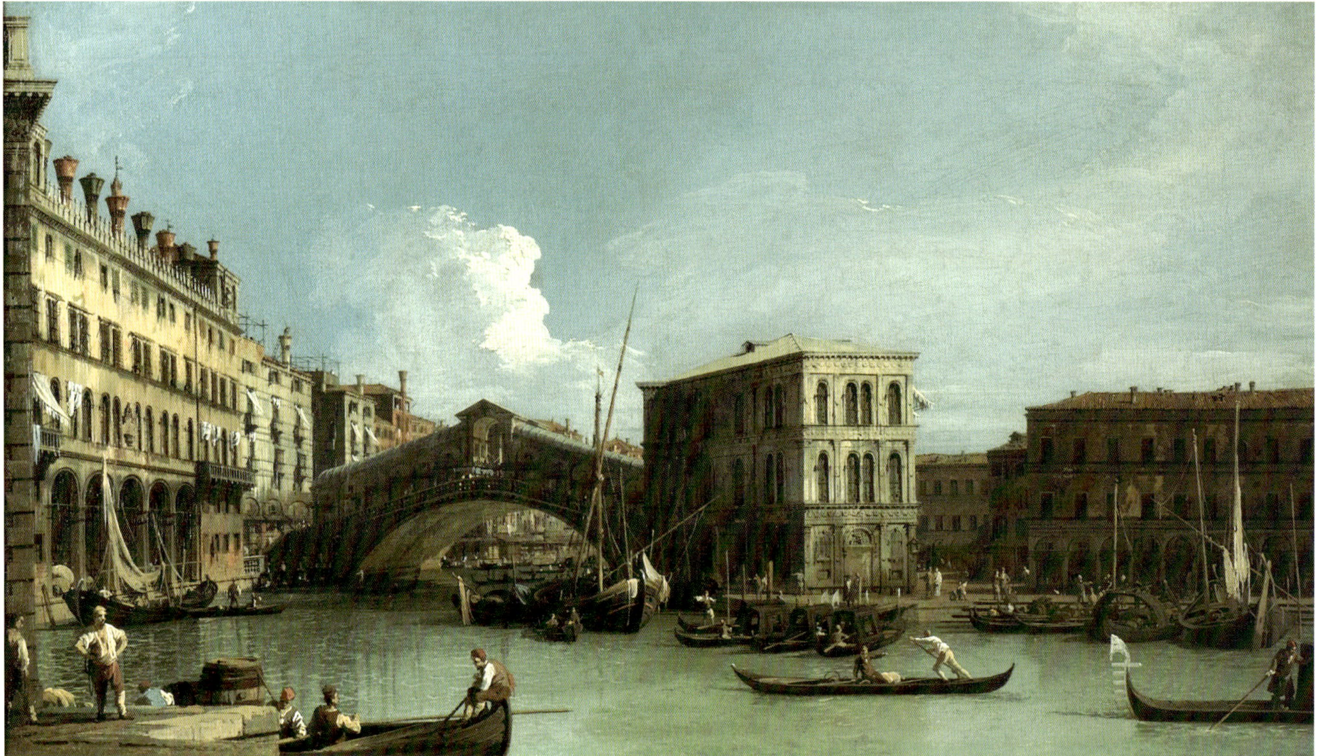

Canaletto has often been perceived as a keenly objective observer of the eighteenth-century Venetian cityscape.[1] The intensity of his pictorial description— be it of an illusionistic relief on a building cornice, an impossibly detailed rooftop seen from a far distance, or an uncannily fresh observation of an oarsman at rest—compels the viewer to believe, as the Irish art dealer Owen McSwiney famously did, that Canaletto painted "things which fall immediately under his eye."[2] So it is with *Rialto Bridge,* which is minutely rendered down to its subtle aqueous reflections of an arcade along the Grand Canal. Canaletto's paintings seduce the viewer into seeing their fiction as reality. For his works are, of course, artful constructions, marvelously calculated to convey the *nature* of Venetian life.

Here Canaletto takes a southwesterly view of the bridge, which until the mid-nineteenth century was the only one to span the Grand Canal. As a result, its surrounding neighborhoods and waterways comprised the commercial heart of the city, making it the perfect location for Canaletto to scrutinize the urban scene. Indeed, he seems to relish the depiction of gondoliers, oarsmen, and merchants of all manner of costume and character, who navigate through and around the bridge and gesture at one another. Even the people resting on a nearby quay do not escape his brush.

Conveying persuasively the physical essence of Venice, however, often involved compromising topographical accuracy. Canaletto was known to rearrange viewpoints, alter rooflines, modify the contours of the Grand Canal, and simplify (or even eliminate) architecture to suit his vision. In the Philadelphia Museum of Art picture, he conflates a series of viewpoints along the canal in order to capture the major structures. The position of the Rialto Bridge, with the Fondaco dei Tedeschi on its left and the Palazzo dei Camerlinghi on its right, is consistent with a view that likely was provided by the small dock—still accessible today—on which the boatmen in the left corner of the painting stand.[3] However, the angle and proximity in the painting of the Fabbriche Vecchie—the long set of civic offices adjacent to the Palazzo dei Camerlinghi—is inconsistent with that view, since when standing on the dock one can see only the first of the Fabbriche's fifteen bays. Thus to depict such a broad portion of the façade Canaletto must have worked from a second spot, farther down the Grand Canal. Though minor, this perspective modification allows for a more dramatic panorama than the single viewpoint would have afforded.

Canaletto painted several variations on the Rialto Bridge theme, particularly early in his career.

(Doubtless, this immediately recognizable view was highly popular among his many Grand Tourist patrons.) His first known such composition was done for the textile merchant Stefano Conti in 1725 (see fig. 5, p. 15). But the circa 1726–27 canvas that was in the large group of works sold by the British consul Joseph Smith to King George III in 1762 (engraved by Antonio Visentini; see cat. 13h) bears the strongest architectural and lighting similarities to the Philadelphia painting (fig. 19.1).

AL

Notes

1. On this perception of the artist, see Michael Levey, "Canaletto as Artist of the Urban Scene" in New York 1989, 17–29.

2. On November 28, 1727, Owen McSwiney wrote to the second Duke of Richmond, "his Excellence lyes [sic] in painting things which fall immediately under his eye." W. G. Constable first transcribed the extant letters from McSwiney to the second Duke of Richmond in Constable 1962, 1: 173–76.

3. See Bomford and Finaldi in London et al. 1998, 14, figs. 6–8

Provenance: George A. F. Cavendish-Bentinck [1821–1891]; (sold, Christie's, London, July 11, 1891, lot 629, as *A View of the Rialto*); Martin Colnaghi [1821–1908]; with Marlborough Gallery, London; John G. Johnson [1841–1917], Philadelphia.

References: Constable 1962, 284, under no. 236 (b); Constable 1976, 302, no. 236 (b); Constable and Links 1989, 302, no. 236 (b); Philadelphia Museum of Art 1994, 184–85.

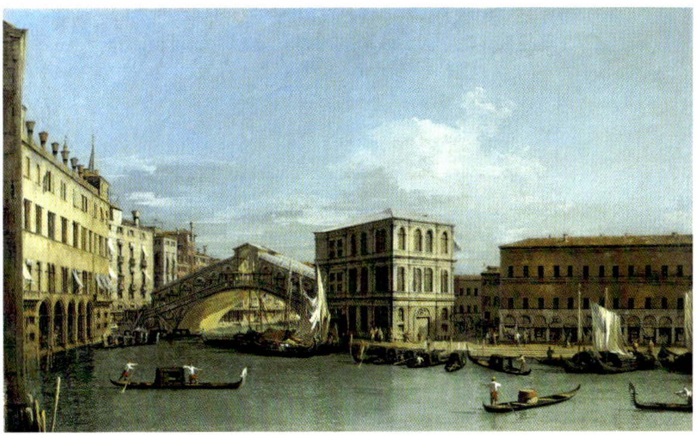

Fig. 19.1
Canaletto (Giovanni Antonio Canal)
The Rialto Bridge from the North, ca. 1726–27
Oil on canvas, 18 1/2 x 31 1/2 in. (47 x 80 cm)
The Royal Collection, Her Majesty Queen Elizabeth II RCIN 400668

20. Canaletto (Giovanni Antonio Canal), 1697–1768
   The Grand Canal from the Campo San Vio, ca. 1740
   Oil on canvas, 44 7/8 x 63 1/2 in. (114 x 161.3 cm)
   Memphis Brooks Museum of Art; Gift of the Samuel H. Kress Foundation 61.216

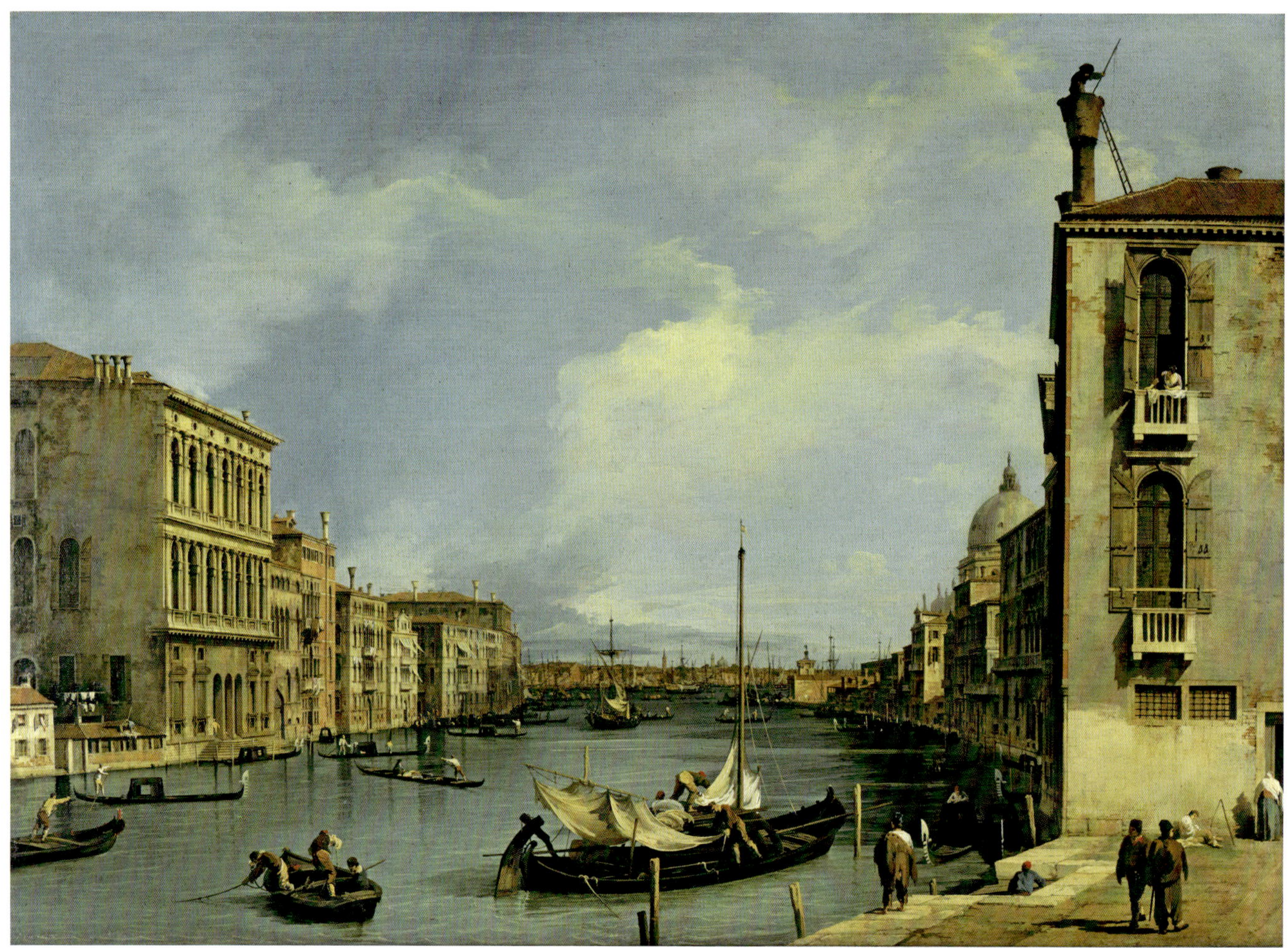

One of Canaletto's most popular subjects was the Grand Canal as viewed looking east from the Campo S. Vio; at least ten versions by his hand are known, not to mention numerous related works.[1] Also, Antonio Visentini included it in the *Prospectus Magni Canalis Venetiarum* (1735), his famous portfolio of etchings after paintings by Canaletto (cat. 13e). Views from the campo are among the artist's earliest documented canvases, one example of which—in the Museo Thyssen-Bornemisza, Madrid—is dated by at least one scholar to as early as 1719.[2] As Martin Clayton noted in his discussion of the version in Britain's Royal Collection, which was produced a few years later and most closely resembles the Memphis Brooks Museum of Art canvas, the composition's popularity is surprising, given the absence of any recognizable monuments (see fig. 4, p. 28).[3] A possible explanation is that the campo is one of the few public spaces in Venice offering an unobstructed view of the lower Grand Canal.[4]

The Campo S. Vio is a small piazza on the south side of the Grand Canal that takes its name from the Church of SS. Vito e Modesto, located there. On the right side of this painting, Canaletto depicts a corner of the campo—over which looms a wall of the Palazzo Barbarigo. He animates it with the figures of a woman leaning over a window railing, another woman stooping to open a door, and a chimney sweep at work. Beyond the palazzo, the line of buildings facing the canal recedes toward the Church of Sta. Maria della Salute, its dome just visible above these façades. This line of buildings terminates with the distinctive outline of the Dogana del Mar, the customs house for maritime trade. Behind it, and beyond the Bacino di S. Marco and dozens of ships, lies the distant Riva degli Schiavoni. The Palazzo Corner della Cà Grande, attributed to Jacopo Sansovino, dominates the left side of the painting.

As the art historian Michael Levey observed, Canaletto's views of the Grand Canal from the Campo S. Vio are repetitions of the same composition but "with minor shifts of the viewpoint and changes in Staffage."[5] By continually reinterpreting the light, brushwork, and color in these similar works, the artist succeeded in making each version singular in some way. Here, he conveys the sense of deterioration that pervades Venice: he lavishes attention on the derelict wall of the Palazzo Barbarigo, giving an almost tactile quality to its weathering brick, plaster, and wood. He balances the airy elegance of the painting with shabbily dressed servants and workmen and with ragged laundry drying on lines. Canaletto's willingness to depict decay and his attraction to the mundane are evident even in his earliest work and reflect his personal affinity for all aspects, however humble, of Venetian life.[6]

ST

Notes

1. For the various versions as well as the related paintings and drawings, see Constable and Links 1989, 2: 274–79, nos. 182–92.

2. Links 1977, 21.

3. Clayton 2005, 64.

4. The view seems to have held a particular appeal for George Proctor, who commissioned not only the Memphis Brooks Museum of Art picture and its pendant but also a smaller pair of paintings, one of which is a nearly identical view of the Grand Canal as seen from the Campo S. Vio. That picture, *Looking East, from the Campo di San Vio,* and its pendant, *The Molo: From the Bacino di San Marco,* are in the collection of Proctor's descendents. Those two works, both of which measure 18 1/2 x 31 in. (47 x 78.5 cm), are considerably smaller than the Brooks Museum canvas. Presumably these pictures also date to about 1740, during Proctor's sojourn in Venice. See Constable and Links 1989, 2: 237 and 278, nos. 106 and 190, respectively. See also London 1957, 34.

5. Levey 1959, 58.

6. Links in London and Washington 1994, 219.

Provenance: Probably executed for George Proctor [ca. 1670–1744], in Venice, ca. 1740; by descent to Sir Reginald Proctor-Beauchamp [1853–1912], Langley Hall, Norfolk; by descent in Proctor-Beauchamp family; (sold at Sotheby's, London, June 11, 1947, no. 26); R. F. Watson; (sold at Sotheby's, London, March 23, 1955, to "Betts"); David Koetser, New York, before 1957; Kress acquisition, 1957.

References: *Arts Magazine* 1958, 36; Suida 1958a, 48; Pallucchini 1960, 104; *Connoisseur* 1961, 286, ill.; Shapley 1961, 41; Constable 1962, 2: 262, no. 187; Memphis and Lexington 1965, 56; Suida and Davis 1966, 56; Puppi 1970, no. 72D, 96; Shapley 1973, 161 K2173; Memphis 1984, 68; Constable and Links 1989, 2: 276–77, no. 187; Memphis 2004, 90–91.

21.‡ Canaletto (Giovanni Antonio Canal), 1697–1768
View of the Molo, ca. 1740
Oil on canvas, 44 1/2 x 63 1/4 in. (113 x 160.6 cm)
El Paso Museum of Art, Gift of the Samuel H. Kress Foundation 1961.1.49

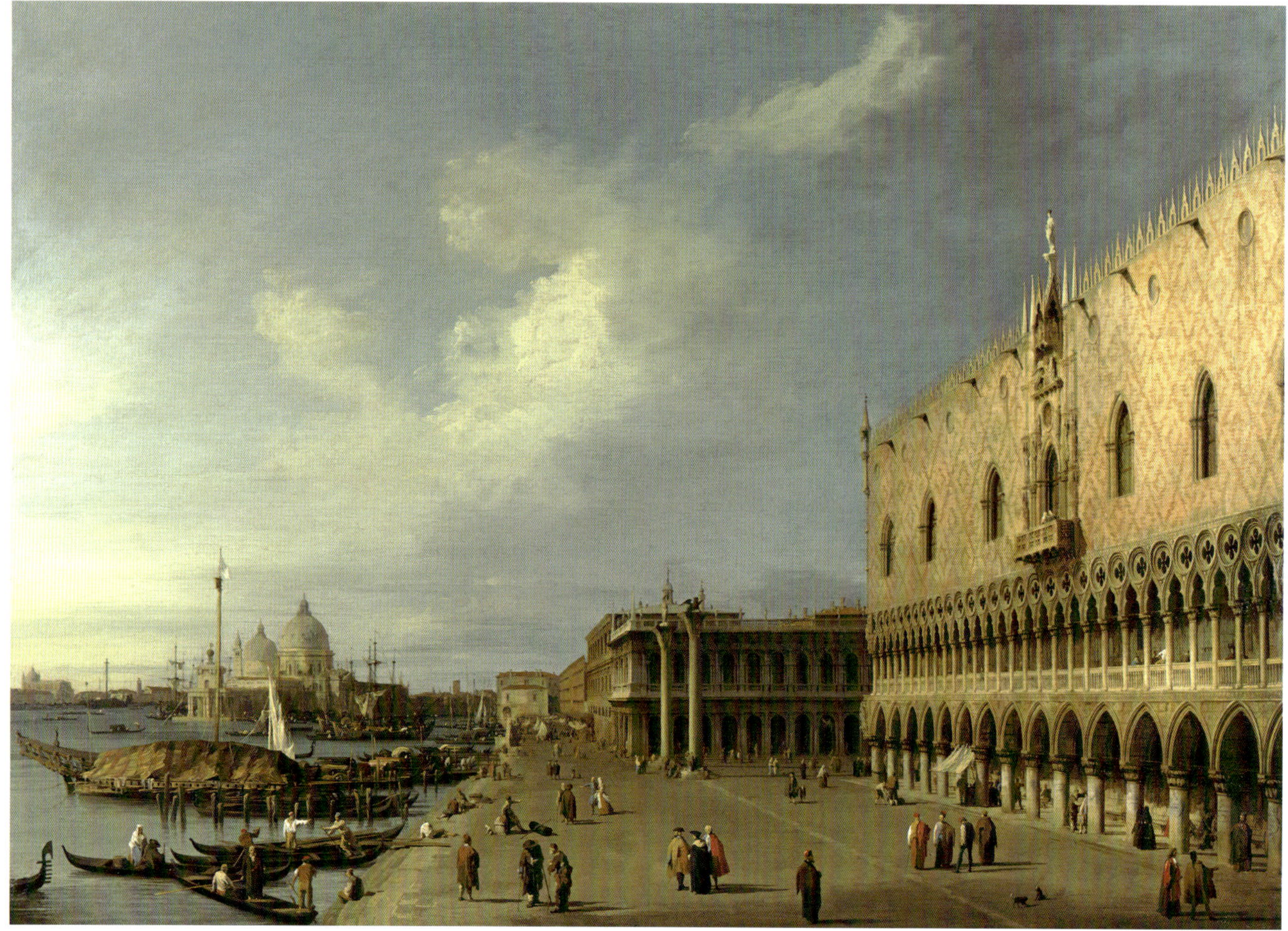

Views of the Molo, the broad stone quay fronting the Bacino di S. Marco, were common in Canaletto's oeuvre.[1] Among the most recognizable sites in Venice, the Molo accommodated commercial and passenger boats, and provided a pleasant and lively locale for walks. More significantly, it functioned as a ceremonial landing place for important officials and distinguished visitors. As such, it appears repeatedly in Canaletto's depictions of the arrival of dignitaries and of public festivals. The El Paso Museum of Art painting is one of about ten showing the Molo from the east, dominated on the right by the Doge's Palace and looking down its length toward the entrance to the Grand Canal.[2]

The richly ornamented Gothic façade of the Doge's Palace, with its distinctive pink and white marble walls, dominates the picture. At the end of its arcade, near the center of the canvas, are the two massive granite columns bearing, respectively, statues of the city's patron saints: the winged lion of St. Mark, and St. Theodore. These stand at the intersection of the Molo and the Piazzetta, the small plaza that adjoins the expansive Piazza S. Marco. The Biblioteca Marciana (National Library of St. Mark's), designed by Jacopo Sansovino, is visible directly behind the columns. Just beyond, and overlooking the Bacino di S. Marco, are the Zecca, or mint, and the red-brick façade of the Graneri Publici, or public granaries. The simple, unadorned wall and arched door of the Fonteghetto della Farina mark both the end of the Molo and the entrance to the Grand Canal. Most of the structures along the canal proper in this painting are unidentifiable, but the square tower rising from the line of hazy façades belongs to the Palazzo Vernier della Toreselle.[3] The Church of Sta. Maria della Salute (designed by Baldassare Longhena), seen on the left side, dominates the gateway to the Grand Canal. In front of it is the Dogana del Mar, or maritime customs house, with its distinctive tower crowned by a globe and statuary. The island of Guidecca, site of Il Redentore, a monastic church designed by Andrea Palladio, is visible at the far left.

Traditionally, scholars have dated *View of the Molo* and its pendant, *The Grand Canal from the Campo San Vio* (cat. 20), to the early 1730s.[4] However, archival information about George Proctor, the English merchant and entrepreneur who originally owned the pair, indicates that he probably commissioned them in Venice around 1740.[5] This corresponds to the style of the pictures, which exhibit the sunny tonalities and crisp execution that were so popular with Canaletto's English patrons.

It is worth noting that the vantage point in *View of the Molo* is from a site almost directly opposite the perspective used for its pendant. That is, the former looks down the Riva degli Schiavoni along the Bacino di S. Marco, past the Dogana del Mar and Sta. Maria della Salute along the Grand Canal and toward the Campo S. Vio in the distance.

ST

Notes

1. Constable and Links reproduce twenty-eight views of the Molo, taken from different vantage points, not including festival scenes in which this site serves as a backdrop. Constable and Links 1989, 2: 225–40, nos. 85–110.

2. Constable and Links list a number of versions of the composition that are known to be by Canaletto's hand, along with several related works. Of these, the version now in the Gemäldegalerie, Berlin, and dated to about 1730 is probably closest to the El Paso Museum of Art painting. Constable and Links 1989, 2: 225–40, nos. 85–100.

3. The tower, erected in the fifteenth century, no longer stands. It is much more distinctly depicted in the Antonio Visentini etching (after Canaletto) that shows the entrance to the Grand Canal, looking west (cat. 13g). See also Madrid 2001, 237, no. 88.

4. Pallucchini (1960, 104) posits that the work belongs to the years "before 1735." Shapley (1973, 161, no. K2174) concurs with this dating but also notes that the "finished effect" of the painting suggests a later period in Canaletto's career. In a 1956 letter, W. G. Constable noted that Proctor's descendents traditionally believed he had purchased all four of his paintings (this picture and its pendant [cat. 20], plus the pair of smaller Canalettos still with the family; see note 5, p. 30) while in Venice. Constable therefore surmises that the Englishman must have been there in the 1730s. See W. G. Constable to David Koetser, January 10, 1956, El Paso Museum of Art curatorial files. Instead of dating the painting to a specific period in the artist's career, Constable and Links (1989, 2: 227, nos. 87 and 88) point out the work's similarity to a version of the subject in the Gemäldegalerie, Berlin, that they date to about 1730.

5. For early provenance information, and particularly a discussion of archival sources associated with Proctor and the Proctor-Beauchamp family, see Thomas essay, p. 25.

Provenance: Probably executed for George Proctor [ca. 1670–1744], in Venice, ca. 1740; by descent to Sir Reginald Proctor-Beauchamp [1853–1912], Langley Hall, Norfolk; by descent in Proctor-Beauchamp family; (sold at Sotheby's, London, June 11, 1947, no. 25, to "Major Abbey"); David Koetser, New York, before 1957; Kress acquisition 1957.

References: Moschini 1954, pl. 28 (ill. only); Pallucchini 1960, 104; Shapley 1961, 41; Constable 1962, 2: 219, no. 88; Shapley 1973, 161–62, no. K2174; Constable and Links 1989, 2: 227–28, no. 88.

22. Canaletto (Giovanni Antonio Canal), 1697–1768
   The Riva degli Schiavoni Towards the East, ca. 1760
   Oil on canvas, 14 3/4 x 10 1/8 in. (37.5 x 25.7 cm)
   The John and Mable Ringling Museum of Art, Sarasota; Bequest of John Ringling, 1936, SN187

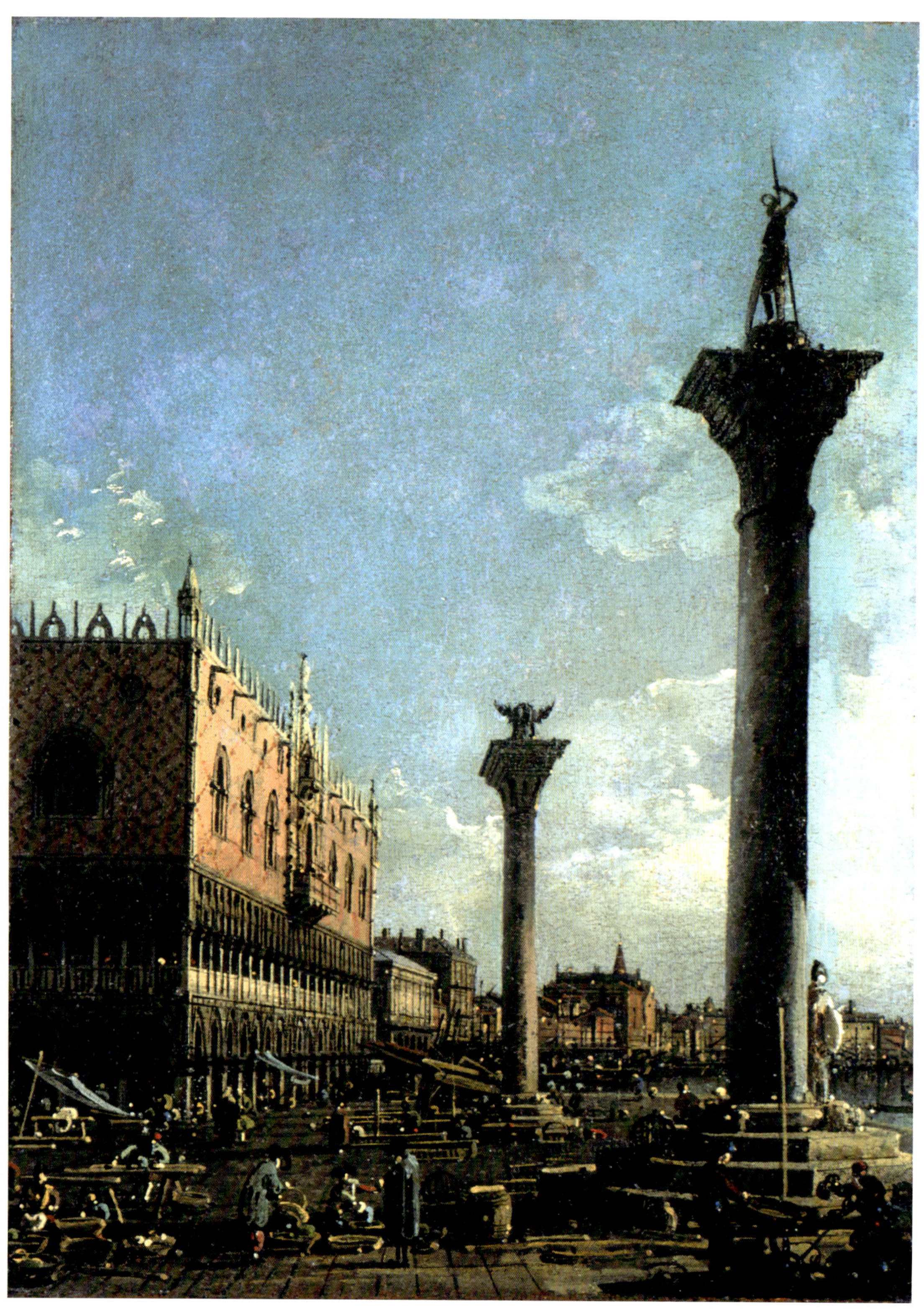

Among the many views Canaletto painted of the Riva degli Schiavoni, most look east from a point near the Piazzetta. The Ringling picture—pendant to *Piazza San Marco Seen from the Campo San Basso* (cat. 23)—is one of only three such views that include both columns commemorating Venice's two patrons, St. Theodore (pictured in the foreground with his spear and shield) and St. Mark (represented in the background as a winged lion, the apocalyptic symbol of the Evangelist).[1] The Doge's Palace, distinguished by its sunlit pink-and-white southern façade, and the adjacent prison together frame a sidelong view of the city's popular waterside promenade. The impression given by this painting is that the artist stood directly in front of Jacopo Sansovino's Biblioteca Marciana (National Library of St. Mark's) when composing this scene.

Most of Canaletto's Venetian paintings do not accurately depict actual topography, yet the illusions they produce are, as the art historians David Bomford and Gabriele Finaldi observed, "so complete that we cannot resist testing them against reality."[2] So it is with this work. If, for example, one compares the distance Canaletto suggests between the St. Theodore column and the library steps (the implied vantage point) to the actual distance (approximately ten feet), it becomes clear that he has drastically altered the scale of the column. In reality, when standing by the library steps, one can see only the lowest portion of the St. Theodore column and nothing of the St. Mark column.

A drawing in a Swiss private collection that is closely related to the Ringling *Riva degli Schiavoni* further demonstrates the extent to which Canaletto manipulated the proportions of this pair of monuments. In the drawing, the St. Theodore column appears to be more steeply angled than in the painting, where its capital and pedestal are barely visible.

Canaletto's frequent distortion of proportion in order to heighten his paintings' effects has long been a topic of scholarly discussion. On this point, the connoisseur J. G. Links remarked that "[Canaletto's] were pictures painted *in* Venice rather than pictures painted *of* Venice" (emphasis mine).[3] Thus the resizing of the columns for the present painting must have been done to serve a larger compositional purpose: to convey as direct and convincing an image of the paired monuments as possible. Additionally, the altered scale creates a perfectly descending angle that silhouettes the columns, thereby offering a more fluid, cohesive view than does the relatively severe drawing referred to above.

Riva degli Schiavoni was probably painted during the last decade of Canaletto's life, as it bears all the hallmarks of his late work, including the cool blond tone that resulted from his use of a pale underpaint and the perfunctory shorthand that describes each figure. Employing tiny dabs of paint to indicate heads and hands and just a few quick strokes to suggest clothing, Canaletto created doll-like figures that only vaguely resemble the individualized and varied characters he had portrayed early in his career.

AL

Notes

1. Of the other two, one is in the Wallace Collection and the other is in the collection of Mr. and Mrs. John P. Pomerantz. Baetjer and Links in New York 1989, 198, neglect the Ringling picture, asserting that the Wallace and Pomerantz paintings are the only two eastward-looking views of the Riva degli Schiavoni that include both columns.

2. Bomford and Finaldi in London et al. 1998, 61.

3. Links 1982, 34.

Provenance: A. J. Pilkington, Parkmore, County Antrim-Cavan, Ireland, by 1930; (sold, Christie's, London, July 25, 1930, no. 30); John Ringling [1866–1936], Sarasota, 1930–36.

References: Vilas 1942, 68; Suida 1949, no. 187, 158–59; Austin 1955, n.p., ill.; Henry in Pittsfield 1960, n.p., no. 23; MacAgy in Dallas 1961, 48, fig. 38, no. 39; Constable 1962, 1: 73, 232, no. 116 and 2: 199, 443; Constable in Toronto et al. 1964, 142, no. 118; Berto and Puppi 1968, 120, no. 343; Puppi 1968, 121, no. 343; Fredericksen and Zeri 1972, 43, 637; Constable 1976, 1: 73, pl. 29, no. 116 and 2: 243, no. 116; Tomory 1976, 85–86, no. 82; Shore 1980, no. 178; Links 1981, 94, no. 318; New York and Tampa 1981, 15, no. 8, 72, pl. 40; Corboz 1985, 2: 747, no. P.482; Constable and Links 1989, 1: 73, pl. 29, no. 116 and 2: 243, no. 116; New York 1989, 338; Links 1998, 50; Merling 2002, 155; Borys 2008, 101.

23. Canaletto (Giovanni Antonio Canal), 1697–1768
Piazza San Marco Seen from the Campo San Basso, ca. 1760
Oil on canvas, 14 3/4 x 10 1/8 in. (37.5 x 25.7 cm)
The John and Mable Ringling Museum of Art, Sarasota; Bequest of John Ringling, 1936, SN186

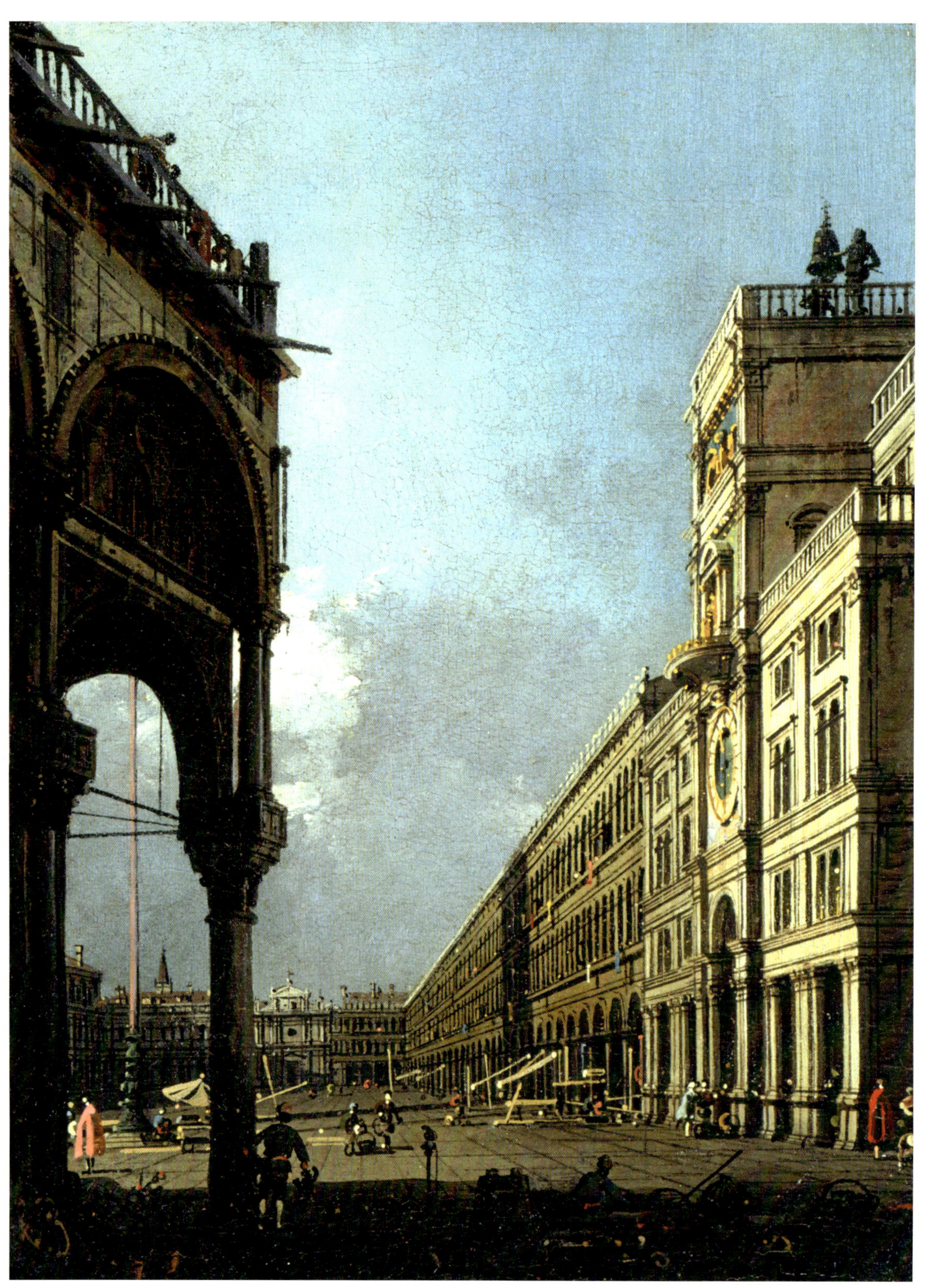

Beginning with his earliest recorded commission for the Irish entrepreneur Owen McSwiney in 1722, Canaletto showed a preference for creating paired, or pendant, paintings.[1] The practice of painting in pairs, particularly on smaller canvases that tourists could easily transport, is most characteristic of Canaletto's late career.[2] Typically, these pendant pictures offered different views from the same general location, thereby presenting a more dramatic panorama than a single scene could afford. The Ringling pendants differ slightly from other paintings in this practice because their views—of the Campo S. Basso and the Piazzetta—were taken from two spots adjacent to the Piazza San Marco rather than from a single vantage point.

The occurrence of views in and around the Piazza S. Marco in Canaletto's oeuvre is second in frequency only to his images of the Grand Canal.[3] This picture, however, is one of three works that locate the viewer at the Campo S. Basso, looking west.[4] Seen in the center of the composition is the Church of S. Geminiano, with the Campanile of S. Moise visible through the arcade. To the right, in vertiginously steep perspective, is the official dwelling of the Venetian republic's doges (chief magistrates). Nearest the viewer, on the north side of the piazza, is Mauro Coducci's Torre dell'Orologio (clock tower) with its great bronze bell. Flanking the tower are the so-called Moors. Below them is the lion of Venice, the Virgin and Child, and the elaborate clock that, besides telling time, shows the phases of the Sun and Moon and displays the signs of the zodiac.

Built toward the end of the fifteenth century and expanded to include east and west wings early in the sixteenth century, the Torre dell'Orologio appears prominently in numerous Canaletto *vedute*. Depicted here above the east wing is the extra story that was added in 1753—a sign that the painting cannot have been executed earlier than 1755, when Canaletto returned from a five-year sojourn in England. Further, its use of cool muted tones and strong black outlining for topographical and architectural details fixes the painting within his style of the early 1760s. Finally, the canvas bears such a striking resemblance to the right side of what is generally believed to be Canaletto's final rendering of this subject, *Piazza San Marco: Looking South and West* (see fig. 14, p. 21)—signed and dated 1763—that it is reasonable to suggest it was painted no later than that year.

A probable study for the Ringling painting is in the collection of the Musée Condé, Chantilly (fig. 23.1). Except for the absence of masts in front of the Basilica of S. Marco and a slight altering of figures—for example, the workman in the foreground of the drawing stands rather than sits—the compositions of the drawing and painting are virtually identical.

AL

Notes

1. The early McSwiney commission consisted of twenty-four "tomb paintings" (as they came to be called) collaboratively created by Canaletto, Giovanni Battista Cimaroli, Giovanni Battista Piazzetta, Giovanni Battista Pittoni, and Marco and Sebastiano Ricci. Canaletto's contribution was minor, involving perspective and landscape work on two of the canvases. For more on this project, see Haskell 1956, 296–300; Links 1967, 453–58; idem 1982; Baetjer and Links in New York 1989; and Constable and Links 1989.

2. Another Canaletto pendant pair of about 1760 whose dimensions are close to those of the Ringling companion pieces is in the National Gallery, London: *Piazza San Marco: Looking East from the Southwest Corner* and *Piazza San Marco: Looking East from the Northwest Corner*. See Links 1982, 195–216.

3. For the many views Canaletto painted of these two major subjects, see Constable and Links 1989.

4. One was at Castle Howard in England but was destroyed by fire in 1940. See Constable 1962, 2: 199, no. 40. The second, in the collection of the Los Angeles County Museum of Art, offers both a south and a west fish-eye panorama. J. G. Links considers that work to be a capriccio, given the impossibly wide angle and tufts of foliage sprouting from the northern column of the Basilica of S. Marco. See Links 1982, 207–9; and idem 1989, 274–75, no. 84.

Provenance: A. J. Pilkington, Parkmore, County Antrim-Cavan, Ireland, by 1930; (sold, Christie's, London, July 25, 1930, no. 30); John Ringling [1866–1936], Sarasota, 1930–36.

References: Vilas 1942, 68; Suida 1949, no. 186, 158–59; Austin 1955, n.p.; Constable 1962, 1: 232 and 2: 199, no. 41, 443, no. 534; Constable in Toronto et al. 1964, 143, no. 119; Berto and Puppi 1968, 120, no. 342; Puppi 1968, 121, no. 342; Fredericksen and Zeri 1972, 43, 637; Constable 1976, 1: pl. 19, no. 41 and 2: 204, no. 41, 484, no. 534; Tomory 1976, 85–86, no. 81; Links 1981, 92, no. 317; New York and Tampa 1981, 15, no. 7, pl. 39; Corboz 1985, 2: 747, no. P.481; Constable and Links 1989, 1: pl. 19, no. 41 and 2: 204, no. 41, 484, no. 534; New York 1989, 338; Garnier-Pelle in Chantilly 2001, 82, no. 52; Merling 2002, 155; Borys 2008, 101.

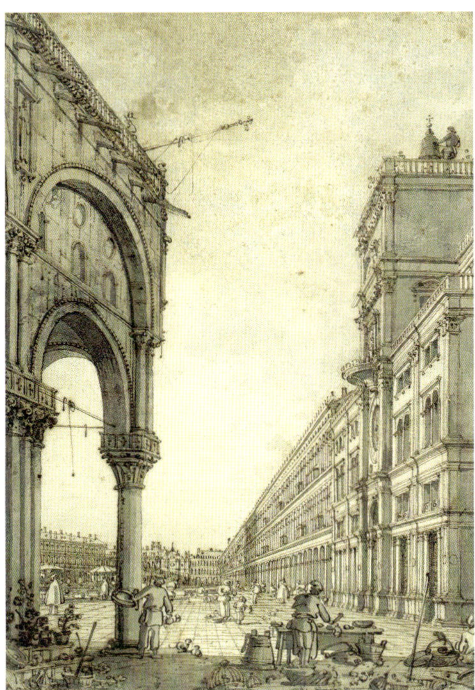

Fig. 23.1. Canaletto (Giovanni Antonio Canal)
Venice: Piazza San Marco, Seen from Campo San Basso, 18th century
Wash with India ink, 14 5/8 x 10 1/4 in. (37.2 x 26.3 cm)
Musée Condé, Chantilly, France

24. Pietro Longhi, ca. 1701–1785
The Music Lesson (The Bird Cage), ca. 1740–45
Oil on canvas, 22 x 17 in. (55.9 x 43.2 cm)
Fine Arts Museums of San Francisco, Gift of Mortimer Leventritt, 1952.83

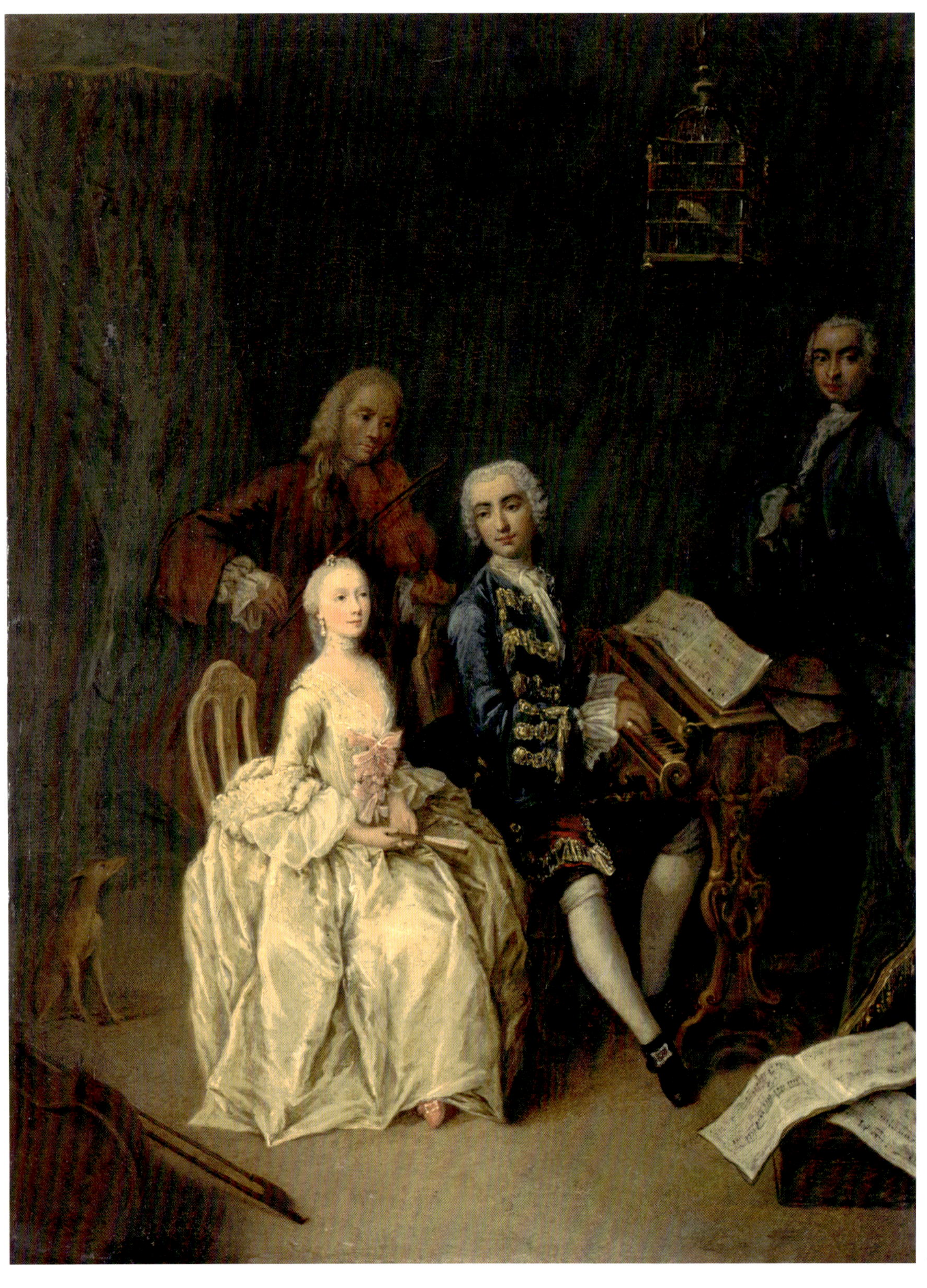

Pietro Longhi often depicted concerts or musical instruction in his paintings, whether as features of everyday life or as elements in family portraits. This canvas is one of six distinct genre scenes by the artist that bear the very same title, all of which portray women receiving music lessons.[1] The young lady, whose fair skin and pale dress stand out against the dark room and the somber clothing of her companions, is the focus of this composition. In 1990 the man at the piano was tentatively identified as the famous castrato Carlo Broschi, commonly known as Farinelli.[2] Yet while his carefully delineated features may imply a portrait and his prominent placement and rich clothing suggest celebrity, this identification is tenuous; more recent scholarship has revealed that the painting dates to about twenty years after Farinelli's visit to Venice.[3]

Longhi's subjects often tend to be enigmatic. Here, the woman presumably receiving instruction holds a fan rather than playing an instrument. The harpsichordist and violinist apparently are awaiting her cue, but the man on the right—perhaps a music master—looks toward the viewer, as if a visitor has interrupted their practice session. The small dog gazing at the group offers a clue about the scene's implicit meaning. In Venetian art of the eighteenth century, lapdogs often symbolized the amorous attentions of men toward women; in this instance, the dog's demeanor is probably meant to underscore the pianist's desires.[4] In addition, the birdcage—a title that has sometimes been assigned to the San Francisco painting—seems to reinforce this interpretation. Caged birds rarely appear in Longhi's work and then only in seduction scenes, where they hang above beautiful young women and their male admirers.[5] With its combination of sexuality and music making, the painting echoes the Longhi *Music Lesson* in the collection of the Walters Art Museum (cat. 26).

The setting of *The Music Lesson*—a rather shallow room with little furniture and no windows—is typical of Longhi's interiors, which are similarly constrictive and seemingly artificial spaces. Some scholars contend that because Longhi depicted interiors that resemble stage sets—spaces populated with a handful of people who appear to be acting out mundane dramas—his paintings can be linked to the plays of the popular contemporary Venetian writer Carlo Goldoni (1707–1793), whose work involved everyday characters and situations.[6] Although both men were keen observers of their fellow Venetians, the painter's imagery lacked the writer's sarcastic wit; Longhi chose to record the lives of upper-class Venetians without overt criticism or irony. Although they seem to illustrate stories, Longhi's paintings are not so much narratives that follow plots as images that hint at intriguing relationships.[7]

An undated preparatory sketch for a parrot and cage is in the collection of the Museo Correr, Venice (see fig. 26.1, p. 119).

ST

Notes

1. Four canvases are in the collections of: Petworth House, West Sussex; the Staatliche Museen, Berlin; the Museo Correr, Venice; and the Walters Art Museum, Baltimore. The Walpole Gallery, London, offered the sixth painting for sale in 1990; its present location is unknown. For the painting on the London art market, see London 1990, 76–78, no. 34.

2. London 1990, 76.

3. Venice 1993, 100.

4. In his article on Longhi genre paintings in the Metropolitan Museum of Art, Rolf Bagemihl discussed the importance of the lapdog as a symbol of flirtatious attentions paid by suitors to young women. Bagemihl 1988, 235–36.

5. See for example *Milord's Salad* (ca. 1760, Aldo Crespi Collection, Milan), in which a caged bird is positioned above a beautiful young woman who is ogled by a well-dressed aristocrat. Terisio Pignatti (1974, 78) called that work "piquant" due to its flirtatious overtones. Historically, caged birds have symbolized female sexuality and are often associated with lost virtue. See Shefer 1991, 446–47.

6. Pignatti 1996, 169.

7. Paulson 1975, 110.

Provenance: Mortimer Leventritt, San Francisco.

References: Fort Worth 1954, 54; San Francisco 1960, 20; Pignatti 1969, 84; Fredericksen and Zeri 1972, 633; Pignatti 1974, 87; Manning 1980, 193–94; Venice 1993, 100.

25. Pietro Longhi, ca. 1701–1785
   Masked Party in a Courtyard, 1755
   Oil on canvas, 24 1/2 x 19 7/8 in. (62.2 x 50.5 cm)
   Saint Louis Art Museum, Museum Purchase, 32:1939

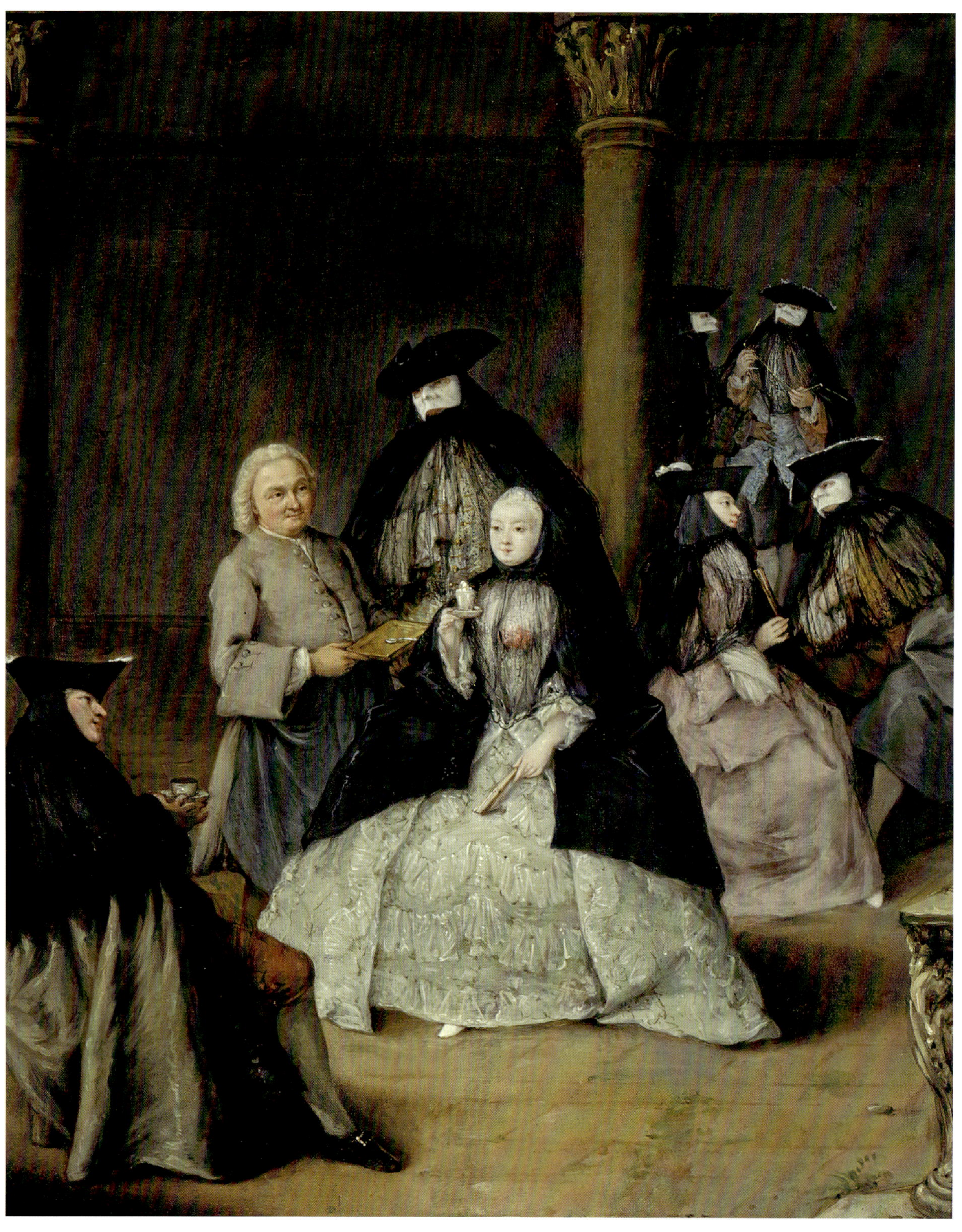

Although Pietro Longhi executed portraits as well as religious and history paintings during his long career, he is best known for his small-scale, gently satirical genre pictures of contemporary Venetian life. As the art historian Michael Levey famously noted, the artist "virtually *is* genre painting in Venice for the major portion of the [eighteenth] century."[1]

Here, Longhi captures a small group of people conversing and drinking coffee or tea in a domestic courtyard during Carnival season. He often centered his scenes on a female figure surrounded by a few individuals who offer her their attention and services. This painting is also typical of his work in that it contrasts the radiant whiteness of a woman's face and the pale fabric of her gown with the rather dim setting. In his written instructions to Giambattista Remondini, who published engravings after Longhi's paintings, the artist encouraged the printmaker to "make the central figure aglow!"[2]

Except for the servant who delivers a covered cup to the woman, all the figures are dressed in the *bautta* costume, which consisted of a black tricorn hat, a *volto* (a mask made of waxed white cloth), a veil, and, usually, a cloak.[3] Worn by both men and women over their clothing, it was probably the most popular form of Carnival attire. The *bautta* disguised both clothing and faces, although the transparent veil—seen on several figures in this painting—afforded a tantalizing glimpse of the wearer's torso while concealing his or her face.

Many of Longhi's genre paintings focus on pleasurable activities, ranging from gambling to parlor games, but at least one scholar has sensed an underlying current of boredom in these works.[4] Whether taking refreshment, flirting, or conversing, the figures often seem nearly lifeless, as if they were fashionably dressed dolls posed in artificial settings—such as this courtyard devoid of sunlight and a view of the sky. These works may be interpreted as subtle metaphors for Venetian aristocratic life and, indeed, for the city itself. Longhi portrays an upper class that was trapped in a culture whose power and importance were waning. At least one writer detected an almost sinister aura in the Saint Louis Art Museum painting, noting how the canvas, with its tenebrous, fading light and mysterious masked figures, anticipates the disturbing, even nightmarish images that Francisco Goya would create later in the century.[5]

ST

Notes

1. Levey 1980, 137.

2. Venice 1995, 46. Pignatti (1968, 52) includes the entire letter, which offers the engraver a range of advice on how to improve his work.

3. For the *bautta* and its origins, see Mazzarotto 1980, 110; and Reato 1988, 43, 103.

4. Paulson 1975b, 112.

5. Moschini 1956b, 28.

Provenance: Papadopoli Collection, Venice; Paul Drey, New York, 1939.

References: Rogers 1939, 43–47; St. Louis 1944, 111; Bacchelli 1953, 72–73; Morassi 1953, 55–56; St. Louis 1953, 69; Bordeaux 1956, 13–14; Moschini 1956b, 28; Donzelli 1957, 135; Pallucchini 1960, 181; Pignatti 1968, 38, 167; Fredericksen and Zeri 1972, 630; St. Louis 1972, n.p.; Pignatti 1974, 95; St. Louis 1975, 112; no. 95; Mann 1997, 53–55, 62.

26.† Pietro Longhi, ca. 1701–1785
    The Music Lesson, ca. 1760
    Oil on copper, 17 9/16 x 22 11/16 in. (44.6 x 57.6 cm)
    The Walters Art Museum, Baltimore, 37.397

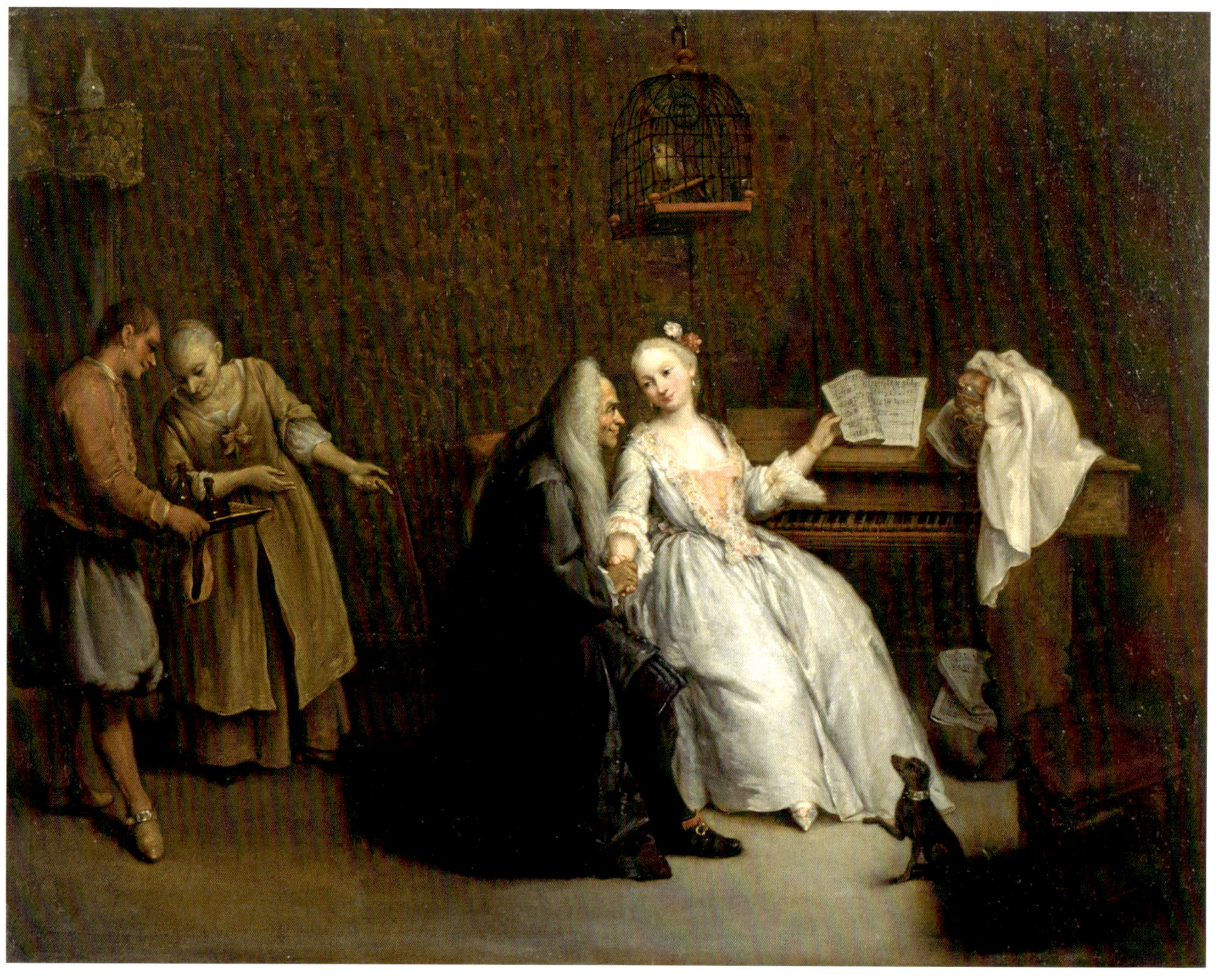

Reflecting the abiding desire of scholars to identify particular subject matter in works of art, early Walters Art Museum catalogues assign the title *Voltaire chez la princesse de Condé* to this painting, presumably because of the perceived similarity of the old man's visage to documented portraits of Voltaire.[1] Despite the never-substantiated assumption that the pretty young girl and old man represent famous French individuals, the painting is actually one of Longhi's typical genre scenes. Such works depict neither specific people nor even a particular theme but simply record episodes of daily life. Here, employing gentle humor, Longhi shows an elderly and rather lecherous music teacher with his beautiful young student. Taking advantage of the servants' momentary inattention, he squeezes the pupil's hand and gazes lustfully at her.

The lapdog—traditionally associated in Western European art with women, the home, and fidelity—raises its paw in alarm. Although such a pet could in certain contexts symbolize playful flirtation, here it almost certainly is meant to underscore a threat to female virtue.[2] The caged bird above the harpsichord, traditionally a symbol of lost virginity, further underscores the painting's sexual theme.[3] Significantly, this bird is a brightly colored parrot, an exotic creature that often positively represented divine salvation or fluent wisdom. However, because the parrot is tightly confined, its presence carries connotations that are less benign.[4]

As the art historian Terisio Pignatti noted, Longhi worked for a relatively small circle of wealthy Venetians, often providing glimpses into the luxurious world of his patrons. The sumptuous clothing worn by the young woman in *The Music Lesson* is matched by the furnishings, particularly the gilded harpsichord and the porcelain vases atop the valance on the left. Additionally, the walls are hung with *cuori d'oro*—literally, heart of gold; made of embossed, painted, and gilded leather, such wall coverings adorned the most opulent Venetian rooms during the eighteenth century.

The Music Lesson is one of only two images Longhi is known to have painted on a copper plate—a rather expensive medium.[5] An undated preparatory sketch by him of a parrot and cage is in the collection of the Museo Correr, Venice (fig. 26.1).[6] Longhi also incorporated the parrot and cage into another version of this subject (cat. 24).

ST

Notes

1. Additionally, early Walters catalogues (which were compiled based on notes by William Thomas Walters) classify this painting as "French School, eighteenth century." See, for example, Walters 1922, no. 397. Federico Zeri (1966, 444) rejected the subject-matter identification and attribution alike, conclusively attributing the picture to Longhi.

2. Lapdogs could mimic the actions and desires of honorable suitors. For the positive role of these animals in eighteenth-century Italian art, see Bagemihl 1988, 235–36. On the other hand, they could signify loss of innocence and marital infidelity. For example, a lapdog figures prominently in Giuseppe Maria Mitelli's etching *La vita infelice della mererice* (1692), which depicts an innocent young woman's tragic transformation into a prostitute. See Kurz 1952, 144–45.

3. For a discussion of this symbolism, see Shefer 1985, 446–47.

4. See Lloyd 1971, 25–27, 47.

5. Longhi's other known painting on copper is an anonymous portrait of a violinist, dated to about 1760. Pignatti (1969, 80–81) recorded it as being in the collection of Robert Manning, Long Island.

6. See Zeri 1976, 564.

Provenance: Henry Walters [1848–1931], Baltimore, before 1909 (mode of acquisition unknown); Walters Art Museum, 1931, by bequest

References: Walters 1909, no. 397; Walters 1922, no. 397; Walters 1929, no. 397; Zeri 1966, 444; Pignatti 1972, 56; Pignatti 1974, 97, no. 150; Boles in Baltimore 1976, 49, no. 84; Zeri 1976, 2: 564, no. 452, ill. 294; Spike in Fort Worth 1986, 205; Pignatti 1987, 69, no. 973 and 128–30, nos. 1055, 1056; Zeri 1987, 107; Zafran 1988, 78, no. 30; Venice 1993, 126; Hansen and Spicer 2005, 156–57, no. 45.

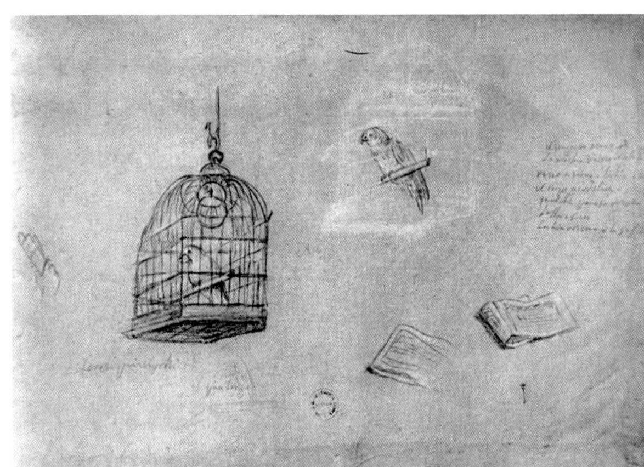

Fig. 26.1. Pietro Longhi
Cage and Parrot, n.d.
Black and white chalk on buff paper, dimensions unavailable
Museo Correr, Venice

27. Pietro Longhi, ca.1701–1785
     The Display of the Elephant, 1774
     Oil on canvas, 19 x 23 3/4 in. (48.3 x 60.3 cm)
     Sarah Campbell Blaffer Foundation, Houston BF.1980.03

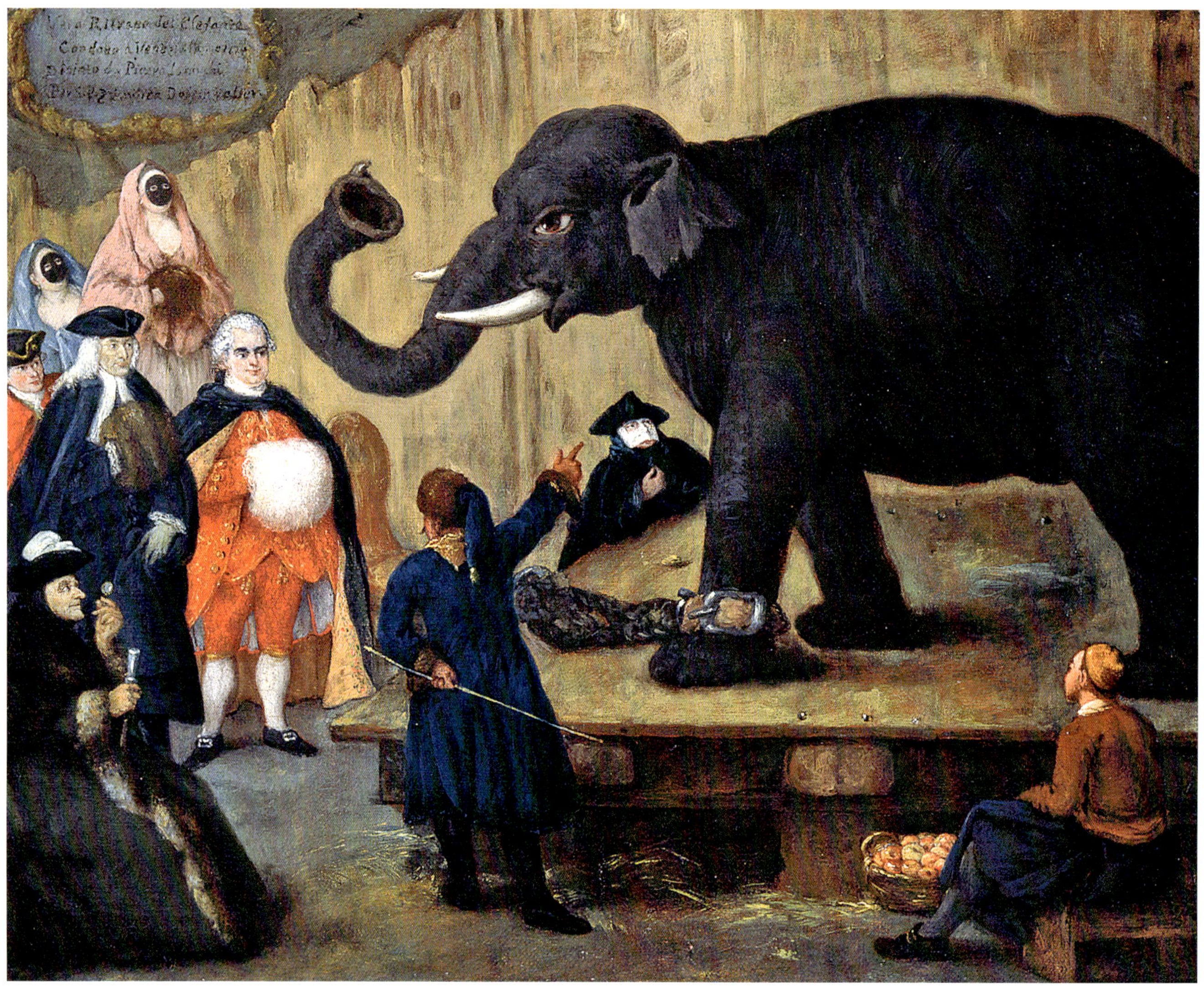

Safely chained to a heavy wooden platform, an elephant enthralls a group of Carnival revelers. The setting is probably the Piazzetta or the Piazza S. Marco, where the public could view exotic animals within temporary enclosures made of heavy planks.[1] In keeping with the pachyderm's exotic origins, its trainer wears a turban; his assistant also appears to be clothed in Eastern garb. Longhi gives special prominence to a portly man in red holding a large, white fur muff by placing him directly in front of the elephant; this may be Andrea Dolfin Valier, who presumably commissioned the painting and whose name apparently is included in the elaborate inscription at the upper left.[2] As translated, it reads, "True depiction of the elephant / Brought to Venice in 1774 / Painted by Pietro Longhi / For S. P. Z. Andrea Dolfin Valier."[3]

The masked costumes indicate that the scene is taking place during Carnival season. Both the old woman seated in the foreground—telescope in hand to improve her viewing—and the man at the back of the platform staring up at the animal wear the long, veiled black cloak, tricorn hat, and white mask of the *bautta*.[4] She, however, has placed the costume's mask atop her hat. Two women in the background wear *moretta*, black-velvet facial coverings.[5] A small bit or button clinched in the teeth secured these masks, which concealed the entire face.

Until the early nineteenth century, there were very few elephants in Western Europe.[6] Before and during the Renaissance, Eastern monarchs often presented exotic and unusual animals as diplomatic gifts to their Western counterparts; for example, both Charlemagne and the Holy Roman emperor Maximilian II were given elephants.[7] The arrival of these rare creatures inevitably attracted public attention, and artists often documented such events for posterity. Longhi also painted at least two images of the celebrated rhinoceros Clara while she was on display in Venice during the Carnival season of 1751,[8] and he also depicted an apparently tame lion performing with a group of small costumed dogs.[9]

The Display of the Elephant is one of four known Longhi paintings of Carnival revelers admiring pachyderms in public settings.[10] Probably the most famous of these, also dating to 1774, is in the Gallerie di Palazzo Leoni Montanari, Vicenza. All four are similar in terms of overall composition and rendering of the elephant itself—suggesting that they were based on the same drawing.[11] The inscriptions appearing on this and the Vicenza canvases are identical, except that the latter notes Marina Sagredo Pisani as the person for whom it was made. Despite these similarities, the groups viewing the elephant in each version are quite different. This is likely because the individual patrons asked not only that their own likenesses be included but possibly also those of their family members.

ST

Notes

1. Venice 1995, 62.

2. Pignatti 1985, 198.

3. The inscription on the present painting reads, "Vero Ritratto del Elefante/Condotto a Venezia a. o 1774/Dipinto da Pietro Longhi/Per S. P. Z. Andrea [?] Dolfin Valier." This area of the canvas is badly worn and hard to read. Pignatti's reading of the first name as "Andrea" indicates that a man commissioned the picture. This accords with the part of the abbreviation S. P. Z. that precedes the full name. The S and P almost certainly stand for Signore Procuratore, an inherited masculine title in Venice. The Z may be an abbreviation for Zuan, which is "Giovanni" in the Venetian dialect. I am grateful to Professor William Barcham for providing this information.

4. Mazzarotto 1980, 110. See also Reato 1988, 43, 103.

5. The name of this mask stems from the expression *servetta muta*—literally, dumb-maid servant. See Mazzarotto 1980, 107–9.

6. For a history of the elephant in Europe, see Druce 1919.

7. Hans Burgkmair the Elder included Emperor Maximilian's elephant in woodcut images of the ruler's triumphal entries and processions. These date to the early 1500s. See Nickel 2002, 87. Likewise, an elephant given to Pope Leo X was the subject of works by several Renaissance artists, including Giulio Romano and Raphael. See Bedini 1981, 75–90.

8. For Clara, see Pignatti 1968, 90.

9. For *The Booth of the Lion* (1762, Pinacoteca Querini Stampalia, Venice), see Venice 1995, 62, no. 15.

10. One of these versions is now in the Gallerie di Palazzo Leoni Montanari, Vicenza. See Pignatti 1968, 97; and Sgarbi 1982, 30. Of the other two, one is in an Italian private collection and the remaining one was recently on the art market. See, respectively, Gorizia 2008, no. 58; and San Marco Casa d'Aste (Venice), *Old Master Paintings, Furnitures, Sculptures,* Sunday, 29 March, lot 45.

11. Pignatti 1968, 85, pl. 255. Writing about the present painting, Pignatti (1985, 198) noted that Longhi included an image of himself sketching the animal in the Vicenza version.

Provenance: Collection Andrea [?] Dolfin Valier, Venice*; Collection Rawdon Brown; (Christie's, London, May 30, 1884, 185); private collection, Paris**; David Hargreaves; Colnaghi Gallery, London, 1980.

* The name of the painting's original owner can be discerned only by examining the inscription on the canvas itself, where the first name of the person for whom it was painted is badly worn and barely legible. Martini read it as "Domenica." More recently, Pignatti interpreted it as "Andrea." The latter reading seems correct. See Martini 1982, 546, n. 326; and Pignatti 1985, 198.

** Martini (1982, 546, n. 326) records the work as being included in a private collection in Paris. This unnamed collection might be synonymous with that of David Hargreaves, the next owner of the picture, but Martini could in fact have been referring to notes possibly taken during the 1970s or 1980s, that is, before Hargreaves owned the work.

References: Martini 1982, 546, n. 326; Pignatti 1985, 198–99; Daxecker 2004, 325–27.

28. Francesco Guardi, 1712–1793
   View up the Grand Canal Toward the Rialto, ca. 1785
   Oil on canvas, 25 3/4 x 35 7/16 in. (65.4 x 90 cm)
   Minneapolis Institute of Arts, The William Hood Dunwoody Fund
   and a gift of Mr. and Mrs. Theodore W. Benne, 56.41

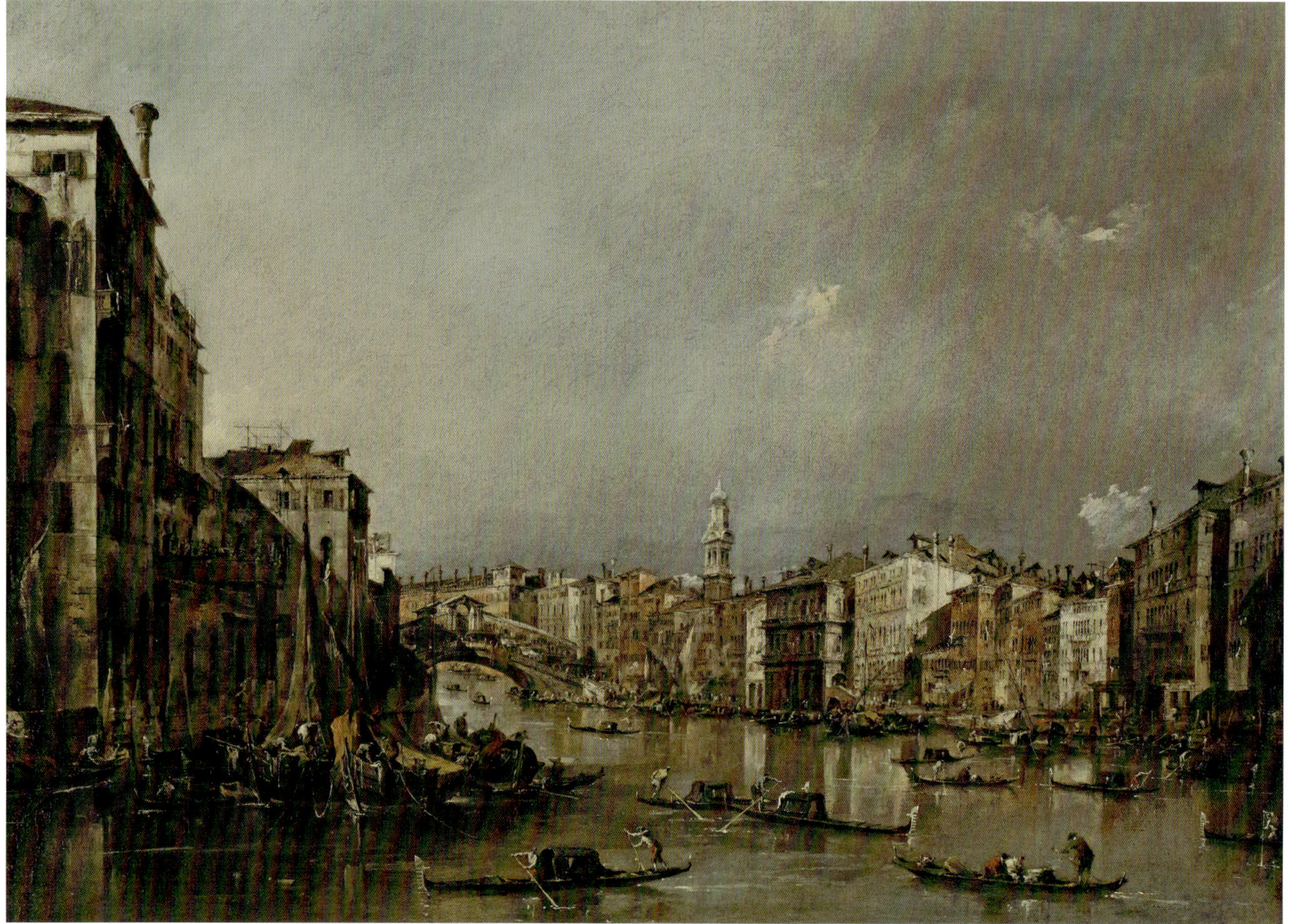

Francesco Guardi was nearly fifty years old when he began creating *vedute* (view paintings). A member of a family of Venetian artists, he trained first as a figure painter, only occasionally executing a landscape or capriccio (imaginary view) starting in the 1750s.[1] However, after the death in 1760 of his brother Antonio (who had headed the fraternal workshop), Francesco was able to dedicate himself fully to becoming a *vedutista* (view painter), producing more than 600 such works during the last thirty years of his career.

Although he was never a pupil of Canaletto—contrary to the oft-cited assertion of one contemporary, Pietro Gradenigo—Francesco Guardi was profoundly influenced by the master.[2] His brilliant atmospheric effects, strong tonal contrasts, and lively brushwork more closely recall Canaletto's early pictures, such as *View of Piazza San Marco* (see fig. 4, p. 14), than they do his later ones, such as *Piazza San Marco Seen from the Campo San Basso* (cat. 23). It has been suggested that these qualities may have been the embodiment of Guardi's criticism that Canaletto's late manner was cold and linear.[3] Indeed, the freedom and energy of Guardi's style and technique make his works akin to those of Giovanni Battista Piazzetta, Sebastiano Ricci, and Giambattista Tiepolo—the other great Venetian painters of the eighteenth century.

In the Minneapolis picture, the artist presents a long view of the Grand Canal, looking toward the Rialto Bridge. The view is northeasterly, offering a sweeping vista of the Riva del Carbon that begins at the Palazzo Farsetti (seen at the far right, in deep shadow). Farther north is the sun-drenched façade of the Palazzo Bembo and, adjacent to that, the Palazzo Dolfin-Manin—plunged into darkness.[4] The bell tower of the Church of S. Bartolommeo dominates the horizon just beyond the two palaces, while the many chimneys of the Fondaco dei Tedeschi appear directly behind the bridge. On the left winds the steeply foreshortened Riva del Vin, so called because that was where wine barrels shipped in from the mainland were unloaded—an activity detailed here.

An earlier Guardi painting of this same subject, now in the Musée Fabre, Montpellier (fig. 28.1), offers a much closer view of the Riva del Carbon, one that begins at the Palazzo Dolfin-Manin. However, the left side of the composition, showing the Riva del Vin, is virtually identical to that of the Minneapolis painting. Like Canaletto, Guardi was not primarily concerned with topographical accuracy. Manipulating proportion, perspective, and light to suit his aesthetic purposes, he achieved artistry—as did Canaletto—through the creation of compositional cohesion and sheer beauty.

AL

Notes

1. As early as 1731, the workshop was referred to as the "fratelli Guardi," indicating Francesco's presence. It is likely the younger brother, Nicolò, also worked there. See Sinding-Larsen 1962, 183.

2. In his diary, Procurator Pietro Gradenigo identified Francesco as a "buon scolaro del rinomato Canaletto" (good pupil of the celebrated Canaletto). Gradenigo's words have been frequently quoted in Canaletto scholarship. See, for example, Links 1977, 93; and Pedrocco 2002, 198, 233–34, no. 78.

3. Mitchell Merling, "The Brothers Guardi" in London and Washington, D.C. 1994, 315.

4. Jacopo Sansovino built the palazzo for the Dolfin family in the mid-sixteenth century. It was later occupied by Ludovico Manin, who became Venice's last doge in 1797, just months before the republic voted to accept Napoleon's demand for capitulation.

Provenance: Charles Tyson Yerkes [1839–1905], Chicago and New York, by 1910; (Yerkes sale through the American Art Association, New York, April 5, 1910, lot 181, no. 330); Harry Payne Whitney [1872–1930], New York, 1910–30; by inheritance to Cornelius Vanderbilt Whitney [1899–1992] and Gertrude Vanderbilt Whitney [1875–1942], New York, 1930–55; (with M. Knoedler and Co., Inc., New York, London, and Paris, stock no. 6210, 1955–56).

References: Yerkes 1910, n. 33; Moschini 1952, 9, ill.; Thomas 1957, 53–65; New York and Palm Beach 1957, n.p., ill.; Shaw in Houston 1958, no. 19; Selvig 1963, 37–38; Berenson 1968, 18–19, ill.; Minneapolis Institute of Arts 1970a, 458–59, no. 244; Minneapolis Institute of Arts 1970b, 28, 108, no. 27; Fredericksen and Zeri 1972, 96; Morassi 1973, 409, no. 533, 2: fig. 520; Bortolatto 1974, no. 549, ill.; Lipschultz 1988, 130, ill.

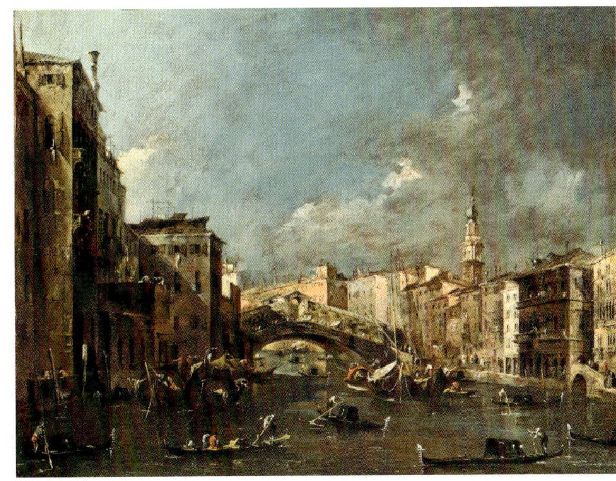

Fig. 28.1. Francesco Guardi
View of the Grand Canal and of the Rialto Bridge, Venice, 1770–80
Oil on canvas, 15 5/8 x 21 1/8 in. (39.5 x 53.5 cm)
Musée Fabre, Montpellier, France, 837.1.19

29. (a, b) Francesco Guardi, 1712–1793
        Allegory of Abundance, 1747
        Oil on panel, 62 1/2 x 30 1/2 in. (158.7 x 77.5 cm)
        Allegory of Hope, 1747
        Oil on panel, 63 1/2 x 30 3/4 in. (161.3 x 78.1 cm)
        The John and Mable Ringling Museum of Art, Sarasota; Bequest of John Ringling, 1936, SN190 and SN189

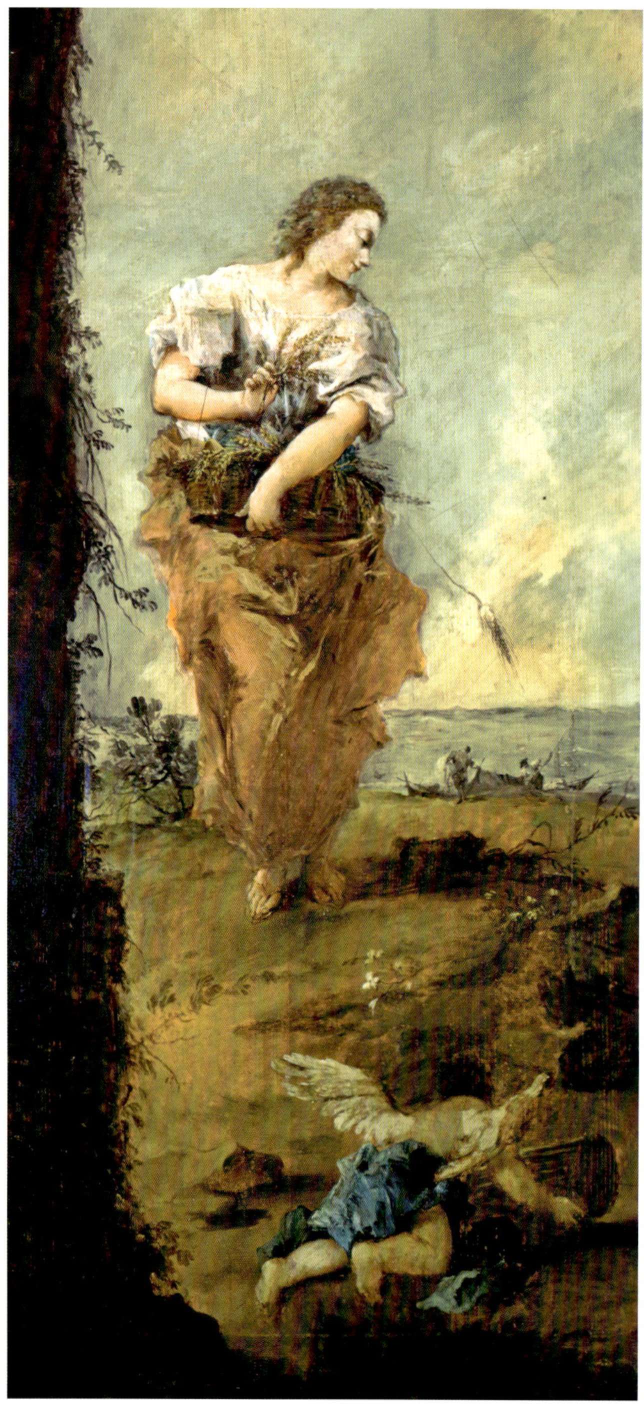
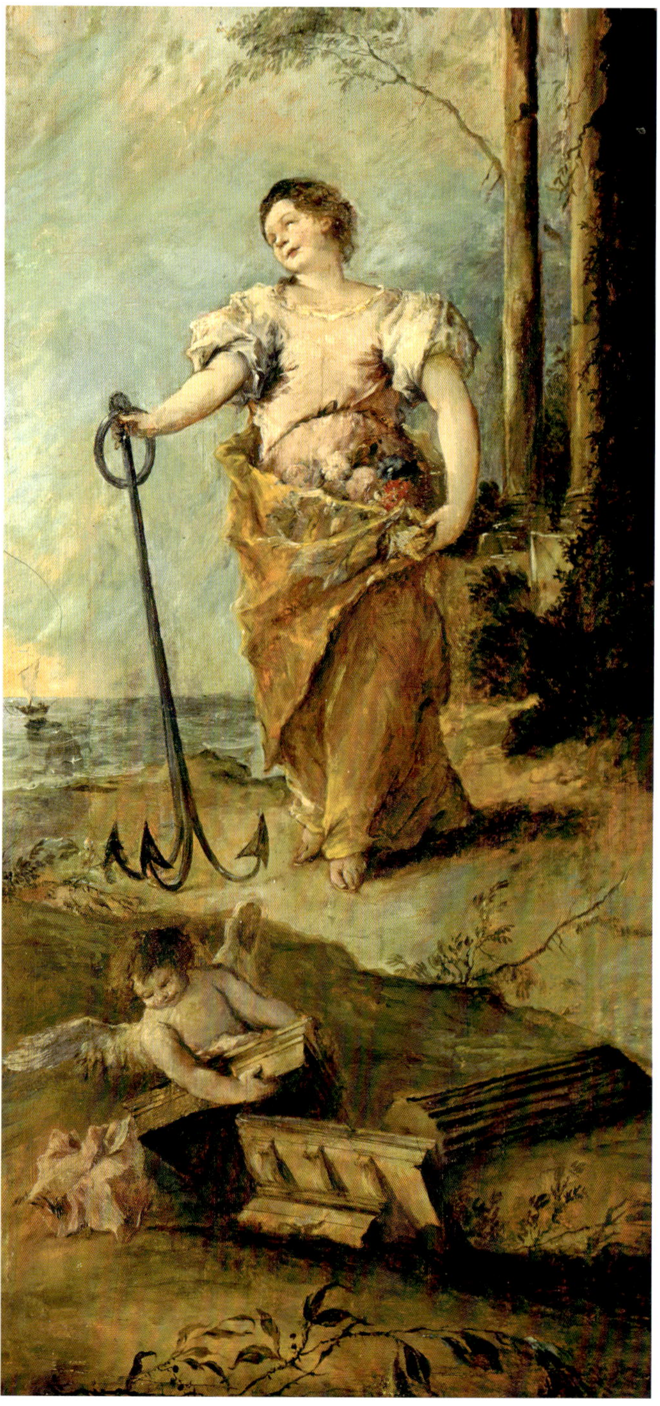

The pair of figures in these pendant works loosely correspond to descriptions of the virtues Hope and Abundance in *Iconologia*, Cesare Ripa's popular sourcebook of symbolic images.[1] Abundance (on the left) bears a sheaf of grain, a harbinger of plentitude and delight. Hope (on the right) gazes heavenward, a multicolored bouquet of flowers gathered in her left hand. The flowers denote the promise of a rich harvest, while the anchor she leans upon with her other hand suggests stability in the face of adversity. The two putti below Abundance and Hope convey the idea that love assists both these virtues.

Although Francesco Guardi was best known for the atmospheric *vedute* (view paintings) and verdant capriccios he created during the last thirty years of his career, he first trained as a history painter in the workshop of his brother, Antonio Guardi (1699–1760). The two collaborated on numerous religious and allegorical commissions from the 1730s until 1760, the year Antonio died, copying works by famous Venetian artists as well as producing original imagery.

An inscription removed in 1949 from the column fragment at the lower right in the Hope panel dated the pendants to 1747.[2] By that time, Francesco had worked alongside Antonio for more than a decade, and while he had developed a distinct artistic personality, it appears he was experimenting here with several of the Rococo touches favored by his brother. Particularly reminiscent of Antonio's style is the agitated angular drapery, which he used to define the figure of Erminia in their collaborative painting *Erminia and the Shepherds* (fig. 29.1). Unlike the older Guardi, however, Francesco approached figure painting with greater precision and commitment to solidity. Abundance's and Hope's arms are firm and robust, and although clothing covers much of their figures, the viewer nonetheless clearly senses their substance shape and volume and weight. Furthermore, Abundance and Hope are painted with the dense and varied brushwork, laid on in quick strokes, that was a hallmark of Francesco's technique.

It is uncertain where the paintings originally were located. In 1927 Giuseppe Fiocco suggested that they might have served as the shutters on the organ in the Church of S. Angelo Raffaele, Venice. Antonio

Morassi (1949) rejected that idea, citing the difference between the combined dimensions of the panels and those of the organ's aperture.[3] Fernanda de'Maffei (1951) bolstered Morassi's argument, noting the lack of any evident hinging on the instrument's shutter posts. Subsequently, Fiocco abandoned his notion but suggested in 1966 that the paintings instead had functioned as cupboard doors in the Confraternità del Sacramento of the same church. This, too, seems unlikely, given the acute perspectival angle of the images—which would have necessitated the cupboard being placed at an impractical height—and the likelihood that such an important commission would have gone to Antonio, as head of the workshop, rather than to his younger sibling.

AL

Notes

1. Ripa 1645, 589.

2. When John Ringling purchased the paintings in 1927, the column fragment in the Hope panel bore the inscription *F. Guardi f L'anno 1747*. When the paintings were cleaned in 1949 with "a very light solvent" (Ringling Museum file notes), the inscription came off, leading the Ringling conservator Cesari Dorio to declare it had been a false one. However, the fact that the inscription came away so easily is not necessarily an indication of its historical inaccuracy. It could have reproduced a lost original, as de'Maffei (1948), Nicolson (1965), and Heinemann (1965) posited. Or, as Mahon suggested (1967, 85), Guardi could have added it to the painting in a soluble medium after applying his final allover coat of varnish.

3. The panels measure 126 x 61 1/4 in. (320 x 156 cm). The organ's aperture measures 141 3/4 x 121 1/4 in. (360 x 308 cm).

Provenance: (with Eugene Glaenzer, New York, nos. P.768–69), by 1911 (each as "panneau decorative: femme"); Arabella Duval Huntington [1850–1924], New York, 1911–24*; by inheritance to Archer M. Huntington [1870–1955], 1924–26; (sold, Anderson Galleries, New York, April 15, 1926, sale lot 2057, nos. 78, 79); (with Julius Böhler, Munich, by 1927); John Ringling [1866–1936], Sarasota, 1927–36.

* I am grateful to Shelley Bennett, former curator of British and European art at the Huntington Library, Art Collections, and Botanical Gardens, San Marino, California, and currently a senior research associate at that institution, for helping me research Mrs. Huntington's part in this provenance.

References: Hadeln 1927, 254–55, 259, ill.; Fiocco 1927, 52; Fiocco 1929, 66, 106, pl. 83; Morassi 1929, 299; Lasareff 1934, 52; Goering 1938, 289–315; Pach in New York 1940, 24, nos. 27, 28; Tietze 1940, 25; Vilas 1942, 65–66, nos. 154, 155; Pallucchini 1943a, 19, 40; Pallucchini 1943b, 19, 40; Arslan 1944, 1–8, 144; Goering 1944, 22, 29, 79, no. 38 (SN190); Suida 1949, 160–61, nos. 189–90; Nicolson 1950, 203, n. 2 (SN189); de'Maffei 1948, 94–99, 132, figs. 34, 35; de'Maffei 1951, 93–99, figs. 34, 35; Morassi 1951, 212, 215–16; Byam Shaw 1952, 300; Morassi 1953b, 263, n. 1; Ragghianti 1953, 6, 9, 10–13, 22–23, 27, 35, 37; Thomas 1954, 159, n. 1; Moschini 1956, 12, 14, 18, figs. 20, 21; Fiocco 1958, 29, 35; Byam Shaw in Houston 1958, n.p., nos. 3, 4 (SN 189); Muraro 1958, 7, n. 19; Pallucchini 1960, 131, 135–36, 139, nos. 341, 342; Morassi 1960, 255, n. 3; Muraro 1960, 424, n. 17; Sinding-Larsen 1962, 183–84; Gállego 1965, 162; Heinemann 1965, 241; Nicolson 1965, 472; Pallucchini 1965, 218, 226; Zampetti in Venice 1965, xxxviii, xli, xlvi, 74, 140, 141, nos. 70, 71; Cailleux 1966, i–ii, fig. 3 (SN189); Fiocco 1966, 46–47, figs. 46, 47; Hannegan 1966, 252; Mahon 1967, 85–87, 98, 99, 103, 104, 109, 151–55, pls. 44, 45; Ragghianti 1967, 228; Sinding-Larsen 1967, 201, 204; Zampetti 1967, 217; Fenyö 1968, 66; Maxon and Rishel in Chicago et al. 1970, 66; Fredericksen and Zeri 1972, 97, 637; Dania 1973, 383; Morassi 1973, 1: 144–45, 348, pls. 229–31; Bortolatto 1974, 109, nos. 334, 335; Tomory 1976, xi, 92–95, nos. 90, 91; Janson 1986, 60–61; Washington, D.C. 1986, n.p.; Pedrocco 1992, 47, 72, 79; Borys, 2008, 104.

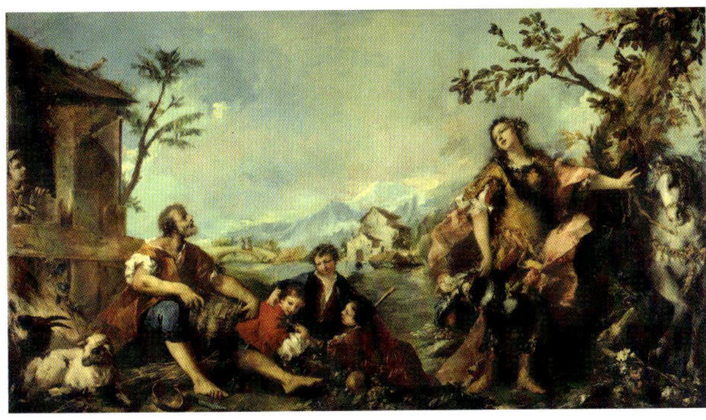

Fig. 29.1. Francesco Guardi and Antonio Guardi
Erminia and the Shepherds, 1750–55
Oil on canvas, 99 x 174 1/8 in. (251.5 x 442.2 cm)
Ailsa Mellon Bruce Fund, National Gallery of Art, Washington, 1964.21.2

30. Domenico Maggiotto, 1713–1794
   Head of a Girl with a Spindle, ca. 1735–40
   Oil on canvas, 18 3/4 x 14 3/4 in. (47.6 x 37.5 cm)
   The John and Mable Ringling Museum of Art, Sarasota; Bequest of John Ringling, 1936, SN183

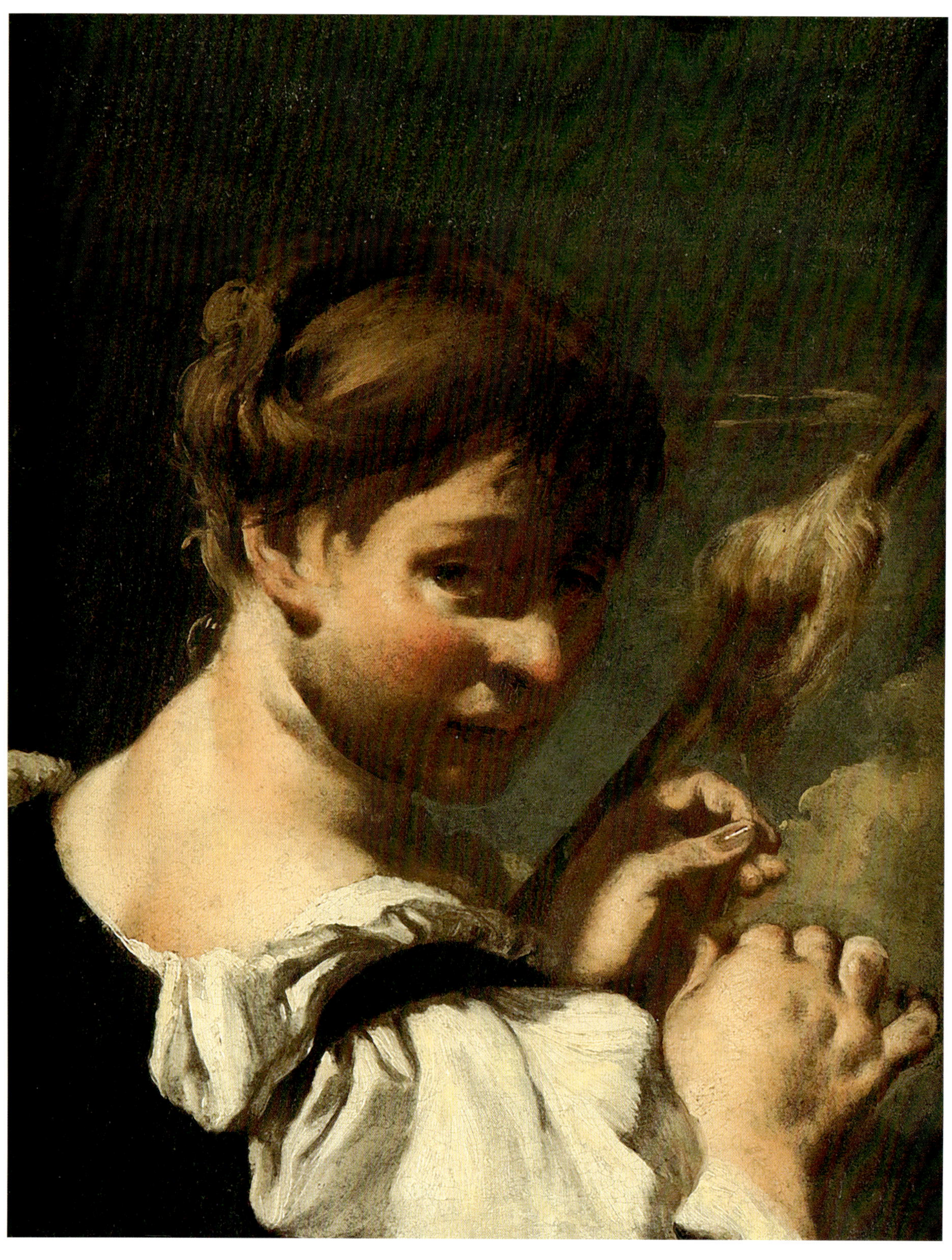

The young woman in this portrait holds a spindle, the rounded stick used to twist yarn in wool spinning. Dressed as a Venetian *popolana,* or peasant girl, she is evidently a domestic servant.[1] She engages the viewer with a casual turn of the head, her soft eyes and parted mouth charmingly conveying the impression that this brief encounter is unexpected but not unwelcome. Although she is a peasant, she is not prosaic. Indeed, this image bears little kinship with conventional European genre painting, which largely focused on low or base subject matter.

Genre painting was little explored in Venice before the early 1700s. Yet during the eighteenth century, as tastes increasingly turned toward private life, an interest developed in pictures of intimate, domestic scenes. Rather than depicting low culture, however, Venetian genre painting tended to be scenic and pleasing and to assume a level of fantasy that was characteristic of Venetian art in general. Only a handful of artists capitalized on this burgeoning market; one of them was Domenico Maggiotto. A student of the Venetian genre master Giovanni Battista Piazzetta (1683–1754), he relied heavily on the expressive formulas developed by his teacher. Pictures featuring bust- or half-length portrayals of quotidian figures are most typical in Piazzetta's oeuvre, as are strong modeling, an "aggressive" naturalism, a chiaroscuro reminiscent of the Baroque, and a certain Arcadian sentimentality.[2] Particular to Maggiotto's work is the dense use of warm browns and hot reds—evident here in the young woman's face and hair.[3] A plasticity of form and strong chiaroscuro are also characteristic of Maggiotto, particularly his early style (late 1730s–40s), which is often considered to be his most successful.[4]

AL

Notes

1. For Venetian dress and the *popolana*, see Morazzoni 1931, pl. 94; and Bulgarelli 1973, 223.

2. Pallucchini 1960, 62.

3. On a 1969 visit to the Ringling, Terisio Pignatti, vice-director of Musei Civici Veneziani d'Istoria e dell'Arte, pronounced this picture to be by "Domenico Maggiotto. Definitely" (Ringling Museum curatorial files). Disregarding Pignatti, Fredericksen and Zeri, in their 1972 *Census of Pre–Nineteenth-Century Italian Paintings in North American Public Collections* (637), cited the painting as a work by Piazzetta. The first firm attribution to Maggiotto came four years later, in Peter Tomory's catalogue of Italian paintings in the Ringling Museum collection (98). However, Suida had suspected as early as 1949 that Maggiotto might have painted it (155).

4. Zampetti 1970, 3: 65.

Provenance: Elia Volpi [1858–1938], Palazzo Davanzati, Florence, by 1917; (sold, American Art Association, New York, December 17, 1917, no. 439, as by Piazzetta); John Ringling [1866–1936], Sarasota, 1917–36.

References: Vilas 1942, 67, no. 246 (as by Piazzetta); Suida 1949, 155, no. 183 (as by Piazzetta); Fredericksen and Zeri 1972, 163, 637 (as by Piazzetta); Tomory 1976, 98, no. 96 (as by Maggiotto); Ferrazza 1994, 119, fig. 117.

31. Bernardo Bellotto, 1721–1780
Capriccio with a Roman Arch, ca. 1745
Oil on canvas, 23 x 36 in. (58.4 x 91.4 cm)
Columbia Museum of Art, Columbia; Gift of the Samuel H. Kress Foundation, CMA 1962.22

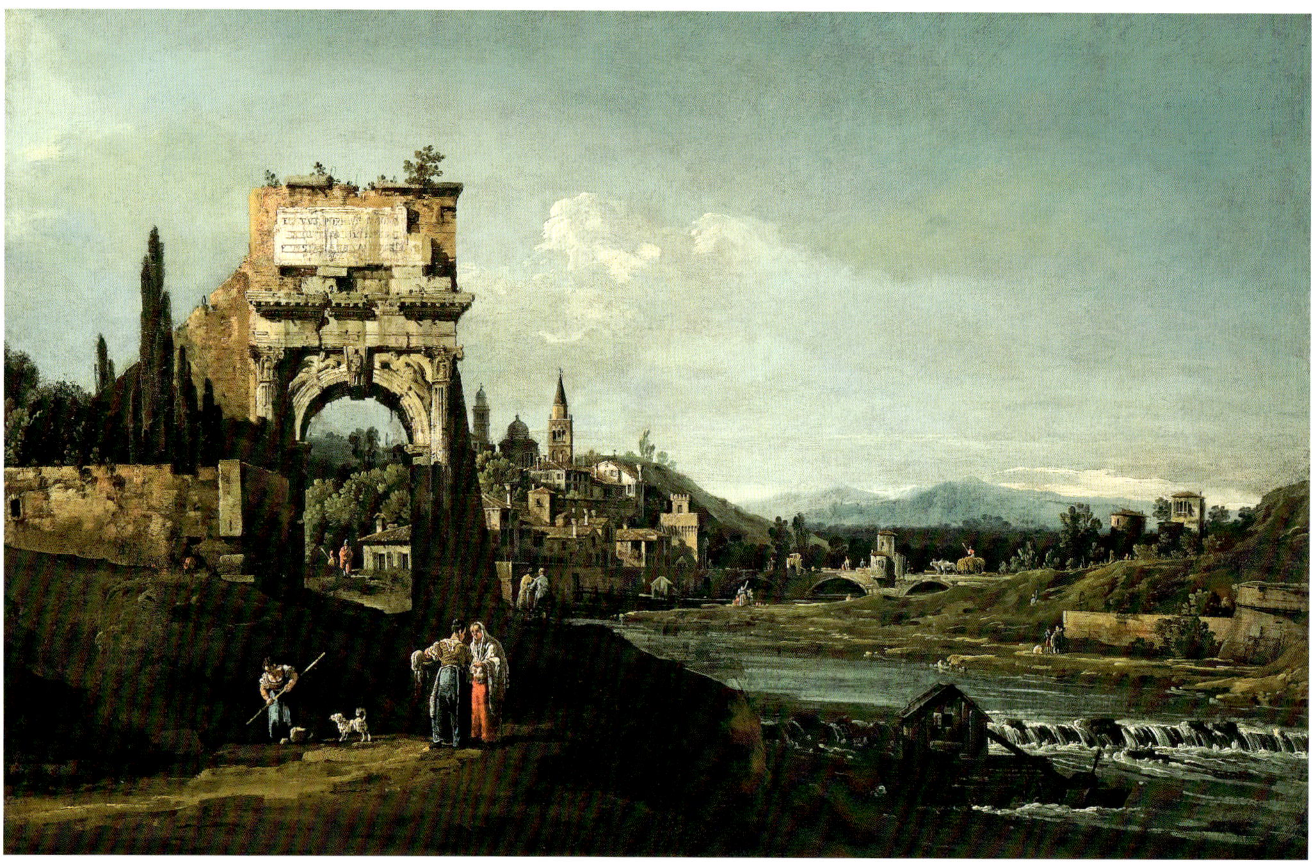

Bellotto's *Capriccio With a Roman Arch* belongs to a group of works that mark a crucial phase between the artist's initial views of Venice and his later images of northern European capitals.[1] The artist trained with Canaletto, who was his uncle; as Michael Levey noted, Bellotto's early paintings are close to being "counterfeits" of the older master's canvases.[2] However, even then Bellotto's evolving style was evident in his darker, richer palette and cooler, more crystalline light. After 1742 Bellotto left Venice, spending several months in Rome, where he made *vedute,* or view paintings, of the city, including its classical ruins. Soon the artist's own expressive impulses asserted themselves, although all his paintings betray a debt to his training with Canaletto.

After his sojourn in Rome, Bellotto spent several months traveling in northern Italy, particularly the regions of Piedmont, Lombardy, and Verona. *Capriccio* is one of several townscapes, capricci, and countryside views he painted before 1747, when he left Italy for good. Canaletto's influence is unmistakable in this painting, even though it combines a variety of rustic landscape elements drawn from different sources with the Arch of Titus, a Roman monument that actually stands on the Via Sacra in Rome. The minutely detailed architecture, the handful of anonymous figures populating the scene, and the subtle composition—which masterfully directs the viewer through the arch toward the town, bridge, and mountains beyond—all suggest the elder artist's effect on his young student. But it is the splendid passages of light and shade that gently illuminate the crumbling buildings and distant hills, as well as the nuanced, cloudy sky, that most clearly reveal Bellotto's debt to his uncle.[3]

If *Capriccio* reflects Bellotto's training, it also bears the hallmarks of a distinct and powerful artistic personality. In place of Canaletto's more ordered world, in which nature is often a backdrop for grand churches, palazzi, and canals, Bellotto emphasizes lush forests, rough winding roads, rushing streams, and distant mountains. Rather than Canaletto's warm yellow light, he instead describes the landscape in rich but cooler greens, blues, and browns.

The swift-moving river, lustrously shadowed foreground, and misty hills imbue this painting with an almost brooding sense of drama, a characteristic of Bellotto's pictures long noted by scholars. For instance, in 1940 Louise Burroughs described these tendencies as not just distinct from but actually "alien to Canaletto's genius."[4] To some extent, the dramatic, at times tenebrous qualities of his paintings may reflect his interest in northern European Baroque landscapes. During his time in Rome, Bellotto may have seen the oeuvre of the influential Dutch view painter Gaspar van Wittel (called Vanvitelli, 1653–

1736), who resided in the city.[5] Like many northern Baroque landscape paintings, Bellotto's canvases often elicit an emotional response: the apparent movement of shadows and light symbolizes the impermanence of life and insignificance of human existence. Paintings such as *Capriccio* both reflect the Baroque past of landscape painting and prefigure the future of the genre. As several scholars have noted, Bellotto's remarkable ability to capture the natural world and subtly imbue it with emotional content looks forward to the Romantic period and particularly to works by the plein-air painters of the Barbizon School.[6]

ST

Notes

1. For the most recent discussion of the picture and its relation to other paintings Bellotto produced during this phase of his career, see Bowron in Venice and Houston 2001, 130. See also Kozakiewicz 1972, 1: 100, no. 133.

2. Levey 1959, 122.

3. Kozakiewicz 1972, 1: 45.

4. Burroughs 1940, 33.

5. Paulson 1975, 338.

6. Kozakiewicz considered some of Bellotto's work as precursors to nineteenth-century painting (1972, 43). However, earlier authors, such as Burroughs and Bialostocki, also noted the artist's apparently proto-Romantic tendencies. See Burroughs op. cit., 33 and Bialostocki 1964, 289. Likewise in his discussion of Bellotto, Bowron noted that the artist's work has often been interpreted as a "prefiguration of German Romanticism." See Edgar Peters Bowron in London and Washington, D.C., 1994, 372.

Provenance: English private collection; Caspari's, Munich 1930; J. M. Heimann, New York; Paul Drey's, New York, 1938; Samuel H. Kress [1863–1965], 1948.

References: Fritzsche 1936, VG 12; Bonacossi 1962, 107; Kozakiewicz 1972, 1: 45 and 2: 100, no. 132; Shapley 1973, 169, no. K1589; Marini in Verona 1990, 72, no. 11; Bowron in Venice and Houston 2001, 130, no. 22.

32. Vezzi Factory, ca. 1720–27
    Teapot, ca. 1724
    Hard-paste porcelain, 5 3/4 (with cover) x 7 1/16 in. (14.6 x 17.9 cm)
    The Metropolitan Museum of Art, Purchase,
    Friends of European Sculpture and Decorative Arts Gifts, 1999 (1999.92ab)

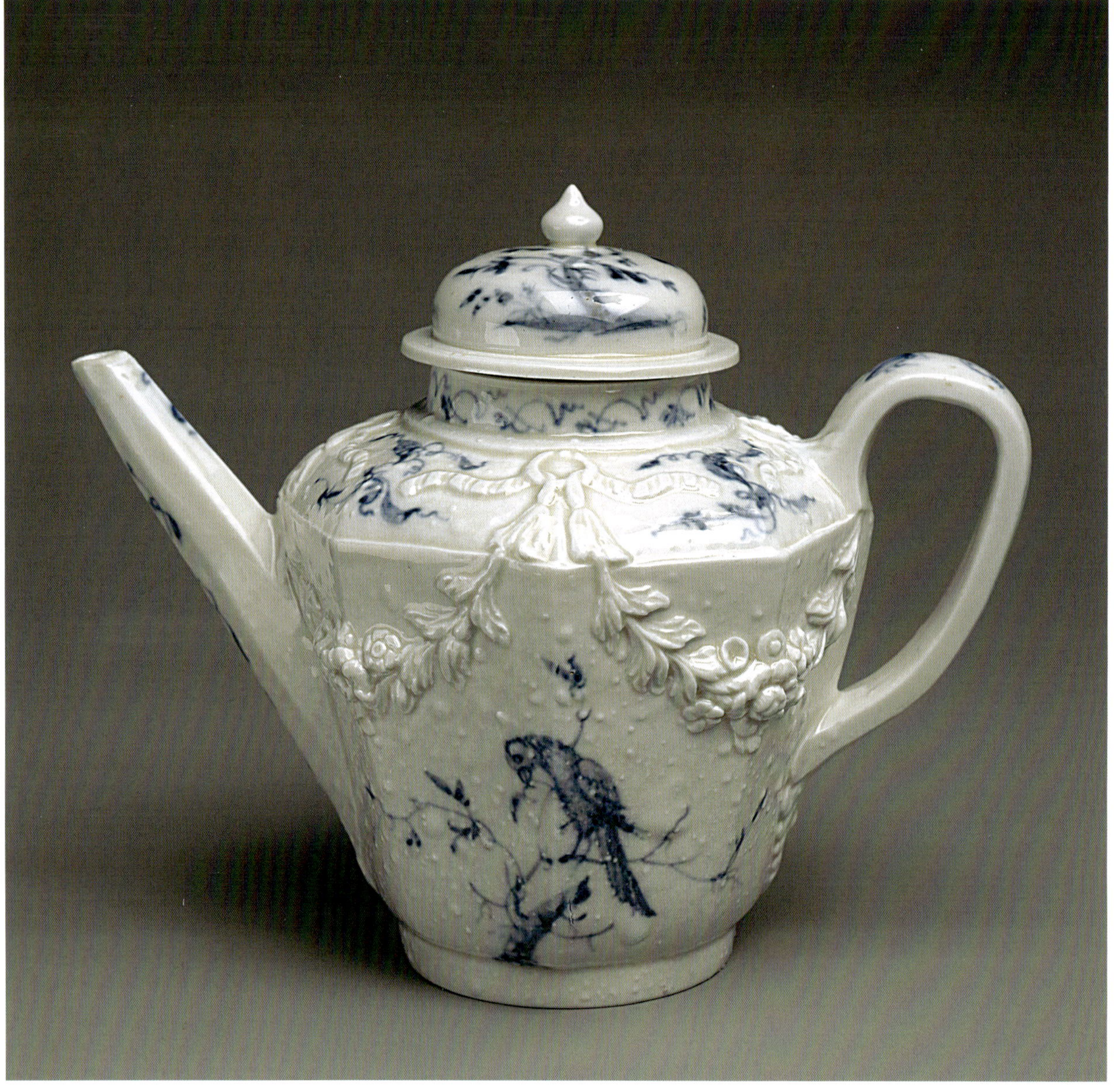

The factory founded around 1720 by Francesco Vezzi (1651–1740) was the third in Europe to produce true hard-paste porcelain. Vezzi backed the venture with part of the fortune he had amassed as a successful goldsmith and with funds from other investors.[1] For technical expertise he relied upon Christoph Conrad Hunger, a Saxon porcelain decorator. At the time, the formula for making porcelain was a closely guarded secret. Hunger, who had initially worked at Meissen—the first European factory to produce the translucent ceramic—divulged trade secrets to Vezzi and others, helping them found companies in both Venice and Vienna.[2] The Vezzi Factory, which operated for only about seven years, mainly produced tableware; it was especially renowned for making beautiful and imaginatively formed teapots such as this example.[3]

Like many early pieces of porcelain manufactured in Europe, the teapot recalls Chinese models. Its delicately painted bird and branch motifs evoke Ming Dynasty ceramics, as does its use of a blue underglaze. Indeed, this decorative technique is rather unusual in a Vezzi object; more commonly, the factory's ceramics are decorated with polychrome overglazes. The teapot's octagonal form and ribboned garlands of flowers and leaves reveal its Western origins.[4] The vessel's uneven, imperfect surface reflects the fact that European porcelain manufacture was at that time still in its infancy.

The teapot's cover is not original. Although the lid is by the Vezzi factory and appears to have been decorated by the same painter, its rounded form does not match the polygonal shape of the main vessel.

ST

Notes

1. Reginald Haggar noted that one of the investors was Vezzi's brother Giuseppe. Although the factory ultimately failed, Francesco's will stipulated that the investors be repaid from his personal fortune. Haggar 1960, 489.

2. Coutts 2001, 90–91. The most recent and comprehensive study of the Vezzi factory is Melegati 1998.

3. A similar Vezzi teapot, showing the same imaginative handling of molded decoration, is found in Stazzi 1967, pl. 48. The Metropolitan Museum of Art collection includes an additional example by the firm that likewise shows its innovative approach to modeling (acc. no. 06.362ab).

4. The teapot's octagonal form is possibly based upon models produced at the Du Paquier porcelain factory in Vienna. Christoph Conrad Hunger had worked there before moving to Venice. See Metropolitan Museum of Art 1999, 34–35.

Provenance: English private collection; (sold, Lacy Scott and Knight, Bury St. Edmunds, March 28, 1998, lot 118); W. Agnew and Co., London, 1998–99.

Reference: Metropolitan Museum of Art 1999, 34–35.

33. Venetian Workshop
   Armchair, late 18th century
   Carved, gessoed, and gilt walnut; upholstered in modern Genoese velvet,
   54 1/2 x 33 3/4 x 35 3/4 in. (138.4 x 85.7 x 90.8 cm)
   The J. Paul Getty Museum, Los Angeles, 87.DA.2.3

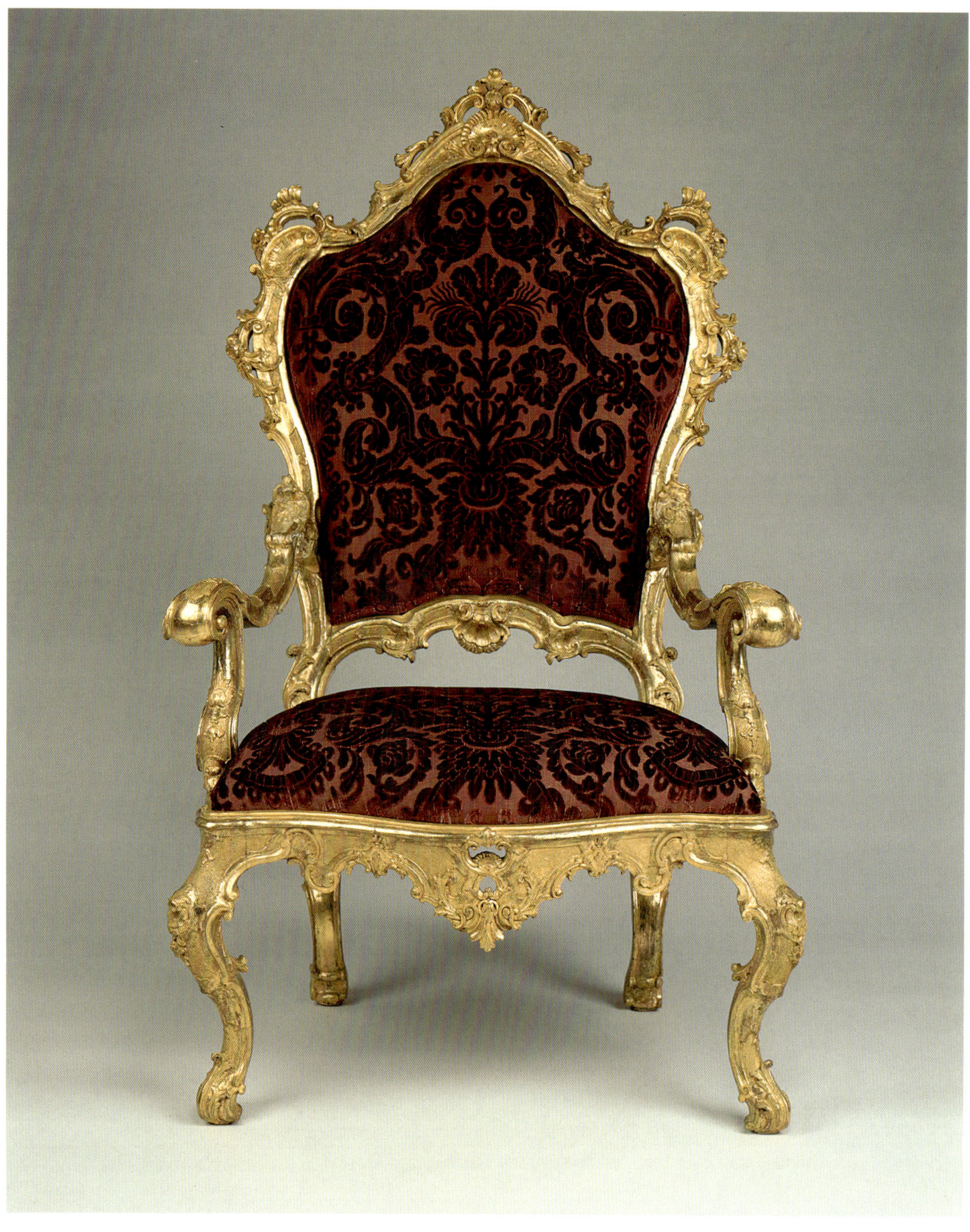

The distinctive shape and ornamentation of this armchair tell us it was made in Venice during the fourth quarter of the eighteenth century. The rearward-leaning, shield-shaped back is found on other Venetian chairs of the period, most notably on those belonging to the set of furniture made in or just before 1779 for Paolo Renier, the penultimate doge (chief magistrate) of Venice.[1] Such precise dating is possible thanks to the oil sketch and resulting portrait of the man—now in the collections of the Civiche Raccolte, Milan, and the Museo Civico, Padua (fig. 33.1), respectively—that Ludovico Gallina painted on the occasion Renier's election as doge that year; both images show him standing beside a chair and side table from this set.[2] The inclusion of this furniture in the portraits indicates how much he must have valued the objects. Luxury and authority are conveyed as much by what surrounds Renier as by what he wears: the ducal *corno* (horn-shaped hat) and an ermine *mozzetta* (short winter cape).

The form of the Renier armchair is nearly identical to that of the J. Paul Getty Museum piece, with two significant differences: the Renier chair's legs are linked by undulating cross-stretchers surmounted by a carved finial while the Getty chair has no stretchers. Also, the Renier chair is "populated" with four putti while elaborate scrollwork and foliate ornamentation adorn the Getty example. The sculpted infant boys are swathed in drapery: those on the forelegs appear to support the seat rail, and the two that flank the back serve to accentuate the outward swell of the shield shape. Such a sculptural conceit—incorporating human figures into the structure of furniture—is among the most imaginative aspects of Italian furniture, particularly pieces dating to the Baroque period.[3] In contrast, the Getty armchair is marked by a rich and refined ornamentation more typical of the Rococo: broken "S" and "C" scrolls recombined and augmented with pierced and entwined foliage, rocailles, pods, acanthus leaves, and shells. Moreover, the fact that the undulating stretchers similar to those in the Renier piece appear on earlier chairs made in the Veneto suggests that the Getty armchair postdates the Renier furniture by several years.[4]

At the turn of the nineteenth century, most European furniture was decidedly Neoclassical in style, and within two decades Gothic and other revival styles would emerge. The fact that the Rococo lingered in Venice in those years perhaps reflects the isolated nature of the city at a time when, avid tourists notwithstanding, its mercantile power had declined and political dominion waned. The once-defiant republic was invaded by Napoleon's forces in 1797.

The Getty chair underwent conservation treatment in Paris in the mid-1980s. At that time, the upholstery was replaced and at least two layers of later gilding were removed. The original layer of gilding was then patched and unified with sections of gesso, bole, and gold. This procedure resulted in the revival and renewal of the original surface, which had been protected under over-gilding for perhaps more than a century. Indeed, as restored, the gilding displays beautifully subtle variations of shiny burnished areas against stippled matte ones.

Several other identical armchairs exist: three further examples are in the Getty Museum's collection; another from the same suite and handled by the same London dealer entered the Detroit Institute of Arts collection in 1991 (fig. 33.2);[5] and two were in the collection of Barbara Piasecka Johnson, New Jersey (now Monte Carlo), which sold at auction in 1992.[6] Many such pieces were brought to England in the eighteenth century, testifying to Venice's popularity among British Grand Tourists.

CH

Notes

1. Alberici 1980, 28–37.

2. Ibid., pls. 35a, 35b.

3. Colle 2000.

4. González-Palacios 1984, pl. 38a, reproduces an armchair of about 1643 that is in the collection of the Scuola Grande di S. Rocco, Venice.

5. Darr and Albainy 2000, 408.

6. Sotheby's, New York, May 21, 1992, lot 72.

Provenance: Private collection, England, after ca. 1780–1984; Alexander and Berendt, Ltd., London, 1984–87.

References: J. Paul Getty Museum 1988, no. 78, 180–81, ill.; Bremer-David 1993, 192, no. 326; Bremer-David 1997, 76, no. 57; J. Paul Getty Museum 1997, 264–65.

Fig. 33.2. Venetian Workshop
Armchair
Carved, gessoed, and gilt walnut; upholstered in modern Genoese velvet, 55 3/8 x 33 7/8 x 34 5/8 in. (140.5 x 86 x 88 cm)
The Detroit Institute of Arts, Founders Society Purchase, with funds from the Joseph M. de Grimme Memorial Fund, the Visiting Committee for European Sculpture and Decorative Arts, Mr. and Mrs. Stanford C. Stoddard, Mrs. Howard J. Stoddard, and the European Sculpture and Decorative Arts General Fund, 1991.132

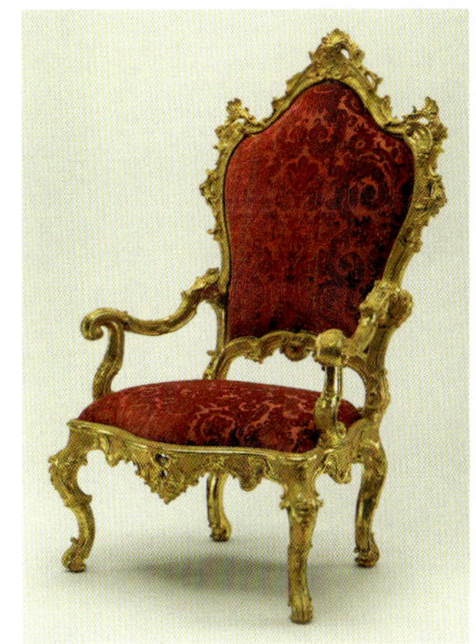

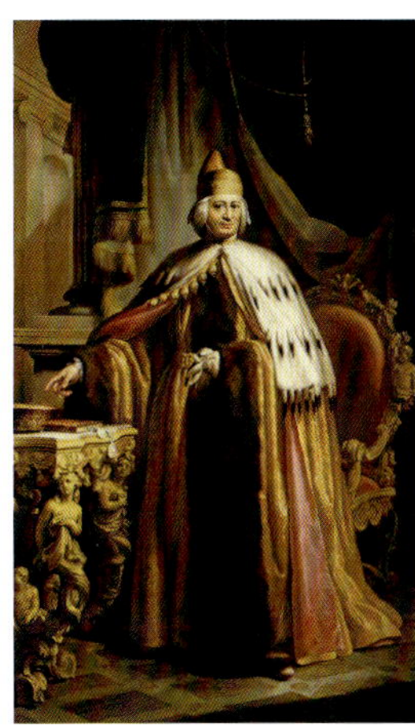

Fig. 33.1. Ludovico Gallina
Doge Paolo Renier, 1779
Oil on canvas, dimensions unavailable
Museo Civico, Padua

34. Venetian Workshop
   Console Table, ca. 1725–50
   Carved and gilded wood, 31 x 48 in. (78.7 x 121.9 cm)
   The John and Mable Ringling Museum of Art, Sarasota; Museum Purchase, 1949, SN1531

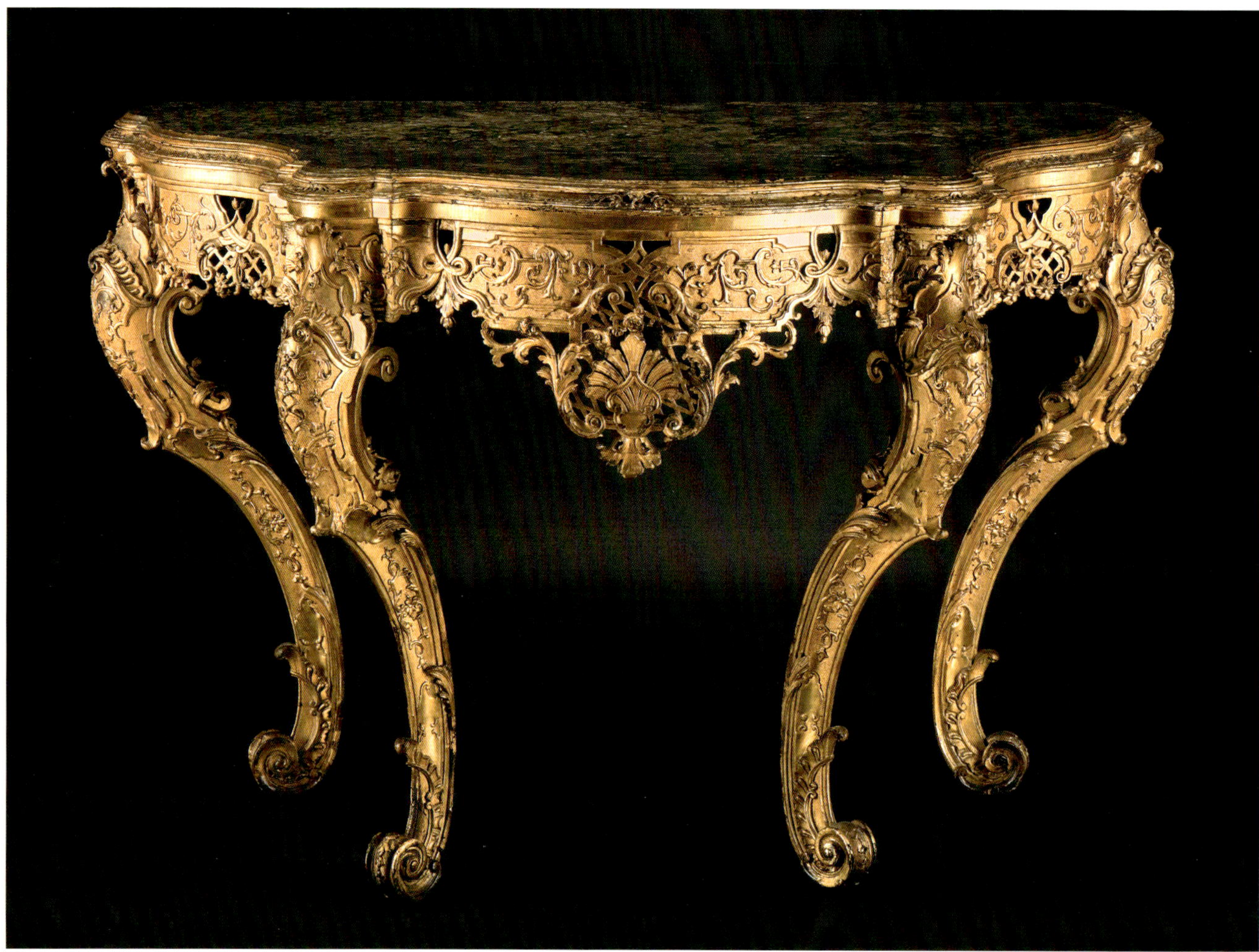

The eighteenth century was a particularly felicitous period for the production of Venetian furniture. Bright, whimsical designs along with lavish carving and rich gilding yielded some of the most graceful and extravagant objects of the Rococo. This elegant, expertly crafted console table is among the finest Venetian decorative objects of that time. Combining highly sculptural relief work with delicate shape and line, it reflects the transition from heavy Baroque form to graceful Rococo design. This is particularly evident in the painted faux-marble top, which bestows on the piece a lightness that is both figurative and literal.

The table was in the collection of Count Lionello von Hierschel de Minerbi, who was the final private owner of Venice's historic Cà Rezzonico (today a museum of eighteenth-century Venetian art), located on the Grand Canal. He purchased it in 1906 from the son of the English poet Robert Browning; the latter lived there from 1880 until his death nine years later. Soon after moving in, de Minerbi, an avid collector of antiques and works by Old Masters, began refurnishing the rooms according to the fashions of the eighteenth century. Unfortunately, in the early 1930s he encountered significant financial difficulties that forced him to sell pieces from his collection and, finally, the palazzo itself. The Comune di Venezia (Municipality of Venice) purchased the property in 1935.

AL

Provenance: Count Lionello von Hierschel de Minerbi, Palazzo Rezzonico, Venice, 1906; Adolf Loewi, Los Angeles, by 1946.

References: Morazzoni 1927, n.p., pl. 43; Sarasota 1953, n.p., no. 46; Duval in Sarasota 1982, 152, no. 147.

35. Giuseppe Briati, 1686–1772
   Dessert Decoration in the Form of a Glass Garden, ca. 1760
   Opaque white, opalescent colorless, and opaque colored glass; lampworked, assembled; wire, adhesive
   Approximately: 26 3/4 x 37 in. (68 x 94 cm)
   The Corning Museum of Glass, Corning, 2002.3.19

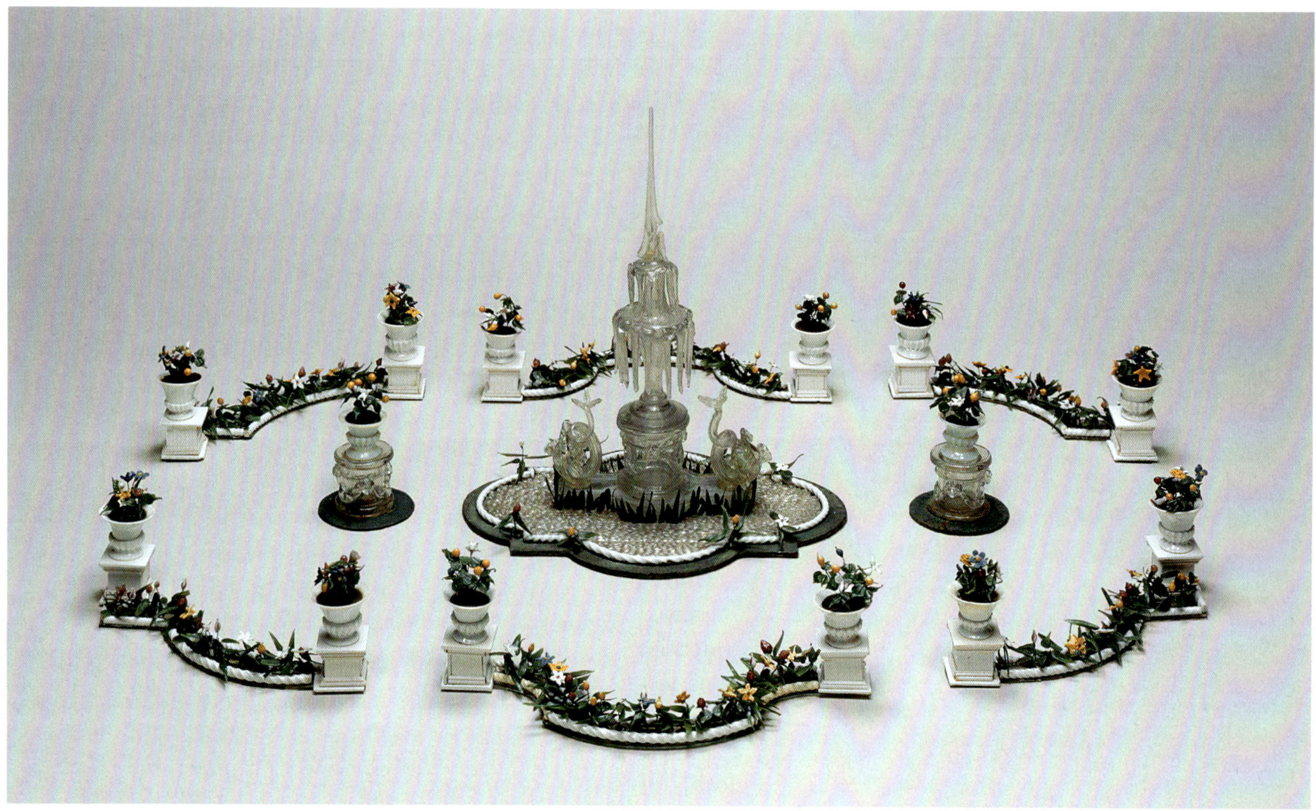

Frivolous and fanciful, this glass garden suggests the enjoyment of luxury and pursuit of pleasure that characterized eighteenth-century Venice. Artisans created such sets to ornament tables during the dessert course of a formal meal. They not only enhanced the appearance of the sweets but also lent an air of fantasy and caprice to the repast. The present example includes colorful flowers set within urns and borders, and three fountains—one of which features a pair of crystal dolphins frolicking in cascading water. The number of delicately crafted elements in a dessert-decoration set that graced a given table depended upon the occasion. The scale and relative simplicity of this set suggests it may have been made for private use. Other surviving glass gardens were clearly executed for grander, more public events. For instance, an enormous example preserved in the Museo Correr, Venice, consists of dozens of features, including tall, elaborately worked archways and pavilions (fig. 35.1).

Because of their fragility, eighteenth-century Venetian glass dessert-decoration sets are relatively rare.[1] Some of the finest of those that remain are attributed to Giuseppe Briati, who was one of the most technically proficient and innovative glassmakers working in Venice during the eighteenth century. Although the city had been a renowned center of glass production for several hundred years, by the early 1700s, the craft was in decline. In 1736, aiming to reverse this trend, Briati requested and received municipal privileges to help revive and modernize the industry.[2] Among the master's innovations was the introduction of clearer, more durable crystal and the manufacture of chandeliers incorporating a metal body covered with glass. Decorative arts historians traditionally have credited Briati with producing the first mirrors with glass frames; these, like his chandeliers, came to characterize eighteenth-century Venetian glasswork.

Briati also was famous for his dessert decorations, which, like the other objects he made, often featured intricately formed white, clear, and polychrome glass. He excelled at lampwork, a technique that uses an open flame to melt and manipulate glass so that it resembles realistic objects such as flowers and leaves. The Venetian government commissioned him to create dessert decorations for presentation as diplomatic gifts; one of these was a service given to the royal house of the Kingdom of the Two Sicilies.[3]

Briati's work often emulated actual outdoor spaces in Venice. For example, the balanced arrangement of meticulously shaped flower beds and pathways seen in the Corning dessert decoration recalls the expansive garden of the Palazzo Contarini dal Zaffo, as depicted by Francesco Guardi (fig. 35.2).

ST

Notes

1. Another surviving example, which is very similar to the Corning's, is discussed in Dorigato 2002, 142-43.

2. Zecchin 2004, 162.

3. Ibid., 161.

Provenance: By purchase, Venice 2002.

References: Corning 2002, 2; JOGS 2003, 207; Zecchin 2004, 164–65.

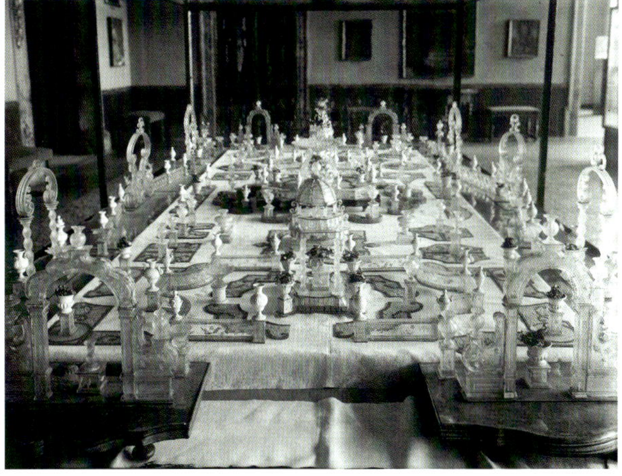

Fig. 35.1. Venetian Workshop
Table Decoration in the Form a Glass Garden, n.d.
Opaque white, opalescent colorless, and opaque colored glass; lampworked, assembled, and glued, dimensions unavailable
Museo Correr, Venice

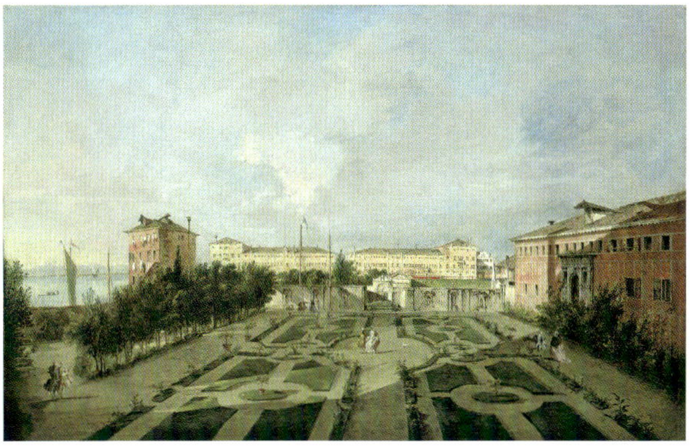

Fig. 35.2. Francesco Guardi
The Garden of the Palazzo Contarini dal Zaffo, ca. 1780
Oil on canvas, 19 x 30 11/16 in. (48 x 78 cm)
The Art Institute of Chicago, Gift of the Marian and Max Ascoli Fund, 1991.112

36. (a, b) Factory of Geminiano Cozzi, active Venice, 1764–1812
Vase with Neptune, 1769
Hybrid soft-paste porcelain, 11 13/16 x 10 1/2 in. (30 x 26.7 cm)
Vase with Personification of Venice, 1769
Hybrid soft-paste porcelain, 11 3/4 x 10 3/4 in. (29.8 x 27.3 cm)
The J. Paul Getty Museum, Los Angeles, 88.DE.9.1.1 and 88.DE.9.2.1

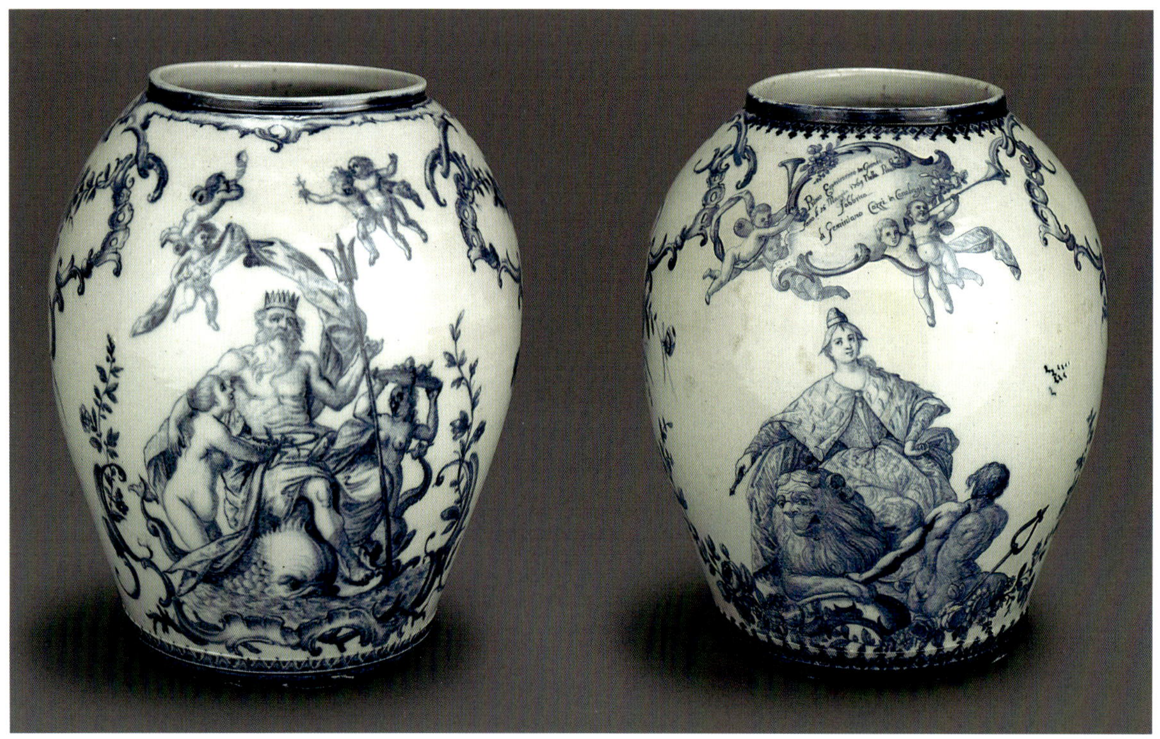

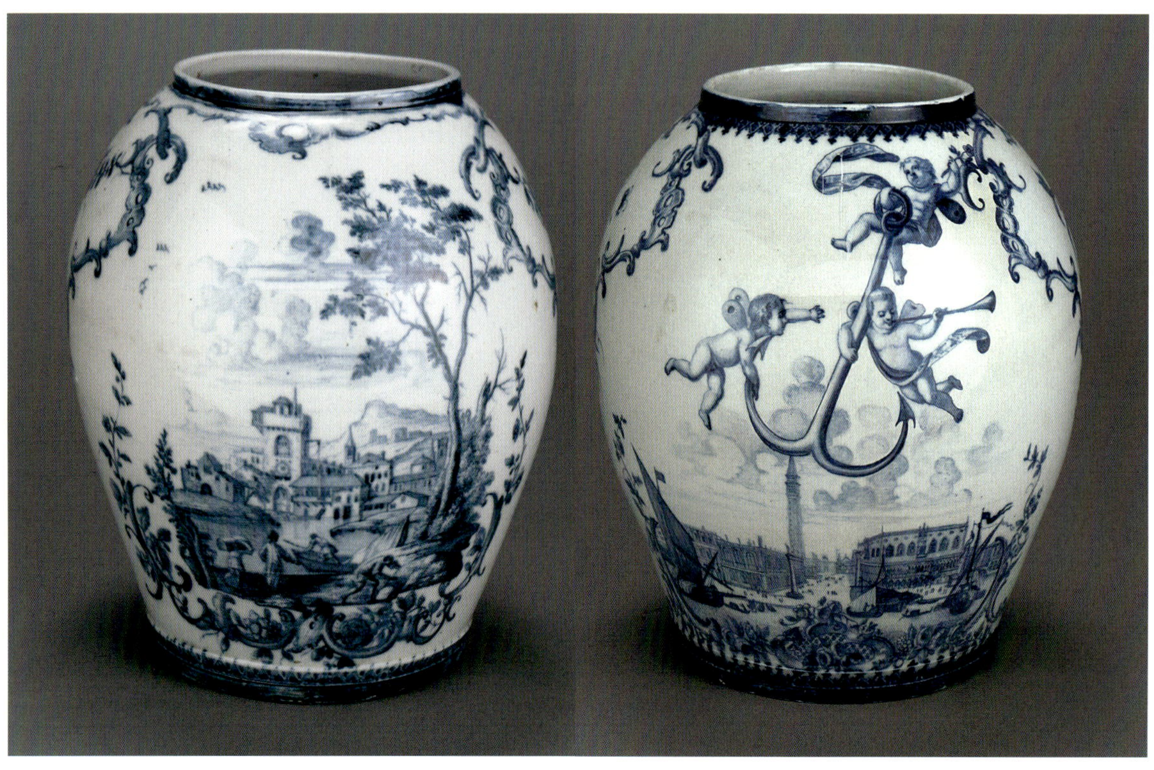

Elaborate allegorical personifications of the Adriatic Sea and Venice ornament this pair of vases. On one vessel Venice is portrayed as a benevolent ruler. She is shown seated on a recumbent lion and clad in rich damask and an ermine cape. A symbol of her supremacy over the surrounding sea is the *corno*, or ceremonial hat with which she is crowned. According to Catherine Hess, author of the authoritative work on these vases, the figure of Venice is based on an engraving by Giambattista Albrizzi.[1] She sits comfortably on the lion—rather like a grande dame ready to receive visitors in her salon. Below her, with one hand touching the lion's paw, is a nude. Because the figure's back is turned, it is impossible to discern its gender, but the stylized triton it holds suggests it might be one of the Nereids fathered by the Greek sea god Neptune. If so, its appearance here emphasizes the city's reliance on sea trade. Above, four putti—two of whom trumpet the glory of Venice—hold a rocaille-edged cartouche with an inscription that translates as "First large-scale experiment executed May 15, 1769, in the privileged factory of Geminiano Cozzi in Cannaregio"(fig. 1).[2]

Visually linked by flowers, vines, butterflies, and rocaille motifs, the theme of Venetian commerce continues on the back of this vase, where three putti frolic around a massive anchor. The anchor is both the mark of the Cozzi factory and a reference to maritime travel. Below this scene is a view of the Bacino di S. Marco showing ships along the Molo, and the Piazzetta, the Biblioteca Marciana (National Library of St. Mark's), the Doge's Palace, and the Campanile beyond.

Complementing the personification of Venice on the vase discussed above, the other vessel depicts Neptune, triumphant upon a dolphin-drawn chariot and flanked by gift-laden sea Nereids. Above him romp four putti; one blows on a shell to proclaim the sea god's glory while another bears his flowing drapery. As on the companion vase, Rococo decorations link Neptune and his retinue to the back. Beyond the image of workers laboring on a dock is a picturesque river village filled with rustic buildings, a church, and a clock tower. The townscape was probably based upon engravings after Marco Ricci taken from an artist's model book published by Albrizzi.[3]

Many cultural centers and royal courts in Europe aspired to produce porcelain, the lustrous, exotic, and precious ceramic imported from the Far East. Europeans recognized the value of manufacturing the material both as a symbol of prestige and as a profitable trade commodity. During different periods of the eighteenth century, several ceramics firms operated in Venice, one of which was the third in Europe to produce true porcelain.[4] The factory of Geminiano Cozzi (1728–1797) was founded around 1765, soon after the departure of Nathaniel Friedriche Helwecke, the Saxon potter from Meissen from whom Cozzi probably learned ceramic production.[5] Hess notes that Cozzi was initially a Modenese banker, but his talents as a shrewd businessman and entrepreneur led to his career change.[6] He soon secured not only privileges from the Venetian board of trade but also financial support and a monopoly on porcelain production. The inscription noted above, dated to a few years after the firm was founded, refers to the special status granted Cozzi and also indicates that these works were his first large-scale experiments. Despite the dimensions of these pieces and their elaborate decoration, the inscription makes no mention of a patron or dedication. Hess convincingly argues that the pair remained at the factory, where Cozzi displayed them to advertise the quality and innovation of his firm's wares.[7]

ST

Notes

1. For Albrizzi and images associated with him see Hess 1990, 154.

2. The original inscription reads: "Primo Esperimento in Grand fotto li 15 Maggio 1769 Nella Privil [egiata] fabbrica di Geminiano Cozzo in Canaleregio." Cannaregio—the modern spelling of Canaleregio—is the northernmost of the six historic *sestieri*, or districts, of Venice.

3. Hess 1990, 152. An anonymous note in the object file at the Getty Museum suggests the scene was taken from a collection of engravings after works by various artists published by Albrizzi in 1750. See Albrizzi 1750, n.p.

4. Battie 1990, 102–3.

5. Coutts 2001, 35.

6. Hess 1990, 145.

7. Ibid., 156.

Provenance: Cetanini, Venice, by 1889; private collection, Budapest, until the end of the 1930s, then stored in Switzerland during World War II; recovered by the owners after World War II and brought to Rome; by inheritance in the same family, Rome; Edmund de Unger, 1988.

References: Raffaele 1889, 151; Molfino 1976, 27; Stazzi 1982, 53; J. Paul Getty Museum 1989, 146; Battie 1990, 9–10; Hess 1990, 141–56; J. Paul Getty Museum 1991, 217; Coutts 2001, 135.

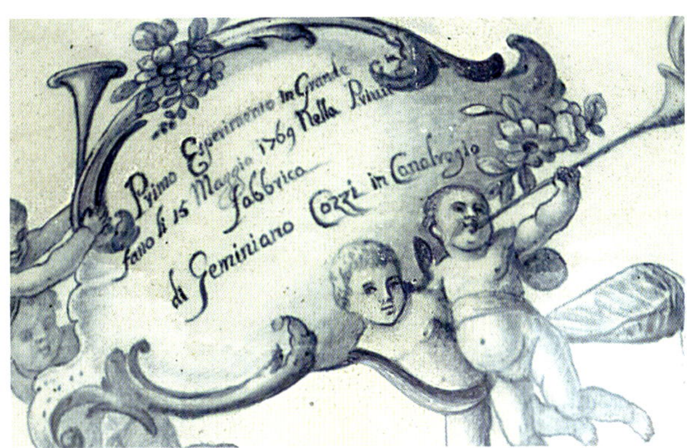

Fig. 36.1. Factory of Geminiano Cozzi, active Venice, 1764–1812
Vase with Personification of Venice (det.), 1769
Hybrid soft-paste porcelain, 11 3/4 x 10 3/4 in. (29.8 x 27.3 cm)
The J. Paul Getty Museum, Los Angeles, 88.DE.9.2.1

37. Venetian Workshop
Commode, mid-18th century
Painted and varnished pine carcass with spruce drawers; later brass pulls, locks, escutcheons,
and linen drawer lining, 29 13/16 x 49 15/16 x 22 5/8 in. (75.7 x 126.8 x 57.5 cm)
Isabella Stewart Gardner Museum, Boston, F11s14

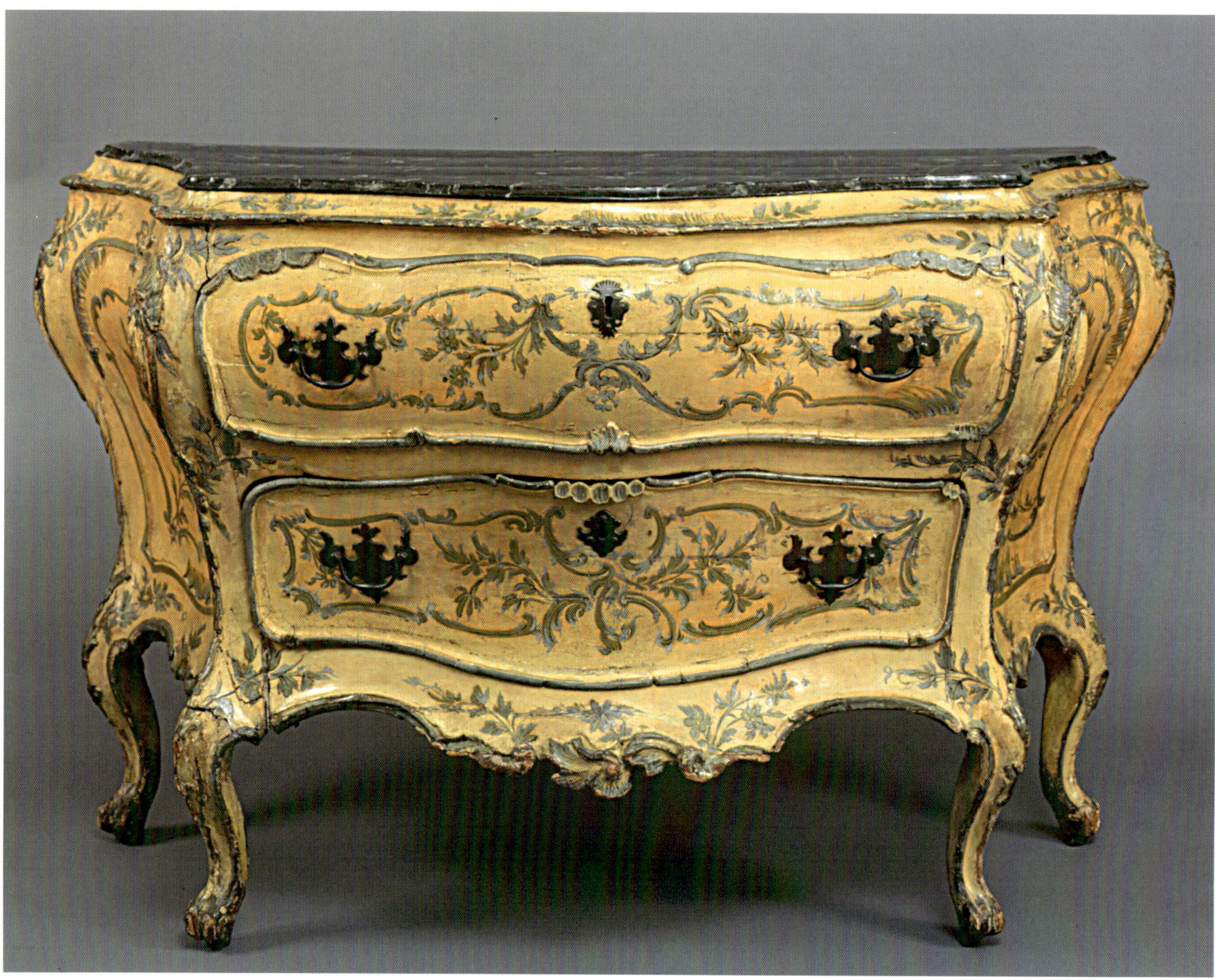

This commode or low chest of drawers beautifully embodies the characteristics of Rococo furniture popular in Venice around the middle of the eighteenth century. The front and sides of the piece gracefully swell outward in bombé fashion, and that flowing, undulating movement continues throughout the top, skirt, drawer fronts, and cabriole legs. Delicately carved moldings incorporating foliate and shell motifs enhance the piece's sinuous lines. The commode is remarkable for its painted decorations of blue, green, and gold set against a yellow ground. These patterns of flowers and leafy tendrils trail across the surfaces to engage or complement the molded decorations. The top preserves its original painted surface, which imitates a richly veined marble.

Eighteenth-century Venetian furniture that had a glossy, translucent covering over a layer of paint is often described as *lacca*, or lacquered. However, this coating is not true lacquer. Properly called *urushi*, authentic lacquer is derived from the sap of the Japanese sumac tree. That durable coating was developed in East Asia and used there for centuries, but it was not produced in Europe before the nineteenth century.[1] Technical analysis of the Gardner Museum's chest of drawers revealed that its finish is actually a coating of resin and turpentine (both derived mainly from European coniferous trees) applied over the painted surface.[2] These substances were common ingredients in varnishes throughout Europe in the eighteenth century, and were frequently used to imitate the appearance of Asian lacquer. The technique is known also as japanning.[3] The varnish on this object was probably somewhat yellow when first applied, but it has darkened over time, giving the underlying paint a more golden cast and causing the bluish tints of leaves and tendrils to appear as a deeper green.

This chest of drawers embodies the evolution in Venetian lacquered furniture that occurred during the early eighteenth century. Until the 1730s, cabinetmakers in Venice favored the Asian-inspired chinoiserie style reflected in works such as the gig chair in the present volume (cat. 38). The Rococo, exemplified by gracefully curved forms and delicate carving, soon replaced that fashion. Venetian Rococo furniture is often painted ivory, yellow, pink, pale green, or light blue, and typically is accented by floral motifs that echo the flowing lines of the overall design. Several public and private collections in Venice—most notably that in the Cà Rezzonico—include similar chests. The fine quality of these objects is a testament to the collaborative efforts of the highly specialized and skilled carpenters, carvers, and painters who adapted Rococo models to meet a growing demand.

In eighteenth-century Italy, chests of drawers were known as *casettone* or *comò*. The latter is derived from the French word *commode*, which is the French chest of drawers on which Italian examples are based. Created for the court of the King Louis XIV, such pieces of furniture were innovative in design: drawers set at table height and raised on short legs. The commode was adapted by cabinetmakers throughout Europe, perhaps most famously by the Englishman Thomas Chippendale in the early 1760s.[4] Venetian chests of drawers differ from their northern European counterparts in both their exuberantly curving forms and their painted polychrome decorations. Furthermore, Venetian examples are embellished with ornamentation carved directly into—or applied onto—the wood itself, instead of bearing the kinds of bronze and gilded bronze elements found on French commodes. Eighteenth-century Venetian furniture makers often skillfully combined and exploited rather modest yet distinctive materials, such as soft woods, paint, and varnish, to produce a rich overall effect.

FC

Notes

1. For surveys of eighteenth-century lacquered Venetian furniture, see Baccheschi and Levy 1960, Levy 1967, and Santini 2002.

2. Technical analysis conducted in 2003 revealed that the outermost coating of the commode is comprised of a mixture of copal resin and Venice turpentine, typical of eighteenth-century japanning. Gardner Museum conservators Kathrin Kessler and Valentine Talland coordinated investigation of the paint and finishes. Richard Newman, conservation scientist at the Museum of Fine Arts, Boston, performed the analysis. Analytical methods included: polarized microscopy (with visible and UV light), electron-beam microprobe, Fourier-transform infrared reflectography (FTIR), microspectrometry, and gas chromatography/mass spectrometry (GCMS).

3. For a discussion of the history of Western lacquering techniques, and particularly japanning, see Dorge and Carey 1983, 331; and Kühlenthal 2000, 442, 456.

4. For Chippendale's influential commode designs see Chippendale 1949, especially pls. 64–66 and 69. Chippendale identified such chests of drawers as "French Commode Tables." See also Kisluk-Grosheide et al. 2006, 146.

Provenance: Probably Domenico Lorenzetti, Venice, 1892.1*.

* This is probably the commode Isabella Stewart Gardner purchased from Lorenzetti in 1892 for 70 lire. Object file, Isabella Stewart Gardner Museum.

Reference: Longstreet and Carter 1935, 64–65.

38. Venetian Workshop
Chair from a Gig, early 18th century
Painted, gilded, and varnished walnut, modern upholstery, 39 1/4 x 34 3/4 x 18 in. (99.8 x 88.5 x 45.5 cm)
Isabella Stewart Gardner Museum, Boston, F25n13

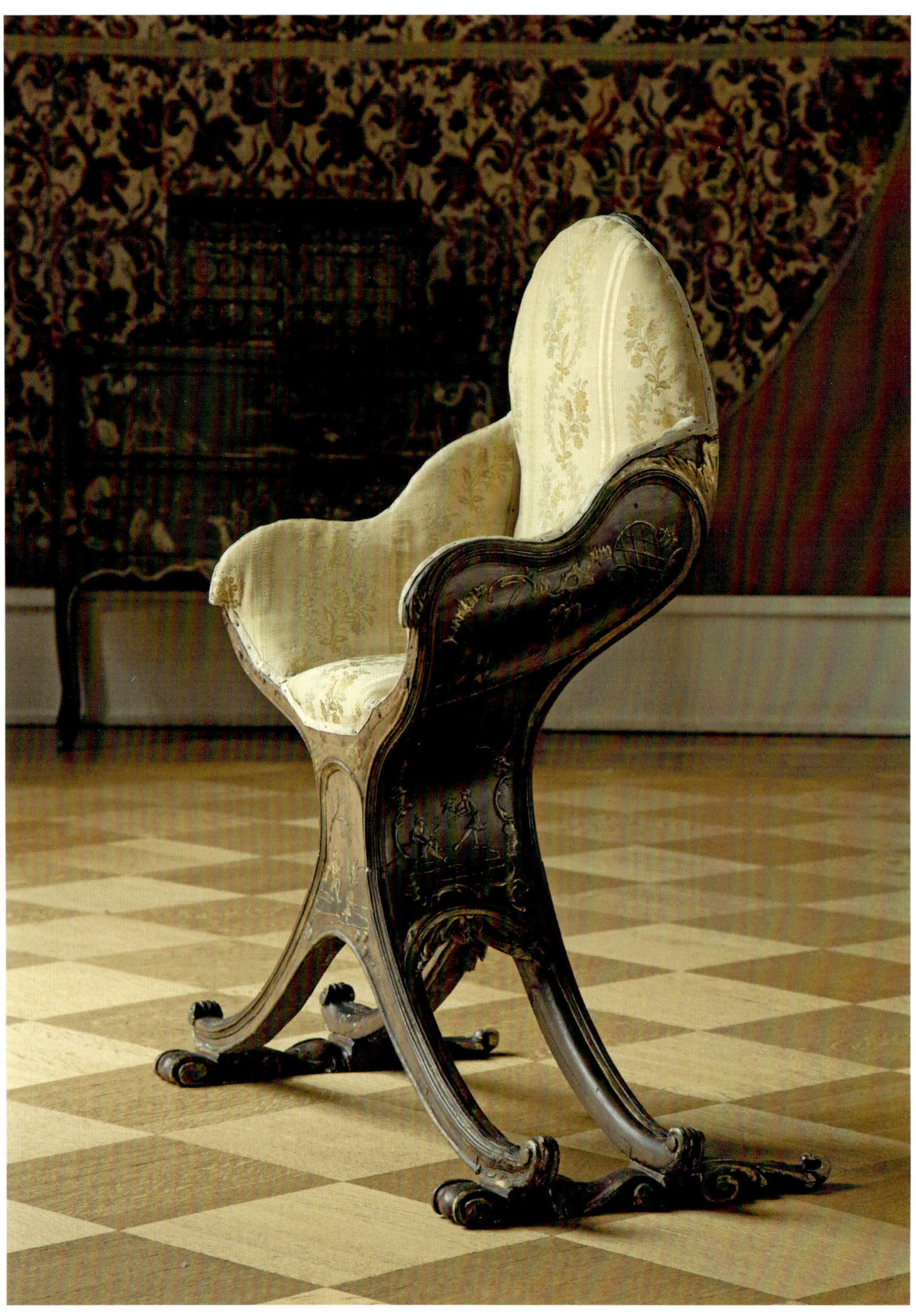

This elegant and unusually shaped chair consists of a seat that rests on a richly decorated base. This in turn is supported by four curved legs set on two gently undulating rails. The distinctive splayed legs and rails, which combine to give the chair considerable stability, indicate that it was originally the seat on a light carriage known as a *sediolo*, or gig. In eighteenth-century Italy, there was a fashion for such carriages, which consist of a seat and two wheels drawn by a single horse. Complete Italian gigs with very similar seats are preserved in the Victoria and Albert Museum, London; the Musée de la Voiture, Compiègne; and the Cà Rezzonico, Venice.[1] A similar gig chair, also decorated in chinoiserie and varnished, is in Waddesdon Manor.[2] The finely decorated example in the Gardner Museum must have originated in an especially luxurious *sediolo*.

The chair's decoration is distinctly Venetian. The wood is painted with a deep red ground. Asian figures in landscapes, accompanied by flowers and shell motifs, are painted or formed by gilded stucco. These chinoiserie elements help date the chair to the early eighteenth century.

FC

Notes

1. For the gig chair in the Victora and Albert Museum, see Straus 1912, fig. after page 142. An example which was formerly in the Museo artistico industriale, Rome (a collection that was absorbed into other Italian state museums) can be found in Ferrari, 1928, 368.

2. See De Bellaigue, 1974, 666–669.

Provenance: Moisè Dalla Torre, Venice, 1899.

References: Longstreet and Carter 1935, 202; De Bellaigue 1974, 666.

39. Venetian Workshop
Armchair, mid-18th century
Carved, gilt, painted, and varnished walnut, modern upholstery, 37 x 26 1/2 x 26 5/8 in. (94 x 66.7 x 65 cm)
Isabella Stewart Gardner Museum, Boston, F25c1

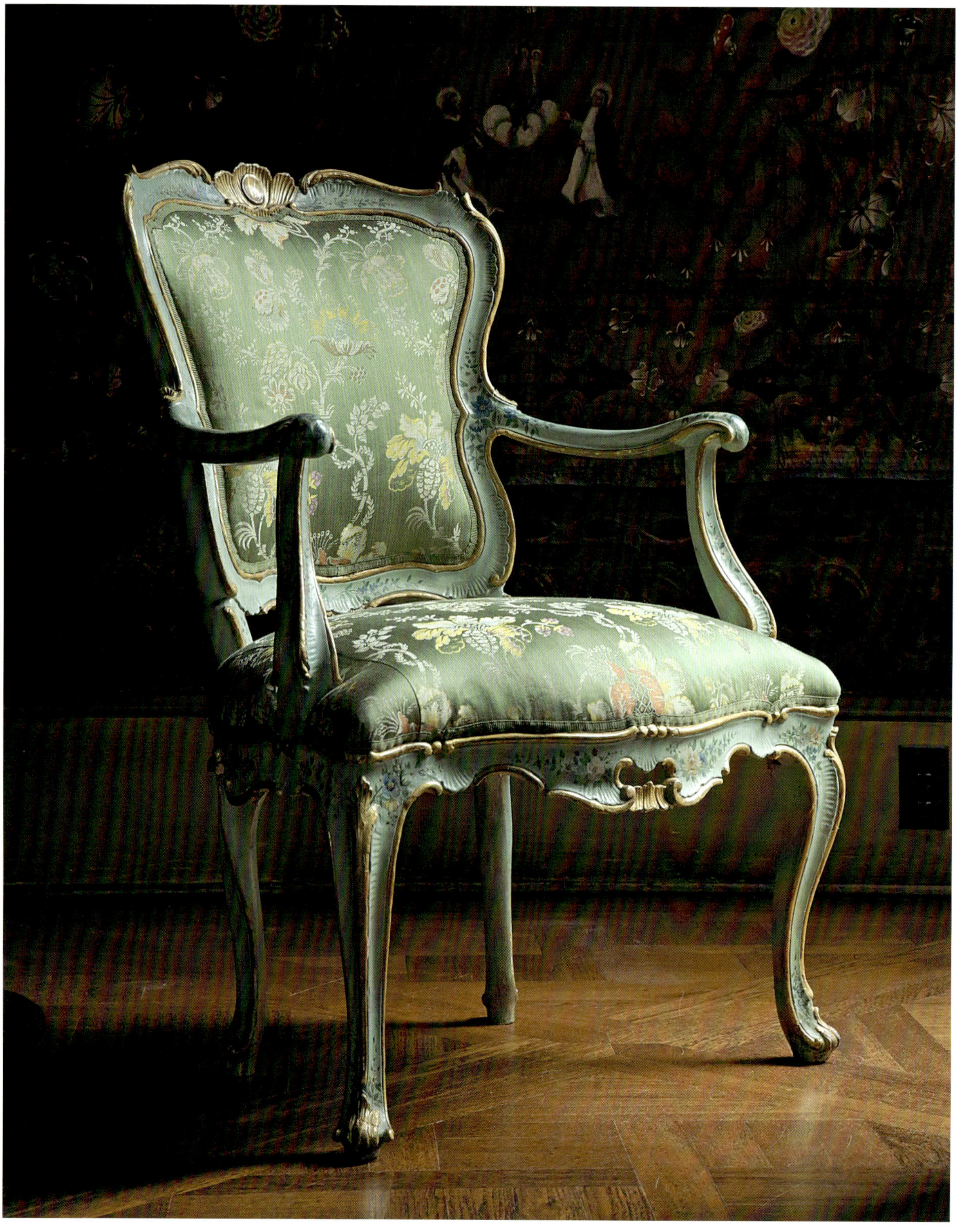

This type of armchair was commonly found in Venetian palazzi from the mid- to the late eighteenth century. The curving lines, cabriole legs, and delicate carved details of the piece suggest the extent to which Venice, more than any other artistic center in Italy, assimilated the international Rococo style.

The chair's graceful frame is accented by carved and gilded moldings that terminate in foliage or spiral into volutes. Stylized shells, beautifully fluted, are scattered across the surface; these are gilded at the crest, apron, and arms. The front apron is pierced with an elegant double oval design, while a gilded cartouche, set on carved shells, marks the crest. The pale blue ground of the frame is painted with flowers and leaves, and varnished with Venetian lacquer. This finish gives the surface a rich, warm patina.

FC

Provenance: Acquired by Isabella Stewart Gardner by ca. 1895.

Reference: Longstreet and Carter 1935, 204.

40. Venetian Workshop
Side Table, late 18th century
Painted and varnished pine, 33 3/8 x 50 13/16 x 24 3/16 in. (84.8 x 129 x 61.4 cm)
Isabella Stewart Gardner Museum, Boston, F3s6

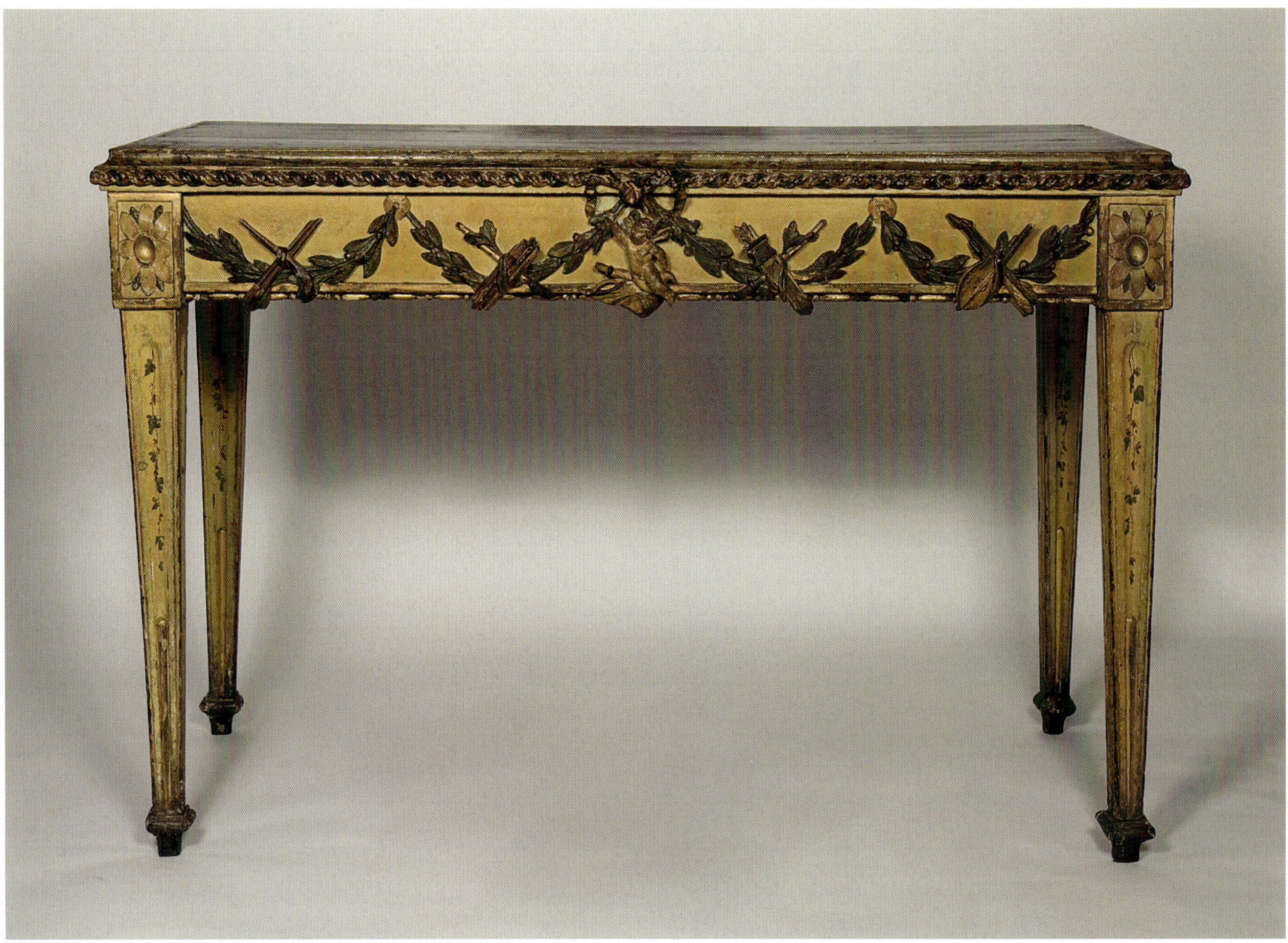

Unfinished at the back, this well-preserved table is of a type called a *tavola a muro*—literally, a wall table, but commonly known in English as a side table or console. Its simple lines and Greek- and Roman-inspired decoration exemplify the Neoclassical style in Venice. The table is particularly noteworthy for its finely carved details, highlighted throughout with contrasting paint and balanced by beautifully proportioned moldings. The aprons bear festoons of olive branches hanging from open flower calices; these garlands support musical instruments, quivers, arrows, clubs, and fasces.[1] In the center is an image of a blindfolded putto—no doubt intended to suggest romantic love. The combined symbols of music, war, and affairs of the heart evoke an allegorical theme about the pains and pleasures of amorous pursuits. *Chandelles* fill the lower portions of the flutes on the gracefully proportioned legs, and above these appear delicate, leafy tendrils. A flower-painted frame and a spiral molding surround the ebonized-wood top.

The table owes much to French Neoclassical designs that were fashionable throughout Europe—and adapted by Venetian craftsmen—beginning in the 1760s. For instance, similarly decorated pieces appear in the drawings of Pietro Antonio Novelli, whose illustrations of popular dramas, such as works by the celebrated playwright Carlo Goldini, document the popularity of this style in Venice.[2] In contrast to the curving forms and elaborate ornamentation of the Rococo style prevalent in Venice during the mid-eighteenth century, Neoclassical pieces such as this one incorporate the simple lines and relatively restrained carving of French models. Tinted varnish over paint imbues the table with a warm, luminous surface; known as Venetian lacquer, this type of finish began to disappear by the end of the century. Compared to richly colored and exuberantly decorated Rococo examples such as the commode in the collection of the Isabella Stewart Gardner Museum (cat. 37), this table exhibits a restrained use of Venetian lacquer and a relatively monochromatic color scheme.

The combination of robust carving with the Neoclassical style makes this *tavola a muro* unusual among Venetian furniture of the period. Indeed, the motifs and putto ornamenting the olive-leaf garlands, as well as the spiral molding circling the tabletop like twisted ribbons, recall the exuberant Baroque taste of the 1600s. The unusual juxtaposition of different stylistic sensibilities suggests this object may have been intended for a provincial setting or for a somewhat modest private room in a Venetian palazzo.

FC

Notes

1. Fasces are an ancient Roman motif comprising a bundle of rods bound around an ax, the blade of which projects outward. Originally, this symbolized governmental authority, but it is used here as a Neoclassical decorative device.

2. Novelli (1729–1804) was a versatile and prolific artist whose extensive output documents popular taste in eighteenth-century Venice. For instance, his suite of thirty drawings illustrating the works of the poet and librettist Pietro Metastasio (1698–1782) are excellent examples of Neoclassical art based on French designs. These drawings were recently on the art market. See Christie's (Paris) *Collection Jean Lignel: dessins et manuscrits, livres anciens et livres d'artistes*, Thursday, 11 December 2008, lot 24.

Provenance: Acquired by Isabella Stewart Gardner by 1915.

Reference: Longstreet and Carter 1935, 26.

41. Venetian Workshop
Toilet Mirror, mid-18th century
Painted, gilt, varnished wood and mirror glass, 33 1/2 x 23 x 8 3/8 in. (85.2 x 58.5 x 21.3 cm)
Isabella Stewart Gardner Museum, Boston, F25s4

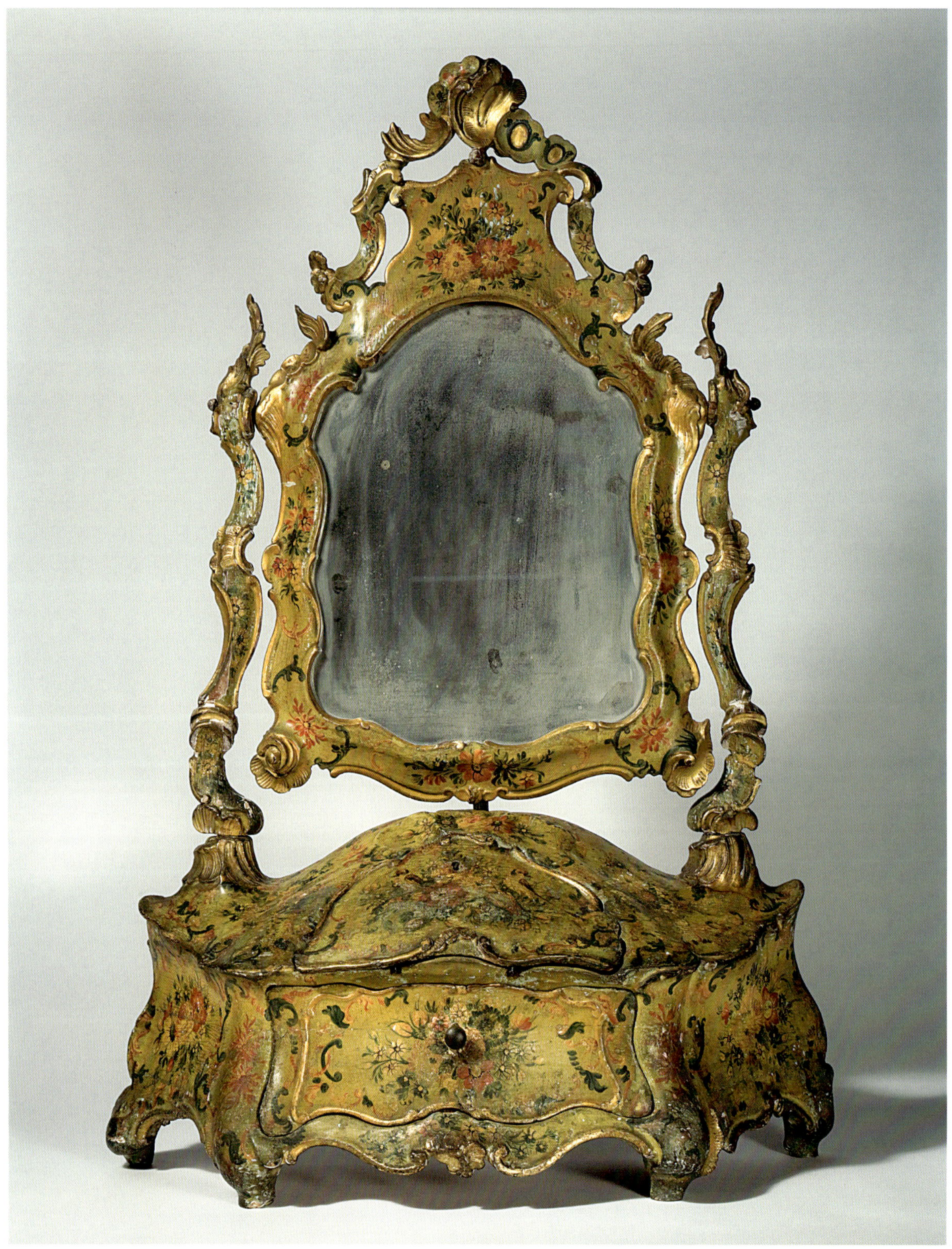

Small toilet mirrors such as this one were indispensable accessories in the bedrooms of eighteenth-century Venetian noblewomen.[1] Typically, the mirror was attached to a small cabinet in which the owner generally stored her jewelry. In this object, the toilet mirror also has a drawer; above it is a compartment that is secured by an arched door with a lock. The outward-curving lines, or bombé form, typify a genre characterized by light, whimsical designs. Another hallmark is the fine carving on the upright elements that hold the mirror—allowing it to pivot—and on the elaborate S-shaped, or cyma, molding that crowns the frame.

The base cabinet is similarly carved with Rococo motifs and scrollwork and is also partially gilded. Foliage and animals are painted on the yellow ground of the surfaces, which are entirely coated with Venetian lacquer (tinted varnish). The piece was originally painted pale blue, but aging of the sandarac resin in the varnish has imparted a yellow tint.

FC

Note

1. For similar mirrors, see Levy 1967, figs. 283–85; and Silva 1997, no. 6.

Provenance: Moisè Dalla Torre, Venice, 1899.

Reference: Longstreet and Carter 1935, 199.

42. (a – d) Style of Michelangelo Pergolesi, active 1777–1801
     Suite of Furniture, ca. 1750
     Carved, painted, and lacquered wood
     a. *Settee* (SN1533): 38 x 63 1/4 x 19 1/4 in. (96.5 x 160.7 x 48.9 cm)
    † b. *Settee* (SN1803): 39 x 54 1/2 x 18 7/8 in. (99.1 x 138.4 x 47.9 cm)
    † c. *Chair* (SN1804): 39 x 17 1/2 x 16 1/2 in. (99.1 x 44.5 x 41.9 cm)
    † d. *Chair* (SN1805): 39 x 17 1/2 x 16 1/2 in. (99.1 x 44.5 x 41.9 cm)
    The John and Mable Ringling Museum of Art, Sarasota; Museum Purchase, 1949, SN1533
    The John and Mable Ringling Museum of Art, Sarasota; Museum Purchase, 1957, SN1803,
    SN1804, and SN 1805

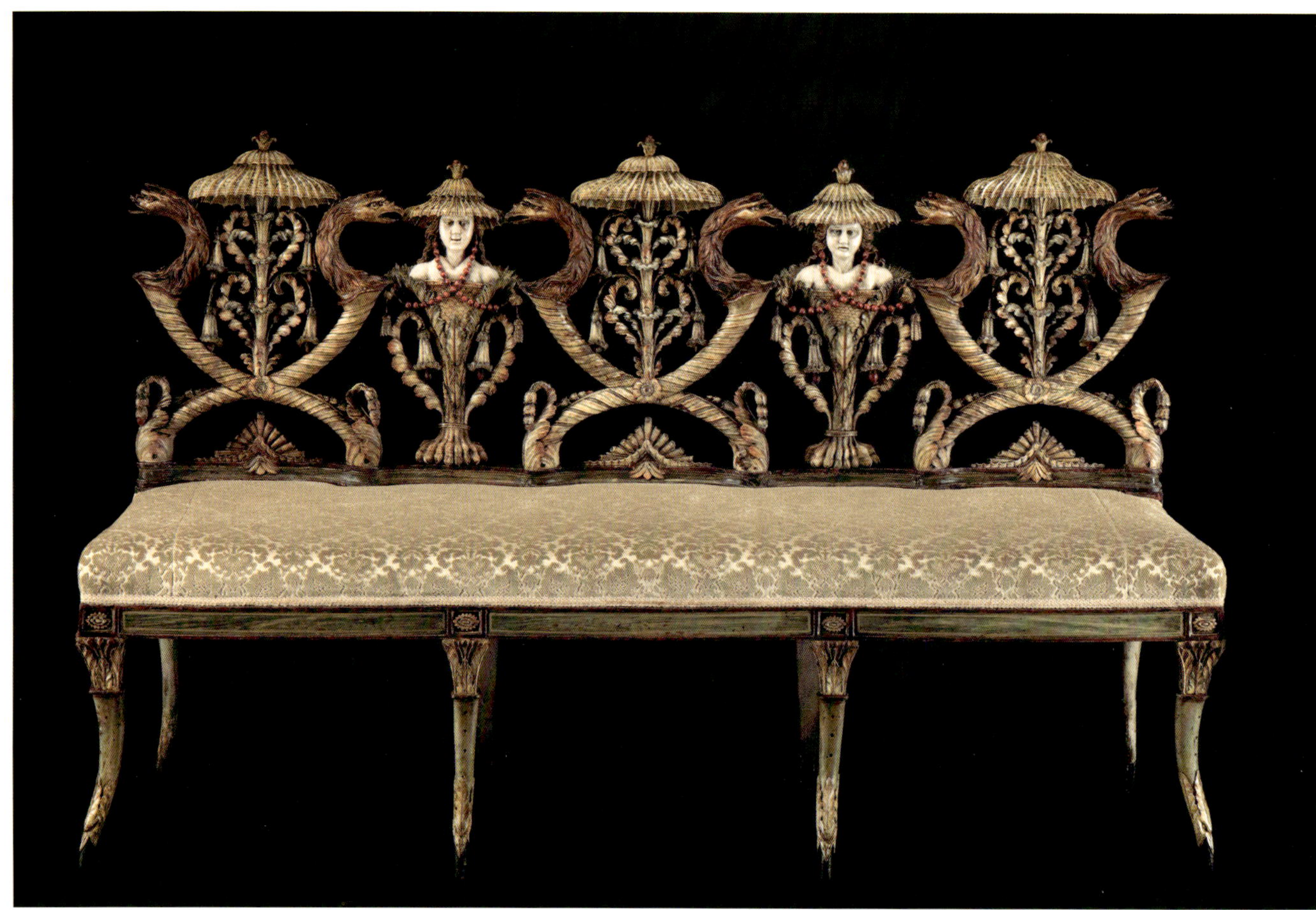

42a.

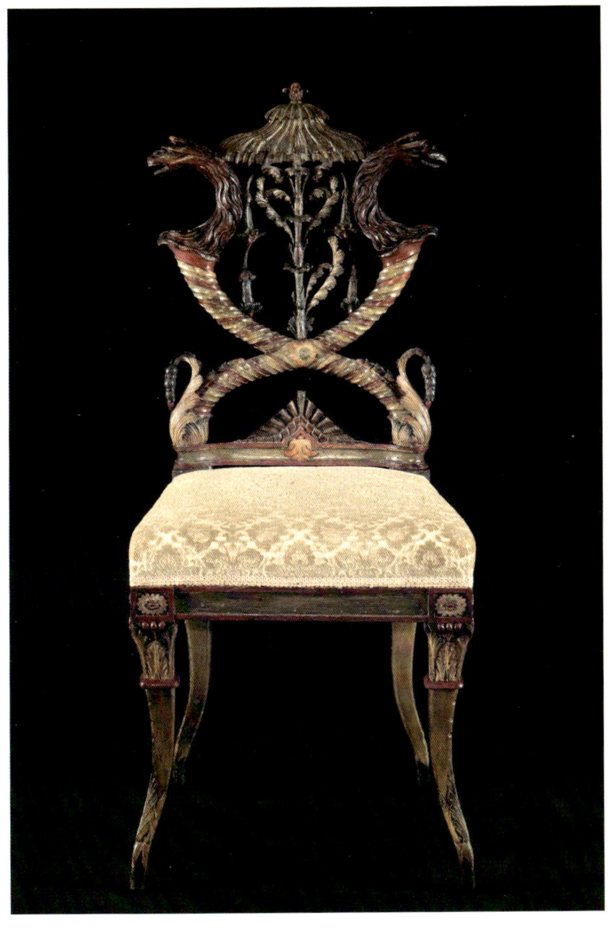

42c.

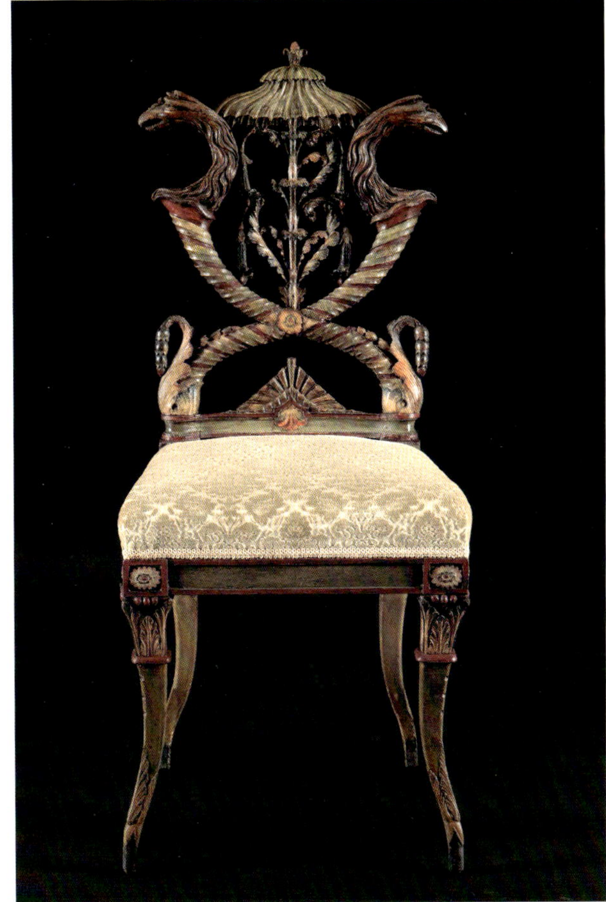

42d.

From the time of Marco Polo's voyage to China in the second half of the thirteenth century, Venetians were fascinated by the Far East. In the arts and crafts, chinoiserie, a vogue for Chinese-influenced styling and motifs, reached its apogee during the eighteenth century, when it expanded from a few specific examples to become a widespread Westernized style that was adapted to various media. Chinoiserie played an integral role in Venetian decorative arts, providing a repertoire of fanciful design elements to artists employed by patrons who were eager to surround themselves with objects that bespoke exotic refinement and luxury.

Elaborately carved and painted, this suite of two settees and two chairs was executed in the manner of the influential Venetian-born decorative artist Michelangelo Pergolesi. Little about him is known, including his birth and death dates, making it difficult to trace his work in Venice.[1] After a successful career there, he moved to London in the 1770s to collaborate with the renowned English designer Robert Adam on several publishing endeavors. However, he authored just one volume of his own, *Designs for Various Ornaments on Seventy Plates* (1777–1801), a pattern book of designs for friezes, doors, ceilings, urns, balustrades, chairs, and settees.[2] Although there are no exact graphic corollaries to this suite of furniture in Pergolesi's publication, chinoiserie-style similarities, such as the intertwined dragon heads, parasol-like canopies, and mandarin-like faces, can be seen between these pieces and several designs in that volume (fig. 42.1).

Artists such as Pergolesi were especially popular among wealthy Venetians. They sought to adorn their apartments, palazzi, and country homes with furniture whose capricious designs reflected notions of prestige during a time when the local sense of patrician identity—like the power and influence of Venice itself—was unraveling. Functionality and comfort generally were of secondary concern, and most such furniture would not actually have been used. The intricacy of carving and fragility of construction seen in the Ringling pieces suggest that they likely served as "props" in a grand Venetian salon; their straight, unelaborated backs indicate that they would have been placed against the walls.

Another chair from this set is in the collection of the Cooper-Hewitt National Design Museum, New York.[3] Console tables belonging to the suite were at "one time" thought to have been at the Vizcaya estate in Miami.[4]

AL

Notes

1. The most thorough biographical sketch of Pergolesi, primarily focused on his time in England, is Thieme and Becker 1907, 412–13. He is also mentioned in the compendia: Guilmard 1880–81, Macquoid 1904–8, Simon 1907, Jessen 1920, and Clouston 1975.

2. A reproduction edition of Pergolesi's pattern book published four decades ago bears no title and only includes sheets from 1777 through 1792. Maser 1970.

3. The chair is described in the Cooper-Hewitt's files as being in the "style of Michelangelo Pergolesi" (accession no. 1924.6.1).

4. A. Everett Austin, Jr., the Ringling Museum's first director, recorded this in his notebook upon purchasing the settee 42a (SN1533) from French and Company, New York, in 1949. The family of the agricultural industrialist James Deering, original owners of Vizcaya, purchased many works from French, and it seems likely Austin learned of the console tables' "one time" presence there from that New York dealer. In 1952 the Deering heirs conveyed the house, its contents, and formal gardens to Dade County; however, there are no console tables fitting the Pergolesi description in the collection of the Vizcaya Museum and Gardens today.

Provenance (SN1533): Mrs. Benjamin Thaw, before 1949; French and Company, New York, by 1949.

Provenance (SN1803, SN1804, and SN1805): Mrs. John Innes Kane [1857–1926], before 1930; French and Company, New York, by 1930; A. Everett Austin, Jr. [1900–1957], Sarasota, 1930–57.

References: Richardson in Detroit and Indianapolis 1952, 84–85, nos. 166 and 167 (SN1804 and SN 1805); Duval in Sarasota 1982, 153, no. 148 (SN1533); Borys 2008, 105 (SN1533).

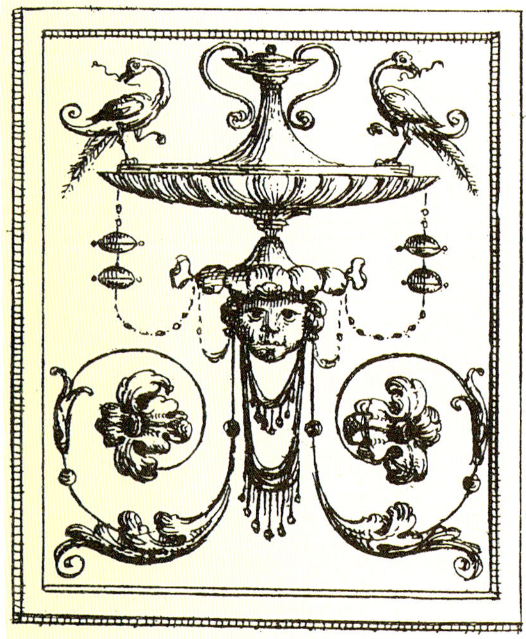

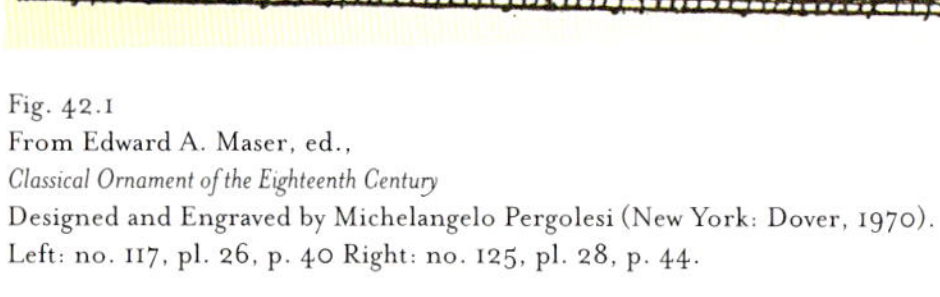

Fig. 42.1
From Edward A. Maser, ed.,
Classical Ornament of the Eighteenth Century
Designed and Engraved by Michelangelo Pergolesi (New York: Dover, 1970).
Left: no. 117, pl. 26, p. 40 Right: no. 125, pl. 28, p. 44.

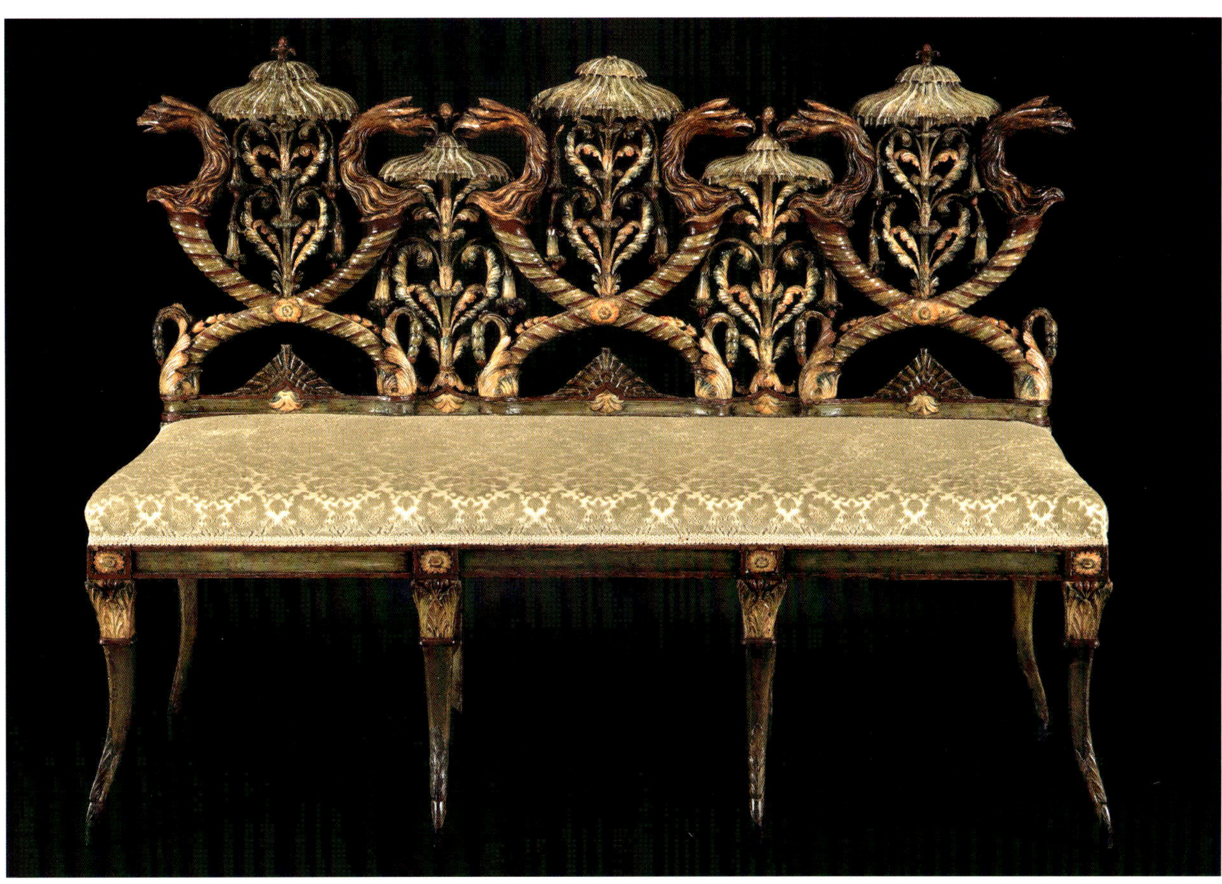

42b.

Bibliography

Agnellini and Baccheschi 1990
Maurizio Agnellini and Edi Baccheschi. *Mobili italiani del Settecento*. Milan, 1990.

Aikema 1984
Bernard Aikema. "Proposte per Sebastiano Ricci e per Nicola Grassi." *Nicola Grassi e il Rococò europeo* (Atti del Congresso internazionale di Studi, 20–22 May 1982). Udine, 1984.

Alberici 1980
Clelia Alberici. *Il Mobile Veneto*. Milan, 1980.

Albrizzi 1750
Giambatista Albrizzi. *Raccolta di paesetti intagliati in rame, parte originali, parte estratti da'migliori autori per uso de'professori e dilettanti di pittura*. Venice, 1750.

Alpers and Baxandall 1994
Svetlana Alpers and Michael Baxandall. *Tiepolo and the Pictorial Intelligence*. New Haven and London, 1994.

Ames 1963
Winslow Ames. "The Villa dal Timpano Arcuato by Francesco Guardi." *Master Drawings* 1, no. 3 (1963), 37–81.

Amsterdam 1990
Painters of Venice: The Story of the Venetian 'Veduta.' Exh. cat. Rijksmuseum, Amsterdam, 1990. By Bernard Aikema and Boudewijn Bakker.

Andrieux 1972
Maurice Andrieux. *Daily Life in Venice in the Time of Casanova*. New York and Washington, D.C., 1972.

Anglo-Saxon Review 1899
Anglo-Saxon Review 2 (1899), 81.

Arslan 1932
Edoardo Arslan, "Appunti su Magnasco, Sebastiano e Marco Ricci." *Bolletino d'Arte* 26 (1932), 200–219.

Arlsan 1942
__________. "Nota breve sul Piazzetta." *Le Arti* 5 (1942), 206.

Arslan 1944
__________. "Per la definizione dell'arte di Francesco e Niccolo Guardi." *Emporium* 100 (1944): 1–8.

Arts Magazine 1958
"A Double Benefaction." *Arts Magazine* 32, no. 8 (1958): 36.

Austin 1955
A. Everett Austin, Jr. *A Popular Guide: Fifty Masterpieces in The John and Mable Ringling Museum of Art*, Sarasota, 1955.

Austin 2006
Blanton Museum of Art Guide to the Collection. Austin, 2006.

Bacchelli 1953
Ricardo Bacchelli. *Teatro e Immagini del Settecento Italiano*. Turin, 1953.

Baccheschi and Levy 1960
Edi Baccheschi and Saul Levy. *Mobili laccati del Settecento veneziano*. Milan, 1960.

Bagemihl 1988
Rolf Bagemihl. "Pietro Longhi and Venetian Life." *Metropolitan Museum Journal* 23 (1988): 233–47.

Baltimore 1958
The Age of Elegance: The Rococo and Its Effects. Exh cat. Baltimore Museum of Art, 1959.

Baltimore 1976
Maryland Heritage: Five Baltimore Institutions Celebrate the American Bicentennial. Exh. cat. Maryland Historical Society, Walters Art Gallery, Baltimore Museum of Art, Peale Museum, and Maryland Academy of Sciences, 1976.

Barcham 1977
William Barcham. "Canaletto and a Commission from Consul Smith." *Art Bulletin* 59, no. 3 (September 1977), 383–93.

Barcham 1979
__________. "Giambattista Tiepolo's Ceiling for S. Maria di Nazareth in Venice: Legend, Traditions, and Devotions." *Art Bulletin* 61, no. 3 (September 1979): 430–47.

Barcham 1992
__________. *Giambattista Tiepolo*. New York, 1992.

Battie 1990
David Battie. *Sotheby's Concise Encyclopedia of Porcelain*. London, 1990.

Beckford 1834
William Beckford. *Italy; with Sketches of Spain and Portugal*. 2 vols. London, 1834.

Bedini 1981
Silvio A. Bedini. "The Papal Pachyderms." *Proceedings of the American Philosophical Society* 125, no. 2 (April 30, 1981): 75–90.

De Bellaigue 1974
Geoffrey De Bellaigue. *Furniture, Clocks, and Gilt Bronzes. The James A. Rothschild Collection at Waddesdon Manor*. Friburg, 1974.

Berenson 1968
Bernard Berenson. *Seeing and Knowing*. Greenwich, 1968.

Beresford and Raissis 2003
Richard Beresford and Peter Raissis. *The James Fairfax Collection*. Sydney, 2003.

Berto and Puppi 1968
Giuseppe Berto and Lionello Puppi. *L'opera complete del Canaletto*. Milan, 1968.

Bialostocki 1964
Jan Bialostocki. "Bernardo Bellotto in Dresden and Warsaw." *Burlington Magazine* 106, no. 735 (1964): 289–91.

Bibliotheca Sanctorum 1987
"Filippo Neri." *Bibliotheca Sanctorum, Prima Appendice*, Rome, 1987, 759–90.

Birmingham 1952
Samuel H. Kress Collection: Birmingham Museum of Art, Birmingham, 1952.

Birmingham 1993a
Canaletto and England. Exh cat. Birmingham Gas Hall Exhibition Gallery, Birmingham, 1993. By Michael Liversidge and Jane Farrington.

Birmingham 1993b
Masterpieces East and West: From the Collection of the Birmingham Museum of Art. Exh cat. Birmingham Museum of Art, Birmingham, 1993.

Birmingham and Springfield 1978
The Tiepolos: Painters to Princes and Prelates. Exh. cat. Birmingham Museum of Art, Birmingham, and Museum of Fine Arts, Springfield, 1978.

Black 1992
Jeremy Black. *The British Abroad: The Grand Tour in the Eighteenth Century*. London, 1992.

Blackburn 1780
Francis Blackburn. *Memoirs of Thomas Hollis*. London, 1780.

Bober 1999
Jonathan Bober. "The Suida-Manning Collection in the Jack S. Blanton Museum of Art at the University of Texas at Austin." *Burlington Magazine* 141, no. 1156 (1999), 445–52.

Bober 2001
__________. *Capolavori della Suida-Manning Collection*. Milan, 2001.

Bober and Rubenstein 1986
Phyllis P. Bober and Ruth Rubenstein. *Renaissance Artists and Antique Sculpture: A Handbook of Sources*. Oxford, 1986.

Bonacossi 1962
Antonio Contini Bonacossi. *Art of the Renaissance from the Samuel H. Kress Collection*. Columbia, 1962.

Bordeaux 1956
De Tiepolo à Goya. Exh cat. International Festival, Bordeaux, 1956. By Gilberte Martin-Méry.

Bortolatto 1974
Luigina Rossi Bortolatto. *L'opera complete di Francesco Guardi*. Milan, 1974.

Borys 2008
Stephen D. Borys. *Guide to the Collections: The John and Mable Ringling Museum of Art*. Sarasota, 2008.

Bremer-David 1993
Charissa Bremer-David, ed. *Decorative Arts: An Illustrated Summary Catalogue of the Collections of the J. Paul Getty Museum*. Malibu, 1993. [Revised edition]

Bremer-David, 1997
__________. *Masterpieces of the J. Paul Getty Museum: Decorative Arts*. Los Angeles, 1997.

Brülmeyer 1965
Hermann Brülmeyer. *Das Heiligenkreuzer Chorgestühl von Giovanni Giuliani*. Vienna, 1965.

Brunel 1991
Georges Brunel. *Tiepolo*. Paris, 1991.

Bulgarelli 1973
Maria Angela Bulgarelli. "Profilo di Domenico Maggioto." *Arte Veneta* 27 (1973), 220–35.

Burroughs 1940
Louise Burroughs. "View of Vaprio D'Adda by Bellotto." *Metropolitan Museum of Art Bulletin* 35, no. 2 (February 1940), 32–34.

Byam Shaw 1952
James Byam Shaw. "Review: *Gian Antonio Guardi* by Fernanda de'Maffei." *Burlington Magazine* 94, no. 595 (1952), 300.

Cailleux 1966
Jean Cailleux. "The Guardi Brothers: Dating and Documentation." *Burlington Magazine* 108, no. 758 (1966), i–ii.

Calabi 1915
A. Calabi. "Da Venezia a Padova in 'Burchiello.'" *Emporium* 43 (1915), 226–33.

Çelik et al. 1994
Zeynep Çelik, Diane Favro, and Richard Ingersoll, eds. *Streets: Critical Perspectives on Public Space*. Berkeley, 1994.

Chaloner 1950
W. H. Chaloner. "The Eagertons in Italy and the Netherlands, 1729–1734, with Two Unpublished Letters from Joseph Smith, Sometime H.M. Consul in Venice." *Bulletin of the John Rylands Library* 32 (March 1950), 157–70.

Chantilly 2001
Paysages: chefs-d'oeuvre du Cabinet des dessins du musée Condé à Chantilly. Exh. cat. Musée Condé, Chantilly, 2001. By Nicole Garnier-Pelle.

Chicago et al. 1970
Painting in Italy in the Eighteenth Century: Rococo to Romanticism. Exh. cat. Art Institute Chicago; Minneapolis Institute of Arts; and Toledo Museum of Art, 1970. By John Maxon and Joseph J. Rishel.

Chippendale 1949
Thomas Chippendale. *The Ornamental Designs of Chippendale, from the Gentleman and Cabinet-Maker's Director, 1762*. London, 1949.

Christiansen 1982
Keith Christiansen. "The Baptism of Christ." *Metropolitan Museum of Art: Notable Acquisitions 1981–82*. New York, 1982.

Clark 1964
Anthony M. Clark. "Imperiali." *Burlington Magazine* 64, no. 734 (1964), 226–33.

Clayton 2005
Martin Clayton. *Canaletto in Venice*. London, 2005.

Clouston 1975
K. Warren Clouston. *The Chippendale Period in English Furniture*. Paris, 1975.

Colle 2000
Enrico Colle. *Il mobile barocco. Arredi e decorazioni d'interni dal 1600 al 1738*. Milan, 2000.

Connoisseur 1961
"The Kress Collection." *Connoisseur* 148, no. 598 (December 1961), 284–94.

Constable 1962
W. G. Constable. *Canaletto: Giovanni Antonio Canal, 1697–1768*, 2 vols. Oxford, 1962.

Constable 1976
__________. *Canaletto: Giovanni Antonio Canal, 1697–1768*. 2 vols. Oxford, 1976. [Revised edition]

Constable and Links 1989
W. G. Constable and J. G. Links. *Canaletto: Giovanni Antonio Canal, 1697–1768*. 2 vols. Oxford, 1989. [Revised edition]

Corboz 1985
André Corboz. *Canaletto: Una Venezia immaginaria*. 2 vols. Milan, 1985.

Corning 2002
Annual Report, 2002. Corning Museum of Glass, Corning, 2002.

Costa 1747
Gianfrancesco Costa. *Le delizie del fiume Brenta nei palazzi e casini situati sopra le sue sponde dalla sua sboccatura nella laguna di Venezia infino alla città di Padova*. Venice, 1747.

Coutts 2001
Howard Coutts. *The Art of Ceramics: European Ceramic Design, 1500–1830*. New Haven and London, 2001.

Crivellato 1962
Valentino Crivellato. *Tiepolo*. New York, 1962.

Croft-Murray 1962–1970
Edward Croft-Murray. *Decorative Painting in England 1587–1837*. 2 vols. London 1962; Feltham 1970.

Dallas 1961
The Art That Broke the Looking Glass. Exh. cat. Dallas Museum for Contemporary Arts, Dallas, 1961. By Douglas MacAgy.

Dania 1973
Luigi Dania. "Some Unpublished Drawings by Francesco Guardi in Private Collections." *Master Drawings* 11, no. 4 (Winter 1973), 383–86, 442–48.

Daniels 1969
Jeffery Daniels. "Sebastiano Ricci: The Last Phase." *Apollo* 89 (January–June 1969), 6–11.

Daniels 1974
__________. "English Baroque Sketches at Marble Hill." *Burlington Magazine* 116, no. 856 (1974), 421–22.

Daniels 1976a
__________. *Sebastiano Ricci*. Hove, 1976.

Daniels 1976b
__________. *L'opera complete di Sebastiano Ricci*. Milan, 1976.

Daniels 1976c
__________. "Ricci in England." *Atti del congresso internazionale di studi su Sebastiano Ricci e il suo tempo*. Milan, 1976.

Daniels 1984
__________. "Direct or Indirect." *Nicola Grassi e il Rococò europeo (Atti del Congresso internazionale di Studi)*. Udine, 1984.

D'Arcais 1973
Francesca D'Arcais. "I complessi decorativi fiorentini di Sebastiano Ricci III." *Saggi e Memorie de Storia dell'Arte* 12 (1973), 10–13.

D'Arcais 1976
__________. "Un libro su Sebastiano Ricci." *Arte Veneta* 30 (1976), 254–56.

Darr and Albainy 2000
A. Darr and T. Albainy. "Acquisitions of European Sculpture and Decorative Arts at the Detroit Institute of Arts, 1988–99." *Burlington Magazine* 142, no. 1167 (2000), 405-412.

Daxecker 2004
Franz Daxecker. "Ein Einglas auf einem Bild des Pietro Longhi im Museum of Fine Arts in Houston." *Berichte des naturwissenschaftlich-medizinischen Vereins in Innsbruck* 91 (November 2004), 325–27.

De Grazia and Garberson 1996
Diane De Grazia and Garberson, eds. *Italian Paintings of the Seventeenth and Eighteenth Centuries: The Collections of the National Gallery of Art, Systematic Catalogue*. Washington, D.C., 1996.

de'Maffei 1948
Fernanda de'Maffei. *Gian Antonio Guardi: Pittore di figura*. Verona, 1948.

de'Maffei 1951
__________. *Gian Antonio Guardi: Pittore di figura*. Verona, 1951. [Revised edition]

Dent 1905
Edward J. Dent. *Alessandro Scarlatti: His Life and Works*. London, 1905.

Descamps 1772
J.-B. Descamps. *Voyage pittoresque de la Flandre et du Brabant avec des réflexions relativement aux arts et quelques gravures*. Amsterdam, 1772.

Detroit and Indianapolis 1952
Venice 1700–1800: An Exhibition of Venice and the Eighteenth Century. Exh. cat. Detroit Institute of Arts, Detroit, and John Herron Art Museum, Indianapolis, 1952. By Edgar P. Richardson.

Devisse and Mollat 1979
Jean Devisse and Michel Mollat. *The Image of The Black in Western Art: Volume II.* New York, 1979.

D'Onofrio 1967
Cesare D'Onofrio. *Gli obelischi di Roma.* Rome, 1967. [2nd edition]

Donzelli 1957
Carlo Donzelli. *I pittori del seicento véneto.* Florence, 1957.

Dorge and Carey 1998
Valerie Dorge and Howlett F. Carey. *Painted Wood: History and Conservation.* Los Angeles, 1998.

Dorigato 2002
Attilia Dorigato. *L'Arte del Vetro a Murano.* Arsenale, 2002.

Draper et al. 1987
James David Draper, James Parker, Johanna Hecht, Clare Le Corbeiller, Jessie McNab, William Rieder, and Clare Vincent, "European Sculpture and Decorative Arts." *Recent Acquisitions: A Selection, 1986–1987* (Metropolitan Museum of Art), 1987, 28.

Druce 1919
G. C. Druce. "The Elephant in Medieval Legend and Art." *Archeological Journal* 76 (1919), 1–73.

Duchartre and Weaver 1966
Pierre-Louis Duchartre and Randolph T. Weaver. *The Italian Comedy; The Improvisation, Scenarios, Lives, Attributes, Portraits, and Masks of the Illustrious Characters of the Commedia Dell'arte.* New York, 1966.

Düsseldorf and Hannover 1992
Venedigs Ruhm im Norden: die grossen venezianischen Maler des 18. Jahrhunderts, ihre Auftraggeber und ihre Sammler. Exh. cat. Kunstmuseum, Düsseldorf, and Forum des Landesmuseums, Hannover, 1992. By Meinolf Trudzinski.

Earle and Lowe 2005
T. F. Earle and K. J. P. Lowe, eds. *Black Africans in Renaissance Europe.* Cambridge, 2005.

Eglin 2001
John Eglin. *Venice Transfigured: The Myth of Venice in British Culture, 1660–1797.* New York, 2001.

Erculei 1889
Raffaele Erculei. *Arte ceramica e vetraria: Catalogo delle opera esposte.* Roma, 1889.

Fagiolo dell'Arco 1978
Maurizio Fagiolo dell'Arco. *Great Baroque and Rococo Sculpture.* New York, 1978.

Fahy 1973
Everett Fahy. *The Wrightsman Collection, vol. 5: Paintings, Drawings.* New York, 1973.

Fahy 2005
__________. *The Wrightsman Pictures.* New York, 2005.

Farmer 1983
David Hugh Farmer. *The Oxford Dictionary of Saints.* Oxford and New York, 1983.

Fenyö 1968
Ivan Fenyö. "An Unknown Processional Banner by the Guardi Brothers." *Burlington Magazine* 110, no. 779 (1968), 60, 63–69.

Ferrari 1928
Giulio Ferrari. *Il legno e la mobilia nell'arte italiana.* Milan, 1928.

Ferrazza 1994
Roberta Ferrazza. *Palazzo Davanzati e le collezioni di Elia Volpi.* Florence, 1994.

Finberg 1920
Hilda F. Finberg. "Canaletto in England." *The Ninth Volume of the Walpole Society, 1920–1921.* London, 1921.

Finberg 1934
A. J. Finberg, ed. *The Twenty-second Volume of the Walpole Society, 1933–1934: Vertue Note Books, Volume III.* Oxford, 1934.

Finberg 1938
__________. *The Twenty-sixth Volume of the Walpole Society, 1937–1938: Vertue Note Books, Volume V.* Oxford, 1938.

Fiocco 1927
Giuseppe Fiocco. *Burlington Magazine for Connoisseurs* (letter; cf. Hadeln) 51, no. 293 (1927), 52.

Fiocco 1929
__________. *Le Pittura veneziana de seicento e settecento.* Florence, 1929.

Fiocco 1952
__________. "Il problema di Francesco Guardi." *Arte Veneta* 6 (1952), 99–120.

Fiocco 1958
__________. *Francesco Guardi: L'Angelo Raffaele.* Turin, 1958.

Fiocco 1966
__________. "Le pitture dell'angelo Raffaele e la confraternita del Sacramenti." *Paragone* 197, no. 17 (1966), 45–57.

Fiorani 1980
Fabio Fiorani. *Vedute di Venezia alla fine del '600.* Rome, 1980.

Fogolari 1931
Gino Fogolari. "Il Bozzetto del Tiepolo per il Trasporto della Santa Casa di Loreto." *Bollettino d'Arte* 25 (July 1931), 18–32.

Ford 1958
Brinsley Ford. "Italy and the Grand Tour at Norwich." *Burlington Magazine* 100, no. 666 (1958), 316–19.

Fort Worth 1954
Inaugural Exhibition. Exh. cat. Fort Worth Art Center, Fort Worth, 1954.

Fort Worth 1986
Giuseppe Maria Crespi and the emergence of genre painting in Italy. Exh. cat. Kimbell Art Museum, Fort Worth, 1986. By John T. Spike, Mira P. Merriman, and Giovanna Perini.

Fort Worth 1993
Giambattista Tiepolo: Master of the Oil Sketch. Exh. cat. Kimbell Art Museum, Fort Worth, 1993. Edited by Beverly Louise Brown.

Frankfurt et al. 1989
The Consul Smith Collection: Masterpieces of Italian Drawing from the Royal Library, Windsor Castle: Raphael to Canaletto. Exh. cat. Schirn Kunsthalle, Frankfurt; Kimbell Art Museum, Fort Worth; Virginia Museum of Fine Arts, Richmond; and National Gallery of Scotland, Edinburgh, 1989. By Frances Vivian.

Franzini 1725
Girolamo Franzini. *Les merveilles de la ville de Rome.* Rome, 1725.

Fredericksen 1995
Burton B. Fredericksen ed. *Masterpieces of Painting in the J. Paul Getty Museum.* Malibu, 1995. [3rd ed.]

Fredericksen and Zeri 1972
Burton B. Fredericksen and Federico Zeri. *Census of Pre–Nineteenth-Century Italian Paintings in North American Public Collections.* Cambridge, 1972.

Freedberg 1980
David Freedberg. *Dutch Landscape Prints of the Seventeenth Century.* London, 1980.

Fritzsche 1936
Hellmuth Allwill Fritzsche. *Bernardo Belotto detto il Canaletto.* Berg, 1936.

Gállego 1965
Julián Gállego. "La esposición Guardi, en Venecia." *Goya* 69 (November–December 1965), 156–63.

Garas 1964
Klára Garas. "New Documents Concerning Sebastiano Ricci." *Burlington Magazine* 106, no. 732 (1964), 130–31.

Gemin and Pedrocco 1993
Massimo Gemin and Filippo Pedrocco. *Giambattista Tiepolo: i dipinti: opera complete.* Venice, 1993.

Georgelin 1978
Jean Georgelin. *Venise au siècle des lumières.* Paris and The Hague, 1978.

Gheltof 1889
Urbani de Gheltof. "Note storiche ed artistiche sulla ceramica italiana." *Arte ceramica e vetraria*, Raffaele Erculei, ed. Rome, 1889.

Ghidiglia Quintavalle 1956–57
Augusta Ghidiglia Quintavalle. "Premesse giovanili di Sebastiano Ricci." *Revista dell' Instituta Nazionale d'Archeologica* 5/6 (1956–57), 395–415.

Ghidiglia Quintavalle 1961
__________. "Sebastiano Ricci a Parma, ritravato e da ritrovare." *Arte Antica e Moderna* 4 (1961), 448–52.

Gibson 2000
Walter S. Gibson. *Pleasant Places: The Rustic Landscape from Bruegel to Ruisdael.* Berkeley, 2000.

Goering 1938
Max Goering. "Francesco Guardi als Figurenmaler." *Zeitschrift für Kunstgeschichte* 7, no. 4 (1938), 289–315.

Goering 1944
__________. *Francesco Guardi.* Vienna, 1944.

Goethe 1989
Johann Wolfgang von Goethe. *Italian Journey.* Trans. Robert R. Heitner. New York, 1989. [1st ed., 1813–17]

González-Palacios 1984
Alvar González-Palacios. "The Furniture of Doge Paolo Renier." *Furniture History, The Journal of the Furniture History Society* 20 (1984), 28–51.

Gorizia 2008
Le meraviglie di Venezia: dipinti del '700 in collezioni private. Exh. cat. Palazzo Della Torre, Gorizia, 2008. By Dario Succi and Annalia Delneri.

Guilmard 1880–81
Désiré Guilmard. *Les maîtres ornemanistes, dessinateurs, peintres, architectes, sculpteurs et graveurs . . .* Paris, 1880–81.

Hadeln 1927
Baron Detlev von Hadeln. "Two Allegorical Figures by Francesco Guardi." *Burlington Magazine* 50 (1927), 254–59.

Haggar 1960
Reginald G. Haggar. *The Concise Encyclopedia of Continental Pottery and Porcelain.* London, 1960.

Hannegan 1966
Barry Hannegan. "Exhibition Review: Guardi at Venice." *Art Bulletin* 48, no. 2 (1966), 248–52.

Hansen and Spicer 2005
Morten Steen Hansen and Joaneath A. Spicer. *Masterpieces of Italian Painting: The Walters Art Museum.* Baltimore, 2005.

Haskell 1956
Francis Haskell. "Stefano Conti, Patron of Canaletto and Others." *Burlington Magazine* 98, no. 642 (1956), 296–300.

Haskell 1960
__________. "Francesco Guardi as Vedutista and Some of His Patrons." *Journal of the Warburg and Courtauld Institutes* 23 (1960), 256–76.

Haskell 1963
__________. *Patrons and Painters: A Study in the Relations between Italian Art and Society in the Age of the Baroque.* New York and London, 1963.

Haskell 1980
__________. *Patrons and Painters: A Study in the Relations between Italian Art and Society in the Age of the Baroque.* 1980. [Revised edition]

Haydon 1967
Harold Haydon. *Great Art Treasures in America's Smaller Museums.* New York, 1967.

Heinemann 1965
F. Heinemann. "Mostra dei Guardi." *Kunstchronik* 18, no. 9 (1965), 235–49.

Heller 1997
Karl Heller. *Antonio Vivaldi: The Red Priest of Venice.* Portland, 1997.

Herbermann 1913
Charles G. Herbermann, ed. *The Catholic Encyclopedia, vol. 7.* New York, 1913. [Revised edition]

Hess 1990
Catherine Hess. "'Primo Esperimento in Grande': A Pair of Vases from the Factory of Geminiano Cozzi." *J. Paul Getty Museum Journal* 18 (1990), 141–56.

Hiskey 1997
Christine Hiskey. "The Building of Holkham Hall: Newly Discovered Letters." *Architectural History* 40 (1997), 144–48.

Houston 1958
The Guardi Family. Museum of Fine Arts, Houston. Exh. cat. 1958. By James Byam Shaw.

Howard 1951
Catalogue of the Opening Exhibition, April 8 through June 3, 1951. Birmingham Museum of Art, Birmingham, 1951. By Richard Foster Howard.

Ingamells 1997
John Ingamells. *A Dictionary of British and Irish Travelers in Italy, 1701–1800*. New Haven and London, 1997.

Ithaca 1971
Views of Venice. Exh. cat. Andrew Dickson White Museum of Art, Cornell University, Ithaca, 1971. By J. G. Links.

J. Paul Getty Museum 1988
"Acquisitions/1987." *J. Paul Getty Museum Journal* 16 (1988).

J. Paul Getty Museum 1989
"Acquisitions/1988." *J. Paul Getty Museum Journal* 17 (1989).

J. Paul Getty Museum 1991
J. Paul Getty Museum Handbook of the Collections. Malibu, 1991.

J. Paul Getty Museum 1997
J. Paul Getty Museum Handbook of the Collections. Los Angeles, 1997.

J. Paul Getty Museum 2001
Summary Catalogue of European Decorative Arts in the J. Paul Getty Museum. Los Angeles, 2001.

Jameson 1867
Anna Brownell Jameson. *Legends of the Madonna as Represented in the Fine Arts: Forming the Third Series of Sacred and Legendary Art*. London, 1867.

Janson 1986
Anthony F. Janson. *Great Paintings from The John and Mable Ringling Museum of Art*. Sarasota, 1986.

Jeromack 2000
Paul Jeromack. "Panorama del collezionismo pubblico nell'America del Nord, 1990–1995." *Pittura italiana antica. Artisti e opere del Seicento e del Settecento*. Alessandro Morandotti, ed. Milan, 2000.

Jessen 1920
Peter Jessen. *Der Ornamentstich*. Berlin, 1920.

JOGS 2003
"Recent Important Acquisitions." *Journal of Glass Studies* 45 (2003), 207.

Jones 1981
Leslie Marion Jones. *"The Paintings of Giovanni Battista Piazzetta."* 3 vols. Ann Arbor, 1981. [Ph.D. diss., New York University, 1981]

Kisluk-Grosheide et al. 2006
Daniëlle O. Kisluk-Grosheide, Wolfram Koeppe, and William Rieder. *Highlights of the European Furniture Collection in the Metropolitan Museum of Art*. New Haven, 2006.

Knox 1968
George Knox. "G. B. Tiepolo and the Ceiling of the Scalzi." *Burlington Magazine* 110, no. 784 (1968), 394–403.

Knox 1992
__________. *Giambattista Piazzetta 1682–1754*. Oxford, 1992.

Knox 1995
John Knox. *Antonio Pellegrini, 1675–1741*. Oxford, 1995.

Kozakiewicz 1972
Stefan Kozakiewicz. *Bernardo Bellotto*. Greenwich, 1972.

Kühlenthal 2000
Michael Kühlenthal. *Japanische und europäische Lackarbeiten: Rezeption, Adaption, Restaurierung : Deutsch-Japanisches Forschungsprojekt zur Untersuchung und Restaurierung historischer Lacke, gefördert durch das Bundesministerium für Bildung, Wissenschaft, Forschung und Technologie*. Munich, 2000.

Kurz 1952
Hilde Kurz. "Italian Models of Hogarth's Picture Stories." *Journal of the Warburg and Courtauld Institutes* 15, nos. 3–4 (1952), 136–68.

Lach and Van Kley 1993
Donald F. Lach and Edwin J. Van Kley. *Asia in the Making of Europe*. Chicago, 1993.

Lane 1973
Frederic C. Lane. *Venice: A Maritime Republic*. Baltimore and London, 1973.

Lasareff 1934
Victor Lasareff. "Francesco and Gianantonio Guardi. I.-Figure Compositions." *Burlington Magazine for Connoisseurs* 65, no. 377 (1934), 53–55, 57–59, 62–64, 66–68, 70–72.

Lawrence 1955
German and Austrian Sculpture of the Eighteenth Century. Exh cat. University of Kansas Museum of Art, Lawrence, 1955.

Levesque 1994
Catherine Levesque. *Journey through Landscape in Seventeenth-Century Holland*. University Park, 1994.

Levey 1959
Michael Levey. *Painting in XVIII Century Venice*. London, 1959.

Levey 1962
__________. "Canaletto's Fourteen Paintings and Visentini's *Prospectus Magni Canalis*." *Burlington Magazine* 104 (1962), 333–41.

Levey 1980
__________. *Painting in Eighteenth-Century Venice*. New York, 1980.

Levey 1986
__________. *Giambattista Tiepolo: His Life and Art*. New Haven and London, 1986.

Levey 1994
__________. *Painting in Eighteenth-Century Venice*.
New Haven and London, 1994.

Levy 1967
Saul Levy. *Lacche veneziane settecentesche*. 2 vols. Milan, 1967.

Levy 1996
__________. *Il mobile veneziano del settecento*. Milan, 1996.

Lewis 1979
C. Douglas Lewis. *The Late Baroque Churches of Venice*.
New York and London, 1979.

Links 1967
J. G. Links. "The View Paintings Return to Venice."
Burlington Magazine 109, no. 773 (1967), 453–58.

Links 1971
__________. *Views of Venice by Canaletto, Engraved by
Antonio Visentini*. New York, 1971.

Links 1977
__________. *Canaletto and His Patrons*. New York, 1977.

Links 1981
__________. *Canaletto: Every Painting*. New York, 1981.

Links 1982
__________. *Canaletto*. Ithaca, 1982.

Links 1998
__________. *A Supplement to W. G. Constable's Canaletto:
Giovanni Antonio Canal, 1697–1768*. London, 1998.

Lipschultz 1988
Sandra LaWall Lipschultz. *Selected Works: The Minneapolis
Institute of Arts*. Minneapolis, 1988.

Lloyd 1971
Joan Barclay Lloyd. *African Animals in Renaissance Literature and
Art*. Oxford, 1971.

London 1950
Paintings and Silver from Woburn Abbey. Exh. cat. Royal
Academy, London, 1950.

London 1951
Eighteenth-Century Venice. Exh cat. Whitechapel Art Gallery,
London, 1951

London 1954
European Masters of the Eighteenth Century. Exh. cat. Royal
Academy of Arts, London 1954.

London 1957
*European Pictures from an English County: In Aid of the British
Red Cross Society, Hampshire Branch*. Exh. cat. Thomas Agnew
and Sons, London, 1957.

London 1970
Italian Drawings from the Ashmolean Museum. Exh. cat.
Wildenstein Gallery, London, 1970. By Denys Sutton.

London 1978
Works by Sebastiano Ricci from British Collections. Exh. cat.
Colnaghi and Company, London, 1978. By Terence Mullaly.

London 1981
Canaletto: Paintings and Drawings. Exh. cat. Queen's Gallery,
Buckingham Palace, London, 1981.

London 1982
Second Sight. Exh. cat. National Gallery, London, 1982.
By Michael Helston.

London 1990
Venetian Baroque and Rococo Paintings. Walpole Gallery,
London, 1990.

London 1993
*A King's Purchase: King George III and the Collection of Consul
Smith*. Exh. cat. Queen's Gallery, Buckingham Palace,
London, 1993.

London and Washington, D.C. 1994
The Glory of Venice: Art in the Eighteenth Century. Exh. cat.
Royal Academy of Arts, London, and National Gallery of Art,
Washington, D.C., 1994. By Jane Martineau and Andrew
Robison.

London et al. 1998
Venice Through Canaletto's Eyes. National Gallery, London; York
City Art Gallery, York; and Glynn Vivian Art Gallery, Swansea,
1998. By David Bomford and Gabriele Finaldi.

Longstreet and Carter 1935
Gilbert Wendel Longstreet and Morris Carter. *General Catalogue:
The Isabella Stewart Gardner Museum*, Fenway Court. Boston,
1935.

Los Angeles 2005
For Your Approval: Oil Sketches by Tiepolo. Exh. cat. J. Paul Getty
Museum, Los Angeles, 2005. By Jon L. Seydl.

Los Angeles et al. 1968
*Image and Imagination. Oil Sketches of the Baroque: Collection
of Kurt Rossacher*. Exh. cat. Los Angeles County Museum of
Art; Nelson Gallery-Atkins Museum, Kansas City; and Toledo
Museum of Art, 1968.

Louisville 1948
A Gallery of Eighteenth Century Venetian Paintings.
J. B. Speed Art Museum, Louisville, 1948.

Macquoid 1904–8
Percy Macquoid. *A History of English Furniture, vol. 4*.
London, 1904–8.

Madrid 2001
Canaletto: "Una" Venezia Imaginaria. Exh. cat. Museo
Thyssen-Bornemisza, Madrid, 2001. By Dario Succi
and Annalia Delneri.

Mahon 1967
Dennis Mahon. "The Brothers at the Mostra dei Guardi . . ."
*Problemi guardeschi: Convegno di studi promosso dalla Mostra dei
Guardi*. Venice, 1967.

Mann 1997
Judith Walker Mann. "Baroque into Rococo: Seventeenth and
Eighteenth Century Italian Paintings." *Saint Louis Art Museum
Bulletin* 22, no. 2 (Winter 1997), 53–62.

Manning 1980
Bertina Suida Manning. "A Panorama of Italian Painting."
Apollo 111 (March 1980), 193–94.

Manning 1961
Robert Manning. *Venetian Paintings of the Eighteenth Century.*
New York, 1961.

March 1911
Earl of March. *A Duke and His Friends.* 2 vols. London, 1911.

Mariette 1851–60
Pierre Jean Mariette. *Abécédario.* Philippe de Chennevières and
Antone de Montaiglon, eds., Paris, 1851–60.

Mariuz and Pallucchini 1982
Adriano Mariuz and Rodolfo Pallucchini. *L'opera completa del
Piazzetta.* Milan, 1982.

Martini 1964
Egidio Martini. *La pittura veneziana del settecento.*
Venice, 1964.

Martini 1982
__________. *La pintura del Settecento Veneto.* Udine, 1982.

Martorelli 1732–33
Pietro Valerio Martorelli. *Teatro storico della Santa Casas
nazarena.* Rome, 1732–33.

Maser 1970
Edward A. Maser, ed. *Classical Ornament of the Eighteenth
Century. Designed and Engraved by Michelangelo Pergolesi.*
New York, 1970.

Mazza 1976
Barbara Mazza. "Le vicenda dei 'Tombeaux des Princes': Matrici,
storia e fortuna della serie Siny tra Bologna e Venezia." *Saggi e
memorie di storia dell'arte* (Fondazione Giorgio Cini, Venice) 10
(1976), 79–102, 141–51.

Mazzarotto 1980
Bianca Tamassia Mazzarotto. *Le feste veneziane: i giochi popolari,
cerimonie religiose e di governo.* Florence, 1980.

Melegati 1998
Luca Melegati. *Giovanni Vezzi e le sue porcellane.* Milan, 1998.

Memphis 1984
*Painting and Sculpture Collection: Memphis Brooks Museum of
Art.* Memphis, 1984.

Memphis 2004
Collection Highlights from the Memphis Brooks Museum of Art.
Memphis, 2004.

Memphis and Lexington 1965
Sebastiano and Marco Ricci. Exh. cat. Brooks Memorial Art
Gallery, Memphis, and University of Kentucky Art Gallery,
Lexington, 1965. By Michael Milkovich.

Merling 2002
Mitchell Merling. *Ringling: The Art Museum.* Sarasota, 2002.

Metropolitan Museum of Art 1999
Metropolitan Museum of Art. *Recent Acquisitions: A Selection,
1998–1999.* New York, 1999

Miami Beach 1953
Old Masters from the Ringling Collection. Exh cat. Miami Beach
Art Center, Miami Beach, 1953.

Minneapolis Institute of Arts 1970a
*Catalogue of European Paintings in the Minneapolis Institute
of Arts.* Minneapolis, 1970.

Minneapolis Institute of Arts 1970b
A Guide to the Galleries: The Minneapolis Institute of Arts.
Minneapolis, 1970.

Molfino 1976
Alessandra Mottola Molfino. *L'Arte della porcellana in Italia.*
Milan, 1976.

Morassi 1929
Antonio Morassi. "Francesco Guardi as a Figure Painter."
Burlington Magazine 55, no. 321 (1929), 293–95, 298–99.

Morassi 1950
__________. "Settecento inedito (II). VIII. Quattro 'Ville' del
Guardi." *Arte Veneta* 4 (1950), 85–98.

Morassi 1951
__________. "Conclusione su A. e F. Guadri." *Emporium* 114
(1951): 212, 215–16.

Morassi 1953a
__________. *Una Mostra del Settecento Veneziano à Detroit.*
Venice, 1953.

Morassi 1953b
__________. "A Signed Drawing by Antonio Guardi and the
Problem of the Guardi Brothers." *Burlington Magazine* 95, no.
605 (1953), 260–67.

Morassi 1960
__________. "Aggiunta al Guardie: Le cinque 'Storie' delle
Gerusalemme liberata." *Emporium* 131 (1960), 247–56.

Morassi 1962
__________. *A Complete Catalogue of the Paintings of G. B.
Tiepolo, Including Pictures by His Pupils and Followers Wrongly
Attributed to Him.* London, 1962.

Morassi 1973
__________. *Guardi. Antonio e Francesco Guardi.* Venice, 1973.

Morassi 1975
__________. *Guardi, Tutti I desegni di Antonio, Francesco,
e Giacomo Guardi.* Venice, 1975.

Morassi 1984
__________. *Guardi. I dipinti.* Milan, 1984. [2nd edition]

Morazzoni 1927
Giuseppe Morazzoni. *Il Mobile Veneziano del '700.*
Milan, 1927.

Morazzoni 1931
__________. *La moda a Venezia nel secolo XVIII.* Milan, 1931.

Morse 1979
John D. Morse. *Old Master Paintings in North America: Over
3000 Masterpieces by 50 Great Artists.* New York, 1979.

Moschini 1952
Vittorio Moschini. *Francesco Guardi*. Milan, 1952.

Moschini 1954
__________. *Canaletto*. Milan, 1954.

Moschini 1956a
__________. *Francesco Guardi*. Milan, 1956.

Moschini 1956b
__________. *Pietro Longhi*. Milan, 1956.

Mras 1956
George P. Mras. "Some Drawings by G. B. Tiepolo." *Record of the Art Museum, Princeton University* 25 (1956), 41–44.

Munich 1931
Ausstellung Altvenezianischer Malerei: München. Exh. cat. Julius Böhler. Munich, 1931.

Muraro 1958
Michelangelo Muraro. "An Altar-Piece and Other Figure Paintings by Francesco Guardi." *Burlington Magazine* 100, no. 658 (1958), 3–10, 13.

Muraro 1960
__________. "The Guardi Problem and the Statutes of the Venetian Guilds." *Burlington Magazine* 102, no. 691 (1960), 420–29.

Murray 1951
Marian Murray. *The Ringling Museums: a Magnificent Gift to the State of Florida*. Sarasota, 1951.

Museums, Libraries, and Archives Council 2008
Museums, Libraries, and Archives Council. *Acceptance in Lieu Report, 2007/2008*. London, 2008.

Neale 1820
J. P. Neale. *Views of the Seats of Noblemen and Gentlemen*. London, 1820.

da Nembro 1958
Padre Metodio da Nembro, OFM Cap. "Note sulla sacra predicazione in Italia nel Settecento." *L'Italia francescana* 33 (1958), 117–30.

New Haven and London 2006
Canaletto in England: A Venetian Artist Abroad, 1746–1755. Exh. cat. Yale Center for British Art, New Haven, and Dulwich Picture Gallery, London, 2006. Edited by Charles Beddington.

New Orleans 1966
The Samuel H. Kress Collection. New Orleans Museum of Art, New Orleans, 1966.

New Orleans 1980
Handbook of the Collection. New Orleans Museum of Art, New Orleans, 1980.

New York 1929
Medieval and Renaissance Art: Paintings, Sculpture, Armor and a Few Pieces of Furniture from the Federico Spitzer Collection. Exh. cat. Anderson Galleries, New York, 1929.

New York 1940
Masterpieces of Art: Catalogue of European and American Paintings, 1500–1900. Exh. cat. New York World's Fair, New York, 1940. By Walter Pach, Christopher Lazare, Anne A. Wallis, Marion Haviland, and Simonetta de Vries.

New York 1971
Drawings from New York Collections III: The Eighteenth Century in Italy. Exh. cat. Metropolitan Museum of Art, New York, 1971. By Jacob Bean and Felice Stempfle.

New York 1989
Canaletto. Exh. cat. Metropolitan Museum of Art, New York, 1989. By Katharine Baetjer and J. G. Links.

New York 1994
A Gift to America: Masterpieces of European Painting from the Samuel H. Kress Collection, New York, 1994

New York 1996
Giambattista Tiepolo, 1669–1770. Exh. cat. Metropolitan Museum of Art, New York, 1996. Edited by Keith Christiansen.

New York and Palm Beach 1957
Painting and Sculpture from the Minneapolis Institute of Arts. Exh. cat. Knoedler Galleries, New York, and the Society of the Four Arts, Palm Beach, 1957.

New York and Tampa 1981
Masterworks from The John and Mable Ringling Museum of Art. Exh. cat. Wildenstein Gallery, New York, and the Tampa Museum, Tampa, 1981. By Denys Sutton.

Nickel 2002
Helmut Nickel. "Miss America's Brother and His Club." *Metropolitan Museum Journal* 37 (2002), 83–88.

Nicoletti 1890
G. Nicoletti. "Lista di nomi d'artisti tolta dei libri di tanse o liminarie delle Fraglie dei Pittori." *Ateneo Veneto* (1890), 33.

Nicolson 1950
Benedict Nicolson. "Mannerism at the Arcade Gallery." *Burlington Magazine* 92, no. 568 (1950), 203–5.

Nicolson 1965
__________. "The Guardi Brothers as Figure Painters." *Burlington Magazine* 107, no. 750 (1965), 470–72.

Niero and Rugolo 2006
Antonio Niero and Ruggero Rugolo, eds. *Tre artisti per un tempio: Santa Maria del Rosario—Gesuati, Venezia*. Venice, 2006.

Northampton 1965
Chinoiserie. Exh. cat. Smith College Museum of Art, Northampton, 1965. By Hugh Honour and Nelly Schargo Hoyt.

Norwich 1982
John Julius Norwich. *A History of Venice*. New York, 1982.

Norwich 1985
Norfolk and the Grand Tour: Eighteenth-Century Travelers Abroad and Their Souvenirs. Exh. cat. Norwich Castle Museum, Norwich, 1985. By Andrew W. Moore.

Omaha et al. 1997
Hot Dry Men, Cold Wet Women: The Theories of Humors in Western European Art, 1575–1700. Exh. cat. Joslyn Art Museum, Omaha; Arkansas Arts Center, Little Rock; and The John and

Mable Ringling Museum of Art, Sarasota, 1997. By Zirka Z. Filipzcak.

Orlandi 1753
Pellegrino Antonio Orlandi. *Abecedario pittorico*. Venice, 1753.

Osti 1950
Cornelia Osti. "Sebastiano Ricci in Inghilterra." *Commentari* 2 (1950), 119–23.

Ovid 2004
Ovid. *Metamorphoses*. A. S. Kline, ed. Ann Arbor, 2004. [Revised edition]

Padua 1994
Luca Carlevarijs e la veduta veneziana del Settecento. Exh. cat. Palazzo della Ragione, Padua, 1994. By Isabella Reale and Dario Succi.

Pagaro 2006
Roberto Pagaro. *Alessandro and Domenico Scarlatti: Two Lives in One*. Hillsdale, 2006.

Pallucchini 1968
Anna Pallucchini. *L'Opera completa di Giambattista Tiepolo*. Milan, 1968.

Pallucchini 1942a
Rodolfo Pallucchini. *Giovanni Battista Piazzetta*, 1942. [2nd edition]

Pallucchini 1942b
__________. "Unbekannte Werke Piazzettas." *Pantheon* 29 (1942), 49–55.

Pallucchini 1943a
__________. *I disegni del Guardi al Museo Correr di Venezia*. Venice, 1943.

Pallucchini 1943b
__________. *Guardis Zeichnungen im Museum Correr zu Venedig*. Venice, 1943.

Palluchini 1952
__________. "Studi Ricceschi Iº Contributo a Marco." *Arte Veneta* 9 (1952), 63–84.

Pallucchini 1956
__________. *Piazzetta*. Milan, 1956

Pallucchini 1960
__________. *La pittura veneziana del Settecento*. Venice, 1960.

Pallucchini 1965
__________. "Note all mostra dei Guardi." *Arte Veneta* 19 (1965), 215–37.

Pallucchini 1981
__________. *La pittura veneziana del Seicento*. Venice, 1981.

Pallucchini 1995
__________. *La pittura nel Veneto: Il Settecento*. 2 vols. Milan, 1995.

Paris 1956
Le cabinet de l'amateur organisé par la Société des Amis du Louvre en souvenir de M.A.S. Henraux . . . février–avril 1956. Exh. cat. Orangerie des Tuileries, Paris, 1956.

Parker 1956
K. T. Parker. *Catalogue of the Collection of Drawings in the Ashmolean Museum, vol. II: Italian Schools*. Oxford, 1956.

Paulson 1975a
Ronald Paulson. "Types of Demarcation: Townscape and Landscape Painting." *Eighteenth-Century Studies* 8, no. 3 (Spring 1975), 337–54.

Paulson 1975b
__________. *Emblem and Expression: Meaning in English Art of the Eighteenth Century*. Cambridge, Mass., 1975.

Pavanello 2008
Giuseppe Pavanello. *Canaletto: Venezia e i suoi splendori*. Venice, 2008.

Pedrocco 1992
Filippo Pedrocco. *Antonio Guardi*. Milan, 1992.

Pedrocco 2002
__________. *Venetian Views*. New York, 2002.

Philadelphia 1994
Paintings from Europe and the Americas in the Philadelphia Museum of Art: A Concise Catalogue. Philadelphia Museum of Art, 1994.

Pignatti 1968
Terisio Pignatti. *Pietro Longhi*. Milan, 1968.

Pignatti 1969
__________. *Pietro Longhi: Paintings and Drawings: Complete Edition*. London, 1969.

Pignatti 1972
__________. "Aggiunte per Pietro Longhi." *Arte Illustrata* 47 (January 1972), 156–59.

Pignatti 1974
__________. *L'opera completa di Pietro Longhi*. Milan, 1974.

Pignatti 1985
__________. *Five centuries of Italian painting: 1300–1800; from the collection of the Sarah Campbell Blaffer Foundation*. Houston, 1985.

Pignatti 1987
__________. "Risveglio della dama di Pietro Longhi." *Bolletino dei Musei Civici Veneziani* 31 (1987), 87–90.

Pilo 1966
Giuseppe Maria Pilo. "Sebastiano and Marco Ricci in America." *Arte Veneta* 20 (1966), 304–5.

Pilo 1976
__________. *Sebastiano Ricci e la pintura veneziana del settecento*. Pordenone, 1976.

Pittsfield 1960
Canaletto and Bellotto. Exh. cat. Berkshire Museum, Pittsfield, 1960. By Stuart C. Henry.

Pollak 1932
Ludovico Pollak, ed. *Collezioni Simonetti: quadri, mobili e oggetti d'arte*. Rome, 1932.

Posner 1971
Donald Posner. *Annibale Carracci: A Study in the Reform of Italian Painting around 1590*. 2 vols. London, 1971.

Povoledo 1951
E. Povoledo. "La scenografia architettonica del Settecento a Venezia." *Arte Veneta* 52, no. 7 (1951), 126–30.

Precerutti-Garberi 1971
Mercedes Precerutti-Garberi. *Frescoes from Italian Villas*. New York, 1971.

Préclin and Jarry 1955–56
Edmond Préclin and Eugène Jarry. *Les luttes politiques et doctrinales aux XVIIe et XVIIIe siècles*. Paris, 1955–56.

Princeton 1980
Italian Baroque Paintings from New York Private Collections. Exh. cat. Art Museum, Princeton University, Princeton, 1980. By John T. Spike.

Puppi 1968
Lionello Puppi. *The Complete Paintings of Canaletto*. New York, 1968.

Puppi 1970
__________. *The Complete Paintings of Canaletto*. London, 1970.

Ragghianti 1953
L. Collobi Ragghianti. "Epiloghi guardeschi." *Annali della Scuola Normale Superiore di Pisa* 2, no. 22 (1953), 6, 9, 10–13, 22–23, 27, 35, 37.

Ragghianti 1967
__________. "Situazione dei Guardi." *Problemi guardeschi: Convegno di studi promosso dalla Mostra dei Guardi*. Venice, 1967.

Raleigh et al. 1994
A Gift to America: Masterpieces of European Painting from the Samuel H. Kress Collection. Exh. cat. North Carolina Museum of Art, Raleigh; Museum of Fine Arts, Houston; Seattle Art Museum, Seattle; and the Fine Arts Museums of San Francisco, 1994. By Chiyo Ishikawa, Marilyn Perry, and Edgar Peters Bowron.

Rasmo 1967
Nicolò Rasmo. "Osservazioni e proposte sulla formazione pittorica dei Guardi." *Problemi guardeschi: Convegno di studi promosso dalla Mostra dei Guardi*. Venice, 1967.

Reato 1988
Danilo Reato. *Le maschere veneziane*. Venice, 1988.

Redford 1996
Bruce Redford. *Venice and the Grand Tour*. Princeton, 1996.

Richardson and Grigaut 1953
E. P. Richardson and Paul L. Grigaut, eds. "Accessions of American and Canadian Museums." *Art Quarterly* (1953), 248–58.

Ripa 1645
Cesare Ripa. *Iconologia*. Giovanni Zaratino Castellini, ed., Venice, 1645.

Ripa 1709
__________. *Iconologia*. P. Tempest, ed., London, 1709.

Rizzi 1963
Aldo Rizzi. "Contributo alla conoscenza del primo Carlevarijs." *Emporium* 87, no. 821 (May 1963), 201–9.

Rizzi 1967
__________. *Luca Carlevarijs*. Venice, 1967.

Rizzi 1989
__________. *Sebastiano Ricci*. Milan, 1989.

Rogers 1939
Meyric R. Rogers. "Il ridotto by Pietro Longhi (1702–1785)." *Bulletin of the City Art Museum of Saint Louis* (1939), 43–47.

Rollin 1839
Charles Rollin. *The Ancient History of the Egyptians, Carthaginians, Assyrians, Babylonians, Medes and Persians, Grecians, and Macedonians: Including a History of the Arts and Sciences of the Ancients*. New York, 1839.

Rome and Venice 2002
Gaspare Vanvitelli e le origini del vedutismo. Exh. cat. Chiostro del Bramante, Rome, and Museo Correr, Venice, 2002. By Fabio Benzi and Claudio Strinati.

Ross 1993
Nicholas Ross. *Canaletto*. London, 1993.

Rowan 1988
Alistair Rowan. *Robert Adam*. London, 1988.

Russell 2001
Francis Russell. "Canaletto and Bellotto. Venice and Houston." *Burlington Magazine* 143, no. 1183 (2001), 654–57.

Sack 1910
Eduard Sack. *Giambattista und Domenico Tiepolo, ihr Leben und ihre Werke; ein Beitrag zur Kunstgeschichte des achtzehnten Jahrhunderts*. Hamburg, 1910.

St. Louis 1944
Handbook of the Collections: The City Art Museum of Saint Louis. City Art Museum of St. Louis, St. Louis, 1944.

St. Louis 1953
Handbook of the Collections: The City Art Museum of Saint Louis. City Art Museum of St. Louis, St. Louis, 1953.

St. Louis 1972
Venice in Saint Louis. Exh. cat. City Art Museum of Saint Louis, St. Louis, 1972. By Nancy W. Neilson.

St. Louis 1975
Handbook of the Collections: The City Art Museum of Saint Louis. City Art Museum of Saint Louis, St. Louis, 1975.

Salzburger Residenzgalerie 1975
Salzburger Residenzgalerie mit Sammlung Schonborn-Buchheim, Salzburger Residenzgalerie, Salzburg, 1975.

San Francisco 1960
Handbook of the Collections. California Palace of the Legion of Honor, San Francisco, 1960.

San Francisco 1964
Man, Glory, Jest, and Riddle. Exh. cat. California Palace
of the Legion of Honor, San Francisco, 1964.

Santa Barbara 1958
Guardi in America. Exh. cat. Santa Barbara Museum of Art,
Santa Barbara, 1958.

Santifaller 1974
Maria Santifaller. "Le Soprapporte dei Tiepolo nel Palazzo
Canossa di Verona." *Arte Veneta* 28 (1974), 283–84.

Santifaller 1975
__________. "Die Gruppe mit die Pyramid in Giambattista
Tiepolos Treppenhausfresko der Residenz zu Würzburg."
Münchner Jahrbuch für Bildende Kunst (1975), 193–207.

Santifaller 1976
__________. "Giandomenico Tiepolos 'Hl. Joseph mit dem
Jesuskind' in der Staatsgalerie Stuttgart und seine Stellung
in der Ikonographie des Barock." *Jahrbuch der Staatlichen
Kunstsammlungen in Baden-Württemberg* 13 (1976), 65–86.

Santini 2002
Clara Santini. *Mille mobili veneti: L'arredo domestico in
Veneto dal sec. XV al sec. XIX*. 3 vols. Venice and Milan, 2002.

Sarasota 1953
The Artful Rococo. Exh. cat. John and Mable Ringling
Museum of Art, Sarasota, 1953.

Sarasota 1972
Central Europe 1600–1800. Exh. cat. John and Mable
Ringling Museum of Art, Sarasota, 1972. By Kent Sobotik.

Sarasota 1979
*The Arts of Europe: 1600–1780: Painting and Decorative Arts
from the Ringling Museums*. Exh. cat. John and Mable
Ringling Museum of Art, Sarasota, 1979. By Cynthia Duval
and David Butler.

Sarasota 1982
500 Years of Decorative Arts from the Ringling Collections.
Exh. cat. John and Mable Ringling Museum of Art,
Sarasota, 1982. By Cynthia Duval.

Scarpa 1991
Annalisa Scarpa. *Marco Ricci*, Milan, 1991.

Scarpa 2006
__________. *Sebastiano Ricci*. Milan, 2006.

Scharf 1890
George Scharf. *A Descriptive and Historical Catalogue of the
Collection of Pictures at Woburn Abbey*. London, 1890.

Schiller 1966
Gertrud Schiller. *Ikonographie der christlichen Kunst Inkarnation,
Kindheit, Taufe, Versuchung, Verklarung, Wirken und Wunder
Christi*. Gutersloh, 1966.

Schmidt 1974
Volkmar Schmidt. "Zu Tiepolos Asien-Darstellung in
Würzburg." *Zeitschrift für Kunstgeschichte* 37, no. 1 (1974),
52–62.

Scirè 1991
Giovanna Nepi Scirè. *Treasures of Venetian Painting.
The Gallerie dell'Accademia*. London, 1991.

Scott-Elliot 1959
A. H. Scott-Elliot. "The Statues from Mantua in the Collection
of King Charles I." *Burlington Magazine* 101, no. 675 (1959),
214, 218–227.

Selvig 1963
Lawrence Selvig, ed. *European Paintings from the Minneapolis
Institute of Arts*. Minneapolis, 1963.

Sgarbi 1982
Vittorio Sgarbi. *Pietro Longhi: The Paintings in the Palazzo Leoni
Montanari*. Venice, 1982

Shapley 1961
Fern Rusk Shapley. *The Samuel H. Kress Collection*. El Paso,
1961.

Shapley 1973
__________. *Paintings from the Samuel H. Kress Collection:
Italian Schools XVI–XVIII Century*. London and New York,
1973.

Shapley 1979
__________. *Catalogue of the Italian Paintings*. 2 vols. National
Gallery of Art, Washington, D.C., 1979.

Shefer 1991
Elaine Shefer. "The 'Bird in the Cage' in the History of
Sexuality: Sir John Everett Millais and William Holman Hunt."
Journal of the History of Sexuality 1, no. 3 (January 1991),
446–80.

Shore 1980
Leslie Shore, ed. *Small Paintings of the Masters: Masterpieces
Reproduced in Actual Size*. New York, 1980.

Silva 1997
Tullio and Lucia Silva. *Lacche veneziane del Settecento, vol. 1*.
Milan, 1997

Simon 1907
Constance Simon. *English Furniture Designers of the 18th
Century*. London, 1907.

Sinding-Larsen 1962
Staale Sinding-Larsen. "Four Paintings by the Guardis in Oslo . . ."
Acta (Institutione Romanum Norvegiae) 1 (1962), 183–85.

Sinding-Larsen 1967
__________. "L'Elemento paesistico in opera figurative dei
Guardi." *Problemi guardeschi: Convegno di studi promosso dalla
Mostra dei Guardi*. Venice, 1967.

Smekens 1973
Frans Smekens. "Giovanni Antonio Pellegrini (1675–1741)."
Antwerpen: Tijdschrifte der Stad Antwerpen (July 1973), 74–78.

Stazzi 1967
Francesco Stazzi. *Porcellana della Casa Vezzi*. Munich, 1967

Stazzi 1982
__________. *Le porcellane veneziane di Geminiano e Vincenzo
Cozzi*. Venice, 1982.

Straus 1912
Ralph Straus. *Carriages and Coaches: Their History and Their Evolution*. Philadelphia, 1912.

Succi 1993
Dario Succi. *Francesco Guardi. Itinerario dell'avventura artística*. Cinisello Balsamo, 1993.

Suida 1949
William E. Suida. *Catalogue of Paintings: The John and Mable Ringling Museum of Art*. Sarasota, 1949.

Suida 1950
__________. "The Samuel H. Kress Collection." *Philadelphia Museum of Art Bulletin*, 46, no. 227 (1950).

Suida 1953
__________. *The Samuel H. Kress Collection in the Isaac Delgado Museum of Art*. New Orleans, 1953.

Suida 1954
__________. Art of the Italian Renaissance from the Samuel H. Kress Collection: *Catalogue for the Columbia Museum of Art*. Columbia, 1954.

Suida 1958a
__________. *The Samuel H. Kress Collection: Brooks Memorial Art Gallery*. Memphis, 1958.

Suida 1958b
__________. *Italian Paintings and Northern Sculpture from the Samuel H. Kress Collection*. Atlanta, 1958.

Suida 1965
__________. *Masterpieces in the High Museum of Art*. Atlanta, 1965.

Suida 1966
__________. *The Samuel H. Kress Collection*. New Orleans, 1966.

Suida and Davis 1966
Wilhelm Suida and Mary M. Davis. *The Samuel H. Kress Collection*. Memphis, 1966.

Sutton 1985
Julia Sutton. "The Minuet: An Elegant Phoenix." *Dance Chronicle* 8, no. 3–4 (1985), 119–52.

Tallahassee 1951
Masterpieces from the Ringling Museum of Art. Exh cat. Florida State University Art Museum, Tallahassee, 1951.

Terpitz 1998
Dorothea Terpitz. *Giovanni Antonio Canal, Known as Canaletto: 1697–1768*. Cologne, 1998.

Thieme and Becker 1907
Ulrich Thieme and Felix Becker, eds. *Allgemeines Lexikon der bildenden Kunstler*. Leipzig, 1907.

Thomas 1954
Hylton A. Thomas. "Review: The Drawings of Francesco Guardi by J. Byam Shaw." *Art Bulletin* 36, no. 2 (1954), 158–60.

Thomas 1957
__________. "View of the Grand Canal by F. Guardi." *Minneapolis Institute of Arts Bulletin* 46, no. 4 (Winter 1957), 53–65.

Tietze 1940
Hans Tietze. "Venetian Painting at Toledo." *Parnassus* 12, no. 3 (1940), 22–25.

Tivaroni 1888
Carlo Tivaroni. *L'Italia prima della rivoluzione francese, 1753–1789*. Turin and Naples, 1888.

Tomory 1976
Peter Tomory. *The Italian Paintings before 1800*. Sarasota, 1976.

Toronto et al. 1964
Canaletto: Giovanni Antonio Canal, 1697–1768. Exh. cat. Art Gallery of Toronto; National Gallery of Canada, Ottawa; and the Montréal Museum of Fine Arts, 1964. By W. G. Constable.

Turin 2008
Canaletto e Bellotto. Exh. cat. Palazzo Bricherasio, Turin, 2008. By Bożena Anna Kowalczyk.

Twickenham 1974
English Baroque Sketches. Exh. cat. Marble Hill House, Twickenham, England, 1974. By John Simon.

Udine 1971
Mostra del Tiepolo dipinti. Exh. cat. Villa Manin di Passariano, Udine, 1971. By Aldo Rizzi.

Udine 1995
Luca Carlevarijs: Le fabriche, e vedute di Venezia. Soprintendenza BAAAAS Friuli-Venezia Giulia, Udine, 1995. By Isabella Reale.

Udine and Rome 1963
Disegni, incisioni e bozzetti del Carlevarijs. Exh. cat. Loggia del Lionello, Udine and Gabinetto Nazionale delle Stampe, Rome, 1963. By Aldo Rizzi.

Veit 1976
L. Veit. "Der Königskopf mit der Stirnbinde auf Münzen und Siegeln der Stauferzeit und des augsehenden Mittelalters. Ein Herrschaftszeichen und heraldisches Symbol." *Anzeiger des Geramnischen Nationalmuseums* (1976), 22–30.

Venice 1929
Il Settecento Italiano. Exh. cat. Palazzo della Biennale, Venice, 1929.

Venice 1951
Mostra del Tiepolo. Exh. cat. Unknown venue, Venice, 1951. By Giulio Lorenzetti.

Venice 1965
Mostra dei Guardi. Exh. cat. Palazzo Grassi, Venice, 1965. By Pietro Zampetti.

Venice 1969
Dal Ricci al Tiepolo: I pittori di figura del settecento a Venezia. Exh. cat. Palazzo Ducale, Venice, 1969. By Pietro Zampetti.

Venice 1982
Canaletto: disegni, dipinti, incisioni. Exh. cat. Fondazione Giorgio Cini, Venice 1982. By Alessandro Bettagno.

Venice 1986
Canaletto e Visentini: Venezia e Londra. Exh. cat. Cà Pesaro, Galleria Internazionale d'Arte Moderna, Venice, 1986. By Dario Succi.

Venice 1993
Pietro Longhi. Exh. cat. Museo Correr, Venice, 1993.
By Adriano Mariuz, Giuseppe Pavanello, and
Giandomenico Romanelli.

Venice 1995
Pietro Longhi, Gabriel Bella: scene di vita veneziana. Exh.
cat. Palazzo Grassi, Venice, and Palazzo Aperto, Venice, 1995.
By Giorgio Busetto.

Venice 2001
Canaletto: Prima Maniera. Exh. cat. Fondazione Giorgio
Cini, Venice, 2001. By Bożena Anna Kowalczyk.

Venice and Houston 2001
Bernardo Bellotto and the Capitals of Europe. Exh. cat. Museo
Correr, Venice, and Museum of Fine Arts, Houston, 2001.
By Irina Artemieva and Edgar Peters Bowron.

Venice and New York 1996
Giambattista Tiepolo, 1696–1770. Exh. cat. Museo del
Settecento Veneziano di Ca' Rezzonico, Venice, and the
Metropolitan Museum of Art, New York, 1996.
Edited by Keith Christiansen.

Verona 1990
Bernardo Bellotto: Verona e le cittá europee. Exh cat.
Museo di Castelvecchio, Verona, 1990. By Sergio Marinelli
and Gisela Barche.

Vienna 2005
Giovanni Giuliani, 1665–1744. Exh. cat. Liechtenstein
Museum, Vienna, 2005. By Luigi A. Ronzoni.

Vilas 1942
Curtis N. and Naomi R. Vilas. *A Guide to the Collection:
The John and Mable Ringling Museum of Art.* Chicago, 1942.

Vivian 1962
Frances Vivian. "Joseph Smith and Giovanni Antonio
Pellegrini." *Burlington Magazine* 104, no. 713 (1962),
328, 330–333.

Vivian 1971
__________. *Il console Smith: mercante e collezionista.*
Vicenza, 1971.

Walsh and Gribbon 1997
John Walsh and Deborah Gribbon. *The J. Paul Getty Museum
and Its Collections: A Museum for the New Century.*
Los Angeles, 1997.

Walters 1909
W. T. Walters. *The Walters Collection.* Baltimore, 1909.

Walters 1922
__________. *The Walters Collection.* Baltimore, 1922.

Walters 1929
__________. *The Walters Collection.* Baltimore, 1929.

Wardropper and Roberts 1991
Ian Wardropper and Lynn Springer Roberts. *European Decorative
Arts in the Art Institute Chicago.* Chicago, 1991.

Washington, D.C. 1941
Preliminary Catalogue of Paintings and Sculpture. National
Gallery of Art, Washington, D.C., 1941.

Washington, D.C. 1959
*Paintings and Sculpture from the Samuel H. Kress Collection.
National Gallery of Art, Washington.* National Gallery of Art,
Washington, D.C., 1959.

Washington, D.C. 1961
Art Treasures for America. National Gallery of Art, Washington,
D.C., 1961.

Washington, D.C. 1965
Summary Catalogue of European Paintings and Sculpture.
National Gallery of Art, Washington, D.C., 1965.

Washington, D.C. 1968
European Paintings and Sculpture, Illustrations. National Gallery
of Art, Washington, D.C., 1968.

Washington, D.C. 1975
European Paintings: An Illustrated Summary Catalogue. National
Gallery of Art, Washington, D.C., 1975.

Washington, D.C. 1985
European Paintings: An Illustrated Summary Catalogue. National
Gallery of Art, Washington, D.C., 1985.

Washington, D.C. 1986
*Baroque Paintings from The John and Mable Ringling Museum of
Art.* Exh. cat. National Gallery of Art, Washington, D.C., 1986.

Watson 1952
F. J. B. Watson. "Reflections on the Tiepolo Exhibition."
Burlington Magazine 94, no. 587 (1952), 40–44.

Watson 1954
__________. "English Villas and Venetian Decorators." *Journal
of the Royal Society of the Institute of British Architects* 61 (1954),
171–76.

Watson 1963
__________. "Book Reviews: G. B. Tiepolo: Pioneer of
Modernism." *Apollo* 77 (March 1963), 244–48.

Watson 1967
__________. "Guardi in England." *Problemi guardeschi: Atti del
convegno di studi promosso dalla Mostra dei Guardi.* Venice, 1967.

Wescher 1962
Paul Wescher. *Le Prima Idea. Die Entwicklung der Ölskizze
von Tintoretto bis Picasso.* Munich, 1962.

Whinney and Millar 1957
Margaret Whinney and Oliver Millar. *English Art.*
Oxford, 1957.

Whitley 1928
William Thomas Whitley. *The Baptists of London, 1612–1928.*
London, 1928.

Wollheim 1964
R. Wollheim, ed. *Hume on Religion.* Cleveland and New York,
1964

Worcester 2005
*Hope and Healing: Painting in Italy in a Time of Plague, 1500–
1800.* Exh. cat. Worcester Art Museum, Worcester,
2005. By Gauvin A. Bailey and Sheila Barker.

Wright 1992
Christopher Wright. *The World's Master Paintings: From the Early Renaissance to the Present Day*. 2 vols. London and New York, 1992.

Yerkes 1910
Charles T. Yerkes. *The C. T. Yerkes Collection of Ancient and Modern Paintings*. New York, 1910.

Zafran 1988
Eric M. Zafran. *Fifty Old Master Paintings from the Walters Art Gallery*. Baltimore, 1988.

Zampetti 1967
Pietro Zampetti. "Il Problema dei Guardi: La ricerca della verità." *Problemi guardeschi: Convegno di studi promosso dalla Mostra dei Guardi*. Venice, 1967.

Zampetti 1969
__________. "Un capolavoro del Lotto." *Arte Veneta* 2 (1957), 75–81.

Zampetti 1970
__________. *A Dictionary of Venetian Painters*. Leigh-on-Sea, 1970.

Zanetti 1733
Antonio Maria Zanetti. *Descrizione di tutte le pubbliche pitture della città di Venezia e isole circonvicine . . . .* Venice, 1733.

Zanetti 1771
__________. *Della Pittura Veneziana e delle Opere Pubbliche dei Veneziani Maestri*. Venice, 1771.

Zanotto 1989
Francesco Zanotto. *Storia della predicazione nei secoli della letteratura italiana*. Modena, 1989.

Zecchin 2004
Paolo Zecchin. "I 'deseri' di cristallo a Venezia nel Settecento." *Journal of Glass Studies* 46 (2004), 159–71.

Zeri 1966
Frederico Zeri. "The Italian Pictures: Discoveries and Problems." *Apollo* 84 (December 1966), 28.

Zeri 1976
__________. *Italian Paintings in the Walters Art Gallery*. Baltimore, 1976.

Zeri 1987
__________. *Dietro l'immagine: conversazioni sull'arte di leggere l'arte*. Milan, 1987.

Zorach 2008
Rebecca Zorach. *The Virtual Tourist in Renaissance Rome: Printing and Collecting in the Speculum Romanae Magnificentiae*. Chicago, 2008.

The Memphis Brooks Museum of Art and The John and Mable Ringling Museum of Art wish to thank the museums, galleries, and collectors that supplied us with images and granted us permission to reproduce artwork from their collections. Information regarding copyright and photography credits is listed below.

© The Art Institute of Chicago (Fig. 35.2)

Alinari / Art Resource, NY / Photo: Mauro Magliani, 1998 (Barcham, Fig. 1); Eric Lessing / Art Resource, NY (Barcham, Fig. 2; Barcham Fig. 3; Fig. 15.1); Scala / Art Resource, NY (Fig. 2.1 and Fig. 12.1); Bildarchiv Preussischer Kulturbesitz / Art Resource, NY / Photo: Jörg P. Anders (Fig. 3.1); Réunion des Musées Nationaux / Art Resource, NY / René-Gabriel Ojéda (Barcham, Fig. 5); Alinari / Art Resource, NY (Fig. 14.2); Bildarchiv Preussischer Kulturbesitz / Art Resource, NY / Photo: Roman Beniaminson (Fig. 16.1); Réunion des Musées Nationaux / Art Resource, NY (Fig. 23.1)

Blanton Museum of Art, The University of Texas at Austin, Photo: Rick Hall (Fig. 4; Fig. 10)

The Bridgeman Art Library, (Libby, Fig. 9); © Dulwich Picture Gallery, London, UK / The Bridgeman Art Library (Libby, Fig. 13)

© The Trustees of the British Museum (Fig. 4.1)

Image courtesy of the Columbia Museum of Art (Fig. 6; Fig. 31)

© 2009, Detroit Institute of Arts (Fig. 33.2)

© His Grace the Duke of Bedford and the Trustees of the Bedford Estates (Fig. 18.1)

© Fondazione Pinacoteca Giovanni e Marella Agnelli (Libby, Fig. 5; Libby, Fig. 6)

Gallerie dell' Accademia, courtesy of the Minister of Arts and Culture (Fig. 14.1)

© J. Paul Getty Trust (Fig. 36)

© The Goodwood Estate Company Limited (Libby, Fig. 10; Libby, Fig. 11)

© Isabella Stewart Gardner Museum, Boston (Fig. 37 - 41)

© 2009 Museum Associates / LACMA (Libby, Fig. 14)

© 2009 Memphis Brooks Museum of Art (Libby, Fig. 3) Photos: Murray Riss Photography (Fig. 13a-o)

© The Metropolitan Museum of Art (Fig. 32)

© Musée Fabre, Montpellier Agglomération / F. Jaulmes (Fig. 28.1)

© Museo Thyssen-Bornemisza, Madrid (Libby, Fig. 4; Thomas, Fig. 3)

© 2009 Museum of Fine Arts, Boston (Libby, Fig. 12)

National Gallery of Art, Washington, Images courtesy of the Board of Trustees, (Fig. 5; Fig. 12); Photo: Bob Grove (Barcham, Fig. 6); Photo: Philip A. Charles (Barcham, Fig. 7); Photo: Richard Carafelli (Fig. 29)

© NTPL/John Bethell (Libby, Fig. 7; Libby, Fig. 8)

Philadelphia Museum of Art, Photo: Lynn Rosenthal (Fig. 19)

© Rijksmuseum, Amsterdam (Johnson, Fig. 3)

The Royal Collection © 2009, Her Majesty Queen Elizabeth II (Johnson, Fig. 2; Thomas, Fig. 4; Fig. 19.1)

© The Royal Hospital Chelsea, London (Barcham, Fig. 4)

Staatliche Kunstsammlungen, Gemäldegalerie Alte Meister, Dresden, Photo: Elke Estel / Hans-Peter Klut (Fig. 11.1)

© Tate, London 2009 (Johnson, Fig. 1)

© J. S. Thomas (Thomas, Fig. 1; Thomas, Fig. 2)

© The Walters Art Museum, Baltimore (Fig. 26)

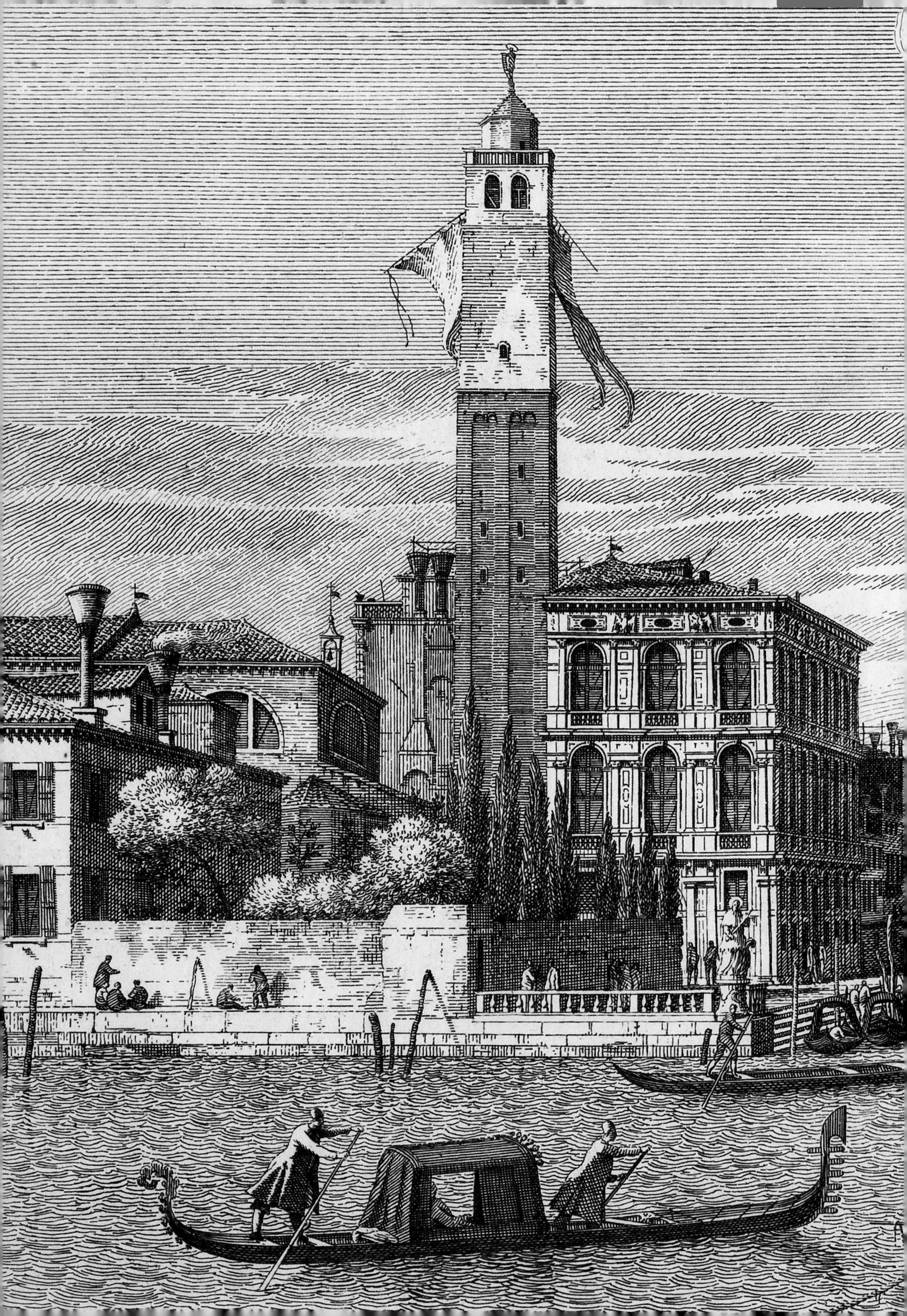